MERTON & JUDAISM

MERTON &JUDAISM

Recognition, Repentence, and Renewal
HOLINESS IN WORDS

Compiled and Edited by
Beatrice Bruteau

With a foreword by
Victor A. Kramer

FONS VITAE

The Fons Vitae Thomas Merton Series:
Merton & Sufism: The Untold Story, 1999
Merton & Hesychasm: The Prayer of the Heart, 2003
Merton & Judaism: Holiness in Words, 2003

Future Thomas Merton Editions:
Merton & Buddhism • *Merton & Taoism* • *Merton & Art*

This edition printed and distributed by
Fons Vitae, Louisville, Kentucky

Printed in Canada

Library of Congress Control Number: 2003105992

ISBN-1-887752-55-2

This edition published by
Fons Vitae
49 Mockingbird Valley Dr.
Louisville, KY 40207-1366
fonsvitaeky@aol.com
www.fons vitae.com

Dedicated to
furthering
mutual respect
among the world's
sacred traditions
by sharing matters of
spiritual sustenance.

Fons Vitae is grateful to
Eleanor Bingham Miller and her family,
Rowland, Rowland II, Worth and Hannah
who have made the publication of this volume
a gift in honor of Dr. Kenneth Zegart,
beloved Obstetrician and Gynecologist,
and his family, Shelly, Terri and Amy.

ACKNOWLEDGMENTS

The Editor and the Publisher gratefully acknowledge the following permissions to reprint material previously published:

America Press: "Letter from the Council," by Donald R. Campion, S.J., was originally published in *America*, October 31, 1964. "Thomas Merton and Judaism," by William H. Shannon, was originally published in *America*, October 6, 1990. These pieces are reprinted with permission of America Press, Inc. Copyright 1964, 1990. All rights reserved: www.americamagazine.org

Citadel Press/Kensington Publishing Corp.: *The Way of Man According to the Teaching of Hasidism,* by Martin Buber, Third Paperbound Edition 1970. Copyright © 1976 by The Citadel Press. First published in England 1950 by Routledge & Kegan Paul, Ltd. Second Impression 1963. Published by Vincent Stuart Publishers, Ltd., 45 Lower Belgrave Street, London SW1. All rights reserved.

Cistercian Studies: "The Eclipse of Difference: Merton's Encounter with Judaism," by Karl A. Plank, Vol. 28.2 (1993), 179-191.

Samuel Dresner: Abraham Joshua Heschel, *The Circle of the Baal Shem Tov*, ed. Samuel H. Dresner, 1985.

Reprinted by permission of Farrar, Straus, Giroux, LLC:
Excerpts from MORAL GRANDEUR AND SPIRITUAL AUDACITY by Abraham Joshua Heschel. Copyright © 1996 by Sylvia Heschel.
Excerpt from a PASSION FOR TRUTH by Abraham Joshua Heschel, Copyright © 1973 by Sylvia Heschel.
Excerpts from THE HIDDEN GROUND OF LOVE: THE LETTERS OF THOMAS MERTON ON RELIGIOUS EXPERIENCE AND SOCIAL CONCERNS by Thomas Merton,

edited by William H. Shannon. Copyright © 1985 by the Merton Legacy Trust.

Excerpt from A VOW OF CONVERSATION: JOURNALS 1964–1965 by Thomas Merton. Copyright © 1988 by Thomas Merton.

Excerpt from WITNESS TO FREEDOM by Thomas Merton. Copyright © 1994 by the Merton Legacy Trust.

Griffin House: "Contemplative Inwardness and Prophetic Action: Thomas Merton's Dialogue with Judaism," by Edward K. Kaplan, published in the book *Thomas Merton: Pilgrim in Process,* eds. Donald Grayston and Michael W. Higgins, 1983.

Harper Collins: Excerpts from pages 142-43 and page 162 from *Dancing in the Water of Life: The Journals of Thomas Merton, Volume Five 1963-1965,* by Thomas Merton and edited by Robert E. Daggy. Copyright © 1997 by The Merton Legacy Trust. Reprinted by permission of Harper Collins Publishers, Inc. Excerpts from pages 175-177 from A *Search for Solitude: The Journals of Thomas Merton, Volume Three 1952-1960,* by Thomas Merton and edited by Patrick Hart. Copyright © 1996 by The Merton Legacy Trust. Reprinted by permission of Harper Collins Publishers, Inc.

Indiana University Press: "People Today and the Jewish Bible," by Martin Buber, in *Scripture and Translation,* by Martin Buber and Franz Rosenzweig, tr. L. Rosenwald with E. Fox, 1994.

Louisville Eccentric Observer: "Beating 'Constantine's Sword' into a Spiritual Plowshare," by Terrence A. Taylor, February 13, 2002.

The Liturgical Press: *Opening the Bible,* by Thomas Merton. Copyright © 1970 by The Order of St. Benedict, Inc. Published by The Liturgical Press, Collegeville, Minnesota. Reprinted with permission.

The Merton Legacy Trust: Thomas Merton, telegram to Abraham Joshua Heschel, October 28, 1964. Transcription, by Paul Pearson, of Merton Sunday Afternoon Lecture, October 29, 1967. *Contemplation in a World of Action*, by Thomas Merton, 1973.

New Directions: "*Chant To Be Used in Processions Around a Site* With Furnaces" (excerpt), by Thomas Merton, *from THE COLLECTED POEMS OF THOMAS MERTON, 1963, by The Abbey of Gethsemani, Inc., 1977, by The Trustees of the Merton Legacy Trust.*
"*The Fasting of the Heart*" *(51 word excerpt)*
"*When A Hideous Man...*"
"The Empty *Boat*" *(15 line excerpt)*
"*Keng's Disciple*" *(20 line excerpt) by Thomas Merton, from THE WAY OF CHUANG TZU, copyright* © *1965 by The Abbey of Gethsemani.* Used by permission of New Directions Publishing Corporation.

The Rabbinical Assembly: "Abraham Joshua Heschel and Thomas Merton: Heretics of Modernity," by Shaul Magid. Reprinted from *Conservative Judaism,* Vol. L, no. 2-3 (Winter/Spring 1998) with permission. Copyright by The Rabbinical Assembly.

The Editor and the Publisher gratefully acknowledge permission from the following to publish letters to Thomas Merton:
Sylvia Heschel for Abraham Joshua Heschel
Prof. Maimon Schwarzschild for Rabbi Dr. Steven S.
 Schwarzschild
Lou Hackett Silberman
R.J. Zwi Werblowsky.

CONTENTS

THE FONS VITAE
THOMAS MERTON SERIES

Professional theologians and lay readers, scholars and spiritual seekers in a broad spectrum of religious practice regard the Cistercian monk Thomas Merton (1915–1968) as one of the most important spiritual writers of the last half of the twentieth century. The writing impelled by his monastic life's interests in the world's religious traditions are recognized as a seminal and continuing catalyst for inter-religious dialogue in the twenty-first century.

Ewert Cousins, a distinguished Professor of Religion and the General Editor of the World Spirituality Series, has called Merton an "axial figure" who bridges within his own experience and theological work the contemporary estrangements between religious and secular perspectives. Dr. Cousins has publicly shared his opinion that Thomas Merton means almost more today to many than he actually did in his lifetime. He is becoming an iconic figure who models inter-religious dialogue for those who are seeking a common ground of respect for the varied ways in which human beings realize the sacred in their lives. Merton's life and writing, especially when it focuses on the contemplative practices common to the world's major religions, have indeed become a forum, or a "bridge" in Cousins' term, upon which those engaged in inter-religious dialogue can meet and engage one another.

In his reaching out to living representatives of the world's various religious traditions by correspondence, and by his immersing himself in the study of religious traditions other than his own Roman Catholicism, Merton models the inclusivity of intellect and heart necessary for fruitful inter-religious dialogue. His personal journal for April 28, 1957 witnesses his zeal for a unity of learning and living as a method of personal "inner work" for ensuring communication and respect among religious persons:

If I can unite *in myself*, the thought of the East and the West, of the Greek and Latin Fathers, I will create in myself a reunion of the divided Church, and from that unity in myself can come the exterior and visible unity of the Church. For, if we want to bring together East and West, we cannot do it by imposing one upon the other. We must contain both in ourselves and transcend them both in Christ.

The Fons Vitae publishing project for the study of world religions through the lens of Thomas Merton's life and writing brings Merton's timeless vision of all persons united in a "hidden ground of Love" to a contemporary audience. The first volume in this multi-volume series, *Merton and Sufism: The Untold Story*, included essays by world-renowned scholars and practitioners of Islam's contemplative traditions. Merton's own writing about Sufism over various genres – essays, poetry and transcriptions of his conferences to monastic novices – were collected to indicate the depth and range of Merton's intellectual and affective encounter with Islam. This first volume has received critical acclaim and, more importantly for the project, has become another catalyst for the study of Islam's contemplative religious practices.

Merton & Hesychasm: The Prayer of the Heart, volume two in the series, gathered essays by renowned scholars of Thomas Merton's interests in their traditions of the Christian East. The volume collected for the first time Merton's own essays across his career that bear witness to the significance of Merton's encounter with Russian and Greek orthodoxy for his contemplative practice.

This third volume, *Merton and Judaism: Recognition, Repentance, and Renewal, Holiness in Words*, consists of papers presented at a conference organized and chaired by Edward K. Kaplan of Brandeis University, held at Adath Jeshurun Synagogue in Louisville, Kentucky in February 2002, sponsored by the Thomas Merton Foundation. Additional material includes essays, journal entries, letters, poetry, and church documents. A keynote presentation by James Carroll, author of *Constantine's Sword*, highlights the volume.

Succeeding volumes in this series will include studies on Merton and Buddhism, Merton and Taoism, Merton and Protestantism, and Merton and Art. We hope that the Fons Vitae Thomas Merton Series will find a place in the library of anyone who studies and practices one of the contemplative religious traditions.

Gray Henry and Jonathan Montaldo
General Editors

MERTON'S DEVELOPING EXPRESSION OF HIS JEWISH BROTHERHOOD: A HOPEFUL VISION

Victor A. Kramer

This gathering of revised essays derives from a 2002 Thomas Merton Foundation initiated conference and is of value for several reasons. These thoughtful essays demonstrate once again Merton's prophetic role in being able to pursue a particular line of interest which then shines as a beacon to guide others in the decades following. His vision of Jewish–Catholic brotherhood is respectful and hopeful. Just as Merton led lay Catholics to appreciate solitude and monasticism in the 1940s and then led still more persons in the 1950s to become concerned with the virtues of silence, during the 1960s his concern for others exploded into many additional different areas, fronts not much explored earlier in race relations, and about war, liturgy, poetry and ecumenism. Throughout these articles evidence accumulates to show Merton was especially interested in other religions, particularly as that inquiry would relate to his own living faith, rooted in Judaism.

FINDING PARALLELS

Merton's journal entries, a massive project of thirty years, reveal facets of his concerns about the parallels which exist in other faith journeys. He described these from the perspective of his own journey, which kept raising questions for him. One of the most startling parallels with his own career and love of the mystical was the love which he nurtured and celebrated in his thirty-five year long friendship with Bob Lax, who was born Jewish, converted to Catholicism and, we must assert, became one of Merton's best friends, a fellow-hermit and journeyer on the road of solitude toward sainthood. In *The Seven Storey Mountain* there are beautiful pages, which recount Merton's early pleasure when Lax came to the Abbey of Gethsemani to visit and Merton learned that Lax had been baptized, mirroring closely Merton's road of conversion. Merton subsequently celebrates his friendship with the man he admired and called a prophet. Their collected correspondence joyfully records their embrace.

One sees in Lax an emblem of Merton's change toward wider and ecumenical relationships. Merton learned a lot from Lax, and the reverse as well. In the final decade of Merton's life (1958-1968) he was able to find a bit more time for leisure and in that contemplative leisure he widely explored his relationships with others, culturally, religiously, politically, and above all with other Christians. More and more he saw that other philosophies and religions were not so much different from his beloved Catholicism as they were parallel ways of being. Most especially is Judaism such a gift. In these forms of worship and praise, he found a common foundation to cherish.

This book demonstrates that the foundation of Christianity, Judaism, is to be pondered, recognized, and celebrated. Merton's appreciation of the gifts given to him, to us, to all western culture at a time which revealed a critical need for dialogue, is repeated and developed in these studies. At the core of our freedom, as Merton argues in *The New Man* (1961), is the fundamental need to recognize God's presence in others. God's Spirit moves all our beings.

UNIFICATION OF CULTURE

In so many of his commentaries about Judaism, Merton stressed that to a significant degree no Christian can avoid being a Jew. It is part of our spiritual heritage:

One has either to be a Jew
Or stop reading the Bible.
The Bible cannot make sense

To anyone who is not "spiritually
A Semite."
The spiritual sense of the Old Testament is
Not and cannot be a simple emptying
Out of its Israelite content.

Quite the contrary.
The New Testament is the fulfillment
Of that spiritual content...[1]

Emphatically, Merton acknowledges that his own belief and continuing support from God are dependent on their foundation in Judaism. This realization is a basic ingredient in his own continuing formation. Merton was never naive in his assessment of the relationship of Catholicism to other faiths and to aspects of culture which have clouded our own manifestation of belief. He would agree with those who claim that our contemporary Western variety of Christianity is, at best, a version within Capitalism, and as such, not a religion much inclined to dealing with pain, anger and mystery. In fact, to a significant degree, Merton might be seen as holding that we have so compartmentalized our religious beliefs and our business that it is often impossible for Americans to see the contradictions. Recourse to the Jewish foundation would correct this, directing us to the unity of culture available in the Abrahamic root, where the realities of human life are the very medium of the divine revelation.

Merton's call for Mercy, the word and concept he best loved, is his recurring word of praise to the God, not just of Jesus, but of all those with whom a covenant has been made and then sustained in more than one manner even down to the present, most especially Jews.

A LIVING FAITH

James Carroll's spirited address about Merton's fascination with Jews and Carroll's admiration of Merton who has led him to a demand for "a full Christian Teshuva" is an excellent, but also at

---

1 Merton, *Conjectures of a Guilty Bystander* (New York: Doubleday, 1966), p. 17. (This is prose arranged here for my emphasis as verse.)

some places an exaggerated rallying speech for Christians to become aware of their complicity in a history which remains so mysterious and clouded for many in the 21st century. This is especially true for Westerners unaware of the complexity of their own religious roots both in Judaism and in the imperial mentality of those Christians who would be conquerors.

Carroll's work is, like Merton's, not the thought of a systematic scholar, yet his reading of the times is a plea which allows us to see our involvement in the complexity of religion and misunderstandings in a world we were once encouraged to think was so very simple. Essentially, Carroll argues, little has changed for 700 years. It is not quite that simple.

Carroll uses a 1990 article by William Shannon to establish the context for his argument. I can remember the particular address out of which this article developed as it was given at the 1989 First General Meeting of the International Thomas Merton Society and, as well, doubts which were expressed by some in that audience about the accuracy of Shannon's assertions. In a recent homily by Msgr. Shannon (August 18, 2002) he spoke eloquently again of the fact (not desire) that as Christians we have an obligation to accept *all* people. As Christians we are not given an option of choosing to love only those for whom we have been foreordained to care. Our Christian group is part of all, insists Shannon. Thus, *all* must be included, praised, and embraced.

William Shannon's essay "Thomas Merton and Judaism" does an excellent job of preparing the reader of this book to encounter the central mystery of Israel and our relation (not in the past) but today with the mystery of an Israel with a lived history in recent years. Much of what Shannon has written about in relation to Merton focuses on the living foundation of a common faith.

The two articles, by Shannon and Karl A. Plank, placed early in this gathering, together provide the setting for observing Merton's loving engagement with Judaism. Merton would, in fact, like the word "correspondence" employed here. He sometimes played around with the word "conversation" when he thought about his monastic vow of a continuing "conversion" of manners. *A Vow of Conversation*, his edited journal gathering materials for 1964 and 1965, reveals this and shows his openness to dialogue.

Our continuing conversion requires a constant conversation if we are going to make progress toward recognizing parallels and correspondences in faith. That Merton forty years ago was able to articulate this continuing need so well is documented in these two studies. That this is but the beginning of our cultural need for dialogue is apparent: we must, as Plank writes, *not* oversimplify as, he argues, Merton did to some significant degree. Plank surely does not need to derogate Merton's contribution to Jewish and Christian relations. He does wisely underscore the difficulty of the challenge that those relations bring: to live in kinship without eclipsing the difference that makes relation possible and which infuses it with importance.[2]

Placed to follow this pair of opening essays which work so well together, two more are nicely edited so that they too reverberate. Donald Grayston's "Thomas Merton: The Holocaust, and the Eclipse of Difference" is a placement of Merton's Jewish awareness within the far broader context of ecumenism and Merton's recognition of world religions. Karl Plank's gentle letter, written as a friend, establishes precisely the right tone for a continuing conversation which (not just for Grayston and Plank but for all readers) must be continued in love and friendship.

CONTINUING DIALOGUES OF MYSTERY

As if engaging talk was the best way to get an audience to listen, the next two pieces included in this collection demonstrate "Merton's Opening to Judaism" as a dialogue which in being opened is *now* in process of being continued. Edward K. Kaplan admits that in many ways Merton's work of the 1960s is only a beginning: "[d]ialogue...mutual understanding takes place in the world where contradictions are not resolved."[3] This ability to embrace contradictions is at the core of Merton's thrust and our own engagement.

Karl Plank's careful analysis of Merton's reading of Buber and the Bible stands as a model of such a serious continuing

2 p. 78.
3 p. 123.

conversation. We are reminded that there are no easy fixed answers. The "Thou" demands receptivity and "personal engagement."[4] Plank's discussion allows us to see that the best of Scripture can render the text as person. It is not dead, but a living human document. While we are unsure what Merton knew of Buber's work, which had preceded his own, it is clear they are parallel voices listening to the voices of the past which become living spokespersons today.

As this collection develops, it is as if we *must* first return to some old stories and the retelling of those stories. Lucien Miller does an excellent job of drawing the reader into the way various readers do read Israel's holy mountains. All these storytellers, as surveyed here – Heschel, Buber, and Merton – "are creative interpreters of 'holiness' in words"[5] yet all of them demonstrate great respect for their original sources.

In fact, it is even more than a concern for sources and a retelling in the spirit of the original sources. These storytellers "experience a personal turning or *teshuva* as they listen or retell folk tales and legends, and they invoke that *teshuva* spirit of conversion, repentance and forgiveness in their audience" as well.[6] Thus, we see that a spirit of respect for the original voice would eventually lead Merton to a careful rewording of Chuang Tzu so that this classic Taoist, too, could be alive for contemporary readers.

Mary Heléne P. Rosenbaum examines some of Merton's many pertinent letters to isolate their "Hasidic themes" within his exchanges with Jewish correspondents. This gathering stands as an invitation to other scholars to investigate more completely Merton's fondness for Erich Fromm, Abraham Joshua Heschel, Zalman Schachter-Shalomi, Steven S. Schwarzschild and others.

CORRESPONDENCES ABOUT INWARDNESS

We know, as Jonathan Montaldo has written in his "Introduction" to *The Intimate Merton*, that so much of what made Merton a monk was his very writing about being a monk. Thus, an awareness of the correspondence between Merton and

4 p. 150.
5 p. 176.
6 p. 178.

Abraham Joshua Heschel is especially significant since they both acknowledge the need for a process of spiritual development.

Those letters are immediate, definite, specific and often urgent. What is magnificent is that the issues addressed in these letters are often not just issues of that moment, but issues about universal questions. Thus, what we have revealed here is a prophetic exchange. The piece which follows, "Abraham Joshua Heschel and Thomas Merton: Heretics of Modernity," by Shaul Magid, reveals true boldness.

Awareness of the wider, and often terrifying contemporary culture, dialogue, and prayers, provide the template for this relationship between the monk and the rabbi. The article which follows, "Contemplative Inwardness and Prophetic Action: Thomas Merton's Dialogue With Abraham Joshua Heschel" by Edward K. Kaplan, reminds us that out of the depths of suffering (for Christian and Jew) comes the ability to dialogue, cherish, even change and praise.

Three more pieces, the article by Brenda Fitch Fairaday called "Thomas Merton's Prophetic Voice: Merton, Heschel and Vatican II," Ron Miller's "Merton, a Pioneer of Pluralism," and the Interview with Rabbi Zalman Schachter-Shalomi (done November 19, 2001 in Boulder, Colorado), demonstrate the valuable truth of Merton's continuing need for conversation. Merton's continuing dialogue goes on now in those pieces. In looking at all of these articles, we see convergence of mind and spirit. The Fairaday essay is necessarily an overview. The power of her summary is that we are reminded of Merton's prescient way of intuiting exactly what needed to be said at Vatican II.

The document *Nostra Aetate* for the first time officially recognized the historical and living relationship between Christians and Jews as a "permanent preciousness."[7] All of a sudden 20th-century Christians were reminded (and again through this essay and this new book) that *all* of Jewish teaching *is* astoundingly significant for Christians.

What is most astounding is that Merton realized so much of this so early throughout his career and in his writings.

In the pieces placed toward the end of this collection the rhythm of the book's dialogue becomes still clearer. Edward K.

7 p. 271.

Kaplan's "Contemplative Inwardness and Prophetic Action" positions us in the direction that Merton so frequently stresses. Our call is to work both directly and indirectly in talk and in prayer.

Those of us who are serious Christians and modern Jews, both rooted in the Abrahamic Tradition, must go forward not in isolation but in communion with our historic brothers. Merton's enthusiastic correspondence, as Fairaday clearly demonstrates, is evidence of his continuing dialogue. The correspondence of Merton and Abraham Joshua Heschel is the pinnacle of this spiritual engagement and, as has been demonstrated, led to the diligent and careful (and indeed sometimes painful) work which grew out of Vatican II and the many subsequent follow-up documents about Judaism and Catholicism.

Fairaday's article is an important complement to both what precedes as background and what follows in this gathering of pieces which investigate Merton's study, absorption of key insights and the fluency of his surprising perceptions which remain valuable right down to the present moment.

PROPHECY

The last parts of the book, an introduction to a tape by Merton on "Jewish/Christian Existentialism" transcribed and edited by Paul M. Pearson, along with a poem by Paul Quenon and three appendices, are excellent supplements to the main parts of the book. Appendix A, "The Four Versions of *Nostra Aetate*," with Notes and Commentary provided by James M. Somerville, form a useful resource for understanding the history of this development. These documents provide knowledge of history and the stumbling blocks to communion. The other appendices, a report on speeches by Pope John Paul II and Chief Rabbi Elio Toaff (1986) and excerpts from The National Council of Synagogues and Delegates of the U.S. Catholic Bishops Committee on Ecumenical and Interreligious Affairs (2002), are promising steps forward as dialogue.

All this will prove to be valuable as research material for further study. The growth of the four versions, slowly building toward a more affirmative and true stance is truly significant. We suspect that a combing of Merton's letters about Judaism, some of which were omitted from the five selected volumes as edited, and likewise examination of the journals as they have been printed in the new complete versions, will also yield considerably more data to be interpreted.

The recent digitalization of The Merton Reading Notebooks, begun at the Pitts Theology Library of Emory University in cooperation with the Aquinas Center of Theology, also at Emory, eventually will make it possible to do further study of still more primary material which relates to so many aspects of Merton's fascination with comparative religion. As I suggested earlier, Merton's love and admiration of his Jewish-Christian friend, Bob Lax, is a book length study about mutual needs and appreciation waiting to unfold as a paradigm of one tradition's need for another.

The interview with Rabbi Zalman Schachter–Shalomi, conducted by Edward K. Kaplan and Shaul Magid, is a magnificent record too. Here's happiness, here's friendship and hope. It is encouragement to persons engaged in any religious dialogue: witty, clean, clear and as well a plea for interfaith friendship and openness. "We need all these flavors," says the Rabbi. Strong, inclusive and challenging, Zalman Schachter tells us: "The God you don't believe in, I don't believe in either."[8] His point, and Merton's, we are sure, is that convergences and parallels are far more important than differences.

A CALL TO MUTUAL SUPPORT

Finally, we can assert that Merton's work stands as a catalyst for the drawing up of a blueprint for the kind of living building of seekers, which in the contemporary world we must have. We must install our living beliefs in such a new place of openness if we are to gather strength not from separation or isolation, but in a brotherhood of living stones.

Throughout Merton's *Conjectures of a Guilty Bystander* he seeks ways to deal with the fact that as a society we are often revealed as unaware of our common traditions, especially common religious traditions. Most poignantly is this the horrible case with our knowledge of the continuity of our Judeo-Christian inheritance. Merton's monastic study of scripture, ritual, liturgy and the intense

8 p. 314.

need to be aware of God's continuing presence is documented in the reworked and embellished pieces of journal there crafted into *Barth's Dream* (his working title), a dream of the late Western theological mind to ratify and codify and understand theology. Merton would argue the core of life's gift from God remains a mystery.

Our job is now to think of brother chanting to brother, facing one another in the quiet of a choir stall repeating in alternating rhythms a song of wonder for God's power and our awe, yet also our anger, in His absence. Think of the continuous presence of God's gifts of prayer, psalms, and prophecy – lived with and sung for over three thousand years.

Merton's point clearly is that as 'solitary wayfarers' we can never be fully alive and connected. However, the solitude and the desert, the diaspora and fear, can also be signs of God's love preparing us for even greater possibilities of embrace with him and others.

All the articles edited for this gathering about parallel questions concerning the Rabbinical Tradition, along with Merton's joyous embrace of text and tales and ambiguity and of their combining and continuing relationships, contribute to our developing knowledge of culture and reveal both pain and love. Such wonder affirms the mystery of our covenants with the God of creation. They also reveal Merton's growing conviction that in no way are we, as western and ever so rational perpetrators of order, able to penetrate fully the mystery of our chosen brotherhood with one another. At the same time, to honor such relationships and mystery is fundamental, necessary, and indeed religious.

This book began with a conversation I had with Brother Paul
Quenon of Gethsemani Abbey, who is also a board member of the
Merton Foundation. He was telling me about the series of books
on *Merton and Sufism*, *Merton and Hesychasm*, Fons Vitae had begun.
I had recently compiled *Jesus Through Jewish Eyes* (Orbis, 2001), so
I suggested that a volume on Merton and Judaism would be
valuable. Brother Paul thought well of the idea and brought Ed
Kaplan, who happened to be visiting the Abbey at the time, into
the conversation. We planned that Paul would ask the Merton
Foundation to sponsor a conference, which Ed Kaplan would
organize, and that I should compile and edit a book including the
papers of the conference plus other material on the same topic.

The Merton Foundation agreed to sponsor such a conference
and arranged with Adath Jeshurun Synagogue in Louisville to host
it. Ed Kaplan then chose and invited the speakers, and Terry Taylor
of the Foundation organized the infrastructure. Furthermore, both
Ed and Terry gave steady and generous assistance at all phases of
the book project, providing needed materials and wise counsel,
and I am most grateful to them and also to Paul Pearson of the
Merton Center for similar help. We are fortunate in having Victor
A. Kramer, outstanding Merton scholar and long time Editor of
The Merton Annual, to write the Foreword, putting our work in
perspective among Merton studies.

The congregation of Adath Jeshurun Synagogue and their
spiritual leader, Rabbi Robert Slosberg, were exceedingly gracious
to us, presenting beautiful music and a fine dinner to add to our
celebration of this joint venture. We thank them for their
friendship, hospitality and generosity.

The book is organized to show thematic unity and dramatic
development from beginning to end. It is launched with James
Carroll's account of his and Merton's journey from innocence of
the Christian/Jewish history to this strong call for Christian
teshuva, a thorough **recognition** of the ill done and deep

repentance for it. Then we move through several papers that examine this in some detail and approach the central climax, Merton's interaction with Abraham Joshua Heschel and their common concern for the production of *Nostra Aetate* during Vatican II. It is in connection with this, Merton's most crucial relation to Judaism – and the hope and the challenge growing out of it – that the appendices are so important; they reveal the struggle within the Church, in the context of which Merton's intervention was significant.

The book is thus intended to be not only a Merton book but a Jews–and–Christians book, a valuable contribution to that very earnest conversation going on now at a level it has never before enjoyed. In this context the book is intended to reach a Jewish audience as well as a Christian one. The presence of the documentary resources makes it unique as a volume in which the serious reader will find at hand the amazing details of the negotiations that touched the lives of the Jews so profoundly.

For the convenience of readers who are interested to see just what the history of that matter involved, Appendix A contains the successive versions (Latin and English) through which the document on the Jews passed, together with helpful pointers and commentary. I draw attention to the fact that the final (promulgated) version was deliberately designed to exclude an explicit repudiation of the formula *gens deicida* (God-killing people) used through the centuries in Church pronouncements on Jews. (See Cardinal Bea's effort to explain and smooth over this failure to attain what many of the Fathers had wanted.)

So the *teshuva* is not yet as complete as it might be, and the papers in the second half of our book show how there has been movement, much of it provoked by Merton, toward discovery of the grounds for new understandings, interpretations, appreciations in openness to the common mysticism in world religions and to the pluralistic respect with which we must now live together. In particular, we look forward to a full **recognition** by Christians of the Jewish people and their religion in their unique distinctness and permanent preciousness, not to be superseded or completed (see Appendix C).

The book concludes with the interview with Merton's correspondent and friend, Reb Zalman, who is presently energizing a **renewal** movement within Judaism and offering friendly advice to Christians concerned for renewal. The coda is Merton on Zalman and Paul Quenon's poem.

As Wayne Teasdale has so well said,[1] aware people undertake to build bridges across the gaps between religions and lifestyles: they encourage conversation and comfortable companionship. They seek out occasions for cooperation and sharing. They remember and respect differences but build habits of collaboration. Although what unites us is always more substantial than what divides us, honoring and protecting each one's specialness and uniqueness is in itself a value that unites us.

One of the important things that Christians need to learn in pursuing their interest in Judaism is to go beyond the biblical era. An interest that limits itself to discovering its own roots in the traditions of ancient Israel is not entering into a genuine conversation with its contemporary partner. Judaism has always developed significantly over time; that is one of its identifying characteristics. Leo Baeck, who calls the Hebrew religion "revolutionary," says that its "truest development" is in the "actual progress of its thoughts mid the ever-new forms in which those thoughts find expression." Like everything that is "truly original," a "product of genius," it transcends itself by continually forcing the mind and conscience that receive it to wrestle with it. "Again and again in different eras [people] are laid hold of by it, and they cannot let it go until it blesses them."[2]

James Carroll truly struck the keynote for the hopes of all of us that there would indeed be a full *teshuva,* a deep recognition, acknowledgment, penitence and grief for the Christian persecution of Jews over centuries and throughout Europe, and that following this cleansing, there would be equally deep healing and friendship. *Teshuva,* often translated "repentance," literally means "turning" or "returning" to God, seeking inner holiness and social justice, the great values that characterized the conversations of Thomas Merton and his Jewish friends, absolute commitment to God and love of all our neighbors.

1 Wayne Teasdale, *A Monk in the World* (Novato, CA: New World, 2002), p. 21.
2 Leo Baeck, *God and Man in Judaism* (New York: Union of American Hebrew Congregations, 1958), pp. 9, 21.

It is in this hope and these sentiments that I offer a portion of Psalm 122 as a dedication of the volume. Let us pray for the "peace of Jerusalem," not only for a just and favorable resolution for all parties to the current distress, but for Jerusalem considered as the mythic capital, the City of Peace to which "all the tribes" go up to be united as "kin and friends" in the security, prosperity, and gladness figured by "the House of the Lord."

Beatrice Bruteau
Pfafftown, NC
April, 2003

Pray for the peace of Jerusalem:
"May they prosper who love you.
Peace be within your walls,
And security within your towers."
For the sake of my relatives and friends
I will say, "Peace be within you."
For the sake of the house of the Lord our God,
I will seek your good.

Psalm 122:8
NSRV

BEATING "CONSTANTINE'S SWORD" INTO A SPIRITUAL PLOWSHARE

Terrence A. Taylor

Thomas Merton once said: "One has either to be a Jew or stop reading the Bible. The Bible cannot make sense to anyone who is not spiritually a Semite."

Dramatic words, to be sure, but they take on even more power when you realize that they were written not by a Jew but by a Christian – and 40 years ago at that. For 27 years in the middle of the 20th century, the man who wrote those words was a monk at the Abbey of Gethsemani just 50 miles south of Louisville.

On February 17–18, 2002, a broad group of Christians and Jews convened in Louisville at Adath Jeshurun Synagogue to learn more about the pioneering interfaith work of Merton and to discuss what can be done by Christians to make amends for past wrongs to Jews.

LOOKING AT HISTORY AND CALLING ON CHRISTIANS FOR REPENTANCE

The keynote speaker at the "Thomas Merton and Judaism" meeting was James Carroll, best-selling author of *Constantine's Sword: The Church and the Jews*. His book details the long and often troubling relationship between Christians and Jews over the last two millennia. Carroll's topic was, "Thomas Merton and a Full Christian Teshuva."

Teshuva is a Hebrew word that refers to a sort of repentance that not only seeks forgiveness but acts to uncover the root of the sinner's transgression. In this context, Carroll's address picks up where his book left off.

For Carroll, this Teshuva means that Christians must acknowledge the horrors that have been perpetrated in the name of their faith. It also means Christians must realize that God's new covenant with Christians does not invalidate the original covenant that God made with the Jewish people. Carroll recognizes that a full Teshuva requires major steps that would take decades to complete, and he points to Merton as a person who took some of the first steps in the process of healing.

"Merton was key to the basic kinds of change necessary," Carroll said. "He was at the heart of the beginning of changes in Christian-Jewish relations in the 20th century."

THOMAS MERTON:"A GOOD JEW UNDER MY CATHOLIC SKIN"

Merton was the focus of the conference because he adopted an attitude toward Jews that was decades ahead of its time. In the early 1960s, he wrote of his desire to be "a good Jew under my Catholic skin." He talked with important Jewish leaders of his day, including such visionary figures as Abraham Joshua Heschel and Zalman Schacter-Shalomi, while also carefully studying the work of Jewish theologians such as Martin Buber.

Merton delved into the Jewish roots of his Catholic faith and spiritual practices. He acknowledged the responsibility of Christians for creating an atmosphere that made the Holocaust possible. He even worked with officials of the Roman Catholic Church who were drafting position papers on the Jewish faith as part of the Vatican II Council.

The following story is but one example of his role in furthering Jewish-Christian relations. In 1964 Rabbi Heschel made an urgent visit to Merton. At the time Heschel was the chief Jewish adviser to the Vatican II officials who were drafting documents on Jewish matters. Heschel was worried the Catholic Church might be taking a position in one of its papers that was offensive to Jews, and he told Merton that he had written to the Council Fathers:"I am ready to go to Auschwitz any time, if faced with the alternative of conversion or death." Heschel asked for Merton's help, and the monk wrote to the Vatican urging the cardinal in charge of the process to act carefully to ensure that the concerns of the Jews were handled in a way that accorded them the dignity, respect and independence they deserved.

"Constantine's Sword": When Christianity
was joined with imperial power

Constantine's Sword" refers to the cross-shaped weapon that became a symbol for the coming together of religious faith and imperial power. The sword belonged to Constantine, a Roman emperor of the fourth century who, according to legend, saw a vision of a cross in the sky and heard the words, "Conquer in this sign." He soon made Christianity a licit religion and put an end to persecution.

Before Constantine, Christianity had co-existed uneasily but more or less peacefully with Judaism for more than 250 years. In the centuries following Constantine's conversion, Christians were led to see Jews as "Christ-killers." Christians blamed Jews for everything from crop failures to the Black Death. Over the next 16 centuries, Jews, already exiled from their homeland, were persecuted, ghettoized and, finally, slaughtered by the millions during World War II.

Overcoming the ignorance that led to anti-Semitism

Some might question why anyone should spend the many hours required to read a lengthy list of sins. The answer is simple: a need to overcome the ignorance and indifference that in the past have led to prejudice and hostility, which in turn have led to genocide.

Many Christians in North America are simply unaware of the pervasive history of anti-Jewish acts associated with their faith. Most of them probably know about the Holocaust and may have some vague notion that anti-Semitism has besmirched American culture in previous decades. But those same Christians probably have no concept of the almost countless ways the practitioners of their faith found to harm Jews in every decade from the mid-300s to the post-World War II era.

Carroll's book hopscotches across the centuries, from country to country, chronicling a long list of anti-Jewish incidents. In it he describes how religious relics were sometimes used as reasons to blame and humiliate Jews. And the Roman Catholic Church is not the only religious group singled out for scrutiny by Carroll. In his book, he notes that at the birth of the Protestant Reformation, Martin Luther himself engaged in vicious anti-Semitic demagoguery.

But the book ends in hope rather than despair. In spite of all that he has described in such painful detail, Carroll acknowledges the enormous strides that have been made in Christian-Jewish relations since World War II. The last few years have seen Pope John Paul II visit a synagogue in Rome and pray at the Western Wall in Jerusalem. The Catholic Church and many other Christian groups have decided to stop trying to convert their Jewish brothers and sisters. In January 2002, the Vatican issued statements recognizing the legitimacy of the Jewish faith, seeming to back away from aspects of *Dominus Iesus,* a document issued by the Vatican in 2001 that some theologians interpreted as calling into question the salvation not only of Jews but of Protestants as well.

Teshuva IN LOUISVILLE

In spite of the healthy relationship between Christians and Jews in Louisville, there is still a need for both to learn – and sometimes grieve – their history. Today, for the first time, many Christians are coming to grips with the fact that Jesus, who was born a Jew, was very much a Jew in his beliefs and practices. Others are rediscovering the roots of their spirituality within historical Judaism.

In a telephone interview, author Carroll said, "Over the centuries, Christians forgot about the Jewishness of Jesus. If Christians had remembered his Jewishness, there could have been no anti-Semitism. We must ask ourselves now if what we are doing is consistent with the Jewishness of Jesus."

A number of mainstream Christian churches are wrestling with whether they should finally acknowledge the fact that other religions, like Judaism, may be just as valid and good as Christianity. But perhaps most importantly, many of those Christians are asking themselves: What is it in the history of Christianity that led to anti-Semitic practices, anti-Jewish violence, and a religious climate that made possible the horrors of the Holocaust?

Such Christians are beginning their own process of Teshuva.

Regarding the need for Teshuva, the Rev. Bill Hammer, Director of the Ecumenical Office for the Archdiocese of Louisville, said: "The process of Teshuva has already begun with the Catholic Church's expression of repentance for past acts of individuals within the Church. A full Teshuva remains our goal. Part of that will be a further, fuller appreciation of our need for repentance throughout the Church."

Professor W. Eugene March, of the Louisville Presbyterian Theological Seminary, said: "Vatican II opened questions related to the relationships between Christians and Jews that had never been asked before. Now, almost all of the major denominations are wrestling with their attitudes toward Judaism and their historical responsibility for attitudes that led to anti-Semitism and ultimately to the Holocaust."

One major step in that process of reconciliation is acceptance of Judaism as a valid religion in its own right. March said there are three primary ways people of one faith can view other religions.

"In an exclusivist view, I believe that mine is the one and only true religion," he said. "In an inclusivist view, I believe that other religions are all right, but that mine is the best. In a pluralist view, I believe that other religions may be just as valid and good as my own."

March has publicly challenged members of his own denomination to begin wrestling with the implications of adopting a pluralist position regarding Judaism and other faiths. He is about to begin work on a book that will deal with this challenging issue.

"Christians have found their own unique truth in Jesus," March said. "But the fact that we have a unique truth doesn't mean that others do not have their own form of truth as well."

He also noted that while other major Christian denominations such as the United Methodists and the Christian Church/Disciples of Christ have not adopted a pluralist stance, they have issued strong statements recognizing the Jewish faith.

To address the question, the Rev. Charles Bockwell, of Fourth Avenue Methodist Church, quoted from his denomination's 1996 document, "Building the New Bridges of Hope," with which he strongly agrees. "Christians and Jews are bound to God through Biblical covenants that are eternally valid. ... We know that judgment as to the ultimate salvation of persons from any faith community, including Christians and Jews, belongs to God alone."

Regarding Teshuva, "Building the New Bridges of Hope"

said, "We deeply repent of the complicity of the Church and the participation of many Christians in the long history of the persecution of the Jewish people."

The Rev. Steven Johns-Boehme, Area Minister of the Christian Church/Disciples of Christ Kentuckiana region, said, "We understand that Christianity was complicit in the Holocaust by giving rise to the anti-Semitism that led to it."

Johns-Boehme stressed that his denomination does not seek to convert Jews. "We need to understand their Jewishness to truly understand our own Christian nature," he said.

Clearly, much has been accomplished by Christians and Jews working together in this city, and yet much remains to be done. In any case, there is one thing on which everyone can agree. As Hammer said, "Perhaps our greatest challenge will be to avoid repeating the mistakes we made in the past."

Louisville Eccentric Observer, February 13, 2002

Edward K. Kaplan

The invitation to organize a conference on "Thomas Merton and Judaism" came from the Thomas Merton Foundation of Louisville, Kentucky, the lay association devoted to conveying the experience and insights of that great Trappist monk into the world at large. It was high time to cherish the Jewish roots of Christianity, for Merton truly embodied the spirit of Vatican II, its ideal of Christian unity, but also its new openness to all religions. Merton's friendship with Abraham Joshua Heschel, Zalman Schachter-Shalomi, and other Jews had brought him into intimate contact with the Hebrew prophetic quest for holiness and justice. Our conference continued those spiritual conversations.

The public meetings on Thomas Merton and Judaism took place on 17-18 February 2002, in the sanctuary of the Adath Jeshurun Synagogue in Louisville, Kentucky. It was indeed a cooperative venture, regional and national, Jewish and Christian, including people of other faiths and traditions – and people of no faith at all. The papers delivered and the discussions they engendered provided remarkable spiritual opportunities. The eloquent introduction to this book by Terrence Taylor of the Thomas Merton Foundation expresses the poignant quest for repentance communicated by our Catholic partners.

The vital spirit of Thomas Merton enriched our proceedings. The Foundation launched this initiative under extraordinary circumstances. In June 2000, responding to Merton's unfulfilled hope to create a contemplative retreat center, which he called Mount Olivet, the Merton Foundation had invited me to join a number of scholars, religious practitioners, and leaders to what they called a "contemplative dialogue." These spiritual and political and social activists came from around North America, and other countries such as India, Brazil, South Africa. We engaged in contemplative dialogue, an exceptional blend of silence, listening, self-expression, and community building.

We were able to reconcile inwardness and moral commitment. Now, contemplation implies solitude and extreme privacy in the individual's relation to God. Our encounters took the form of a private retreat at the Abbey of Gethsemani, but it was not entirely silent. Group communication was facilitated so that we would sit together in stillness, worship briefly together, and then speak to each other from the heart, without an agenda, and without producing a tangible product, such as a statement or manifesto.

In various ways, we harvested the wisdom of Thomas Merton himself. At the end of this Merton 2000 Retreat, as it was called, we participated in a public forum in Louisville at which each of us spoke and shared insights gathered at the Abbey of Gethsemani. We experienced how inwardness and respect for differences can become an element of communication and solidarity. Such was our hope for the conference on Thomas Merton and Judaism, to foster community without violating the integrity of individuals, to strive for mutuality without compromising the distinctiveness of each religious tradition.

We hope that the present book translates into print some of the contemplative dialogue we achieved as Christians and Jews before and during our February 2002 conference. The public program was indeed nourished by Merton's spiritual resources. During the weekend before the public meetings, those of us presenting papers shared an unpublicized retreat at the Abbey of Gethsemani. We celebrated holy time together, the Jewish Sabbath and the liturgical Hours of the Trappist monks. We also got to know each other, and I believe that we began a rare process of understanding – both reciprocal and self-understanding – which readers of this book are invited to enlarge.

Thomas Merton established deep bonds with several Jewish thinkers and teachers such as Rabbi Abraham Joshua Heschel, of the Jewish Theological Seminary in New York, Reb Zalman Schachter-Shalomi, a Lubavitch Hasidic rabbi who was himself reaching out to different traditions and eventually became the founder of the Jewish Renewal movement; Dr. Lou Silberman of Vanderbilt University, a teacher of Karl Plank, a leading Merton scholar; Eric Fromm, the visionary psychoanalyst and social philosopher; Rabbi Steven

Schwarzschild, professor and editor of the quarterly journal, *Judaism*; professor of comparative religion R.J. Zwi Werblowsky of the Hebrew University in Jerusalem; the poet Denise Levertov, and others. Their correspondence, and visits some of them made to the Abbey of Gethsemani, constitute a distinguished chapter of Merton's direct contact with Jews – and with the Judaism to which many of those individuals devoted their lives.

That was history. Merton and Judaism. What could that possibly mean to us today? Why would it matter that an eccentric, though enlightened, Trappist monk, committed heart and soul and body to the rule of strict observance within the Roman Catholic Church, grappled with Judaism as a living tradition? Our authors acknowledge his difficulties and failures as well as his successes.

One obvious and well-documented reason – movingly represented by James Carroll's courageous and compassionate book, *Constantine's Sword* – is the unfinished business of Vatican II, in which the Roman Catholic Church, the most powerful and influential among all Christian institutions, initiated a momentous self-examination during 1962-1965. The good Pope John XXIII personally charged Augustin Cardinal Bea, president of the Secretariat for Christian Unity, with the task of revising the Church's negative teachings about the Jews. Supporters of the "Declaration on the Jews" hoped to repudiate the horrendous charge of deicide and to remove images of the Jews as an accursed people from official doctrine and from the liturgy. During the early 1960s, the great, venerable Roman Catholic Church, not without immense discord, opened its heart – and its theology, its self-definitions – to other faiths, such as Protestantism, Hinduism, Buddhism, and others – including the mother covenant, Judaism.

We witnessed a remarkable process of individual and institutional repentance, what we called *Teshuva*, using the Hebrew word for turning toward God. The practical outcome of that repentance, and at least potential restoration, was encompassed in the version of *Nostra Aetate* ratified by the Second Vatican Council in 1965; but the redemptive goals of that somewhat compromised document remain to be completed. That was one crucial reason why our meeting on Thomas Merton and Judaism had to take place.

For Thomas Merton felt, as intensely and deeply as any

Catholic thinker, the necessity of revering Judaism, its religion, its culture, and its sacred texts and prayers, in order for the Christian spirit to cleanse itself of arrogance, cruelty, and insensitivity to the Other. The personal dimension of our conference was at least equal to the institutional one. Merton taught us by his example how women and men devoted to religious matters – most of us, perhaps all of us – still seek God. Religion is not an answer to our problems but a task, unfinished business.

As a Jew, I need my Christian sisters and brothers – and not only the religious sisters and brothers, the secular folks too – to help inspire my own spiritual odyssey. If God is God, God is the God of every human being. I was honored to join with those who take the contemplative life, and testimonies to the living God, with utmost seriousness.

The world in which we live is marvelous, but it is also ugly, unjust, cruel, insensitive to the sanctity of all human beings. So many people appear to be indifferent to gross injustice, and, as Rabbi Heschel insisted, unmoved by our very inability to be moved. Even worse, it has become increasingly obvious that religion itself can become a lethal problem. We cannot deny the dangers of religious thinking and we must guard against its perversions. That is another reason why Thomas Merton is our teacher. As we share these conversations, Thomas Merton's dialogue with Judaism and with the Jewish people can become our precious guide.

Rabbi Robert Slosberg
of Congregation Adath Jeshurun

One of the great Jewish philosophers and thinkers, a physician as well as a codifier of Jewish Law, was Moses Maimonides. He was the first to articulate a systematic approach to *teshuva*, to a process of repentance. Repentance is not just a one time act but a process that leads to *teshuva,* to "return," to God, or to an individual or group of people, and at the same time to God.

I believe that there is a process of *teshuva* that is taking place right now between Jews and Christians. I believe the process began in the 1960s with the moving declaration of *Nostra Aetate,* a very important document of the Second Vatican Council, which says that the Jewish People are not guilty of deicide or of the death of Jesus. It further says that care must be taken in preaching and teaching not to say anything suggesting that God has in any way repudiated or turned away from his People; on the contrary, the Church is pledged to stand firmly against any hatred, persecution, or display of anti-Semitism at any time and from any source, for no one can call upon God the Father of all who is refusing to love as brothers any portion of the human race. [See Appendix A for the full texts and translations of the four versions through which *Nostra Aetate* passed on its way to the carrying vote in the Council.]

The second stage, I believe, of the process of *teshuva,* was Pope John Paul II's courageous trip to Israel. It was on this occasion that the Church explicitly renounced any attempt to convert the Jews from their religion, for their own Covenant is recognized by the Church as forever intact. At the Holocaust Museum, at *Yad Vashem,* the Pope said: "I assure the Jewish People that the Catholic Church is deeply saddened by the hatred, acts of persecution, and displays of anti-Semitism directed against Jews by Christians at any time and in any place." He went on to say that the Holocaust, the *Shoah* ["the destruction"] as he correctly referred to it, lives on, and its memory burns itself into our souls, into the souls of Christians.

But these very beautiful words of the Pope cry out, "*Darsheni!*" Explain me, interpret me. And it needed the gifts of tonight's speaker, Jim Carroll, an author, a columnist for the *Boston Globe*, and a former priest, to bring the beautiful words of the Pope into focus for us. And through his *New York Times* bestselling book, *Constantine's Sword*, he has done just that. He has helped us in our effort to complete stage three in repentance, in *teshuva*.

I know that all of you are very grateful, as I am, to Todd and Karen Blue for enabling this evening to happen, in honor of their children, Gracie and Isaac. I can't think of a better gift parents could give to their children. And so it is my fervent prayer that Jim Carroll's words will move each of us to a greater understanding of one another and will take us to this new level of repentance that is so needed by all of us. In the words, very beautiful words, sung by *Voces Novae* and my *hazzan*, my cantor, we can say together, "Praised are you, O Lord, our God, Ruler of the universe, who has kept each of us alive and sustained us and enabled us to reach this day in our community's life. Amen."

I

THOMAS MERTON AND
A FULL CHRISTIAN *TESHUVA*

James Carroll

I am deeply honored to be here for reasons that I hope my
remarks will make clear. My text – from Thomas Merton, of
course – is "I wish I knew more about doing teshuva. It is the only
thing that seems to make much sense in these days. And in the
political dark I light a small, frail light about peace and hold it up
in the whirlwinds." This is from a letter to Rabbi Zalman
Schachter-Shalomi, dated December 15, 1961. In 1961 I was a
freshman at Georgetown University in Washington, the Jesuit
college. It was, some of you remember, the year of John F.
Kennedy. I was alive with the thrill of being the young President's
neighbor in Georgetown. It was also for us the thrill of being
young, Americans, Democrats, and Roman Catholics. With John
XXIII our beloved new Pope, and with Kennedy as our leader, we
American Catholics were in the delightful throes of, as they say,
"having arrived."

But for a young man like me, the delight was tempered by, I
admit, a terrible conflict. The glamour of Kennedy..... yes. The
American call to service .... yes. But also tugging at me, the
impulse to follow another path. One I could hardly talk about. It
had something to do with God. I went to see a Jesuit counselor
and I confided in him. Religion. Religious life, perhaps. And the
thought made me shudder, a vocation to the priesthood. The Jesuit
was kind. He helped me relax. And as I recall, it was he who put
into my hands my first copy of *The Seven Storey Mountain* by
Thomas Merton. As was true of so many of my kind, that book
had an explosive effect on me. How to describe it? Most simply,

Thomas Merton made the contemplative life seem glamourous. For me, a glamour that could compete with Kennedy's glamour, believe it or not. In fact, I then embraced my vocation to the religious life and to the Catholic priesthood. Merton was the Pied Piper of a whole generation of young American Catholic men. Throughout the decade of the 50s, and shortly after, we followed him into the cloister of life in the Church, a cohort of thousands.

Thomas Merton embodied the high point moment of American Catholic culture, when our seminaries were so full that we had to build new ones. Those are the big empty buildings that dot the countrysides around the United States and now serve as businessmen's retreats, businesswomen's retreats, or the headquarters of other religious organizations. Like so many of my generation, I spent the novitiate of my seminary years mastering the then-body of Merton's work: *The Waters of Siloe, The Sign of Jonas, Seeds of Contemplation, The Ascent to Truth*. Merton gave me my vocabulary for faith. He was my constant companion at meditation. He stiffened my spine for the religious life. I loved him. I thought of him at first as a spiritual father, then as a brother. Eventually, though of course I never met him, I regarded him as a dependable friend.

And then ... and then ... Kennedy was gone. America betrayed itself. Pope John XXIII's vision for the Church faltered. And I knew that my world had changed drastically when I was finally able to see how drastically Thomas Merton himself had changed. By then, his story and my story were too intertwined for me not to continue my journey with him as a guide. It is not too much to say that I became one kind of Catholic because of Thomas Merton and then became an entirely other kind of Catholic, the kind I am today, because of Thomas Merton.

And that is why I am so grateful to be here. So honored and so humbled. I acknowledge and honor Abbot Damien. And Brother Paul. And Brother Patrick, who has done so much to bring Merton to us. Your presence here tonight is deeply moving to me. And I acknowledge and bow before the men and women, my fellow presenters at this conference, who have had Merton at the center of research and study. Not me, I should say. I am no Merton scholar. Just a son of Merton, way back then, and still.

Although the work that qualifies me to be your speaker, *Constantine's Sword*, a history of the Church and the Jews, represents a direct challenge to the kind of Catholic Christian I was when I first became fascinated by the glamour of the contemplative life because of Merton, I want to assert tonight that Merton's spirit as it developed informs my work still. Especially, I would say, in its most controversial aspect, which is a firm challenge to the Roman Catholic Church in particular, and to Christianity in general, to change. Apology for the sin of anti-Semitism, even including the momentous Papal apology of two years ago, is the beginning, not the end. And now we must root out of the life of the Church those theologies, attitudes and practices that have been and are the sources of anti-Semitism. And before uttering another word of repentance we must go further in accomplishing a full moral reckoning with the dark history of the sacred hatred of Jews. This is, I take it, the work of *teshuva,* a Hebrew word that very few Christians knew in 1961. Certainly I did not. But should we be surprised that one of those few, using it in a letter, was Thomas Merton?

My claim is that Thomas Merton, as much as anyone, put us on this road to change, and that he remains our steady companion in this unfinished journey. I did not know it in 1961, of course, but Merton was already well along on this road, even before I knew that it lay ahead of us. While I was reading his 1948 masterpiece, a monument to a world that had not changed in 700 years, he was using that word, *teshuva* — already a sign of a change he had undergone and a sign that he saw what change was necessary, while I was still enthralled with American virtue and American power. I stood moved to tears in the presence of John Kennedy at his Inauguration vowing with him to go anywhere, fight any foe. That year I was the Outstanding Cadet in the Air Force ROTC at Georgetown University. And Thomas Merton, at that point, had already written to Ernesto Cardenal — the date is November 20, 1961 — "Pray for us. We are starting an American peace movement. It will be very difficult. We are, alas, very late."

Just as the United States Catholic Church embraced the American consensus, Thomas Merton was seeing through it. With Cardenal, he helped sow the seeds of what would become liberation theology: With the Jesuit priest Daniel Berrigan, he sowed the seeds of the Catholic peace movement. With Zen monks, launched the beginning of a new spiritual openness and, one has to say, political openness, West to East. One by one the building blocks of a new kind of Catholicism and, I would say, even a new kind of being American, were being put in place. And wasn't Merton lifting them! I am presuming to speak of it only in terms of its effect on one young Catholic who had learned early to trust what he learned from Thomas Merton. That is my simple testimony. While I was embracing a life of mindless obedience, Merton himself was starting to resist. In a 1960 letter to the great French Catholic philosopher, Jacques Maritain, he described how his Order forbade his collaboration with a Zen Master – prohibiting *communicatio cum infidele*, communication with the infidel. The Father General, Merton wrote, "objected to this kind of dialogue between a member of the Order and Buddhists, Protestants, Jews and so forth. He does not think, apparently, that I have sufficiently the mind of the Church to be able to engage safely in a dialogue of this kind."

"The mind of the Church": for tens of thousands of us, that is exactly what Thomas Merton embodied. He was our second scripture. And when he changed, how could we not? Merton had led us into what was called "the perfect society" of the Church. An alternative world. And an alternative *to* the world. But then he led us into a human church very much *of* the world. This was of course a journey mapped by Pope John XXIII and then charted by the Fathers of the Second Vatican Council. But for Merton the pressure point apparently was no theological category and no religious imperative. Instead, it was overwhelmingly the question of war and peace – as I read him, and admittedly with a bias. This was especially true of nuclear war, which (he wrote again to Cardinal in 1961) "is glorified as Christian sacrifice, as a crusade, as the way of obedience. So much so that now there are many who insist that one is not a good Christian unless he offers a blind and unresisting obedience to every behest of Caesar." I acknowledge that in 1961, as the son of an Air Force General, harboring the hope at first of being an Air Force Chaplain, I was one of those Christians. A model B-52 bomber came with me to the Seminary.

Merton continues, thinking of the likes of me, "This is for me a complete nightmare and I realize that I have to be very careful how I protest. Otherwise, I will be silenced." But protest he did.

In 1965, two handfuls of people came to Gethsemani for a retreat with him, on the theme "The Roots of Protest." That retreat is now remembered as a mythic meeting. Attended by, among others, James Forest, A. J. Muste, and both Berrigan brothers, Philip and Daniel, it would be regarded by many as the birth of the Catholic wing of the anti-Vietnam peace movement. Merton would be frightened and conflicted about the course they embarked upon, opposing, for example, Daniel Berrigan's refusal to condemn as mere suicide the self-immolation of the young Catholic worker, Roger LaPorte, at the United Nations building later that same year. That refusal was the beginning of Berrigan's trouble with Cardinal Spellman. And it was the beginning of his prominence as a leader of the anti-war movement. But Berrigan had learned too, like me and so many others, to listen to Merton. Even when they disagreed, perhaps especially then. About Merton, Berrigan would write, "Still my friend suffered and did what he could. Kept messages coming. Stuffing them in bottles and casting them on the tide. His was, I think, the purest kind of truth telling. The kind that endures even in the empire of the deaf." [1]

If I was no longer totally deaf by then, 1965, I was certainly still hard of hearing. It did not help that Cardinal Spellman was my parents' friend and that their fondest hope was that he would live to ordain me to the priesthood. I confess the guilty relief it was to me, that before that day came, the Cardinal died. Merton was intimidated by Spellman, as he indicated in his letters. And I understand that. It seems ironic that Spellman died one year before Merton did, almost to the day.

The challenge of the Vietnam War was one noise that would drag me out of my "magnum silentium," the great silence. My cloistered self-protection. And I was dragged, as I say, with Merton's help. But there was another. The play *The Deputy* by Rolf Hochhuth broke over us seminarians in that period like a crushing tidal wave. For it called into question the ground of our faith in the Church, in its essential sinlessness. *The Deputy*, as you know,

1 Daniel Berrigan, *Portraits of Those I Love* (New York: Crossroad, 1982), p. 19.

charged Pope Pius XII with effectively collaborating with Hitler in the anti-Jewish genocide. We Catholics prized the image of the Church as Hitler's mortal enemy. And to have the illusion of the Church's heroism questioned, if not ripped away, was traumatic. Indeed, part of what motivated the likes of Philip and Daniel Berrigan was the determination, as they put it, not to repeat the scandal of a Church, which – if only by its silence – had stood by while the Nazi death machine moved into gear.

And so too with Merton. It is not for nothing (as I read it) that his shocking book of 1965 was called *Conjectures of a Guilty Bystander*. Previous to that, as I learned from the work of Monsignor William H. Shannon, Merton had in fact written about *The Deputy,* properly rejecting, I would say, its slanderous characterization of Pius XII, but also accepting the play's challenge to what Merton called "the magic image of Church innocence." In *Conjectures* and in his other book of 1965, also shocking, *Raids on the Unspeakable,* Merton put the trial of Adolf Eichmann at the center of his meditation. And reflecting on Hannah Arendt's account of the trial, so pointed, so controversial, Merton wrote, in *Conjectures,* that the Holocaust requires "a sordid examination of the conscience of the entire West" [see pages 241-43, 286-90]. He began that examination with his own life and he certainly extended it to the Church.

It was in this period that his friendship with Rabbi Abraham Joshua Heschel was so pivotal. This is a story well known to all of you, and made powerfully clear by the work of Professor Edward K. Kaplan of Brandeis. Rabbi Heschel was the first great figure in my own awakening to the reality of Jewish religion as a living religion beyond the dominant Christian caricature of an Old Testament religion. The Old Testament religion, we were effectively taught, was properly left behind, except as a mere foreshadowing of Christian truth. Professor Kaplan's work on Heschel helps me understand, after the fact, why Heschel was so important to me. In Heschel I found, at first, a man to teach me about Judaism: the vitality of Jewish religion, the Rabbinic tradition, the glories of Talmud and Kabbalah, and modern Jewish thought. All this was unknown to Christians like me. Heschel was a living contradiction of the dominant Christian assumption about

Jewish obsolescence. And for that matter, about Jewish victimhood. Heschel was the opposite of what we Christians had been taught about Jews.

Moreover, and even more surprising, Rabbi Heschel then began to teach me about my own faith, my own belief in a God whose search for me, in his phrase, outweighs my search for God.[2] It seems outrageous of me to have to admit it, but with Heschel I discovered that the God of my Christian faith is nothing but the God of Israel. It shames me to admit it. So Heschel was pivotal to my growth in Christian faith and he became an object, still with Merton, of my morning meditation. I was far from alone in this. And I would say that knowing of Merton's regard for Heschel was a key part of what enabled me to open my parochial, supersessionist mind to such a magnificent witness.

When I wonder what effect Heschel had on Merton, all I really have to do is recall the effect he had on me. The most pointed example I will recall with you: that momentous day in July 1964 when Rabbi Heschel went to see Thomas Merton. It was one of a number of Heschel's attempts to raise alarms about what he had seen in his role as an observer at the Second Vatican Council in Rome. John XXIII, you recall, had called for a new relationship between the Church and the Jews. And he had directed the Council Fathers to put the Church's relationship with Jews at the center of their work. But what Heschel also saw, now that Pope John was gone, was ambivalence, resistance, even the old contempt among the Council Fathers as they debated draft after draft of the proposed document. Each draft seemed to be more watered down than the previous one.

Alarmed at this, Heschel apparently poured his heart out to Thomas Merton. There are scholars here who know this better than I. And the next day, as Professor Kaplan and others teach me, Merton urgently wrote a letter to Cardinal Bea [see The Heschel Correspondence], the cardinal in charge of this process at the Council, to plead – no, I would say to demand – that the Council not miss, as he put it, "this opportunity for repentance and for truth." And Merton tied this opportunity for authentic *teshuva* to

2 Abraham Joshua Heschel, *Man's Quest for God* (1954) and *God in Search of Man* (1955).

the opportunity that the Church had already clearly missed under Pius XII. Merton wrote to Bea that understanding the exact centrality of the Church's relationship to the Jewish People is so crucial for the Church's "own true identity" that "the whole meaning and purpose of the Council is at stake." And as you heard Rabbi Slosberg refer to it, the Council Statement on the Church and the Jews, *Nostra Aetate,* was made that next year, in that pivotal year of 1965. Anyone who has paid attention to the debate in the Council or even who reads the text of the Statement, knows that *Nostra Aetate* is not all that it could have been [see Appendix A]. It is not all that it *should* have been. It is not all, certainly, that Heschel hoped for, or for that matter, that many Catholics hoped for.

Yet *Nostra Aetate* could have been defeated. One of the Bishops who spoke up firmly for *Nostra Aetate* – apparently the first thing that he said at the Council – was a young bishop from Poland, until then unnoticed, named Karol Wojtyla [the future Pope John Paul II]. I am told by someone who was there, Father Thomas Stransky, a Paulist brother of mine, that when Wojtyla spoke with that thick Polish accent of his, the Council Fathers listened. He spoke strongly in favor of *Nostra Aetate*, and its cause was advanced. Not all that it could have been, still that Declaration did two things that changed forever official Catholic attitudes toward Jews. It renounced most of the deicide charge,[3] which, after all, had served as the source of gutter anti-Semitism for most of two millennia. And it affirmed the full and permanent integrity of God's covenant with Israel. This was a rejection of the primal source of what you might call religious anti-Judaism in the Christian tradition. And it is important to note that Merton in his writings had anticipated both of these changes. It is not too much to say that he helped prepare the entire Church to embrace them.

What is going on here? One of the ways in which Thomas Merton was most prophetic in relationship to the Catholic tradition is that he responded to a moral problem – war, the *Shoah* – with ethical insight, urging the legitimacy of peacemaking, and the rejection of anti-Semitism. And this led to the necessity of theological change: ethics leading to theology, and not, as was much more typical in our tradition, the other way around. The

3 For details of the struggle over the *gens deicida* language, see Appendix A, pp. 367-68.

1960s in the Catholic Church, and in the Christian world generally, were nothing if not a time of theological revolution. What is not ordinarily appreciated is the way in which that revolution was predicated on – even *centrally*, if inchoately, predicated on – a reckoning with the *Shoah*.

Merton wrote: "Can one look attentively at Christ and not see *Auschwitz?*" He wrote that in his journal, interestingly, during Easter week in 1964. I say "interestingly" because of course in the Christian tradition Easter Week and Holy Week leading up to it were the occasion for the worst of the pogroms, for the obvious reason. And note, Merton did not put it the other way around as Catholics are wont to do. As for example the well-meaning but misguided Carmelites in the 1990s Convent controversy did. To look at Auschwitz and to see Christ is to render those who died there, the overwhelming majority, invisible. Or at best they might be tokens of someone else's piety, someone else's redemption event. No, Merton had it right. It is in looking at Christ that we Christians must see Auschwitz – where, if he had been there, we should recall, he would have died, not as the savior of the world, but as another anonymous Jew with a number on his arm, that's all.

Professor Kaplan suggests that Merton's capacity to move from ethics to theology echoes Rabbi Heschel's insistence on "the inseparability of moral and religious thinking" and thus Ed Kaplan can say that Merton "meets Heschel at the crossroads of inwardness and of history." And here is the challenge that lies ahead for the Church: how the *ethical* recognition that follows from the *Shoah* leads to *theological* change. The *Shoah* is the great epiphany of contemporary times. It is an epiphany to us because it reveals the hidden action that has run beneath the surface of the history "of the entire West," as Merton said. And this epiphany *must* lead to profound theological change. Ethics leads to theology – which is more than saying ethics leads to apology. And that is why I insist that apology is the beginning of something, not the end.

Now it is certainly true that Christians and Jews have made tremendous strides toward reconciliation over the last generation, but many Christians are still lacking in a knowledge of the deep history of the Church's anti-Semitism, and the Church's tragic relationship to the Holocaust. And most Jews are equally ignorant of the tremendous strides that have taken place since Vatican II among Catholics and other Christians, beginning with, but by no means limited to *Nostra Aetate*. The climax of this shift in Church attitudes was seen by all the world when Pope John Paul II visited Yad Vashem [the Holocaust Memorial in Jerusalem]. It was seen even more momentously when he prayed at the Western Wall, as a Jew would pray, without invoking the name of Jesus. Unprecedented. But even this amounts to a mere beginning.

Merton may have seen through to the humanity of the Church, but the Vatican today still insists on the Church-protecting distinction between the "Church as such," which is the Bride of Christ, and therefore incapable of sin, and "sinful members" of the Church who alone are guilty of failure. That moving apology of the Pope's, you will notice, apologized for the acts of Christians, but not for the acts of the Church. Thus anti-Semitism is decried there and in other Church documents, but always as the product of sinners who were violating the Church's law of love when they hated Jews.

But what if anti-Semitism was the product, not of sinners, but of saints, acting exactly in line with the Church's most solemn teaching? Saints Ambrose, John Chrysostom, Anselm, Aquinas, Francis of Assisi even, and many others, were all spouters of the foulest diatribes against Jews, and often against the very God of Israel.

The blanket deicide charge against all Jews from the first century onward has been repudiated, but Christians still do not know how to regard the texts of the Gospels which are themselves its source. We read in Matthew's Gospel that the people in the street were saying, "His blood be upon us and upon our children," – and so it has been. And what are the Gospels if not "the Church as such"? Supersessionism to some extent has been renounced. *Nostra Aetate*'s affirmation of the covenant God makes with Israel is a powerful renunciation. But the implicitly denigrating prophecy-fulfillment structure of Christian thinking remains. It remains enshrined in "Old Testament" versus "New Testament." It remains enshrined in the pattern of liturgy that we Christians observe, making one reading, the Christian reading, bring to completion another reading, the Jewish reading.

The hold that this structure has on the Christian mind is

revealed even in the way that it continued to grip Merton himself, even when so much else had changed. We must not be surprised to find Merton actually still caught in ancient assumptions of supersessionism. That itself is a signal of how far we Christians have to go. Religious pluralism, of which Merton was a particular prophet within Catholicism, remains an especially thorny problem for the Church. We have left behind "No salvation outside the Church." (It was not that long ago, by the way, when Cardinal Cushing excommunicated Father Leonard Feeney in the 1950s for saying "No salvation outside the Church." I remember my mother turning to me and saying, "But that's what we believe!") We have left "No salvation outside the Church" behind, but we still hold to "No salvation outside Jesus," reiterated most recently in the Vatican document *Dominus Iesus*, year before last. Pope-centered Catholic triumphalism inevitably denigrates the religious integrity, not just of Judaism, but of all who find other ways to God. "God is greater than religion," Rabbi Heschel said with such eloquent simplicity. God is greater than religion. And that understanding shoots through especially the later Thomas Merton. Indeed, that understanding is the ground in which his work, toward the end of his life, is planted.

God is greater than religion. All religions, including this one, including Merton's. That has not been the operative assumption of a Church that sees itself as divine. "The Church as such" is held to be above the human condition. Jewish rejection of such Christian claims, especially of the absolute character of Catholic claims, is exactly what has made the Jewish/Christian relationship so fraught with theological tensions. Those claims are at the heart of what must be reexamined and, where necessary, corrected. The Holocaust requires, in that phrase of Merton's, "a sordid examination of conscience of the entire West." That means centrally, I argue in *Constantine's Sword*, an examination of conscience for the Church – "the Church as such." That means necessarily the Roman Catholic Church, but I'm talking broadly of the whole Christian Church.

The dark history of Christian contempt for Jews grows from a first generation view of Israel as the Church's negative "other," to a second generation's mis-remembering of the story of Jesus as a story against the Jews, to the conversion, not so much of

Constantine to Christianity but of the Church to the *Imperium*, to the subsequent targeting of Jews as the Church's special enemy, even the "privileged enemy," according to the formula of St. Augustine, and to Europe's first pogrom, the Crusades. On we rush to the massive medieval movement to convert Jews, to the *conversio* crisis, when Jews finally do begin to convert in large numbers, and to the Inquisition, which is instituted to investigate those conversions. Then comes the charge of "blood impurity," which spawns modern racial anti-Semitism and prepares the way for the Church's use of anti-Semitism in the post-Enlightenment period as a way of opposing social, religious and political change. Finally we come to the 20th century, when this legacy of Christian anti-Jewish contempt is masterfully exploited by godless Nazism, and to the failure of Pius XII, which in the light of this history should be seen as putting a spotlight on a very basic disorder: Christian betrayal of the very people we ought to be honoring and protecting, the people of Jesus the Jew. Our history is a blasphemy before the God of Israel, the God whom Jesus himself worshipped and served.

And the response to all this? Apology, of course. But to repeat, only as the beginning of *teshuva*, the beginning of a real change of all that has made such a history possible. We need change in how we read our scriptures; we need to read anti-Jewish text as if we were Jews. We need change in how we understand Jesus of Nazareth as a faithful Jew, an orthodox Jew until the day he died. Yes, for us Christians, for me, Jesus is the Word of God, the incarnate Word of God. But is he to be seen as one who reverses God's attitude toward creation by the sacrifice of his death? No. No, not *reversing* God's attitude, but *revealing* that God's attitude never needs to be reversed. Toward God's creation, God's attitude is one of constant love. Therefore there is no "old God/new God" split, no God of justice/God of love contrast. There is only One God, as we say in the *Sh'ma,* after all.

And therefore we need change in how we understand the Church, in relation to the religion of the Jews, certainly, but in relation to the religions of others as well. No more Christian triumphalism. No more Pope-centered authoritarianism − in relationship to which, by the way, Jews have always been especially vulnerable and never more so than in modern times. Recall that the last ruler in Europe to maintain the ghetto, which Cardinal Edward Cassidy of the Vatican today calls the antechamber to the death camps, was none other than Pope Pius IX, whom the Vatican beatified [raised towards sainthood] only last year [2001] – an act which itself shows how far we have to go. "The Church as such," in other words, is desperately in need of reform. And reform, remember, means to shape an institution according to its true character.

Merton's place in all this? We needn't sentimentalize him or remember him apart from the context in which he lived. Much of what I take for granted, as required of the Church by this history, would strike Merton, no doubt, as wrongheaded. And he wouldn't hesitate to tell me so. He complained about what he called "extreme progressives." Merton loved to see himself, in good Catholic fashion, as a man of the reasonable middle. But he railed against what he called "unresisting obedience to every behest of Caesar." Here is the bottom line about Merton, at least for Catholics of my generation. Having led us into the true glories of the great Catholic Church, a greatness we will always honor, he led us to see the ways in which the Church also stands greatly in need of reform. And having learned the hard way, he offered such witness, at least toward the end, with full knowledge that he was standing against the sanctified authorities of the Church, to whom he had once believed he owed absolute obedience.

By the end, he stood against crowned heads, as Berrigan put it, of both Church and State. Here is Monsignor Shannon's comment, about what I regard as Merton's greatest contribution to the task that lies before those who call for more change than Church authority can presently contemplate. Shannon said that we should "see in Merton's willingness to state divergent views the beginning of what has become an important reality in the life of the Roman Catholic Church, (though it was scarcely mentioned in Merton's day), namely, the right to dissent from certain 'official' teachings of the Church authority, without forfeiting one's claim to be a true and authentic Catholic."[4]

So, as you see, this has been a lifetime's journey for this one Catholic. It has been a journey for the Church, through the most

4 William H. Shannon, "Thomas Merton and Judaism," *America*, Oct. 6, 1990, p. 222.

heart-breaking and outrageous events of the 20th century. And it is a journey that is far from complete. But what a joy it is to have had all along the way, and still, this dear companion, this holy man, who ushered us into the very presence of God, when we were so young. This courageous man, who nudged us out into the anguished streets of our times, even though he was present to us from a distance. This believing Christian, who was ready to leave anachronistic notions about Hebrew religion behind, in favor of true respect for the living religion of living Jews. This lonely man, for whom friendship, whether with Heschel, Berrigan, Zen masters, or always his brothers in religion, was the motivating force behind his startling openness. Conversion, metanoia, real change, *teshuva*. Thomas Merton, the most famous convert of the age, showed us the real meaning of conversion – metanoia, *teshuva*. His golden witness still makes it possible to believe that it can happen. In our case that means the possibility of authentic separate but fully respectful mutuality between Jews and Christians. For the sake, of course, of no more *Shoah*. *Shoah* never again. But also because this is simply what is required of us as two peoples of the One God.

In his last letter to his beloved Ernesto Cardenal, composed July 21, 1968, a bare few months before he died on the other side of the world, Thomas Merton wrote, "I have a very definite feeling that a new horizon is opening up and I do not quite know what it is." After he wrote those words, in his last gift to us, he set out to learn what the new horizon is – or who. And I firmly believe that he found out. So what can we do except the thing that we have always done, which is, with grateful hearts, to follow him.

2

THOMAS MERTON AND JUDAISM

William H. Shannon

More and more scholars are discovering fresh indications of Thomas Merton's versatility, his breadth of vision and the creative ability he had to engage himself in so many different areas of thought. One of these areas that needs more attention is his relationship to Judaism, in terms of both his contact with Jewish thinkers and his appreciation of Jewish thought. His expression of the desire "to be a true Jew under my Catholic skin," written to Rabbi Abraham Heschel at a time of great strain in Roman Catholic-Jewish relationships, gives some measure of his deep appreciation for the relationship of the church and the synagogue.

Merton's reverence and respect for the Jewish Scriptures carried over into a special esteem and appreciation for Jewish scholars and writers. His contact with such people was fairly extensive, though this is not, I think, sufficiently appreciated.

There are three notable and extensive correspondences. First, there is the correspondence with Rabbi Abraham Heschel. Second, there are the letters to the Hasidic scholar, Zalman Schachter: letters extending over a period of seven years and interspersed with visits to Gethsemani by the rabbi. Third, there is the extensive and important correspondence with Erich Fromm, an author and practicing psychoanalyst. While it seems quite clear that Fromm was not a practicing Jew, still his values and insights into the dignity of the human person and the importance of true freedom belong to the Jewish heritage that was his. He acquiesced when Merton described him as "atheistic mystic." Merton also wrote to him: "Your writings show you to be one who has a very real sense of the God of Abraham and Isaac and Jacob.... Your [writing] would be incomprehensible without an implicitly *monotheistic* foundation" *(The Hidden Ground of Love)*.

The Mystery of Israel

In the face of this evidence it must be said that the "mystery" of Judaism fascinated Merton and called forth his reflections. If he approached the topic of Judaism with a bit of diffidence, it was not lack of interest but a sense of inadequacy in dealing with the issues. In a letter to Rabbi Stevens Schwarzschild (dated Feb. 24, 1962), Merton writes: "I am not worthy yet to write about the mystery of Judaism in our world. It is too vast a subject. I wish I could. Maybe some day. If there is anything I say *en passant* that happens to make sense to you, you can quote it if you like. The article will have to a be thing of the future."

Merton had a unique sensitivity to the Jewish character of the books that we, somewhat presumptuously, call the Old Testament. He respected the Jewish tradition enshrined in these books, not as something crypto-Christian, but as first and foremost a heritage that belonged to the people of Israel. Many of us who are Christians have lost the sense that we *share* a heritage with the Jews, indeed a heritage that we received from them and would not have except that they preserved it. Thus he writes in *Conjectures of a Guilty Bystander:* "One has either to be a Jew or stop reading the Bible. The Bible cannot make sense to anyone who is not 'spiritually a Semite.' The spiritual sense of the Old Testament is not and cannot be a simple emptying out of its Israelite content. Quite the contrary! The New Testament is the fulfillment of that spiritual content, the fulfillment of the promise made to Abraham, the promise that Abraham believed in. *It is never therefore a denial of Judaism, but its affirmation.* Those who consider it a denial have not understood it."

He believed, too, that a shared heritage suggested a shared destiny. He refused to consider the *election* of the "New Israel" as a *repudiation* of the "Old Israel." Thus he says in *Conjectures of a Guilty Bystander:* "The Jews were and remain the people especially chosen and loved by God." And in a Notebook entry in July of 1964 he writes: "[The Jews] remain the people of God, since His promises are not made void nor are they all being transferred *en bloc* to the Church without further ado, the Jews ... are still the object of His special mercy and concern, a *sign* of His concern."

Eschatological Expectations

The entire Bible is full of eschatological expectations. For Christians the death and Resurrection of Jesus represent the beginning of the eschatological age. Is it possible that for the Jews the Holocaust may well be seen as a national death and the rise of the state of Israel, not primarily as a political event but as a religious experience, as a new beginning that in some sense may be seen as an eschatological fulfillment?

Merton's notion of eschatology would be broad enough to embrace such diverse experiences. He explains that eschatology means to him "a belief in the decisive and critical breakthrough in [human] destiny." He goes on: "We are on the verge of this breakthrough, in fact it has begun. But we still do not know what form it will take on the surface of history. Still less can we really *plan* it to come out according to some limited set of ideas. Whatever is happening is happening both with us and without us, in us and beyond us. Our errors and our luck, our good and evil acts, our honesty and our lies, our love and hate, all our injustices and failures enter into the picture. None of it can be repudiated because it is all there" (letter to Dr. Weisskopf, April 4, 1968). Yet Merton goes on to express his own understanding of what all this means: "[My] eschatology says that underlying all of it, in the deepest depths that we cannot possibly see, lies an ultimate ground in which all contradictories are united and all come out 'right.'"

This it is that enables him to see a common destiny for Jews and Christians (and, in fact, carried to its logical consequence, the common spiritual destiny of all peoples – but again, we are in the realm of great mystery). He speaks of what this "ground" means for him. "For a Christian this ultimate ground is personal, that is to say it is a ground of freedom and love, not a simple mechanism or process. But since we are all in potentially *conscious* contact with this deep ground (which of course exceeds all conscious *grasp*) we must try to 'listen' to what comes out of it and respond to the imperatives of its freedom. In doing so, we may not be able to direct the course of history according to some preconceived plan, but we will be in harmony with the dynamics of life and history even though we may not fully realize that we are so. The important thing then is to restore this dimension of existence."

THE HOLOCAUST.

The eschatological direction of the Bible is evident. As Merton reflected on that direction, he came to see ever more clearly that the terrible experience of the Holocaust, forces us to face what we had all too readily brushed aside: the intrinsic relationship of Christianity and Israel and the eschatological expectations of both. The Holocaust makes us realize that it is Israel as a present reality, and not just its past history, that offers both Jews and Christians an eschatological perspective. Writing in 1966, Merton accepts the responsibility that the Holocaust imposes. He makes the point that the fact that he was a contemporary of Auschwitz was something about which he was not consulted. But it is an event, he says, in which – whether he liked it or not – he was deeply and personally involved (*Contemplation in a World of Action*).

The Holocaust, climaxing centuries of anti-Semitism, is, for those who are able and willing to see, the great eschatological sign of our times here and now. It is a sign making clear to us what we lost sight of for centuries – namely, that we cannot separate Israel and Christ. The Suffering Servant of the Songs of Isaiah is Israel and it is also Christ: The wedding feast to which God calls His people is a single wedding feast.

To put it in Merton's words (writing on Feb. 15, 1962, to Rabbi Zalman Schachter): "[The] Jews have been the great eschatological sign of the 20th century. Everything...depends on people understanding this fact, not just reacting to it with a little appropriate feeling, but seeing the whole thing as a sign from God *telling* us. Telling us what? Among other things, telling Christians that if they don't look out they are going to miss the boat or fall out of it, because the antinomy they have unconsciously and complacently supposed between the Jews and Christ is not even a very good figment of the imagination. The Suffering Servant is One: Christ, Israel. There is one wedding and one wedding feast, not two or five or six. There is one bride. There is one mystery, and the mystery of Israel and of the Church is ultimately to be revealed as One. As one great scandal maybe to a lot of people on both sides who had better things to do than come to the wedding."

In this same letter he suggests that Christian anti-Semitism became a problem when Christians began to think of Christ as

Prometheus. Then it was, he says, that they justified wars and crusades and pogroms and the bomb and Auschwitz. Michelangelo's Christ of the Last Judgment in the Sistine Chapel is precisely this Promethean Christ. "He is," Merton writes, "whipping sinners with his great Greek muscles." Merton goes on: "All right, if we can't make it to the wedding feast (and we are the ones who refused), we can blow up the joint and say it's the Last Judgment." Merton comments: "Well, that's the way it is the Judgment and that's the way men [sic] judge themselves, and that's the way the poor and the helpless and the maimed and the blind enter into the Kingdom: when the Prometheus types blow the door wide open for them."

MERTON AND POPE PIUS XII

And if Christians have sometimes used Christ to justify war and persecution, they have also used Him to protect institutional power. In 1963 Merton wrote an article entitled "The Trial of Pope Pius XII." The article was about Hochhuth's play "The Deputy," though it was more a reflection on the deeper meaning of the play than a review of it.

To say anything at all about Hochhuth's play put Merton in an awkward position. He was still "under the ban," imposed by the Abbot General of the Cistercians forbidding him to write on the issues of war and peace. The play touched closely on these issues. The play was clearly an attack on Pius XII and, more than that, on the institution of the papacy itself. The Pope was accused in the play of sacrificing the entire Jewish people in order to achieve a policy of coexistence with Hitler.

Without doubt the play was white-hot with partisanship. Nothing is said about the quiet and unofficial aid and refuge given quietly and effectively to thousands of individual Jews by the Pope. Instead, the Pope is portrayed as a hypocrite, as a man who was avaricious, ambitious and obsessed with a sense of his own power. Merton views the play as an instance of anti-Catholic or at least anti-papal propaganda. At the same time he refuses to dismiss it out of hand. For he feels that, despite its "vulgar polemic," "The Deputy" does raise an issue that must be taken seriously, even though the play itself scarcely ever rises to the level of that issue. "Crudely stated (and

Hochhuth states it crudely) the question is this: When the Church is faced with a critical choice between the most basic of all its moral laws, the love for God and for man, and the practical, immediate options of power politics, is she now so accustomed to choosing the latter that she is no longer able to see the former?"

Merton believed that "The Deputy" is unfair to Pius XII and suggests some of the reasons why the Pope failed to speak out against Hitler. But he also suggests that Hochhuth's pope is not a person, but an institution; and he is more than the institution of the papacy. He stands, Merton says, for "all Fatherhood" or, as we might want to express it today, for all paternalistic ways of exercising authority. It is the papacy as an "image" of this way of exercising authority that is on trial in the play. And Merton asks: "Is it a completely unwarranted reaction to the use of the 'Papal image' to enlist blind obedience to all kinds of temporal and expedient causes that are by no means divine, but which are put forward as if they were God's will, without alternative, because they have been presented in close association with the magic image? Is it not the habit of some who can speak officially in the name of the Church and even of some who cannot to evoke this image in support of interests and projects which are not, to put it mildly, those of God and of the Church?" (I should perhaps point out, that in the first draft of this article Merton wrote "those" who speak officially and "those" who do not for "some" in the final text.)

THE SECOND VATICAN COUNCIL AND
THE DECLARATION ON THE JEWS

The very next year following his writing this article on the "Trial of Pope Pius XII," the same issue – the proper exercise of church authority – occupied Merton's attention in connection with another matter deeply affecting to Jews. The matter at stake was the council's declaration on the relationship of the church to the Jews. An original statement had been drawn up by Cardinal Augustine Bea's Secretariat for Christian Unity. Intended to be Chapter IV of the document on ecumenism, it expressed repentance for anti-Semitism and acknowledged the irrevocable election of Israel by God. Hailed by Jewish leaders as a true breakthrough in Jewish-Christian relations, the statement on the Jews had a stormy journey through the council. A number of council fathers opposed it for various reasons. Probably the principal reason was political: the fear of giving offense to the Arab peoples of the East and making the lot of Christian Arabs more difficult.

On July 13, 1964, Rabbi Abraham Heschel visited Merton at Gethsemani. He had heard rumors of the opposition to the declaration and expressed his concern to Merton. The very next day, July 14, Merton wrote a long letter to Cardinal Bea, indicating that he was deeply concerned, yet still had hope that the council would not miss "this opportunity for repentance and truth which is being offered her and which so many are ready to reject and refuse."

Merton points out that it is especially the church that would gain from this statement on the Jews. He says: "I am personally convinced that the grace to truly see the church as she is in her humility and in her splendor may perhaps not be granted to the council fathers, if they fail to take account of her relationship to the anguished synagogue."

This is not, he suggests, simply a "gesture of magnanimity"; rather, "the deepest truths are at stake." "The very words themselves should suggest that the *ecclesia* is not altogether alien from the *synagogue* and that she should be able to see herself to some extent, though darkly, in this antitypal mirror. Yet she has the power to bring mercy and consolation into this mirror image, and thus to experience in herself the beatitude promised to the merciful."

He then goes on to suggest that the church has on more than one occasion yielded her prophetic role for motives of a temporal and political nature. Merton, in fact, does not hesitate to say that the council might at this juncture be in the very position that Pius XII found himself in and might be accused, as he had been, of acting for diplomatic and political reasons rather than for the truth of the Gospel. Thus, "If [the church] forgoes this opportunity out "of temporal and political motives (in exactly the same way that a recent Pontiff is accused of having done), will she not by that very fact manifest that she has in some way forgotten her own true identity? Is not then the whole meaning and purpose of the council at stake?"

In September of that same year, Heschel wrote a very disturbed letter to Merton, telling him that the original statement, which had been in almost all respects a monumental declaration was being replaced by a watered-down text and, indeed, one that was offensive to the Jews.

Although the text that Heschel sent to Merton in September 1964 was not the text the council adopted a year later, I think that Merton's comments on the text he received from Heschel may, with some reasonableness, also be applied to some of the argumentation that took place at the council and even to the final statement on the Jews approved by the council. The declaration finally agreed upon has without doubt lost something of the strong, eschatological emphasis of the earliest statement. Merton comments on the weakness of the document in his journal, *A Vow of Conversation,* under the date of Sept. 10, 1964. (It should be kept in mind that he is commenting on an interim document that was not accepted). He asks first of all, "Where is the prophetic and therefore deeply humiliated and humanly impoverished thirst for light, that Christians and Jews may begin to find some kind of unity in seeking God's will together?"

He goes on to discuss the role of church authority: "But if Rome simply declares herself complacently to be the mouthpiece of God and perfect interpreter of God's will for the Jews, with the implication that He in no way ever speaks to them directly, this is simply monstrous! It is perfectly true that the church, in the highest sense, can indeed speak a message of prophecy and salvation to the Jews, but to say that the juridical niceties of curial officials and well-meaning council fathers are the only source of light for the Jews today would be a fantastic misunderstanding of the Church's true mission." Merton concludes this reflection in his journal by once again linking this event at the council with the ambiguity of Pius XII's reaction to Nazism. "Reflect that the Church, in this rather imperfect sense, this exterior sense, delivered the Jews over to Hitler without a murmur, here and there helping a few individuals to escape, to make it less intolerable to conscience!"

Final Reflection

I want to conclude with three reflections. The first reflection is somewhat extraneous to the topic of this article, but quite helpful in understanding Thomas Merton, especially in the mid-

1960's. I offer it, therefore, as a kind of parenthesis. The point I want to make is that in those years he came to maturity as a Christian and as a Roman Catholic. This meant, among other things, that he made much stricter demands on church authority. He could no longer accept church pronouncements uncritically. Further, when such pronouncements seemed to conflict with what he experienced and felt others were experiencing, he was not hesitant in stating his views. Indeed, it seems to me that it is not stretching the truth to see in Merton's willingness to state divergent views the beginning of what has become an important reality in the life of the Roman Catholic Church (though it was scarcely even named in Merton's day); namely, the right to dissent from certain "official" teachings of the church authority without forfeiting one's claim to be a true and authentic Catholic. Many people today are strongly convinced that such dissent can be a gift offered to the whole church, deepening her understanding of her own identity and clarifying her presentation of the Gospel to all the world. Were Thomas Merton still writing in our midst, I am confident that he would share this conviction.

The second reflection I would offer – one that flows more directly from what I have said in the bulk of this article – is that the things Merton had to say about Judaism were, in part at least, an expression of his concern for the anguish of his Jewish friends, especially Rabbi Heschel. I would point out that this is no rare thing in Merton's life: his being moved to personal involvement in an issue because it affected people who were dear to him and important in his life.

The third and final reflection I would offer is this: Merton's involvement in the issue of Jewish-Christian relationships went far beyond the personal concern he had for his friends or even the affection he had for the Hebrew Scriptures and the religious perspective those Scriptures embodied. More than these, it was generated by the deep appreciation he had of the religious significance – for Jews and Christians – of the horrible and terrifying eschatological event of the Holocaust. Nowhere does he express this more poignantly than in a brief line, written during Easter week of 1964, in his journal, *A Vow of Conversation:* "Can one look attentively at Christ and not also see Auschwitz?"

"If you realize that God has indeed given you His Spirit as the source of all joy and strength, and trust Him to purify your heart with His presence and love, in great simplicity, He will teach you the joy of being a child of God."

—Thomas Merton, *The Hidden Ground of Love*

3

THE ECLIPSE OF DIFFERENCE: MERTON'S ENCOUNTER with JUDAISM[1]

Karl A. Plank

The publication of Thomas Merton's correspondence, begun with William Shannon's edition of *The Hidden Ground of Love* (1985),[2] startled readers not with the news of Merton's catholicity but with the sheer abundance of its evidence. Written at a time when Cold War mentalities held captive American religion and culture, Merton's letters express a sense of writing with the barriers down and a striking openness to the breadth of human concern. His contemporary journals echo the letters' testimony:

> The more I am able to affirm others, to say "yes" to them in myself, by discovering them in myself and myself in them, the more real I am. I am fully real if my own heart says *yes* to everyone ... If I affirm myself as a Catholic merely by denying all that is Muslim, Jewish, Protestant, Hindu, Buddhist, etc., in the end I will find that there is not much left for me to affirm as a Catholic: and certainly no breath of the Spirit with which to affirm it.[3]

---

1 This paper was presented at the meeting of the International Thomas Merton Society at Rochester, New York, June 13-16, 1991. It was also reprinted in Cistercian Studies. Vol. 28, 2 (1993).
2 *The Hidden Ground of Love. The Letters of Thomas Merton on Religious Experience and Social Concerns*, ed. William H. Shannon (New York: Farrar, Straus, Giroux, 1985).
3 *Conjectures of a Guilty Bystander* (New York: Image, 1968) 144.

As he writes, Merton looks out onto a world not empty of particularity, yet uncloistered in its diversity; he sees a world approachable and inviting in its underlying human claim.

Within its diversity, *Hidden Ground* includes letters to several Jewish thinkers: Zalman Schachter-Shalomi, Zwi Werblowsky, Erich Fromm, and most notably Abraham Joshua Heschel. Too often unnoticed in enthusiasm over Merton's dialogue with eastern religions, his awareness of Judaism merits more study, for there the issue of religious difference intimately involves his own particularity. As a Christian monk, Merton shared a scriptural legacy with his Jewish colleagues and stood within a tradition whose origins were linked to the life of early Judaism. Moreover he was becoming aware of the Christian anti-Judaism and complicities that had prepared the way for the Holocaust and darkened the history of his lifetime. For example, in his 1963 review of Rolf Hochhuth's "The Deputy," Merton recognized the drama's just indictment of the Church's paternalism and its institutional failure to combat anti-Judaism during the war years.[4] Elsewhere he referred to the anti-Judaism creeping into the Liturgical Easter Trope and cloaked in a Christian impulse toward treacherous goodness.[5] Thus, Merton's approach to Judaism inevitably put his identity at stake, implicating his own Christian self-understanding.

William Shannon's selection of Jewish correspondence and, subsequently, his article "Thomas Merton and Judaism," promote closer attention to Merton's encounter with Jews and suggests its importance for Merton's identity.[6] Shannon's article seeks to show Merton's appreciation and involvement with Judaism. Implicitly, he responds to Edward Kaplan's claim that Merton "pursued

4 See "The Trial of Pope Pius XII: Rolf Hochhuth's *The Deputy*," *The Literary Essays of Thomas Merton*, ed. Patrick Hart (New York: New Directions, 1981) 162-67. Merton's criticism of the Church is offered alongside certain reservations concerning Hochhuth's assessment of Pius XII.

5 *See Conjectures of a Guilty Bystander* 134-35 and 170-71. Merton's criticism of the treachery of Christian goodness scores a direct hit on the psychology of anti-Judaism. It does so, however, with an unintended irony: Merton unfortunately refers to the one who embodies this tendency as "the exact replica of the Pharisee" (171).

6 William Shannon, "Thomas Merton and Judaism," *America* 163 (October 6, 1990) 218-22 (a published version of a paper delivered at the first meeting of the International Thomas Merton Society, Louisville, KY, May 25-28, 1989), reprinted in this volume.

dialogue with Jews less actively (or less publicly) than dialogue with atheists and religious of the East.[7] For Shannon, Merton's dialogue with Jews is, in fact, active and substantial, as is evidenced in various ways: his extensive correspondence, reflections on the Hebrew Bible, writings on the Holocaust, and involvement in issues of the Second Vatican Council's Declaration on the Jews.[8] Shannon effectively counters Kaplan's suspicion by collating materials that indicate Merton's active concern for Judaism, a concern which in its own time, prophetically challenged the indifference and prejudice of Christian culture.

Still, a certain flaw lurks in Shannon's article that confuses the merit of Merton's *desire* to appreciate Judaism – and on this there is finally no question – with the value of his actual approach to Jews. Shannon, though he exposes Merton's wide and frequent consideration of Judaism, does not sufficiently probe the concrete effects of Merton's language addressed specifically to Jews or about Judaism. Closer attention to *these* effects reveals a troubling ambiguity in Merton: in his very desire to stand in unity with Jews he tends to efface the integrity of Jewish difference, thus denying the particularity of the same persons to whom he would stand in relation.

In Merton's time the urgency of social questions sanctified even the attempt to overcome estrangements, and one must include Merton's approach to Judaism in this context. The liberation struggles of intervening years, however, now warrant additional sensitivity to particularities of culture, religion, and gender and articulate the concern that those to whom one would relate not be oppressed in the very attempt to relate to them. Precisely here one

7 Edward K. Kaplan, "Contemplative Inwardness and Prophetic Action: Thomas Merton's Dialogue with Judaism," *Thomas Merton, Pilgrim in Process*, ed. Donald Grayston and Michael W. Higgins (Toronto: Griffin House, 1983) 96. Kaplan's article helpfully shows certain affinities between the spiritual and ethical writings of Merton and those of Abraham Heschel, but stays within that scope. Accordingly, he does not attend to Merton's writings on Judaism *per se* or to his actual engagement with Jews, Heschel or any other – limitations that hamper the article's adequacy as an account of "Merton's Dialogue with Judaism."

8 Shannon might have added Merton's invitation to Jewish scholars, such as Leo H. Silberman of Vanderbilt University, to lecture in the novitiate. See Merton's letter of February 7, 1963, to Silberman (Thomas Merton Studies Center, Bellarmine College, Louisville, KY). Merton's frequent appropriation of Martin Buber's *Tales of the Hasidim* in conferences for the novices would provide still another source for inquiry.

must press Merton's dialogue with Judaism. In what follows, the examination of that dialogue takes its issue from Abraham Heschel's challenge to the Church's conversionism during the Second Vatican Council; it then considers Merton's response to Heschel and other dimensions of his writings concerning Judaism. As a postscript, a final section identifies from another portion of Merton's writing a better perspective to inform the task of Christian dialogue with Jews.

HESCHEL, CONVERSION, AND THE ISSUE OF DIFFERENCE

In the first days of September 1964, Thomas Merton received jolting words from his friend Abraham Heschel. Since 1961 Heschel had been working with the American Jewish Committee to assist the Vatican's Cardinal Bea to shape a statement on the Church's relation to Jews. Bea's Secretariat for Christian Unity, in preparation for the second Vatican Council, had been responsive to Heschel's concerns: a) that the Church repudiate its anti-Judaism, particularly its association of Jews with the charge of deicide, and b) that the Church affirm the "permanent preciousness" of the Jews *as Jews.*[9] Still, as the Council proceeded, a certain opposition to the Schema on Ecumenism developed. Shortly before the third session was to open (September 16, 1964), a revision was proposed that introduced a conversionist intent: namely, the Church's hope for reconciliation with Jews through their ultimate conversion. Learning of this, Heschel responded sharply, indicting the Church's proposal as a murderous form of "spiritual fratricide." He continued:

> As I have repeatedly stated to leading personalities of the Vatican, I am ready to go to Auschwitz any time, if faced with the alternative of conversion or death. Jews throughout

9 See Eva Fleischner, "Heschel's Significance for Jewish-Christian Relations", *Abraham Joshua Heschel: Exploring His Life and Thought*, ed. John C. Merkle (New York: Macmillan, 1985) 154; also Marc H. Tannenbaum, "Heschel and Vatican II: Jewish-Christian Relations," paper delivered to the memorial Symposium in honor of Abraham Joshua Heschel, The Jewish Theological Seminary, New York City, February 23, 1983. After Heschel's brief visit to the Abbey of Gethsemani in July 1964, Merton wrote to Cardinal Bea stressing the importance of Heschel's concerns; see *The Hidden Ground of Love*, 433-4. For the shifting fortunes of the deicide charge, see Appendix A, pp. 367 ff.

the world will be dismayed by a call from the Vatican to abandon their faith in a generation which witnessed the massacre of six million Jews and the destruction of thousands of synagogues on a continent where the dominant religion was not Islam, Buddhism, or Shintoism.[10]

Heschel sent a mimeographed copy of these words to Merton who, bewildered with the whole situation, responded: "It is simply incredible. I don't know what to say about it."[11] The protesting silence speaks pointedly, but so had Merton's earlier words to Heschel: "The twentieth century makes it impossible seriously to do this any more, so perhaps we will be humble enough to dig down to a deeper and more burning truth."[12]

One must question whether or not the Church humbly dug down to a deep enough level. With a sense of urgency Heschel flew to Rome to meet with Pope Paul VI, even on the eve of Yom Kippur (September 14, 1964), and his statement does seem to have had some effect: ultimately *Nostra Aetate* avoids reference to Jewish conversion. It still falls short, however, of affirming the "permanent preciousness" of Judaism. Accordingly, this conciliar declaration compromises Heschel's concerns. On the one hand, it importantly denounces anti-Semitism and nowhere endorses proselytizing; on the other, it ambiguously defines Judaism as not "rejected or accursed," a rhetoric whose assertion scarcely affirms. Its limitation can be seen in the warning that anti-Semitism contradicts "the Gospel message" as if the violation were against the Christian

10 Quoted in Fleischner, 156. For full text, see Kaplan 100-1 and the Merton-Heschel Correspondence in this volume.
11 Letter of September 9, 1964, *The Hidden Ground of Love*, 434. Also note Merton's journal entry for the next day, *A Vow of Conversation* (New York: Farrar, Straus, Giroux, 1988) 76-77. See pp. 223-26 in this volume.
12 Letter of January 16, 1963, *The Hidden Ground of Love*, 432. This letter show Merton grappling with the Church's problematic triumphalism, which becomes scandalous in the light of the Holocaust, if nowhere else. Merton's thinking on the Holocaust becomes intensified in March of that same year as he began to work through Hannah Arendt's report of the Eichmann trial (see Karl A. Plank, "Thomas Merton and Hannah Arendt: Contemplation after Eichmann," in *The Merton Annual 3* (1990) 121-50.

principle instead of the intrinsically precious life of the Jew.[13] Thus, Heschel's real challenge goes unmet.

Nostra Aetate ultimately fails because the question of conversion concerns not simply the Church's proselytizing, but the value of the Jew *as Jew*. The conversion issue, at its root, puts at stake the value of difference, the affirmation of otherness that would not only tolerate diversity but recognize the integrity and freedom of an other's existence. Agendas of conversion, Heschel understands, compromise the worth and right of others to live without reference to the norms, needs, and categories that still different persons assume self-evident in *their* own situation. For Heschel, Jewish difference is God-given, a fact that subverts not only the Church's conversionism but also any alleged final importance attributed to the Church's recognition of Judaism. Chosen by God and, thus, free of both the Church's conversion and affirmation, Jewish identity does not need to define itself in Christian categories. Heschel asks:

> Why is so much attention paid to what Vatican II is going to say about the Jews? Are we Jews in need of recognition? God himself has recognized us as a people. Are we in need of a "Chapter" acknowledging our right to exist as Jews? ... It is not gratitude that we ask for: it is the cure of a disease affecting so many minds that we pray for.[14]

The issue that Heschel shared with Merton, especially when understood in terms of difference, takes on further ramifications in current discussions. For example, liberation theologians such as Sharon Welch have understood human difference not only as historical fact but as a condition for political action and power.[15]

13 For the pertinent text of *Nostra Aetate*, the 1965 Declaration of the Council on the relation of the Church to Non-Christian Religions, see *Vatican Council II*, ed. Austin Flannery (Collegeville: Liturgical Press, 1975) 740-2; for commentary, see J.M. Oesterreicher, "Declaration on the Relationship of the Church to Non-Christian Religions," *Commentary on the Documents of Vatican II*, ed. Herbert Vorgrimler (New York: Herder & Herder, 1968) and Franz Mussner, *Tractate on the Jews. The Significance of Judaism for Christian Faith*, transl. Leonard Swidler (Philadelphia: Fortress, 1984) 1-4, 251-3. See also, in this volume, Appendix A.
14 Cited in Fleischner, 157.
15 See Sharon D. Welch, *A Feminist Ethics of Risk* (Minneapolis: Fortress. 1990) 123-51.

Wary of universalisms that reduce human identities to their least common denominator or abstract persons from their history, Welch turns to difference as a basis for solidarity. Her resulting notion, a "communicative ethic," emphasizes "as its standpoint the interaction between 'concrete others.'"[16]

From Welch's point of view, the Church's conversionism would deny for Jews what is most necessary for their well-being, in the same way that universalisms exclude difference: a basic freedom to stand apart from as well as along with others, in order to forge an identity congruent with the distinctiveness of their historical situation. Any compromise, however, threatens their life with more than a loss of freedom. Heschel's words, read through the lens of Holocaust history and liberation theology, remind us that only a short step separates the Church's assertion that the Jew should not be a Jew from saying the Jew should not be.[17] Translated politically, the spiritual fratricide of conversion too easily becomes a literal murder and the exclusion of difference, a death-camp logic.

The centrality of difference thrives in the climate of postmodern theory as well as in liberationist perspectives. Where postmodern critics emphasize the difference between one sign and another as the *sine qua non* for communication, they radicalize this same difference to the point of destabilizing any and every system of signs. In short, the postmodernist sees nothing beyond difference, no underlying metaphysical unity to ground speech and language – only the continual and creative interplay of signs, asserting and subverting their own expression. As Edith Wyschogrod has made clear, such theory plays havoc with traditional formulations of morality by robbing them of any conceptual anchorage in notions of the good or of the right.[18] Still, as she shows, postmodernism affords an ethic rooted not in any concept but in alterity itself, in the living force of the concrete other that decenters the egoism of the self and that summons compassion for that other. She writes:

> The other person opens the venue of ethics, the place where ethical existence occurs. To answer the question

16 Welch, 128.

17 On this point see Karl A. Plank, "The Survivor's Return: Reflections on Memory and Place," *Judaism* 38 (1989) 266.

18 *Saints and Postmodernism: Revisioning Moral Philosophy* (Chicago: University of Chicago Press, 1990).

about whether postmodernism requires some *point d'appui,* this Other, the touchstone of moral existence, is not a conceptual anchorage but a living force. The Other is different from oneself, her/his existence will be shown to carry compelling moral weight. In the context of a postmodern ethics, the Other functions as a critical solvent in much the same way as the notion of difference functions in postmodern metaphysics.[19]

From a postmodern perspective, Heschel's challenge, the expressed difference of a "living force," resists domestication within the Church's conceptual schemes. The Church's attempts to define Judaism relative to the theological claims of Christianity share with conceptual schemes *per se* an arbitrariness and a tendency to imprison the other in a system that is defined by someone else's need and manipulation. As such, the Church's location of Judaism within salvation history shares the same impulse as the more crass and obvious expressions of anti-Judaism: it refuses to meet the Jew as other, as Jew. The postmodern challenge calls for precisely that concrete level of confrontation wherein the difference of a given life, the alterity of Heschel's Jewish identity, must be affirmed.

Merton, Judaism, and the Eclipse of Difference

When read with a sensitivity to difference, Heschel's words laid at Merton's gate a challenge: to approach the Jew as a concrete other for whom alterity and life itself are mutually bound. In that approach, however, Merton's language addressed to and about Jews is problematic. Though he unequivocally supported Heschel's protest and bewailed the Church's proposal as "simply monstrous,"[20] his language yet effaced the Jew he would affirm, allowing a desire for unity to obscure essential difference.

Merton's conversation with Judaism, manifested especially in his correspondence with Heschel, shows his characteristic openness to

---

19 Wyschogrod, xxi. See further Karl A. Plank, "The Human Face of Otherness: Reflections on Joseph and Mary," *Faith and History: Essays in Honor of Paul W. Meyer,* ed. C. Cosgrove and others (Atlanta: Scholars, 1990) 55-73.
20 *A Vow of Conversation,* 76.

ecumenical conversation and his wariness of ecclesial triumphalisms. He sought commonalities and, with compassion, wanted to make Jewish anguish his own, the Council's threatened rejection of Heschel's position being a case in point. On that occasion Merton wrote to Heschel to affirm their unity and to confess his own bewilderment:

> This much I will say: my latent ambitions to be a true Jew under my Catholic skin will surely be realized if I continue to go through experiences like this, being spiritually slapped in the face by these blind and complacent people of whom I am nevertheless a "collaborator."
>
> I must, however, think more of people like Cardinal Bea, who must certainly be crushed by this development.[21]

Here Merton's desire for unity – "to be a true Jew under [his] Catholic skin" becomes difficult. Estrangement is no virtue, particularly if it leads one to be indifferent to another's suffering; but if one overcomes distance by suppressing alterity then one simply creates another form of indifference by effacing the distinctiveness of the other's experience. Desiring to identify with the Jewish anguish, Merton forgets that it is not and cannot be his own, a forgetting that lets his attention slide too quickly from Heschel's grievance to his own frustration. Merton describes himself as "slapped in the face," and he takes note of the certain crushing of Cardinal Bea. Nowhere in the letter, however, does he recognize the particular and more urgent situation of Heschel himself, the concrete situation of the Jew as Jew. Heschel is rendered invisible in Merton's letter, which, at least ostensibly, would respond to *Heschel's* situation, to the offense that the Church directs singularly at his Jewishness.

The eclipse of difference, evident in Heschel's invisibility, often depends on the machinery of analogy to undermine otherness. Analogy brings the other into a frame of reference that seemingly licenses one to stress likeness regardless of difference and thereby to control the other's freedom to appear as different. Merton's inept analogy between anti-Americanism and anti-Semitism, though not

21 Letter of September 9, 1964; *The Hidden Ground of Love*, 434.

intended to manipulate, effectively compromises Jewish difference in this way. He writes: "To identify myself completely with this country [America] is like accepting the fact of a hidden Jewish grandfather in Nazi Germany ... I am, as it were, a Jew with blond hair and blue eyes."[22] Here, the analogy levels Judaism: Americans may be hated in the world, but they face no vulnerability that is comparable to the Jew in Nazi Europe. In this case, the analogy suppresses the Jewish vulnerability to mass death and thus creates a certain indifference to and control of that vulnerability.

Comparable effacements occur in Merton's writings on the *Shoah*. Though he seriously engages the legacy of the Holocaust, his prose and poetry focus almost exclusively on the Nazi evil rather than on the situation of the Jew who has survived or fallen victim to that evil. For example, Merton's most extensive Holocaust writings preoccupy themselves with the specter of Adolf Eichmann, who became for Merton the contra-type of the true contemplative and the perduring force within the banality of the nuclear age.[23] Similarly, his signature "Auschwitz" poem, "Chant to Be Used in Processions Around a Site with Furnaces," depicts the persona of a Nazi commandant, gleaned from William Shirer's quotations of Rudolf Hess.[24] When Merton reflects on the Holocaust in his journals, his perspective continues to be that of Nazi anti-Semitism, thus holding the event captive to the reference point of its perpetrators. These reflections warn of Nazism's technology of death and the perils of propaganda.[25] They cry that Nazism is an attack on Christ, but they conspicuously neglect the fact that before anti-Semitism attacks Christ, it concretely assaults the life of the Jewish other who, for that reason, must be granted primary concern.

22 *Conjectures of a Guilty Bystander*, 281.
23 For a study of these writings, see Plank, "Thomas Merton and Hannah Arendt."
24 *The Collected Poems of Thomas Merton* (New York: New Dimensions, 1977) 345-9. On the source of these poems, see Plank "Thomas Merton and Hannah Arendt" 133. A similar focus is evident in Merton's essay, "Auschwitz: A Family Camp," *The Nonviolent Alternative*, ed. Gordon C. Zahn (New York: Farrar, Straus, Giroux, 1980) 150-9. See p. 87 this volume.
25 *Conjectures of a Guilty Bystander*, 240-3, 133-9.

Clearly, as Merton reminds us, anti-Semitism *is* an attack on Christ.[26] Yet left on its own, such a statement dangerously diverts attention away from those who are concretely vulnerable to that attack, namely the Jews. It again renders them invisible by maintaining a single frame of reference – a Christian lens – that filters out the challenge of difference and itself remains unchallengeable. Merton makes an important journal entry, however, that may in fact counter this tendency in his writing: "Can one look attentively at Christ and not also see Auschwitz?"[27] Though brief and exceptional, the reference suggests Merton's awareness of an alterity that must shape his perception of Christ and qualify the lens of the Christian. In doing so, Merton begins to reverse the tendency of his reflections that keep the other within his frame of reference by asking, in effect, "Can one look at *Auschwitz* and not see Christ?" It is a way of posing the question and keeping the other within his frame of reference.[28]

Merton's writings on the Holocaust do provide an important prophetic critique of Church and culture. Yet these same writings characteristically obscure the concrete situation of the Jewish other, who as a result suffers a double effacement: on the one hand, the near oblivion of the death camps and, on the other, the more subtle eclipse of the Jew in discourse about that very event. Reading the Holocaust simply in terms of Nazism (or Nazism's attack on Christ), even for the sake of significant critique, renders Jews conspicuously absent from the history of their own suffering. Such an understanding constitutes a serious denial of Jewish difference: namely, the way in which the Holocaust remains singularly an event in Jewish history. Though it claims and indicts Christian culture to its very foundations, the Holocaust will not be reduced to an "eschatological sign," for the Church,[29] nor to a foil for the Nazism that the Church should oppose.

Both in his correspondence with Heschel and in his Holocaust

26 *Conjectures of a Guilty Bystander*, 19.
27 *A Vow of Conversation*, 42.
28 More generally on Christ and the Holocaust, see Karl A. Plank, "Broken Continuities: *Night* and 'White Crucifixion,'" *The Christian Century* 4 November, 1987: 963-6.
29 A line pursued in Merton's letter to Zalman Schachter (February 15, 1962); *The Hidden Ground of Love*, 535.

writing, Merton effaces Jewish difference, subordinating it to some frame of reference more nearly his own. Even when preoccupied with the critique of Nazism or the Church's triumphalism, the frame of reference remains distinctly Merton's in its concern to articulate what the Church must learn or oppose. His difficulty in sustaining Jewish difference may derive from his limited and romantic perception of Judaism itself. Characteristically, Merton seems to understand Judaism primarily in terms of its biblical antecedents. At least in his correspondence, he points to the scriptural legacy as a basis for unity.[30] Yet if seeing Judaism as a biblical religion enables a scriptural kinship, it also obscures Jewish particularity from its historical beginnings in the post-biblical mishnaic period through the current period of the *Shoah* and its aftermath. Tying Judaism too closely to its *antecedent* history in the Hebrew Bible screens for Merton the elements of greatest difference and thus probably contributes to the effacements noted earlier. If so, it is also likely that Merton is limited by the misleading notion of a Judaeo-Christian tradition, a notion that reduces the Jewish other to the common denominator with Christianity and typically tries to see that denominator in the common scriptural heritage.[31] The Jew of the Judaeo-Christian tradition, the Jew without full difference, falls short of being the Jewish other that Heschel invites Merton to see as permanently precious.

Shannon's article mentioned earlier appeals to the frequency and breadth of reference to Judaism in Merton's writing to show that Merton's appreciation of Judaism was no minor concern. Still, as a significant concern, his engagement with Judaism remains problematic: Merton's correspondence with Abraham Heschel, precisely on the issues of Vatican II, shows not a special sensitivity to the Jewish situation but an effacement of the Jewish grievance; his writing on the *Shoah*, preoccupied with the reference frames of Nazism and Christianity, similarly effaces Judaism from its own

---

30 For example, *The Hidden Ground of Love* 432, 435, 535-6; note also *Conjectures of a Guilty Bystander*, 90.
31 On the problematic "Judaeo-Christian" tradition, see Arthuer A. Cohen, *The Myth of the Judaeo-Christian Tradition* (New York: Harper & Row, 1963).

history; and his tendency to refract Judaism through a biblical lens leads him to appreciate a Jew who exists without full difference.[32]

Merton intends no harm in pursuing Jewish relations; on the contrary, he desires to diminish suffering and affirm kinship. Yet the consequences of displacing Jewish difference, even and especially in ecumenical conversation, are serious. Those consequences appear most starkly within scenes of Claude Lanzmann's mammoth film, *Shoa*. Lanzmann's film begins with the return of Simon Srebnik to Chelmno, where some four hundred thousand Jews had been murdered during the *Shoa*. Srebnik, sent to Chelmno as a boy of thirteen, was one of only two Jews to survive the imprisonment at this death camp. Now forty-seven years old, Srebnik goes back to where SS guards used to parade him through the village, forcing him to sing with his melodious voice. Outside the church, a festal Marian procession concluding in the background, a group of villagers surround the returning Srebnik, eager to welcome him for "they know all he's lived through."[33] Zealously they rush to give their versions of Srebnik's story as if it were theirs to tell and as if they were not indicted by the very reality they would describe. Once or twice they seek Srebnik's nod of approval, yet without awareness of what they have asked him to confirm. Lost amid their cackle, Srebnik is silent. The villagers, caught in the euphoria of their own noise, do not hear the shattering scream of that silence; thus Srebnik's return goes effectively unmet. No absence of hostility nor overture of welcome masks this reality: to these villagers Simon Srebnik has no greater voice in Chelmno's present than he did in Chelmno's past. Rendered silent, he is robbed of the integrity of difference. Effaced from the telling of his story, he suffers once more a form of the annihilation that that story portrays.[34]

32 One might consider the role played by Merton's memory of at least two of his closest friends at Columbia, Robert Lax and Robert Gerdy. Both Lax and Gerdy were born Jews but later converted to Catholicism. See Michael Mott, *The Seven Mountains of Thomas Merton* (Boston: Houghton Mifflin, 1984) 121.
33 Claude Lanzmann, *Shoa: An Oral History of the Holocaust* (New York: Pantheon, 1985) 95; for the full account of this scene see 95-100.
34 For this description and further discussion of the Srebnik episodes in Lanzmann's film, see Plank, "The Survivor's Return" 270-77.

The Love of the Other: An Other's Love

The point of this critique is not to derogate Merton's contribution to Jewish and Christian relations so much as to underscore the difficulty of the challenge that those relations bring: to live in kinship without eclipsing the difference that makes relation possible and infuses it with importance.[35] Though tempting in its momentary release from conflict, identity, the fusion of groups or individuals irrespective of difference, cannot be the goal of human communities or the base on which they build. To level difference into a low common denominator or to subordinate the difference of one group to the controlling power of another establishes no community but only banality in the first case and imperialism in the second. Not identity, but the relation of genuine others, responds to Heschel's challenge.

Attempts to stand in relation to an other inevitably confront a dialectic that moves between kinship and difference. Merton, scandalized by the gross estrangements of difference that characterized the context of his writings, accented one end of that dialectic. Accordingly, his emphasis on kinship is not so much wrong as partial. The resulting neglect of Jewish difference, in Merton's case, becomes difficult as a conspicuous omission rather than as an intent to wound. Still, in its very habit, the omission alarms with its signal that oppressions – violation or endangerment of the other – may occur unwittingly and repeatedly, all intentions to the contrary notwithstanding. In this regard, to make uncritically of Merton's approach a model for Jewish-Christian relations or, generally, for inter-religious dialogue ignores its one-sidedness and its potential to oppress. At the same time, casually to dismiss the significance of Merton's concern for unity ignores what must remain an essential dynamic in human relation: the perception of the other as one whose difference claims me with a claim kindred to myself.

Our last word is not criticism, but a postscript and an overture. Merton's writing, like his own self, is varied and complex. Though Merton's explicit discourse on Judaism is seriously flawed, fundamental perspectives found in other portions of his writing

---

35 Here and in what follows I draw upon the dialogic perspective articulated by Martin Buber. Though the perspective is refined in Buber's works as a whole, its classic expression occurs in *I and Thou*, transl. W. Kaufmann (New York: Scribners, 1970).

may yet establish better foundations for Christian dialogue with Jews. In *The New Man,* for example, Merton's reflections on the *imago Dei* tradition move toward a reenvisioning of the relation of self to other. That volume's critique of Prometheanism calls into question behaviors that, in effect, would eclipse the difference of other selves.[36] Prometheus, in his heroic attempt to steal back the fire, cannot allow for the generosity of any other and thus renders all others projections of his own desperate egoism. By contrast, the conviction that human beings bear God's image and thus share in God's capacity for speaking freely *(parrhesia)* means that one can never finally control the word of the other or rob it of its difference.[37] At the moment of one's greatest defensiveness, the other may speak with openness and generosity to provide what one most needs but assumed would have to steal.

The task of relation requires recognizing the difference of an other self whose integrity may speak with generosity but must speak with freedom. To affirm that other, then, calls not for the willful pursuit of one's own need to love, but an openness to the prospect of that other's expression of love. Merton writes:

> In the mystery of social love there is found the realization of "the other" not only as one to be loved by us, so that we may perfect ourselves, but also as one who can become more perfect by loving us. The vocation to charity is a call not only to love but to *be loved*.[38]

Here Merton's words address more pointedly the challenge of Jewish and Christian relations and provide a vantage within his own writings from which to consider the critique of his approach to Judaism. To affirm the Jew as Jew does not mean rendering the Jew as an object of Christian charity or subject of Christian discourse, but perceiving in the Jew an other with words to speak – words of his or her own that may challenge from difference and may love

36 *The New Man* (New York: Farrar, Straus & Giroux, 1961) 23-48. Though he does not pursue it in the book, Merton does connect Promethean theology with anti-Semitism in a letter to Zalman Schachter (February 15, 1962); *The Hidden Ground of Love*, 535.

37 *The New Man*, 51-94.

38 *The New Man*, 91.

with freedom. To recognize, in Heschel's terms, the "permanent preciousness" of the Jews realizes the Jew's inalienable right to speak and to love, and to do so particularly as a Jew within a concrete history. Accordingly, Jewish difference challenges Christians not first to speak but to hear speech not their own, not simply to love but to consent to the prospect of being loved by an other. The alternative, finally, is to replicate the haunting scenario of Simon Srebnik's silence outside the village church at Chelmno, to corrupt relation with the death-dealing eclipse of difference – ultimately of God, the final Other.

4

THOMAS MERTON, THE HOLOCAUST, AND THE ECLIPSE OF DIFFERENCE

Donald Grayston

The dark – three meanings.

First, the darkness of the night, and Thomas Merton's reference to the awakening as that of "a mind awake in the dark,"[1] the dark which is both nocturnal darkness and the experienced mystical darkness of contemplation itself.

Second, the divine darkness: as, for example, when the 18-year-old Merton speaks of his time in Rome as a time when he began to pray "to the God I had never known, to reach down towards me out of His darkness,"[2] out of the divine mystery, the context for the darkness of contemplation: this kind of darkness invites the placing beside it of such related terms as transcendence, mysteriousness, inscrutability.

Third, the darkness of the *Shoa*: the darkness of spirit and society which afflicted minds, hearts, wills and bodies in Europe during those dreadful years, when the sky was made dark with smoke from the chimneys of Auschwitz, a darkness visible to which the silence of God was and is for many the non-auditory correlate, a darkness which, like the darkness of contemplation, can be explored but not explained, and which also attracts terms like

1 "Day of a Stranger," in Lawrence S. Cunningham, ed. and introd., *Thomas Merton: Spiritual Master* (New York: Paulist, 1992) 218. Ross Labrie describes Merton's "fascination with darkness" in *Thomas Merton and the Inclusive Imagination* (Columbia: University of Missouri Press, 2001) 159; see also 217.
2 *The Seven Storey Mountain* (New York: Harcourt Brace, 1948) 111.

inscrutability, and subscendence (Arthur A. Cohen's term) if not transcendence. Those years were indeed, in Hannah Arendt's words, "the darkest of times."[3]

With these three dimensions of darkness as givens, I will try in this paper first to recapitulate the challenge presented to students of Merton's views on the Holocaust by Karl Plank, in his challenging and thoughtful article "The Eclipse of Difference: Merton's Encounter with Judaism,"[4] and then look at Merton's three discrete pieces of writing related to the Holocaust, extend this enquiry into a survey of the evidences of his thinking about the Holocaust which we find in his journals and letters, return to Plank's thesis, and conclude with an attempt to place Merton's view of the Holocaust in the larger perspective of his mature practice of interfaith encounter.

THE ECLIPSE OF DIFFERENCE

Plank's basic charge against Merton is clear from the title of his article, "The Eclipse of Difference." While acknowledging Merton's strong and genuine interest in Judaism, his friendship with a number of Jewish thinkers, and his desire to write "with the barriers down,"[5] Plank finds a "troubling ambiguity" in Merton: for, as he says,

> in his very desire to stand in unity with Jews he tends to efface the integrity of jewish [sic] difference, thus denying the particularity of the same persons to whom he would stand in relation.[6]

In other words, Merton tends to downplay the full alterity of Jews *as* Jews, their "permanent preciousness,"[7] their irreducible

---

3 *Men in Dark Times* (New York: Harcourt Brace, 1968) ix, quoted in Karl A. Plank, "Thomas Merton and Hannah Arendt: Contemplation after Eichmann in *The Merton Annual*, v. 3, ed. Robert E. Daggy, Patrick Hart, Dewey Weiss Kramer and Victor A. Kramer (New York: AMS Press, 1990) 138.
4 Presented to the Second General Meeting of the International Thomas Merton Society, 1991, and rpt. in *Cistercian Studies Quarterly* 28.2 (1993) 179-191.
5 "Eclipse," 179.
6 "Eclipse," 181.
7 "Eclipse," 181, 182, 190.

historical distinctness, repeatedly assuming a default position in which Jews are primarily sharers with Christians in a common scriptural legacy, or, even more misleadingly, sharers (and inevitably thereby permanent junior partners) in the so-called Judaeo-Christian tradition.[8] Specifically in relation to Merton's writings on the Holocaust, Plank points to what he calls Merton's almost exclusive focus on the Nazi perpetrators and on his own response to Nazi evil *as a Christian*, rather than on the situation of the Jew who has survived or fallen victim to that evil,"[9] thereby rendering Jews "conspicuously absent from the history of their own suffering."[10] After examining these writings of Merton, and situating them in the context of his thought about the Holocaust as revealed in his journals and letters, we will return to Plank's thesis for reassessment.

CHANT, MEDITATION, CAMP

The three most extended and discrete pieces of Merton's writing on the Holocaust are his found poem (it could also be called a prose poem or an anti-poem[11]), "Chant to be used in processions around a site with furnaces," first published in 1962;[12] his article in response to the Eichmann trial, "A Devout Meditation in Memory of Adolf Eichmann," first published in 1966;[13] and his review of *Auschwitz* by Bernd Naumann,[14] to

8 I note here Plank's reference to Arthur A. Cohen, *The Myth of the Judaeo-Christian Tradition* (New York: Harper and Row, 1963). In a very different context, there is a parallel here to the way some Canadians feel about Canada's relation to the United States, namely, that Canada will never be anything other than a junior partner in any continental endeavor – hence the current (early 2002) resistance on the part of a number of Canadian political leaders to US proposals for full military integration on a continental basis.

9 "Eclipse," 186.

10 "Eclipse," 187.

11 Or, as Plank notes, an example of *assemblage*, a technique utilized in a sculpture movement of that name.

12 *The Collected Poems of Thomas Merton* (New York: New Directions, 1977) 345-349. It was first published in the British Dominican journal, *Blackfriars*, in April 1962.

13 *Thomas Merton on Peace*, introd. Gordon Zahn (New York: McCall, 1975) 160-162. It was first published in the activist magazine, *Ramparts*, in October 1966.

14 Trans. Jean Steigenberg, introd. Hannah Arendt (London: Pall Mall Press, 1966).

which he gave the savage title "Auschwitz: A Family Camp."[15]
From these dates we may situate his attention to the *Shoa* as
particularly active between the trial of Eichmann and Merton's
death, that is, during his four final years as master of novices (1961–
1965) and the years (1965–1968) during which he lived in the
hermitage for which he had so long asserted his need. This was
also the period in which the Second Vatican Council took place
(1962–1965), and in which he corresponded with Abraham Joshua
Heschel[16]on the text of *Nostra Aetate* (the Declaration on the
Relation of the Church to Non-Christian Religions),[17] the fourth
section of which concerns the Jews.

Hannah Arendt, writing about Eichmann and his "work," had
coined the phrase "the banality of evil,"[18]and it is to his disturbance
in response to this banality that Merton gives expression in the
"Chant to be used in processions around a site with furnaces." It
should be noted first of all that the title evokes in the monastic or
even generally Catholic mind a specific liturgical action, a litany, an
imploring of the mercy of God, often in a time of crisis, and typically
sung in procession; and the plural form here, "processions," suggests
that this is an activity that will need to be repeated. I take this as a
statement of self-indictment on Merton's part, an implicit acceptance
of the responsibility of Christians through anti-Judaism and anti-
Semitism for the actions so chillingly catalogued in the poem.

15 *Thomas Merton on Peace*, 150–159. It was first published in the *Catholic Worker*
in November 1967. Merton took the title from a comment (152) of one of
the former SS guards.
16 Merton's letters are included in v.1 of Merton's collected letters, *The Hidden
Ground of Love: The Letters of Thomas Merton on Religious Experience and Social
Concerns*, ed. William H. Shannon (New York: Farrar Straus Giroux, 1985)
430–436. For Heschel's letters, see appendix to Edward K. Kaplan,
"Contemplative Inwardness and Prophetic Action: Thomas Merton's
Dialogue with Judaism," in Donald Grayston and Michael W. Higgins, eds.,
Thomas Merton: Pilgrim in Process (Toronto: Griffin House, 1983) 85–105.
17 *Vatican Council II: The Conciliar and Post-Conciliar Documents*, ed. Austin
Flannery (Collegeville, MN: The Liturgical Press, 1975) 738–742.
18 *Eichmann in Jerusalem*, revised and enlarged (New York: Viking, 1964).

How we made them sleep and purified them

How we perfectly cleaned up the people and worked a
big heater

I was the commander I made improvements and
installed a guaranteed system taking account of
human weakness I purified and I remained decent

How I commanded

I made cleaning appointments and then I made the
travellers sleep and after that I made soap

I was born into a Catholic family but as these people
were not going to need a priest I did not become a
priest I installed a perfectly good machine it gave
satisfaction to many[19]

Thérèse Lentfoehr says that the poem was probably written
with Eichmann in mind, and that it "proceeds in the manner of a
monotone recording of flat statements" uttered by a camp
commander, recording each horror listed in an "unfeeling,
mechanical recitative."[20] Karl Plank corrects the Eichmann
connection, noting that the figure Merton has in mind is not
Eichmann, who was never a camp commandant, but Rudolf Hess,
the notorious cammandant of Auschwitz.[21] Ross Labrie
characterizes the poem as Merton's response to the "unimaginative
use of reason" and "literalism of mind" which in Eichmann

19 *Collected Poems*, 345-346.
20 *Words and Silence: On the Poetry of Thomas Merton* (New York: New Directions,
   1979) 43-44. See also Michael Mott's comments in *The Seven Mountains of Thomas
   Merton* (Boston: Houghton Mifflin, 1984) 304-305.
21 The reference is to Shirer's *The Rise and Fall of the Third Reich*: see Karl Plank,
   "Thomas Merton and Hannah Arendt: Contemplation after Eichmann," in
   The Merton Annual, v. 3, 131, n.22 and 133, n.27. See also Merton's
   reflections on Shirer in *Conjectures of a Guilty Bystander* (Garden City, NY:
   Doubleday, 1966) 219-220.

"underlay a specious sanity,"[22] a "sanity" without love. Labrie writes:

> The poem's dry, understated tone and phrasing mimic the step-by-step process of reason unaided by imagination while showing the ironic contrast between an apparently rational surface order and the moral chaos that can lurk just below that surface.[23]

In the last stanza, however, there is a sudden leap from the time of the Holocaust to Merton's moment of writing in a time of high nuclear anxiety:

> Do not think yourself better because you burn up
> friends and enemies with long-range missiles without
> ever seeing what you have done[24]

Here Merton connects the Holocaust in all its bureaucratic banality to the contemporary mindset – indeed, one still with us[25] – which can calmly contemplate the use of nuclear weapons. Although nuclear weapons have been reduced in numbers since Merton's time, the danger of an intentional nuclear strike or nuclear accident remains very real; and Merton's challenge to the "sane" among us remains intensely germane.[26]

---

22 Labrie, *Thomas Merton and the Inclusive Imagination*, 152. I should note here that for Merton, imagination meant much more than imaginative capacity. "As with Blake and Coleridge, he was interested in the imagination as a means of attaining truth or reality either through imaginative discernment or through the creative joining of things together to restore their original unity, thus regaining a sense of the depth and authority of their being," Labrie, 151-152.
23 Labrie, 153.
24 *Collected Poems*, 349.
25 On this point, see Douglas Ross, "Risk of Nuclear Attack Worsening," *Simon Fraser University News* 23.4 (Feb. 21, 2002) 5, an article which appeared as I was revising this paper.
26 The week before this paper was presented at the conference on Merton and Judaism, President George W. Bush, at a press conference in Washington with the President of Pakistan, issued a stern warning to those nations which possess and would consider the use of "weapons of mass destruction," with no obvious sense of the irony of his words, given that both the United States and Pakistan fall into that category.

These lines take us directly to Merton's essay, "A Devout Meditation in Memory of Adolf Eichmann," in which the acknowledgement of banality and the twisting of language is pervasive. Merton's opening paragraph is memorable.

> One of the most disturbing facts that came out in the Eichmann trial was that a psychiatrist examined him and pronounced him *perfectly sane.* I do not doubt it at all, and that is precisely why I find it disturbing.[27]

Again Merton moves from the Holocaust to his own moment, as he continues to express his horror at the Eichmannian "sanity" which he sees at work in the minds of those who would justify the use of nuclear weapons.

> It is the sane ones, the well-adapted ones, who can without qualms and without nausea aim the missiles and press the buttons that will initiate the great festival[28]of destruction that they, *the sane ones,* have prepared. No one suspects the sane, and the sane ones will have *perfectly good reasons*, logical, well-adjusted reasons, for firing the shot. They will be obeying sane orders that have come sanely down the chain of command. And because of their sanity they will have no qualms at all.[29]

As Karl Plank comments,

> Merton's hermeneutic move from Auschwitz to Hiroshima, from Eichmann to those who parlay nuclear arms, emphasizes again the insight of *Conjectures* with immediacy and urgency: the banality of evil does not stop

27 "A Devout Meditation," 160.

28 I would suggest that by the use of this phrase Merton is ironically assimilating the possible moment of nuclear destruction to the "great festivals" of the Christian liturgical year – Christmas, Easter, and Pentecost, days on which Christians celebrate the most significant moments in salvation history as they understand it.

29 "A Devout Meditation," 161.

with Eichmann, nor is it a peculiar feature of our enemies. It is *ours* in every instance in which we eschew the responsibility for thinking [about] what we are doing or compromise the humanness of life in the name of our own shallow well-being.[30]

Merton, however, does accept this responsibility, and so takes both Auschwitz and Hiroshima into the existential darkness of contemplation. There he can hear the voices of the dying and the banal words of Eichmann, as well as the questions asked in his own anxious voice, the voice of a postmodern Christian with a mind awake in the dark. There too, if God has anything to say, he can hear the voice of God; or, if God continues silent, he can share the divine silence. For contemplation, as Merton understood it, is not a place of peace, or a refuge from conflict or anguish, or even a privileged locus in which to hear the voice of God, but a place of spiritual purgation, and, paradoxically, a place of certitude. As he says, speaking of his own experience,

> the deep, inexpressible certitude of the contemplative experience awakens a tragic anguish and opens many questions in the depths of the heart like wounds that cannot stop bleeding.[31]

Unable to analyze, to explain, to come to any finally satisfying terms with the banality and inscrutability of evil, he remains in the darkness with God, with the victims of Auschwitz and Hiroshima, and with questions of a magnitude that defy any adequate response. It is an act of responsibility, undertaken on the basis of faith, and in the readiness to live with questions that will in fact never be "answered."

The third of these discrete pieces on the Holocaust is "Auschwitz: A Family Camp," a review of Bernd Naumann's book, *Auschwitz*. Even at this remove, it makes dreadful reading, as Merton quotes graphic excerpts concerned with the operation of Auschwitz as a place of brutality, torture and mass extermination.

30 "Thomas Merton and Hannah Arendt," 137.
31 *New Seeds of Contemplation* (New York: New Directions, 1962) 12.

He describes the self-assurance at their trial of certain defendants, former members of the SS assigned to Auschwitz, as they justified their actions, calmly claimed ignorance of orders which they had signed themselves, characterized the camp as indeed a "family camp," and in general took for granted the tacit support and understanding of the German public for the "difficult" situation in which they had found themselves.

As someone concerned with the power of words, Merton was also affronted by the "violence and crude perversion"[32] to which the German language had been subjected. In this "Gestapo doubletalk,"[33] "special treatment" meant extermination, "disinfectants" meant Zyklon B gas used in the gas chambers, and "assigned to harvest duty," used for a member of the SS, meant that he had been posted to Auschwitz.[34] Euphemism, circumlocution, evasion, slogan, cliché, doublethink and doubletalk, of which in any language Merton was a foe, all added up to "officialese" (*Amtssprache*) which Eichmann admitted, even claimed, was his "only language."[35] In fact, Eichmann, unsurprisingly, was simply following the "language rules" which the SS had officially set forth for use in referring to the "final solution."[36]

As with the "Devout Meditation," his reflection on the Naumann book brings him to his own moment, not, this time, in relation to nuclear weapons, but in relation to the civil rights struggle which Martin Luther King, Jr. was then leading.

> At this point, there swims into view a picture taken at another investigation (hardly a trial), in the state of Mississippi. We see the smiling, contemptuous, brutal faces of the police deputies and their colleagues who are allegedly the murderers of three civil rights workers in the

---

32 "Auschwitz: A Family Camp," 155. See also Merton's essay, "War and the Crisis of Language," in *Thomas Merton on Peace*, 234-247.

33 "Auschwitz: A Family Camp," 155.

34 "Auschwitz: A Family Camp," 156.

35 Arendt, 48.

36 "… all correspondence referring to the matter was subject to rigid 'language rules,' and, except in the reports from the *Einsatzgruppen* it is rare to find documents in which such bald words as 'extermination,' 'liquidation,' or 'killing' occur" (Arendt, 85).

summer of 1964, Instead of seeing the Bogers and Klehrs[37]of Auschwitz as fabulous, myth-sized and inhuman monsters, we come to recognize that people like them are in fact all around us. All they need is the right kind of crisis, and they will blossom out.[38]

He concludes by repeating this recognition: that those who "worked" at Auschwitz were "ordinary," not extraordinary, not monstrous. To this he adds that they worked hard at what they did, at "making genocide a success."[39] In the trial they had protested that they were simply carrying out a difficult and regrettable task; but Merton recognizes that their "gratuitous acts of arbitrary cruelty and violence"[40]gave the lie to their claims. His last word is that, given the right conditions in any society, there will be "no need of monsters: ordinary policemen and good citizens will take care of everything."[41] The review represents Merton at his bleakest, his most pessimistic, his most disturbed. In a time when nuclear confrontation was at its height and when the face of racism in all its ugliness was visible to more and more, he found in the Holocaust a paradigm of the dynamics of evil which took him directly to his own moment, and his own sense of responsibility as contemplative, as Christian and as writer.

JOURNALS AND LETTERS

As we look at Merton's complete journals, we see that most of his references to the Holocaust are found in volumes 4 and 5, which cover the years 1960–1965.[42] Many of these references are reproduced or further developed in *Conjectures of a Guilty Bystander*, published in 1966, in which extracts from his journals from 1956 to 1965 were included, and which he characterized as "a personal

37 Boger and Klehr: notorious members of the SS at Auschwitz.
38 "Auschwitz: A Family Camp," 158.
39 "Auschwitz: A Family Camp," 158.
40 "Auschwitz: A Family Camp," 158.
41 "Auschwitz: A Family Camp," 159.
42 *Turning Toward the World: The Journals of Thomas Merton*, vol.4, ed. Victor A. Kramer (San Francisco: HarperSanFrancisco, 1996); *Dancing in the Water of Life: The Journals of Thomas Merton*, vol. 5, ed. Robert E. Daggy (San Francisco: HarperSanFrancisco, 1997).

version of the world in the 1960s."[43] Pertinent to this study is his further reference in the preface to *Conjectures* to the Catholic Church's "turn" to the modern world, and its "seriously taking note of the non-Christian religions in their own terms."[44] He was reading Hannah Arendt, André Schwarz-Bart's magnificent novel, *The Last of the Just*,[45] which he found, as I did, "tremendously moving,"[46] and Salvatore Quasimodo's poem, "Auschwitz."

> Far from the Vistula, along the northern plain,
> love, in a death-camp there at Auschwitz:
> on the pole's rust and tangled fencing, rain
> funeral cold.
>
> No tree, no birds in the grey air
> or above our thought, but limp
> pain that memory leaves
> to its silence without irony or anger.[47]

Here is part of his comment on this poem in *Conjectures*.[48]

> A great classic poem of compassion and reason, not devoid of horror, but contemplative, detached and yet profoundly committed. Auschwitz, a sign of the depraved wisdom of men who judge by the measure of the weapon: "*sapienza dell' uomo che si fa misura d' armi* [man whose knowledge takes the shape of arms]."[49]

The rest of his comment, I confess, is obscure to me. He is struggling with the relation of death and mercy, both of which, he says, "are seen on the Cross." And Auschwitz itself, "a sign of judgment" – a clear enough word – is also "a sign of the Cross –

43 (Garden City, NY: Doubleday, 1966), p. v.
44 *Conjectures*, vii.
45 Trans. Stephen Becker (New York: Bantam, 1960).
46 *Turning Toward the World*, 202
47 Salvatore Quasimodo, *Complete Poems*, trans. and introd. Jack Bevan (London: Anvil, 1983) 166.
48 *Conjectures*, 46.
49 *Complete Poems*, 167.

and also, inscrutably, of mercy. But who can read it? Not I."[50] This immediately calls to memory the struggle in the 1990s between Jews and Polish Catholics over the building of the Carmelite convent at Auschwitz, marked with the sign of the Cross; and for myself, having also read *The Last of the Just*, the very moving passage in which its protagonist, Ernie Levy, responds to the question of his girlfriend, Golda – why Christians hate Jews – by saying that Christians have taken the Cross and turned it into a sword[51] – Constantine's sword, in fact, to pick up on James Carroll's image.[52] This linking of Auschwitz and the Cross could be taken, in Plank's view, as a statement which "dangerously diverts attention away from those … concretely vulnerable [to the threat of Auschwitz], … namely the Jews."[53] Later, however, he cites Merton's question in another journal of the period, *A Vow of Conversation* – "Can one look attentively at Christ and not also see Auschwitz?"[54] – as indicating an awareness on Merton's part of Jewish otherness, one that "must shape his perception of Christ and qualify the lens of the Christian …"[55] How Merton held together Auschwitz, the Cross, Christ and mercy finally remains to us, as to him, inscrutable. However, as a contemplative, a Christian and a man of the twentieth century, he had the courage to hold together in the darkness of his own contemplation what no merely intellectual scrutiny could render simple, acknowledge his own inability to "read" it, and continue to seek dialogue with those most directly affected.

In other pages of *Conjectures* he reflects on Christian anti-Semitism, the Eichmann trial and Shirer on the Third Reich.[56] He

50 *Conjectures*, 46.
51 *The Last of the Just*, 364-365.
52 *Constantine's Sword: The Church and the Jews, A History* (Boston: Houghton Mifflin, 2001). Carroll begins his book by recounting the history of the Auschwitz Cross (3-63).
53 "Eclipse," 187.
54 *A Vow of Conversation: Journals 1964-1965*, ed. Naomi Burton Stone (New York: Farrar Straus and Giroux, 1988) 42, quoted in "Elipse," 187.
55 "Eclipse," 187.
56 *Conjectures*, 153-154, 262-263, 219-220. See also v. 4 of the Journals, 91, 113, 116-117, 306-308; v. 5, 82, 142-143, 165. For his correspondence with Jewish writers, see *The Hidden Ground of Love: Letters of Thomas Merton on Religious Experience and Social Concerns*. Merton's letters to Erich Fromm, Abraham Joshua Heschel, Zalman Schachter [-Shalomi] and R. J. Zvi Werblowsky (but not their letters to him) will be found there alphabetically.

does not interest himself in such large historical questions as intentionalism and functionalism,[57]nor, in an explicit way, with the question of modernity.[58] Throughout, he attempts to maintain his contemplative stance before God, before his own church and before his readership-as-representative-of-the-world. He becomes a Job-like figure who lets the whirlwinds[59]of historical fact and existential challenge blow over and through him; and, whether still able to stand or lying prostrate in anguish, stays with the unanswerable questions which the *Shoa* asked of him. In brief and inadequate summary, I would say that for Merton the Holocaust was a fundamental hermeneutical reality, a historical and spiritual paradigm of evil which moved him powerfully towards contact and dialogue with Jews, toward the sharing of grief and the need for *T'shuvah*[60] [repentance of a full and deep kind] with fellow-Christians, and towards the self-questioning contemplative orientation towards himself and God to which he was committed.

Kinship and Difference

One of Merton's most-quoted statements from the period on which we are reflecting is this:

> If I affirm myself as a Catholic merely by denying all that is Muslim, Jewish, Protestant, Hindu, Buddhist, etc., in the end I will find that there is not much left for me to affirm as a Catholic: and certainly no breath of the Spirit with which to affirm it.[61]

Beside it we may place another comment, less well-known, from his "Devout Meditation."

---

57 See on this Donald L Niewyk, *The Holocaust: Problems and Perspectives of Interpretation* (Lexington, MA: Heath, 1992) 9-53.
58 As does Zygmunt Bauman in *Modernity and the Holocaust* (Ithaca, NY: Cornell University Press, 1991).
59 "… in the political dark I light small, frail lights about peace and hold them up in the whirlwind" – from a letter to Zalman Schachter [-Shalomi], 15 December 1961, in *The Hidden Ground of Love*, 534; cf. Job 38.1.
60 Letter to Schachter, *The Hidden Ground of Love*, 534.
61 *Conjectures*, 129.

And so I ask myself: what is the meaning of a concept of sanity that excludes love, considers it irrelevant and destroys our capacity to love other human beings, to respond to their needs and their sufferings, to recognize them also as persons, *to apprehend their pain as one's own?*[62]

Plank, to whose assertion of the "eclipse of difference" we now return, says that Merton's "emphasis on kinship is not so much wrong as partial,"[63] and, given that there are total and partial eclipses of sun or moon, this seems to me a fair qualification (without which the title of the article might be taken as suggesting a total eclipse, which the article does not assert). Anti-Semitism eclipses kinship; hyper-empathy eclipses difference. Thus when the partial eclipse of difference is acknowledged and we move back from it, we can see how kinship and difference could stand in right relation to each other. To this end, therefore, I will try to place the statements of Merton to which Plank takes exception in the larger context of Merton's temperament and spiritual development, and look at aspects of Merton's subjectivity which, included in the discussion, may lead to a differently nuanced assessment.

As Plank says, Merton "sought commonalities, and, with compassion, wanted to make jewish [sic] anguish his own,"[64] wanted "to be a true Jew under [his] Catholic skin,"[65] wanted to identify with suffering that was not and could not be his own. Even more strongly, in a letter to Erich Fromm, he makes a statement of impossible identification.

Erich, I am a complete Jew as far as that goes: I am steeped in that experience of bafflement, compunction and wonder which is the experience of those who have been rescued from tyranny, only to renounce freedom and in confusion and subjection to worse tyrants, through infidelity to the Lord.[66] For only in His service is there

62 "A Devout Meditation," 161, italics mine.
63 "Eclipse," 189.
64 "Eclipse," 185.
65 Letter of 9 September 1964 to Heschel: *The Hidden Ground of Love*, 434.
66 There seems to be a word or two missing in this sentence between "freedom" and "in confusion."

true freedom, as the Prophets would tell us. This is still the clear experience of the Jews, as it ought to be of the Christians ....[67]

Perhaps he mitigates the offensiveness of this statement by the words "as far as that goes." Even so, I have to say that in these statements I see him crossing the line from empathy to hyper-empathy, from an understanding and sharing of the feelings and situations of the other to an impossible attempt to feel the feelings or situation of the other as his own, and to that extent I agree with Plank. If Merton had been arrested by the Nazis in the time of the Holocaust, he would not – at least not for genetic reasons – have been sent to Auschwitz; and this is something he could appropriately have acknowledged instead of apparently asserting this impossible identification.

However, Plank raises other concerns which I am unable to support, at least to the extent to which he does. He sees Merton, for example, in his correspondence with Heschel, as letting his own frustration at the potential damage to Jewish-Christian relations, which might have resulted from a negative Vatican Council text, prevent him from recognizing "the particular and more urgent situation of Heschel himself, the concrete situation of the Jew as Jew."[68] Here I would have thought that the promptness of his reply (Heschel's mimeographed bulletin is dated 3 September 1964; Merton's reply is dated September 9)[69] was sufficient evidence of his recognition of Heschel's situation, to say nothing of its frank and full agreement with Heschel's concerns. Again, Plank charges Merton with focusing almost exclusively on the Nazi perpetrators "rather than on the situation of the Jew who has survived or fallen victim to that evil."[70] Here I would point to how moved he was by reading *The Last of the Just,* and by his references to Jewish suffering in "Auschwitz: A Family Camp." Plank's assertion that when Merton writes on the Holocaust in his journals, "his *perspective* continues to be that of Nazi anti-Semitism"[71]

67 Letter of 5 December 1961: *The Hidden Ground of Love,* 317.
68 "Eclipse," 185.
69 Kaplan, 100–102.
70 "Eclipse," 186.
71 "Eclipse," 186, italics mine.

must also be challenged as misleading; Plank's earlier term, "focus," could well be substituted here for "perspective." Nor, in my view, does Merton *reduce* the Holocaust, as Plank charges, to an "eschatological sign" for Christians.[72] In the letter to Zalman Schachter [-Shalomi] in which this phrase occurs, Merton is in fact referring to the Jews as such, not specifically to the Holocaust in any isolated way. By his accompanying reference to his recent reading of *The Last of the Just,* it is clear that he is not separating the Holocaust from Jewish history or experience. Finally, I am unable to agree with Plank that Merton's frequent emphasis on the scriptural legacy which Jews and Christians share confines the Jewish reality to the biblical period:[73] his friendship with contemporary Jews and his interest in contemporary Jewish concerns, the Holocaust included, seem to me sufficient evidence to the contrary.

Plank believes that Merton, scandalized by the sufferings that had come to Jews at the hands of Christians, overcompensated for this by an exaggerated emphasis on his kinship with Jews, and by a hyperbolic and impossible identification with Jews in their sufferings, seeking to apprehend their pain as his own,[74] and this I have to grant. On the other side of the scale, however, I would ask Plank to place the title of Merton's article on Thich Nhat Hanh: "Nhat Hanh Is My Brother,"[75] or the oft-quoted comment, made

72 "Eclipse," 187 – the reference is to Merton's comments in a letter of 15 February 1962 to Zalman Schachter: "the Jews have been the great eschatological sign of the twentieth century ... The Suffering Servant is One: Christ, Israel. There is one wedding and one wedding feast, not two or five or six...There is one mystery, and the mystery of Israel and of the Church is ultimately to be revealed as One" (*The Hidden Ground of Love*, 535). The word "ultimately" indicates that Merton here is thinking of *future* eschatology, the time of the consummation of history associated in Jewish thinking with the coming of the Messiah, in Christian thinking with the second coming of Christ ("thy kingdom come"), rather than *realized* eschatology, the bringing into the present moment of the eschatological realities ("thine is the kingdom"). I suggest here that although Merton in this letter used the word "ultimately," his general perspective, in keeping with his existential outlook and his interest in prophecy and in Zen, is that of realized eschatology.

73 "Eclipse," 187-188; although, as Plank noted in his presentation at the conference, the canonical differences between the Jewish and Christian views of scripture constitute a continuing difficulty in this regard.

74 See note 62 above.

75 *Thomas Merton on Peace*, 262-263.

on the eve of his trip to Asia,"I intend to become as good a Buddhist as I can."[76] The source of this overcompensation, then is not something specific to his thinking about Jews, or the Holocaust, but his well-known tendency to permit his astonishing gift for empathy to spill over into inadmissible identifications and indeed, a partial eclipse of difference. Also in that same side of the scale must go Merton's unconcealed triple religious identity as Christian, monk and priest,[77]received, he believed, as a gift at the time of his conversion and entry into the monastery, refined in the fires of his time with the nurse with whom he fell in love in 1966, and returned to him through this experience, renewed.[78]

More fundamental still, however, is the problem of "Christendom."[79] In its social and political dimensions, anti-Judaism and anti-Semitism are intrinsic to the epoch of Constantinian[80] Christianity, the alliance of church and state, explicit or implicit, which began in the fourth century of our era and which in a general sense ended only as recently (in my own view) as 1945.[81] Within the epoch of European Christendom, the

76 Quoted in David Steindl-Rast, "Man of Prayer," in Patrick Hart, ed., *Thomas Merton, Monk* (New York: Sheed and Ward, 1974) 88.

77 "Certainly I have never for a moment thought of changing the definitive decisions taken in the course of my life: to be a Christian, to be a monk, to be a priest" – from the preface to the Japanese edition of *The Seven Storey Mountain* (August 1963), in Robert E. Daggy, ed., *Honorable Reader: Reflections on My Work*, Foreword by Harry James Cargas (New York: Crossroad, 1991) 63.

78 See on this Patrick Hart's comments in his Foreword to *The Asian Journal of Thomas Merton* (New York: New Directions, 1973) xxvii–xxviii; and William M. Thompson's emphasis on Merton's "Christ-fidelity" in "Merton's Contribution to a Transcultural Consciousness," in Grayston and Higgins, *Pilgrim in Process*, 147–151. On his relationship with the nurse, see *Learning to Love: The Journals of Thomas Merton, Volume Six*, ed. Christine M. Bochen (San Francisco: HarperSanFrancisco, 1997) 35-126, 301-348.

79 For a recent comprehensive treatment of Christian Constantinianism as it applies to our subject, see James Carroll, *Constantine's Sword: The Church and the Jews, A History*, already cited.

80 I am very struck by the use Marc Ellis makes of this term in his article, "On the Jewish Civil War and the New Prophetic," *Tikkun* 16.4 (August 2001) 24–28, in which he speaks of "Constantinian Judaism," by which he means a "Judaism" or Jewish mindset, chiefly in Israel and the US, "in service to the state and to power" (25) comparable in certain ways to Christianity in the Christendom period.

81 I choose this date because it is marked by the beginnings of public awareness

only organized and continuing religious traditions were those of
Christians and Jews, in which the Jewish minority was always at
the mercy of or toleration by the Christian majority. From this
period, Christianity carries a hegemonic taint, which would
understandably evoke Jewish resistance to Merton's statement
about being a "complete Jew."[82] By contrast, when Gandhi made
his well-known statement, "I am a Hindu and a Muslim and a
Christian and a Jew," it was not problematic to Christians and Jews
because it carried no evocation of Christendom, although it was
indeed problematic to those Hindus and Muslims who were pitted
against each other in the Indian independence struggle.

In a very different context, and very close to the end of his life,
Merton shows us his increased ability to balance kinship and
difference. I refer here to his encounter with Chadral Rinpoche,
the Tibetan Buddhist teacher of the Nyingma tradition whom he
met at Ghoom, near Darjeeling, India, on 16 November 1968.[83]

> Chatral looked like a vigorous old peasant ... We started
> talking about *dzogchen* [the inner discovery of
> transcendent awareness] ... and soon saw that we agreed
> very well. We must have talked for two hours or more,
> taking in some points of Christian doctrine compared
> with Buddhist....
>
> The unspoken or half-spoken message ... was our
> complete understanding of each other as people who
> were somehow *on the edge* of great realization.... I was
> profoundly moved, because he is so obviously a great man
> ... marked by complete simplicity and freedom. He was
> surprised at getting on so well with a Christian....[84]

of the Holocaust, the dropping of nuclear weapons on Japan, and the
beginning of the end of formally colonial territories of the Christian nations,
so called.

82 See note 67, above.
83 *Asian Journal*, 142-144. The AJ uses the spelling "Chatral," but the rinpoche
himself currently uses the spelling "Chadral," as I discovered when I was
privileged to meet him at his monastery at Salabari, south of Darjeeling, on
December 13, 2000.
84 *Asian Journal*, 143-144.

Here for Merton and Chadral there is no eclipse of difference; there is rather a clear acknowledgement of religious difference, and yet a strong sense of kinship based on Merton's and Chadral's understanding of each other as spiritual practitioners and fellow seekers of the "great realization"[85] of transcendent awareness.

In an address prepared a short time before this meeting, Merton had spoken of interfaith encounter in terms of the personal qualities required of anyone engaging in it seriously. Any such person, he said, must be

> a living example of traditional and interior realization, ... must be wide open to life and to new experience because he has fully utilized his own tradition and gone beyond it. This will permit him to meet a [disciple] of another ... tradition, and find a common ground of verbal understanding .... This I would call "communion."[86]

Of course it is simpler for a Christian and a Buddhist to engage in this kind of dialogue than for a Jew and a Christian, inasmuch as Christians and Buddhists do not have the sad history in common which Christians and Jews do. This being so, Merton's reference to Thich Nhat Hanh or becoming the best Buddhist that he could did not give offense save to the most literal-minded. Even so, I believe we can take this paradigm, as one which held deep meaning for Merton, and apply it retroactively to Merton's dialogue with Jews, a dialogue which necessarily included attention to the Holocaust in all its darkness. We know that we cannot ignore the need for a balance of kinship and difference; but with a word like "communion" we have gone beyond their polarity, yet I would assert, without negating kinship or eclipsing difference. The image of two tables comes to me here: the long, rectangular Christendom table, at which Christians sat at the head of the table, Jews at the

85 *Asian Journal*, 143.
86 *Asian Journal*, 315. The text has "discipline" where it should have "disciple." I have explored the meaning of this statement for Merton and Chadral at greater length in "Thomas Merton, the Global Future and Parish Priorities," Christian Century 101 (August 29-September 5, 1984) 802-804.

foot; and the round table of interfaith dialogue, at which Jews and Christians sit with Buddhists, Muslims, Hindus and other traditions large and small. At such a table there will be differences, of course, perhaps alliances which change from time to time; but there need never again be a polarized situation in which Jews are to be defined by their relationship to a Christian majority. More positively, if Jews and Christians sit side by side at this second table, as history would suggest they might, they will be in a position to recognize in a fresh way those dimensions of their commonality to which their inclusion in a larger conversation draws their attention.

However, "communion" has ecclesial overtones which may make it less than helpful here; and so we should perhaps go to an even stronger and more universal word to which both Merton and Plank direct us: love. In his comments about Eichmann, Merton expresses his opposition to any kind of "sanity" which excludes love; and in *The New Man*, quoted by Plank, he writes:

> In the mystery of social love there is found the realization of "the other" not only as one to be loved by us, so that we may perfect ourselves, but also as one who can become more perfect by loving us. The vocation to charity is a call not only to love but to *be loved*.[87]

Of Merton after his vocation-shaking time with the nurse, his biographer Michael Mott says: "he loved greatly and was greatly loved. He was overwhelmed by the experience and it changed him forever."[88] Of this same dynamic, that of loving and being loved, Plank says that for the Christian

> [T]o affirm the Jew as Jew does not mean rendering the Jew as an object of christian [sic] charity or subject of

87 (New York: Farrar Straus Giroux, 1961) 91, quoted in Plank, "Eclipse," 190. Edward K. Kaplan in his presentation to the Louisville conference drew attention to this same dynamic in Merton's 1958 dream of Proverb, a young Jewish girl by whom Merton felt loved simply for who he was: see Lawrence S. Cunningham, ed., *Search for Solitude: Pursuing the Monk's True Life* (San Francisco: HarperSanFrancisco, 1996) 175-177, 182.
88 Mott, 438.

christian [sic] discourse, but perceiving in the Jew an other
with words to speak – words of his or her own that may
challenge from difference and may love with freedom....
Accordingly, jewish [sic] difference challenges Christians
not first to speak but to hear speech not their own, not
simply to love but to consent to the prospect of being
loved by an other.[89]

Merton loved greatly, and was greatly loved, and it changed him
forever. If I read Plank correctly, he is suggesting – moved to do so
by his reading of Merton – that Christians consciously consent to
the prospect of being loved by Jews, even greatly loved, and so to *be
changed* forever. Given our history as Christians and Jews, in which
we have been beyond any dispute the "other" to each other, and in
which the Holocaust irreducibly occupies the darkest and most
difficult place, this is an astonishing, mysterious and provocative
prospect. Yet it was a possibility which Thomas Merton, possessor of
a mind awake in the dark, affirmed both in his friendships and his
writings, in which, through empathy and imagination, he reached
out in love toward the other. This being so, then for both historical
traditions which seek to honor the God who makes covenant with
humankind, there yet remains before us this challenge from
Merton's larger vision, the task of imagining in concrete terms the
possibility, the prospect, even the necessity of love.[90]

89 "Eclipse," 190–191.
90 I wish here to express my indebtedness to Karl Plank, my virtual *haver* in the
writing of this paper, as well as my gratitude to my research assistant, Lauren
Faulkner, for her valuable assistance in its preparation.

"O God, we are one with You. You have made us one with You. You have taught us that, if we are open to one another, You dwell in us. Help us to preserve this openness and to fight for it with all our hearts. Help us to realize that there can be no understanding where there is mutual rejection."

—from Merton's last written prayer from *Dialogues with Silence: Prayers & Drawings*

5

AN OPEN LETTER TO DONALD GRAYSTON

Karl A. Plank

March 1, 2002

Dear Don,

I am very grateful for your paper, "Thomas Merton, the Holocaust, and the Eclipse of Difference."[1] Your careful attention to my earlier "Eclipse of Difference: Merton's Encounter with Judaism"[2] honors me with its seriousness, encourages me with its shared concerns, and assists me with its insight. No writer, let alone one of a short essay offered over ten years ago, could ask for more. The dialectic of difference and kinship that emerges more clearly in the juxtaposition of our two papers is one that I welcome.

Moreover, I do not think that in fundamental matters we are finally so far apart, though we have accented points differently and have some exegetical questions to ponder in our reading of particular cases. When you write, "Antisemitism eclipses kinship; hyper-empathy eclipses difference," you say well what I, too, would want to say (and in terms of the Holocaust, tried to pursue in my *Mother of the Wire Fence: Inside and Outside the Holocaust*).[3] This is the arena of our shared concern and it is a deep one.

I appreciate your paper's attempt to locate Merton's dialogue with Judaism within the broadening context of his larger

---

1 Presented at the interfaith conference on "Thomas Merton and Judaism," Louisville, KY; February 18, 2002.

2 *Cistercian Studies Quarterly* 28.2 (1993):179-91.

3 Louisville: Westminster John Knox, 1994.

ecumenical style. This reframing—or broad-framing—of the issue
enriches the case in point with the interplay of further texts and
qualifications. Your use of Merton's encounters with Chadral
Rinpoche and with Thich Nhat Hanh is instructive in showing
Merton's capability of expressing kinship without compromising
difference. The same examples, however, raise for me the question
of whether the cultural distance of their Buddhist contexts made
it more natural and pressing for Merton to concede difference
there in a way that he did not feel in his encounter with Jews. The
assumed strangeness of Buddhism and the assumed familiarity of
Judaism may suggest that Merton met these groups from different
starting points of vantage that set up the accents of acknowledged
difference, in the one case, and kinship, in the other. The widening
ecumenical context of Merton's relations show him to be aware of
critical difference, but perhaps more in some instances than others.
Does the particular case of Judaism reflect or vary from the pattern
seen in the Buddhist encounters? And, if it varies, why is that so?

One possible explanation for any assumption of a nearer
Jewish kinship derives from Merton's viewing Judaism through an
assumed Judaeo-Christian lens that reduces both traditions to their
least common denominator. The "myth of the Judaeo-Christian
tradition," as Arthur Cohen put it,[4] depends heavily on reading
both traditions in terms of a common scriptural heritage. Your
paper registers disagreement "that Merton's frequent emphasis on
the scriptural legacy which Jews and Christians share confines the
Jewish reality to the biblical period." Your point, to the contrary, is
that Merton had "friendship with contemporary Jews" and
"interest in contemporary Jewish concerns." I did not mean to
imply that Merton lacked friendship or concern, but that he
tended to perceive the Jewish identity of those contemporary Jews
through a biblical lens that reduced their particularity and created
a difficult assumption of familiarity. Merton did not lack
acquaintance with contemporary Jews, but awareness of the post-
biblical, rabbinic traditions that shaped their religious identity in
decisive, if not normative ways. Apart from dealing with the post-
biblical reality, Merton confined contemporary Jews to the reality

---

4 *The Myth of the Judaeo-Christian Tradition* (New York: Harper and Row, 1963).

of the biblical period, effacing the trajectories of tradition that defined them both in faithfulness and revolt. Attention to the post-biblical shaping of Jewish identity, in effect, would have de-familiarized Merton's contemporary Jews and made effacement of difference less likely.

Though we agree that "hyper-empathy eclipses difference," we may differ in our readings of where and how this applies to Merton. For example, in Merton's correspondence with Heschel over the maneuvers of the Council (September 9, 1964),[5] I find myself still stumbling over Merton's expressions of the Council's actions as slapping "him" in the face and surely "crushing" Cardinal Bea. While I do not doubt the feelings of genuine empathy, I would like to have heard more acknowledgement of what Heschel himself may have felt at the moment. That acknowledgement perhaps goes without saying, mirrored in Merton's sense of being slapped (by what? by what has happened to Heschel), but the rhetoric remains odd. As you note, Merton's prompt reply does express his agreement with Heschel and underscores the urgency of the situation, but his articulation of the concern seems to lack something: an expression that the offense that slaps *him* is first of all an attack on the very Jew to whom he is writing. Where I argued that, in Merton's holocaust writings, "his perspective continues to be that of Nazi anti-Semitism," you suggest that "focus" would be a better category than "perspective." This is a helpful amendment. Anti-Semitism is, understandably, one of the issues he is concerned to write about, for therein he finds the intersection with his own Christianity. But that is a "focusing" of concern or scope more than perspective, which may imply "sharing the viewpoint of" – something that I, of course, did not mean to imply.

I appreciate your going beyond the critique to deal with the challenge of love and, in particular, of welcoming the love of the other. Your conclusion is a wonderful statement of that challenge and captures what I feel is most important in Merton's relations: his envisioning the prospect not only of loving, but of being loved.

5 See Thomas Merton, *The Hidden Ground of Love*, ed. William H. Shannon (New York: Farrar, Straus, Giroux, 1985), 434.

At the moments when the dialectic of difference and kinship was finely tuned, Merton was extraordinary—not just in what he was able to give, but in what he was open to receiving in the presence of the other.

With gratitude, I look forward to our ongoing dialogue and friendship now begun.

As your person so gracefully modeled throughout the Merton and Judaism conference, may every response to an other be also an invitation and overture.

Peace,

Karl

6

"UNDER MY CATHOLIC SKIN..."

THOMAS MERTON'S OPENING TO JUDAISM
AND TO THE WORLD

Edward K. Kaplan

> This much I will say: My latent ambitions to be a true Jew
> under my Catholic skin will surely be realized if I continue
> to go through experiences like this, being spiritually
> slapped in the face by these blind and complacent people
> of whom I am nevertheless a "collaborator." [1]

Thomas Merton to Abraham Heschel,
9 September 1964

Thomas Merton's relationship to Judaism, to Jewish tradition,
and to several Jewish friends provides fertile ground for productive
dialogue as well as for courageous self-examination. In fact his
deepest spiritual and psychological development paralleled historic
transformations in the Roman Catholic Church in the 1950s and
1960s. During this period of extraordinary progress, and in spite of
much resistance and ambivalence, both the Church and the
Trappist monk opened their hearts and minds to modern thought,
to imperatives of social responsibility – that is, to the world – and
recognized the sanctity of other religions.

The historical context of Merton's opening or "turning"
toward Judaism (as the Hebrew word *teshuvah* is often translated)

---

1 Thomas Merton, letter to Abraham Heschel, 9 September 1964, *Hidden Ground
of Love*, pp. 434–35; I published their correspondence, which includes Heschel's
letters to Merton, as an appendix to my article, "Contemplative Inwardness and
Prophetic Action: Thomas Merton's Dialogue with Judaism," in Donald
Grayston and Michael Higgins, eds., *Thomas Merton: Pilgrim in Process* (Toronto:
Griffin House, 1983), pp. 85-105.

is the Second Vatican Council, during which he corresponded with and then met Rabbi Abraham Joshua Heschel, Professor of Ethics and Mysticism at the Jewish Theological Seminary in New York. At that time Heschel was an active consultant with the American Jewish Committee and worked closely with Augustin Cardinal Bea and his Secretariat for Christian Unity.[2] Both Heschel and Merton were appalled at the internal controversy surrounding a declaration on the Jews, a document that might explicitly repudiate the charge of deicide that cursed the Jewish people for centuries. On the other hand, there was hope that the Council might accept the spiritual autonomy of Judaism and abandon its mission to convert the Jews.

The crisis of their mutual concern for the declaration on the Jews took place in September 1964, when a problematic draft was to be presented at the final session later that month. On 9 September, Merton wrote to Heschel, referring to conservative or reactionary pressures exerted by the Vatican Curia: "My latent ambitions to be a true Jew under my Catholic skin will surely be realized if I continue to go through experiences like this, being spiritually slapped in the face by these blind and complacent people of whom I am nevertheless a 'collaborator.'"[3] The following day (10 September 1964) Merton wrote in his diary: "It is precisely in prophetic and therefore deeply humiliated and humanly impoverished thirst for light that Christians and Jews can begin to find a kind of unity in seeking God's will together." Humility was the initial tone of Merton's alliance with Heschel's Jewish distress. This was a first step toward *teshuvah*.

2 See Eva Fleischner, "Heschel's Significance for Jewish-Christian Relations," in John C. Merkle, ed., *Abraham Joshua Heschel: Exploring His Life and Thought* (New York: Macmillan, 1985), pp. 142-64. For the fullest historical context, and with a personal element analogous to my approach to Merton, see James Carroll, *Constantine's Sword: The Church and the Jews: A History* (Boston: Houghton Mifflin Co., 2001).

3 Merton letter to Abraham Heschel, 9 September 1964, see above note 1. The next quotation can be found in Thomas Merton, *Dancing in the Water of Life. The Journals of Thomas Merton*, vol. 5, 1963-1965, ed. Robert E. Daggy (San Francisco: HarperSanFrancisco, 1977), pp. 142-43.

Repentance in Progress

What did Merton mean by asserting that he wanted to become "a true Jew""under his Catholic skin"? I think that Father Louis (as Merton was known at the monastery) dramatically felt the call of repentance, an opening of his spirit to Judaism as Judaism and not principally as a precursor of the Christian revelation. He was undergoing another major conversion, an opening to the Other that anticipated radical changes within the Roman Catholic Church.[4]

Merton's recognition of Judaism as spiritually autonomous in its own right, beloved by God as separate from Christianity, was refined within his monastic vocation. Compulsively self-reflective, he bravely faced the vicissitudes of his conversion of soul – or as I prefer to name it, *teshuvah,* the word Jews ponder during the Days of Awe, from Rosh Hashanah to Yom Kippur, the Day of Atonement, in which we examine our lives, trembling before God, to receive judgment of life or death. (I use the Hebrew word *teshuvah* deliberately to highlight the differences of our traditions as they confront common dilemmas.)

It is a curious fact that Merton's attitude toward secular life also changes from negative to reverential along with his appreciation of Judaism. Accordingly I focus on the period beginning in the late 1950s, which marks his opening to the world, his positive re-valuation of life outside the monastery. In his unusual position as a Trappist monk exposed through his writings to the public, he struggled intensely with normally contradictory needs: an attraction to silence and solitude versus his long-unacknowledged attachment to the world, and, more specifically, a long-suppressed desire for reciprocal love with a woman versus his vow of celibacy.

From my perspective as a Jew, Merton's "latent desire to be a true Jew under [his] Catholic skin" helps me understand the Church's difficult, and still unfinished, repentance, the shift from an exclusive, triumphalist ideology, which is also anti-Jewish, into a truly catholic

---

4 See the lucid article of Anthony T. Padovano, "The Eight Conversions of Thomas Merton," *The Merton Seasonal* 25, 2 (Summer 2000): 9-15; Mitch Finley, "The Joy of Being Catholic: The Relationship of the Conversion of Thomas Merton to the RCIA," *Thomas Merton Annual* 13 (2000): 171-89. The masterful biography by Michael Mott, *The Seven Mountains of Thomas Merton* (Boston: Houghton Mifflin Co., 1984), has been an invaluable research tool.

reverence for Jewish tradition in its own right. And Merton helps me in my struggle to be a true Jew, true in the eyes of God, but also a worthy representative of Judaism within our pluralistic communities.

My point of reference is the famous epiphany at the corner of Fourth and Walnut in downtown Louisville, the set piece in *Conjectures of a Guilty Bystander* (1966) known as "The Vision in Louisville."[5] At that decisive moment Merton overcame his disdain for the corruption outside the cloister and realized that he actually cherished the world. He extols his fellow human beings: "[I] suddenly realized that I loved all these people and that none of them were, or could be, totally alien to me. [...] There is no way of telling people that they are all walking around shining like the sun."

Such was Merton's eventual openness. Published in 1966 after the Second Vatican Council ended, *Conjectures of a Guilty Bystander* ratifies the Church's most progressive stance toward Judaism and other non-Christian religions, as Merton states: "The more I am able to affirm others, to say 'yes' to them in myself, by discovering them in myself and myself in them, the more real I am. I am fully real if my own heart says *yes* to *everyone*."[6]

MESSAGES FROM THE SUBCONSCIOUS

Merton's private, spontaneous writings, before he edited them for publication, reveal how his turning to the world was strongly influenced by subconscious factors, which, for some reason, he strongly associated with Judaism. During the late 1950s, Merton was experiencing a vocational crisis. Not that he wanted to leave the monastery, but rather he sought more solitude and greater spiritual, as well as intellectual freedom. He was struggling with Church censors and with his Abbot, to whom he owed near

5 See Thomas Merton, *Conjectures of a Guilty Bystander* (New York: Doubleday and Co., 1966), pp. 140-42. For a fuller analysis see Mott, op. cit., pp. 311-16.
6 Merton, *Conjectures*, p. 129. Merton continues: "If I affirm myself as a Catholic merely by denying all that is Muslim, Jewish, Protestant, Hindu, Buddhist, etc., in the end I will find that there is not much left for me to affirm as a Catholic: and certainly no breath of the Spirit with which to affirm it."
  As I stress at the end of this paper, Merton's impulse to erase otherness or difference had negative consequences regarding his attitude toward Judaism: see the pioneering article of Karl Plank, "The Eclipse of Difference: Merton's Encounter with Judaism," *Cistercian Studies Quarterly* 28,2 (1993): 179-91.

UNDER MY CATHOLIC SKIN · 113

absolute obedience. All in all, Merton was wrestling with ambivalence in several areas of his life.

As a writer whose subconscious frequently jumps to the surface of his awareness, Merton began to achieve some clarity. On 28 February 1958, after listing complaints about various frustrations at the monastery, he writes in his journal about a dream, which rekindled unresolved longings from his childhood and early youth. For the first time, perhaps, a powerful female (who happens to be Jewish) emerges from Merton's psychological limbo; she will remain in his memory and drastically influence his future commitments. This is how the awakened dreamer first narrates his remembered dream:

> On the porch at Douglaston I am embraced with determined and virginal passion by a young Jewish girl. She clings to me and will not let go, and I get to like the idea. I see that she is a nice kid in a plain, sincere sort of way. I reflect, "She belongs to the same race as St. Anne." I ask her her name and she says her name is Proverb. I tell her that is a beautiful and significant name, but she does not appear to like it – perhaps the others have mocked her for it.
>
> When I am awake, I rationalize it complacently. "*Sapientiam amavi et quaesivi eam mihi sponsam assumere*" [I loved wisdom and sought to make her my wife] – Sophia (it is the <u>sofa</u> on the back porch . . . etc. etc.). No need to explain. It was a charming dream.[7]

"No need to explain" indeed! We must admit immediately that this is a sexual dream. The time period is Merton's student years at Columbia University, perhaps earlier, and the setting is the Long Island home of his maternal grandparents, Pop and Bonnemaman, where he often took refuge from his parents' frequent travels, after his mother's untimely death when he was six, and especially after his father passed away. It was a place of loneliness and thirst for love.[8] In

7 This and the following several quotations can be found in Thomas Merton, *A Search for Solitude. The Journals of Thomas Merton, vol. 3, 1952-1960*, ed. Lawrence S. Cunningham (San Francisco: HarperSanFrancisco, 1996), pp. 175-77.
8 A detailed analysis of this dream is beyond the scope of this paper. For a start

any case, the dreamed event takes place before Merton converted to Catholicism, and long before he became a Trappist monk.

Why is it a *Jewish* woman who embraces him "with determined and virginal passion"? Jewish women were often stereotypically imagined by gentiles as exotic, Oriental, sexually aggressive and uninhibited. But the point here, I believe, is that now – in February of 1958 – the Trappist monk, in his dreams, begins to confront his vow of chastity by acknowledging, even unconsciously, his unassuaged need for affection from women, maternal and otherwise.

He immediately associates the passionate and worldly, though young and innocent, Jewish woman of his dream with Saint Anne and "Sophia" and "Proverb." That she "belongs to the same race as Saint Anne" (mother of the Virgin Mary, in Hebrew, Hannah), and that her name is "Proverb," hardly sublimates the explicitly erotic elements, since the awakened dreamer does associate "Sophia" with the word "sofa" followed by ellipses. Merton's dream reinforces his fascination with another powerful feminine image, *Hagia Sophia* of Greek Orthodoxy who incarnates the Wisdom of the Church and is associated with the Mother of Christ.[9] In addition, Merton was especially fond of the Hebrew Book of Proverbs, in particular chapter 8, which personifies Wisdom as a woman.

In Merton's waking life, the dream of the young Jewish woman became foundational; it took on an indelible mental reality, for the memory of this dream was just as forceful as that of a concrete social experience. Merton manipulates this scenario, consciously or otherwise, as he attempts to reconcile conflicting desires, the most salient of which is the celibate monk's desire for a woman's love and his unmistakable erotic drives – all symbolized by the forbidden religion, Judaism, still "rejected and cursed" by

see Merton's early translation of this locus of familial isolation and loneliness: "The house in Douglaston, which my grandparents had built, . . . was the symbol of a life that had brought them nothing but confusions and anxieties and misunderstandings and fits of irritation. It was a house in which Bonnemaman had sat for hours each day in front of a mirror, rubbing cold-cream into her cheeks as if she were going to the opera – but she never went to the opera . . ." (*The Seven Storey Mountain* [San Diego, New York: Harcourt Brace Jovanovich, 1976], p. 396).

9 See Mott, pp. 307-308, 312-13; on the Hammers' picture of *Hagia Sophia*, see ibid., pp. 326-27, and on Merton's prose poem of that title, pp. 361-64.

the Roman Catholic Church. Merton will labor valiantly to domesticate these reminders of his frustrated desires.

Merton externalizes his intimate battles in writing. With determination he advances his dream work during his intensely self-conscious waking life. About three days later, in his journal (dated 4 March 1958), he composes a long letter to the Jewish woman he calls "Proverb." This is really a love letter that expresses a deeply felt infatuation (even as it remains imaginary) while the author deftly manipulates its symbolic meaning. He addresses the "woman" directly and defines himself, his personality and his desires, in terms of what she represents:

> Dear Proverb,
>
> For several days I have intended to write you this letter, to tell you that I have not forgotten you. Perhaps now too much time has gone by and I no longer exactly know what I wanted to tell you — except that though there is a great difference in our ages and many other differences between us, you know even better than I that these differences do not matter at all. Indeed it is from you that I have learned, to my surprise, that it is as if they never even existed.

Several vexed issues are condensed in this dream and in Merton's subsequent elaborations and we can interpret this opening paragraph as an allegory of Merton speaking to Jewish tradition. He denies the importance of several "differences," among them their ages, their gender, their religious and ethnic origins. Nor does he distinguish between the drama of erotic versus spiritual love (a difficult enough problem for a professed monk). But his attitudes are extraordinarily prescient: he would side with the Jews in the theological controversies of Vatican II (which took place about six years later) and he would fall in love with "Margie" (almost twenty years down the road).

Remember that this is February of 1958. In his journal, Merton claims that these differences do not matter nor did they ever really exist. And yet, difference as such, as Karl Plank rightly insists, is the decisive element: Merton (and the Catholic Church) had not yet accepted Judaism as not superseded by Christianity, nor had they accepted Jews, not as candidates for conversion, but as precious guardians of the mother religion (the first covenant) of which Christianity is a daughter. Merton strives to find common ground with his dreamed Jewish woman. The denial of differences remains his letter's main theme.

But what does that mean in practical terms? In the end, Merton received a most precious gift from this symbolic Jewish woman named "Proverb" – although his feelings might apply to any woman. He becomes liberated from a constraining sense of sin. This is the pivot point of repentance (of *teshuvah*) and his consequent opening to the world. Not only did her love allow him to glimpse the possibility of fuller self-acceptance; more so, she gave him permission to love the world. One can feel the excitement in his prose:

> How grateful I am to you for loving in me something which I thought I had entirely lost, and someone who, I thought, I had long ceased to be. And in you, dear, though some might be tempted to say you do not even exist, there is a reality as real and wonderful and as precious as life itself. I must be careful what I say, for words cannot explain my love for you, and I do not wish, by my words, to harm that which in you is more real and more pure than anyone else in the world – your lovely spontaneity, your simplicity, the generosity of your love.

It is hard to believe that Merton is not infatuated with a real woman! More significantly, however, he interprets his own love letter, for that is what this written response to his dream and waking obsession has become. He feels loved for who he is, namely a man, as a male sexual being: "something which I thought I had entirely lost, and someone, who, I thought, I had long ceased to be." The young woman may not physically exist; literally, she is a dreamed image; or, to translate, Judaism as such may not yet exist theologically for Catholics. But Merton "treasures" in her "the revelation of [her] virginal solitude."

It is not yet clear what Proverb's radical purity, her solitude, means to him. But it does reflect his aspirations to become a hermit, that is, to leave the world, even to separate himself from the community of Gethsemani: "In your marvelous, innocent, love you are utterly alone: yet you have given your love to me, why I cannot imagine. And with it you have given me yourself and all the innocent wonder of your solitude." Merton still believed that to give "all to God" one must reject ordinary passions.

At the same time, the monk's ambivalence is powerful. His logical contradiction is quite significant, for Proverb is both a lover and a solitary, like himself. Merton wants to become a hermit, to preserve an increasing purity of silence, aloneness, and independence; all the while he is falling in love with a woman, as symbolic as she may be. He concludes: "Dearest Proverb, I love your name, its mystery, its simplicity and its secret, which even you yourself seem not to appreciate."

To translate: Is Merton's dreamed Jewish woman aware of her own sanctity? Is Merton sensitive to the sanctity of the world? Can he accept Judaism and God's continuing covenant with the Jewish people?

SPIRITUAL AND EROTIC LIBERATION

Merton's dream of a young Jewish woman thus became the locus for his attempts to acknowledge, and dynamically to integrate several conflicting desires, most of them still forbidden to the Trappist monk: his yearning to be loved by a woman, his own sexual needs (that is, his identity as an erotic man in the world), and his reverence for Judaism, not as yet recognized as spiritually autonomous by the Roman Catholic Church. To say the least, this symbolic Jewish woman named Proverb includes a number of powerful challenges.

There was momentous progress, however, in Merton's self-acceptance and his ability to tolerate the normal ambiguities and uncertainties of his vocation. His acceptance of mystery proclaims an advanced humility. Yet he remains preoccupied with his vocation and draws a line in his Journal while reflecting on his frustrated desire to found a monastery in South America.[10] Soon

---

10 "What do I expect to accomplish – even supposing that I am sent? (I still

after, he summarizes his contradictory state of mind: "*I am no longer in doubt* – yet I am not yet certain. / A great stage, this – into the peace and darkness which is between doubt and certainty. This, in fact, is another kind of certainty, a higher kind – the certainty of what you do not know." These irreducible antitheses and self-contradictions are typical of Thomas Merton. But does anyone ever achieve certainty? Complete purity of heart and will?

And yet, Merton's psychological gain remained sturdy, though far from resolved. He is indeed confronting his sexuality – and especially his desire for love, of which sexuality is only a partial, but necessary, element.[11] Moreover, Merton's Proverb dreams, fantasies, and his acting out in writing constitute a spiritual breakthrough. Through writing he was successful enough in integrating, or at least bringing into productive tension, a great many essential conflicts. The reader of the journal can recognize how the epiphany of Fourth and Walnut, which occurred just two weeks later, actualizes many of these insights.

Merton's definitive conversion of consciousness took place on the city street during a medical visit to Louisville. After returning to the monastery, he described the decisive event in his private journal on 19 March 1958, the Feast of Saint Joseph. He penned this raw version in the tool shed retreat he called Saint Anne's, the prototype of his hermitage.[12]

> Yesterday, in Louisville, at the corner of 4th and Walnut, suddenly realized that I loved all the people and that none of them was, or, could be totally alien to me. As if waking

believe I will be sent.) What great good will be done by a group of people living as more or less frustrated contemplatives? Or else keeping a Rule for the sake of a Rule?

"Someone else can do that. Surely, it is not my mission in life." *Journal*, vol. 3, ibid., p. 177. The next quotation is from the same page.

11 Even a careful reader of the (censored) *The Seven Storey Mountain* would understand that his relationships with women were unsatisfactory, both personally and ethically. Cf. Merton's Christmas dream (26 December 1959), *Journal*, vol. 3, p. 362. For the most deeply contextualized study of the feminine in Merton, including the dream of Proverb, see Robert Jingen Gunn, *Journeys into Emptiness: Dogen, Merton, and Jung and the Quest for Transformation* (New York: Paulist Press, 2000).

12 This and the next quotation are from *Journal*, vol. 3, pp. 181–82.

from a dream – the dream of my separateness, of the "special" vocation to be different. My vocation does not really make me different from the rest of men or put me in a special category except artificially, juridically. I am still a member of the human race – and what more glorious destiny is there for a man, since the Word was made flesh and became, too, a member of the Human Race!

Thank God! Thank God! I am only another member of the human race, like all the rest of them. I have the immense joy of being a man! As if the sorrows of our condition could really matter, once we begin to realize who and what we are – as if we could ever begin to realize it on earth.

It is not a question of proving to myself that I either dislike or like the women one sees in the street. The fact of having a vow of chastity does not oblige one to argument on this point – no special question arises. I am keenly conscious, not of their beauty (I hardly think I saw anyone really beautiful by special standards) but of their humanity, their woman-ness. But what incomprehensible beauty there is there, what secret beauty that would perhaps be inaccessible to me if I were not dedicated to a different way of life. It is as though by chastity I had come to be married to what is most pure in all the women of the world and to taste and sense the secret beauty of their girl's hearts as they walked in the sunlight – each one secret and good and lovely in the sight of God – never touched by anyone, nor by me, nor by anyone, as good as and even more beautiful than the light itself. For the woman-ness that is in each of them is at once original and inexhaustibly fruitful, bringing the image of God into the world. In this each one is Wisdom and Sophia and Our Lady – (my delights are to be with the children of men!).

We must clarify some essential elements of this complex passage, for Merton himself was still in the process of discovering their meaningful order. Again, he felt that he had overcome a falsified, inauthentic otherness. He experienced a radical breakthrough in his awareness, of himself and of his relation to ordinary people. The bottom line is that he rejected the negative theology of "sin" that characterized *The Seven Storey Mountain*. What was formerly a defensive "separateness" became a more neutral or positive "difference," so that his Benedictine vow of fidelity to monastic life (and its implicit celibacy) no longer opposed "the world."

Insight in the middle of a crowded street opened the doors of perception. He insists that he is "waking from dream" and he repeats the word "dream" several times, for dream is of course a common metaphor of an illusory ideology. But the journal entry also introduces into his description some associative materials drawn directly from the dream of Proverb, connecting the issue of sexuality with the woman's Jewishness. Previously, these two elements of "difference" had been taboo to his vocation: sex versus celibacy, autonomous Judaism versus triumphant Catholicism.

This long, candid description consolidated his attempts to resolve these conflicts by expanding his understanding of, and participation in the femininity of the Church – in the persons of Wisdom, *Sophia*, Saint Anne, and of course the Blessed Virgin. These hypotheses are confirmed by the fact that Merton follows the initial paragraphs on the epiphany at Fourth and Walnut with a second letter to Proverb:

> Dear Proverb, I have kept one promise and I have refrained from speaking of you until seeing you again. I knew that when I saw you again it would be very different, in a different place, in a different form, in the most unexpected circumstances. I shall never forget our meeting yesterday. The touch of your hand makes me a different person. To be with you is rest and truth. Only with you are things found, dear child sent to me by God!

In his dream life and in his private journal, Thomas Merton integrated conflicting needs and desires. We can summarize this breakthrough as a liberation of his *eros,* a powerful feeling of energy connected with spiritual love as well as with sexuality.[13] At

13 See the insightful essay by George Kilcourse, "Introduction: Spirituality as the Freedom to Channel Eros," *The Merton Annual* 13 (2000): 7-15; and the

least inwardly, Merton emancipated his love for the world – which includes typical (non-celibate) male fantasies about women. Merton's *eros* also contains an unmistakable yearning for maternal love, of which he felt deprived while growing up. Perhaps he perceived the Jewish Proverb as the Mother of Christianity.

Whoever she is – and her identity is multiple – Proverb's "touch" made of Thomas Merton another person. He achieved fuller self-acceptance, including enthusiasm for womankind, and he felt a fuller bond with Judaism in its own otherness or "difference." Then he was impelled to write Rabbi Heschel that he wanted to become a "Jew under his Catholic skin." Or so he believed. (To speak personally, Thomas Merton, and this Jewish reader at least, are truly, deeply, brothers, if only for the fact that both Father Louis and myself have been energized, and transformed, by loving a "Jewish woman.")

We can conclude that Merton's dreams of Proverb bespeak a hard-earned conversion (or turning, *teshuvah*), *away* from the defensive self and *toward* the Other. Such is the beginning of authentic dialogue, in Martin Buber's terms, the reciprocal acknowledgment of both distance and relation between partners.[14] Merton's repentance, true *teshuvah*, gave him fuller self-acceptance before God, enhancing his trust of God and strengthening his tolerance of risk. Merton became more able to change, and more able to give and to receive love. In the process he welcomed the voice of Judaism, while still anticipating the touch of her hand.

DIALOGUE AND DIFFERENCE

Merton's struggle to give a voice to Judaism was not easy, nor was it entirely successful. It took active intervention from his subconscious, in the dreamed figure of Proverb, for him to cross

interview with Jane Marie Richardson, SL, ibid., 127-43. For the monk's most developed views on "the feminine" see Thomas Merton, *The Springs of Contemplation. A Retreat at the Abbey of Gethsemani*, (New York: Farrar, Straus & Giroux, 1992; Ave Maria Press, 1997), and the study by R.J. Gunn noted above.

14 See Edward K. Kaplan, "Martin Buber and the Drama of Otherness: The Dynamics of Love, Art, and Faith," *Judaism: A Quarterly Journal of Jewish Life and Thought* 27,2 (Spring 1978): 196-206. The article by Karl Plank, "The Eclipse of Difference" (see above note 6), remains fundamental.

the threshold into Church politics. Influenced by Abraham Heschel and Vatican II, and others, Merton became able to accept his own internalized otherness, his sacramentally suppressed sexuality, and his craving for female affection. But his acceptance of Judaism, as noble and enthusiastic as it was, did not wholeheartedly embrace the spiritual autonomy of the people Israel. How could he, hoping for an eschatological unity beyond human differences?[15] Merton remained secure, as well he should, under and within his "Catholic skin."

We can achieve true dialogue only in this world, and only by acknowledging differences of perspective, differences of understanding, and of course irreducible theological disagreements. These disparities might (or might not) be resolved only by God. Karl Plank, in his pioneering article, "The Eclipse of Difference," insists upon the limitations of Merton's affirmation of Judaism. Here is Plank's summary, minus the nuances: "Merton's correspondence with Abraham Heschel, precisely on the issues of Vatican II, shows not a special sensitivity to the Jewish situation but an effacement of the Jewish grievance; his writing on the

---

15 The question of eschatological unity is a rough one, despite assurance from generous Christian friends that the mysterious end of times does not imply that Judaism should cease to exist before the Messianic return. See the important article of William H. Shannon, "Thomas Merton and Judaism," *America* (October 6, 1990): 218-22. Shannon quotes Merton's letter to Rabbi Zalman Schachter, 15 February 1962: "The Suffering Servant is One: Christ, Israel. There is one wedding and one wedding feast, not two or five or six. There is one bride. There is one mystery, and the mystery of Israel and of the Church is ultimately to be revealed as One," Shannon, p. 220; published in *The Ground of Love*, pp. 535-36.

Related to eschatology, there are significant differences regarding some Christian views of the Holocaust. See Shannon: "Is it possible that for the Jews the Holocaust may well be seen as a national death and the rise of the state of Israel, not primarily as a political event but as a religious event, as a new beginning that in some sense may be seen as an eschatological fulfillment?" p. 220.

Cf. Abraham Heschel, *Israel: An Echo of Eternity* (New York: Farrar, Straus & Giroux, 1969), p. 113: "What would be the face of Western history today if the end of twentieth–century Jewish life would have been Bergen-Belsen, Dachau, Auschwitz? The State of Israel is not an atonement. It would be blasphemy to regard it as a compensation. However, the existence of the State of Israel reborn makes life less unendurable. It is a slight hinderer of hindrances to believing in God."

Shoah, preoccupied with the reference frames of Nazism and Christianity, similarly effaces Judaism from its own history; and his tendency to refract Judaism through a biblical lens leads him to appreciate a Jew who exists without full difference."[16]

I return to our original inquiry into repentance, or *teshuvah*. We must face the frailty of our theologies and acknowledge the ultimate mystery, the living God, Who alone, as Heschel states, provides "the meaning beyond the mystery." Dialogue, I repeat, mutual understanding, takes place in the world, where contradictions are not resolved. We must search our souls boldly, honestly. How can we accept the Other unconditionally if we believe – or if we hope to believe – that only our way is the true path to redemption?

So with gratitude for Thomas Merton's courage, and for the spiritual generosity of his fellow monks and the generous keepers of the Merton legacy, we reach toward true dialogue beyond ideologies, beyond theologies. With gratitude and love and hope, I listen to Rabbi Heschel – Father Louis' friend and spiritual ally, the rabbi who inspired James Carroll,[17] and my spiritual model. Rabbi Abraham Joshua Heschel, in his famous speech "No Religion Is an Island,"[18] affirms the plurality of beliefs: "In this aeon diversity of religions is the will of God."

Thomas Merton and Abraham Heschel establish community at a fundamental level. Nihilism is the common enemy. For most of us, faith is not a given but a task, and we aspire toward holiness by sharing our spiritual dissatisfaction. True dialogue begins as we

16 Plank, op. cit., p. 188. See also Plank's note: "One might also consider the role played by Merton's memory of at least two of his closest friends at Columbia, Robert Lax and Robert Gerdy. Both Lax and Gerdy were born Jews but later converted to Catholicism."

17 James Carroll, *Constantine's Sword* (op. cit.), p. 47: "The deepest change I trace to this rabbi is in my notion of God." See Carroll's chapter 60, Agenda Item 5: Repentance, especially pertinent to this paper.

18 Heschel originally delivered this speech, "No Religion Is an Island," as the inaugural lecture as Harry Emerson Fosdick Visiting Professor at Union Theological Seminary, 10 November 1965; reprinted in Susannah Heschel, ed., *Abraham Joshua Heschel, Moral Grandeur and Spiritual Audacity. Essays* (New York: Farrar, Straus & Giroux, 1996), p. 244; for the next quotation, see ibid., pp. 239-40.

empty the ego before God. Heschel evokes this stance in a long, rhythmical sentence:

> I suggest that the most significant basis for meeting of [people] of different religious traditions is the level of fear and trembling, of humility and contrition, where our individual moments of faith are mere waves in the endless ocean of mankind's reaching out for God, where all formulations and articulations appear as understatements, where our souls are swept away by the awareness of the urgency of answering God's commandment, while stripped of pretension and conceit we sense the tragic insufficiency of human faith.

Heschel envisages a sophisticated humility: "The tragic insufficiency of human faith." We can experience this primal humility as "fear of God" (like Kierkegaard's "fear and trembling"), as we stand morally naked before the Creator. Humility places institutional self-interest and parochialism of any kind into their true light. Perhaps the term "reverence" can summarize its fulfillment.

Thomas Merton came to realize that all religions could fathom the sacred preciousness of humankind. He shares with Heschel's Judaism what can be called *radical reverence*, a humble and loving attitude toward all reality, human and cosmic and divine.[19] Radical reverence combines sacred terror, awe and admiration, and veneration for each and every human being. Merton's dreams of Jewish Proverb and his epiphany at Fourth and Walnut emancipated his radical reverence.

The time is ripe for mutual self-examination, in addition to generosity of spirit, openness to the other. The entanglements of Judaism, the minority tradition, as well as of Christianity, the majority tradition, are rife with ambiguities.[20] As we face our

19 See my essay, "Radical Reverence: A Fulcrum against Fanaticism," *Tikkun* 11,2 (March–April 1996), 57–58, written as a response to the assassination of Yitzhak Rabin. See also the lovely book of Samuel H. Dresner, *Prayer, Humility, and Compassion* (Philadelphia: Jewish Publication Society of America, 1957), deeply influenced by Heschel.
20 See Arthur Green's review essay of James Carroll's *Constantine's Sword* in

differences, together and separately, let us advance, with awe, humility, and moral courage, Thomas Merton's dialogue with Judaism and the world.

Tikkun 16, 3 (2001): 65-67,72. Brandeis University has published this and other responses in a booklet, *Catholics, Jews, and the Prism of Conscience*, ed. Daniel Terris and Sylvia Fuks Fried (Waltham, MA: Brandeis University, Office of Publications, 2001), with essays by Carroll, Arthur Green, Eugene Fisher, Robert Wistrich, Donald Dietrich, Paul Mendes-Flohr, Kanan Makiya, Eva Fleischner, and Irving Greenberg. See also Augustin Cardinal Bea, *The Church and the Jewish People*, trans. Philip Loretz, S.J. (New York: Harper and Row, 1966).

"The message of the Bible is then that into the confusion of man's world, with its divisions and hatred, has come a message of transforming power, and those who believe it will experience in themselves the love that makes for reconciliation and peace on earth."

—Thomas Merton, *Opening the Bible*

7

BREAKTHROUGH OF THE WORD:

THOMAS MERTON AND MARTIN BUBER ON READING THE BIBLE

Karl A. Plank

... [these passages] are somehow claiming that there has been a breakthrough of the ultimate word into the sphere of the human, and that what the Bible is about is this breakthrough, recorded in events, happenings, which are decisive not only for the Jewish people or for the disciples of Christ but for [human]kind as a whole.

—Thomas Merton[1]

All [the Bible's] stories and songs, all its sayings and prophecies are united by one fundamental theme: the encounter of a group of people with the Nameless Being whom they, hearing his speech and speaking to him in turn, ventured to name.

—Martin Buber[2]

LIVING HUMAN DOCUMENTS

Anton Boisen, a pioneer of pastoral psychology, taught his students to consider persons under their care as "living human

1 Thomas Merton, *Opening the Bible* (Collegeville, MN: Liturgical Press, 1970), 25.
2 Martin Buber, "People Today and the Jewish Bible," in Martin Buber and Franz Rosenzweig, *Scripture and Translation*, tr. L. Rosenwald with E. Fox (Bloomington: Indiana University, 1994), 4.

documents." With this image, Boisen sought to encourage his pupils' close attention to the concrete data of human experience, but also to inculcate a hermeneutical approach to the care and cure of persons in need. As people in distress tell the story of their anguish, their situations call for interpretation similar to what readers do with texts set before them. Accordingly, Boisen suggested, counselors and therapists might fruitfully bring to bear perspectives of textual interpretation upon the pastoral conversation. They might find it fitting, for the time being, to regard those in their care as texts whose language, symbols, and structures must all be interpreted—be read—with hermeneutical sensitivity.[3]

The affinity between the interpretation of texts and of personal circumstances invites one to ask if Boisen's image might also run in the opposite direction. Where Boisen's paradigm emphasizes the documentary quality of human situations, could not the image just as well underscore the "living human" or personal dimensions of textuality? Within the Boisen paradigm, one construes persons as texts in order to understand them. The corollary of the image implies: one should also read texts interpersonally, regarding them, if you will, as persons, in order to interpret their meaning. As Stephen Kepnes suggests, one must read "the text as thou."[4]

This paper pursues the workings of an interpersonal hermeneutics in the domain of biblical interpretation. It asks what it means to read the Bible as "thou" or as a "living human document." To do so, it looks at two presentations of reading the Bible: Martin Buber's "People Today and the Jewish Bible" (1926) and Thomas Merton's *Opening the Bible* (1967). Both texts invest the Bible with dimensions of person and emphasize the role of reader as self. As they discuss the Bible, both Buber and Merton make pertinent their views of selfhood to the act of reading scripture and to the dynamics of revelation that may occur in this act. Following a brief introduction to each work, the paper will analyze the two

3 On Boisen's image as a paradigm for pastoral counseling and a significant development of its implications, see Charles V. Gerkin, *The Living Human Document. Re-Visioning Pastoral Counseling in a Hermeneutical Mode* (Nashville: Abingdon, 1984).

4 See Kepnes' study of Martin Buber's hermeneutics, *The Text as Thou* (Bloomington: Indiana, 1992).

presentations in terms of their construals of the Bible and of their ways of relating reading, revelation and self. Though the paper focuses primarily on the issue of interpersonal reading of the Bible, it remains aware that both Buber and Merton present their views from points within their respective Jewish and Christian traditions. Accordingly, it will comment as well on the significance of their statements for conversation between these traditions.

OPENING THE BIBLE

Before becoming the Abbot of Gethsemani in 1973, Timothy Kelly had been a novice under Thomas Merton, later serving as his Undermaster of Novices. Kelly recalls of Merton's work in the novitiate: "He was very hesitant in accepting much of the scriptural work available in English in the early 1960s. His criticism of it as foundational for the spiritual life was harsh."[5] If at odds with a current mode of biblical interpretation, Merton nevertheless continued to engage the Bible intellectually and spiritually: in his teaching of prophetic literature in the novitiate[6]; in his reflections upon the Psalter and its constant presence in the monastic offices[7]; in his encounter with the lectionary throughout the liturgical year; in poetic meditations[8]; and in his concern to keep abreast of recent developments in biblical studies such as the discovery of the Qumran scrolls.[9] Merton was not disenchanted with the Bible, but with the drift toward arid readings that he

5 Timothy Kelly, "Epilogue: A Memoir," in *The Legacy of Thomas Merton*, ed. Patrick Hart (Kalamazoo: Cistercian Publications, 1986), 221. On Fr. Timothy's abbacy, see Dianne Aprile, *The Abbey of Gethsemani. Place of Peace and Paradox* (Winnipeg: Trout Lily Press, 1998), 192-223.

6 See Merton's letter to Abraham Joshua Heschel (12.17.1960), in *The Hidden Ground of Love*, ed. William H. Shannon (New York: Farrar Straus Giroux, 1985), 431.

7 See e.g., Thomas Merton, *Bread in the Wilderness* (Collegeville, MN: Liturgical Press, 1986).

8 See e.g., "Be My Defender" (Psalm 4) and "Earthquake" (Isaias 52) in *The Collected Poems of Thomas Merton* (New York: New Directions, 1977), 692-93 and 701-703.

9 Note e.g., Merton's invitations to Lou H. Silberman of Vanderbilt University to speak to the novices on the Qumran materials. See his letter to Silberman dated 2.7.1963 (Thomas Merton Studies Center, Bellarmine College, Louisville, KY).

found in academic, pious, and cynical circles alike.

In December 1966, Abraham Joshua Heschel offered Merton the opportunity to set out a different approach to reading scripture. Time-Life had begun plans to issue an edition of the Bible and, in its behalf, Heschel sought to commission Merton to write the introductory essay.[10] Merton accepted the assignment, though with resistance, and completed a draft of "Opening the Bible" in 1967.[11] The Time-Life project itself was not fulfilled. Merton's extended essay, however, was published posthumously and stands as his only sustained reflection on the Bible.

Merton begins with the question "What kind of book is this?" (11).[12] He does not pose his question to an audience he perceives to be uninformed about the book as much as deadened to "the existential reality of scripture" (35). Academics and religious persons may know "what kind of book" this is in terms of its literature, history, and theology, yet produce readings that bore (28) and fail to satisfy (11). Shaped by speculative interest (30) or the momentum of religious comfort (36), the habits of reading that Merton contends with impede personal engagement and thus realize neither the claim religious tradition makes for the book – i.e., that it expresses the word of God (11-12) – nor any existential claim at all. Impersonal and shallow reading robs the Bible of its capability to disturb and provoke outrage, features that are essential, in Merton's view, to the book's offering a revealing word. If the Bible is to matter in any vital way, one must discern what this kind of book can *do* (18), what hinders or enables its performance, and what the reader must do to unleash the text's

10 See Merton's letter to Heschel (12.12.1966) in *Hidden Ground of Love*, 435.
11 On Merton's resistance to the project note his letter to Heschel (12.12.96): "I sincerely doubt my capacity to write anything worthwhile on the Bible. I am not a pro." *Hidden Ground of Love*, 435. Merton's protest here may be slightly disingenuous. While he certainly was not a "pro" in biblical studies, the lack of certified expertise rarely restrained him from venturing forth into a widening array of materials with insight and creativity. See, too, his journal entries from the next month, in *Learning to Love*, ed. C. Bochen (New York: HarperCollins, 1998), 186, 188. His earlier letter to Mother M.L. Schroen (11.25.1963) also illumines the resistance. See *The School of Charity*, ed. Br. Patrick Hart (New York: Farrar Straus Giroux, 1990), 185.
12 References to *Opening the Bible* and to "People Today and the Jewish Bible" will be cited parenthetically in the text.

revealing power. For Merton, to ask "what kind of book is this?" does not invoke the question of genre as much as rhetorical function: how the Bible as language *does* something to the life of the one who reads it; how the Bible functions to reveal a divine word and transform (18).[13] Posing the question this way not only helps Merton to deal with the theological claims made for scripture but implicates the Bible's readers in the book's efficacy. It is those readers Merton wants to challenge not with more information about the Bible, but with a call to read differently.

MERTON'S CONSTRUAL OF SCRIPTURE: THE BREAKTHROUGH OF THE WORD

Theological discussion of the Bible generally involves a *construal* of scripture, a selection of some aspect of scripture that establishes the Bible's unity and mode of revelation or authority.[14] Drawing upon prophetic call narratives, Merton construes scripture in terms of the *breakthrough* of the word of God. Thus, he writes: "There has been a breakthrough of the ultimate word into the sphere of the human, and ... what the Bible is about is this breakthrough, recorded in events, happenings, which are decisive not only for the Jewish people or for the disciples of Christ but for [human]kind as a whole" (25). The breakthrough of the ultimate word "is recognized by its transforming and liberating power. The 'word of God' is recognized in actual experience because it does something to anyone who really 'hears' it" (18).

Merton's construal of scripture renders the text as person, as "living human document." He attributes to it the agency of a speaker whose word has efficacy and consequence.[15] It is the subject of active verbs: it *breaks through* the banality of human discourse; it changes and sets free the one who reads its word, "who really 'hears' it." As *breakthrough*, the word that scripture speaks exerts a force that interrupts the pattern of familiar

13 On rhetorical function, see Chaim Perelman, and L. Olbrechts-Tyteca, *The New Rhetoric* (Notre Dame: University of Notre Dame, 1969)

14 On the notion of "construal of scripture," see David H. Kelsey, *The Uses of Scripture in Recent Theology* (Philadelphia: Fortress, 1975).

15 On speech-action as a marker of human identity, see Hannah Arendt, *The Human Condition* (Chicago: University of Chicago, 1958), 175-181.

conversation and thereby demands response. Like the prophets' speech that it expresses, scripture's word claims a human situation and initiates a dialogue that compels answer and change (44). No idle repository of collected words, scripture speaks the words it records. It works in the midst of human history to interrupt, surprise, and claim for transformation. Rendered as person, the Bible acts as prophet, as critic and liberator.

Merton's statements that construe the Bible as *breakthrough* have further implications to note:

1. The Bible has wholeness (70). Through its personification, one can perceive its unity as a sequence of speakings or word-events that work consistently to transform and liberate. In its disparate parts, the Bible speaks a constant, ultimate word that claims its hearers for freedom. It is unified not in its historical condition nor in its literary genres nor even in any theological content. Its wholeness lies in the effects of its word being spoken.

3. As an ultimate word that which the Bible speaks is fundamentally other. It transcends human discourse and, in a paradoxical sense, is a non-Word (25-26), an unvocalized name that appears with mystery and surprise. Accordingly, "we must not therefore open the Bible with any set determination to reduce it to the limits of a preconceived pattern of our own" (69). In its difference, the ultimate word remains pattern-breaking.

3. In its *breaking-through*, the ultimate word interrupts and displaces the discourse of the familiar. As such, it has a critical and interrogative function. Interruption – the breakthrough of a new word – questions the authority of other words to be true, self-evident, or sufficient.

4. Insofar as the ultimate word breaks through in "events and happenings" and is perceived in "actual experience," the Bible manifests a thoroughgoing worldliness. It is worldly in its claim upon human history and recognition of God at the "very center of [human] life" (65). It cannot be spiritualized or confined within the sphere of religion. The Bible's word resists attempts to marginalize it to a sequestered periphery of existence.

5. As "decisive not only for the Jewish people or for the disciples of Christ but for [human]kind as a whole," the Bible is "everybody's book" (38). The Bible is thereby not available to ideological purchase by any one religious tradition or group. Moreover, and beyond the ecumenical point, the Bible's reading cannot be restricted to the religious, even in their diversity. As "everybody's book," the Bible calls for and sanctions reading by the outsider no less than the insider; by the skeptic unbeliever no less than the pious (49-50). It addresses "[human]kind as a whole" in its common predicament of bondage.

6. As a word that effects transformation and liberation, the Bible reveals the "presence of an absolute Freedom" that opposes all that enslaves human life (30). "Both in the Old Testament and in the New the central message is one of liberation, not only from the bondage of Egypt, not only from the corruption of ambitious kings, not only from exile in Babylon, but from everything that corrupts the [human] heart and enslaves. . ." (47-48).

Merton on Reading, Revelation, and the Self

Merton makes clear in his personified construal of the Bible that scripture "*does* something to the one that reads it" (73). This section identifies more precisely what Merton understands it to do, what reading the Bible entails, and how the reader participates in and shapes the meaning-effect of its *breakthrough*.[16]

Merton identifies *breakthrough* with a "collision of wills" between text and reader (75). On the one hand, this provides a cue to what scripture *does* and, on the other, brings into view the pertinence of the reader. In its *breakthrough* scripture provokes conflict with its readers, frustrating the readers' proclivity, if not intention, "to achieve some end which is in conflict with [their] own inner truth, [their] own destiny" (75). If left to their own

16 On the category "meaning-effect," see Daniel Patte, *What Is Structural Exegesis?* (Philadelphia: Fortress, 1976), 21-22. Patte's use of the term brings out the notion that a text's meaning is not so much a fixed entity as an effect performed by the rhetoric of the text. It involves what the text *does* as it speaks rather than simply what it *says*.

momentum, human selves become self-destructive. Scripture
interrupts that momentum with counter-plot and challenging
oracle, making readers aware of the danger and possibility of their
situation. Merton's use of Nathan's parable to David (2 Sam 12:1-
10) is instructive (43). For Merton, the Bible at large functions as
parable, narrating a story that runs counter to human inclination
and expectation. As parabolic word, the Bible traps its readers in a
reversal of vision that, on the one hand frustrates, judges, and
indicts while, on the other, liberates them to struggle with the
freedom of new awareness.[17] The *breakthrough* of such a word
means, if nothing else, that "any serious reading of the Bible means
personal involvement in it. . . And involvement is dangerous,
because it lays one open to unforeseen conclusions" (43).

Reading the Bible requires personal engagement, for its word is
always a question about oneself and one's identity. As Merton writes,
"The curiously oblique yet insistent claims that underlie the very
words of the Bible . . . raise the fundamental question of *identity*"
(26-7). More than making assertions, the Bible interrogates. It breaks
through the screen of abstraction and interrupts the discourse of
easy assurance with questions that are personal, unsettling, and
compelling. The exchange of Nathan and David again provides a
paradigm for the workings of scripture. Nathan tells a story that
seems remote from David's personal existence, a tale of a poor man,
his ewe-lamb, and the transgression of a wealthy man. When David
expresses outrage at the abuse rendered by the person of power,
Nathan's word breaks through: *attah ha-ish* – "You are [that] man" (2
Sam 12:7). Powerfully declarative, Nathan's word yet puts the
personal question of David's identity: "Who are you?" Here occurs
the "collision of wills" that *breakthrough* creates (75). David does have
a sense of his identity, but the story brings into question precisely
that sense by its counter-plot. In the resulting dissonance of
contradiction, David is set free, but only to struggle with the
question he can no longer avoid. The assurances of role and
prerogative collapse in the onset of the prophetic word; his principle
of justice – confirmed in his outrage – offers no escape, for what
seems true in the abstract has crashed in the domain of David's

17 On this view of parable, see J.D. Crossan, *The Dark Interval* (Allen TX: Argus,
  1975).

existence. In the "collision of wills" David cannot hold fast to the identity brought into question without at the same time denying the existential truth of the parable's claim. The text, through its vision and question, compels him to see himself in a new way. In its question, he is brought to a point of struggle with his identity; in that struggle, his identity is transformed.

Merton understands the interrogatory character of scripture in a Barthian fashion: "when you begin to question the Bible you find that the Bible is also questioning you. When you ask: 'What is this book?' you find that you are also implicitly being asked: 'Who is this that reads it?'" (27). The questions one brings the Bible, the Bible transposes into a personal key, making every question reflexive. Likening the dynamic to that of a Zen *mondo,* Merton notes: "one does not go from answer to answer but from question to question. One's questions are answered, not by clear, definitive answers, but by more pertinent and more crucial questions . . . If we approach [the Bible] with speculative questions, we are apt to find that it confronts us in turn with brutally practical questions. If we ask it for information about the meaning of life, it answers by asking us when we intend to start living" (29-30). The *breakthrough* of the word resists responses that are abstract and detached. The voice of the text, itself personified in the image, calls to the person of the reader and compels engaged struggle. Engagement is necessary because the text asks a personal question; struggle is necessary because the text collides with the reader's will and only answers questions with other questions. For Merton, one can approach the Bible with neither the complacency of distance nor the heart's ease of comfort and resolution. The Bible does ultimately liberate, but outrage precedes and accompanies transformation.[18]

The Bible does not reveal and transform in its own right. Transformation requires the personal work of the reader that, if avoided, has the capability to block scripture's revelation. Merton writes, "If this power [of the Bible to transform] appears to have failed and not to have shown its full efficacy, perhaps it is the

18 Thus, Merton writes of "the presence of an absolute Freedom who at once denies and affirms us; who is at once the ground of our freedom and its adversary; who accepts us in proportion as we renounce ourselves and who affirms us in so far as we live at the center of our existence rather than at its periphery." *Opening the Bible,* 30-31.

believers who have failed the Bible and not the other way around"
(22). Readers fail the Bible by pursuing armored strategies of
reading that minimize personal engagement. They deny, on the
one hand, their personal stake in the reading and, on the other, the
Bible as a "living human document" – a text that speaks as person
to person. If personal engagement liberates, however, why do
readers tend to resist and impede it?

Merton explains the resistance in terms of the nature of the
encounter itself. The *breakthrough* is dangerous. As a "living human
document," the Bible voices an ultimate word that is free, other,
and beyond human manipulation. At the point one would attempt
to control its meaning, it asserts itself as an elusive "non-word" (25)
that goes where it wills and draws near as it wants. Unpredictable
and personal, the Bible poses the danger that, as in the case of
David before Nathan, the reader will be thrown into a painful
crisis of identity and never be able to see him- or herself in quite
the same way again. For the Bible to transform the reader, the
reader must become vulnerable to profound change, a yielding to
the death of a false selfhood that, though enslaving, proffers the
temptation of existential ease and stasis.

Here Merton moves from the nature of the encounter to the
problem of the self. In doing so, he brings to bear on the scriptural
breakthrough the contemplative critique of false selfhood that so
characterizes his writing at large.[19] The perspective appears in
shorthand in *Opening the Bible*, but one easily recognizes it. The
revelation of Scripture liberates, but can do so only when "in
reading the Bible, we somehow become aware that we are problems
to ourselves" (80). Yet, in our very human predicament, we are blind
to that awareness. The sin of the human condition divides selves
from their inmost truth and sets them at odds with their own reality.
Merton writes,

---

19 On Merton's sense of contemplation and its critical function, see works such
as his *Contemplative Prayer* (New York: Image, 1971) and especially *New Seeds
of Contemplation* (New York: New Directions, 1961). For discussion of
Merton's perspective see Karl A. Plank, "Thomas Merton and Hannah Arendt:
Contemplation after Eichmann," *The Merton Annual* 3 (1990): 121-150; and
"Thomas Merton and the Ethical Edge of Contemplation," *Anglican
Theological Review* 84/1 (2002): 113-126.

What is called by theological cliché "original sin" is not merely a seemingly unfair moral disability contracted for us by some pristine parent in a balmy grove: it is a spontaneous inclination to resolve the split in ourselves by denying that it exists and by closing ourselves in upon the superficial and exterior unity of the empirical ego. In other words, we affirm our unity on a shallow and provisional level by shutting out other persons and closing off the deepest area of inner freedom where the ego is no longer in conscious control. Thus we cheaply purchase a relative security; we contrive for ourselves an identity we think we can more easily manage and live up to. But it is a false identity because it is only partial and does not even represent that which is authentically personal in us (81–82).

We do not become aware "that we are problems to ourselves" in part because we do not want to: it is dangerous to gain that knowledge. But, in a deeper sense, we fail to attain awareness because of who we are: persons whose problem takes the form of being unable to see the problem that we are. The masking of the predicament is not an appendage to the problem: it *is* the problem.

Society collaborates in the self's deception through its tempting menu of roles that would assure one of well-being, security, and importance. Merton does not miss the opportunity to note that religious society has its own form of defrauding the self. He takes special aim at the religious insiders for whom "the Bible has become a habit" and who "[decide] in advance what they want of the Bible and what it wants of them" (36). In contrast, Merton poses the vantage of the religious outsider who, by virtue of having no necessary expectation of what the Bible must say, approaches it with an openness that allows it to speak freely and exert its own claim.[20] When one reads with openness, Merton wagers, the Bible reveals itself in the form of a crisis-making that does not make one religious as much as more fully human, more fully aware of one's identity in its fragility and prospect. As if with

---

20 Thus, Merton spends significant time in this short work on the readings of Scripture by the Italian Marxist filmmaker Pasolini, Erich Fromm, and William Faulkner.

a personal voice, the Bible brings these readers to the crisis of decision: whether to persist in the false identity of social and religious roles, blind to the ways that persistence enslaves, or to "respond to a 'word' that *breaks through* this comfortable little system and shatters all its precarious selfish values, challenging us to risk a higher and more fundamental freedom" (83).

Merton brings one finally to a paradoxical view of the dynamics of scripture, its reading and revelation. On the one hand, the Bible speaks as a "living document" when read with openness and personal engagement. It must be read with a sense that "we are problems to ourselves" (80) and aware that it speaks to identify us as Nathan to David: You are the one of whom my story speaks. Apart from the reader's personal involvement, the Bible is dead text more than living document. For readers to suppress their sense of person ultimately denies the "personhood" of the text as well, its potential to say, act, and do. Yet, at the same time, it is the very reading of scripture, in its *breakthrough*, that creates such openness and personal engagement in its reader. It is the crisis-making of reading the Bible that awakens one to the awareness of one's predicament and compels attention to the reading as an urgent, personal matter. What revelation requires, revelation enables. What the ultimate word reveals is its own "dynamism of awareness and response, in which lies 'salvation'" (94).

"People Today and the Jewish Bible"

In their respective approaches to reading the Bible, Martin Buber is Thomas Merton's precursor. This does not mean that Merton wrote under direct influence of Buber's biblical work, nor that he even knew of Buber's "People Today and the Jewish Bible."[21]

---

21 What Merton knew directly of Buber's work is hard to determine precisely. One may assume he knew *I and Thou* and clear evidence exists of his use of Buber's Hasidic tales. For example, his lecture to the Gethsemani novices published in recorded form under the title "Losing One's Self in God" reads and expounds upon three of Buber's Hasidic tales: "Tree of Life," "Joyless Virtue,'" and "Abraham and the Idols" (*The Mystic Life,* Tape 10; Electronic Paperbacks , 1976). Citations of *Tales of the Hasidim* are ubiquitous throughout the series of lectures contained in *The Mystic Life*. It is doubtful that he knew of Buber's "People Today and the Jewish Bible." Though gifted in languages, Merton did not read German as readily as other languages (on Merton's

Rather, Buber's writing, as precursor, establishes the precedent for rendering the Bible as a "living human document" – as a Thou – and for implicating the self in the revelation of scripture. In treating Buber as precursor, one becomes aware of a tradition to which Merton's *Opening the Bible* belongs, though one which Merton himself may not have recognized. The link of tradition clarifies Merton's approach to scripture and develops further its implication.

Buber and Franz Rosenzweig published *Die Schrift und ihre Verdeutschung* in 1936.[22] This collection of articles and lectures discussed Buber and Rosenzweig's construal of the Hebrew Bible and questions associated with their biblical translation, a project begun in 1925.[23] As Everett Fox notes, the volume ranges wide in its consideration of matters such as the unity of the Bible and its grounding in the orality, or spokenness, of scripture. Accordingly, it develops a methodology for reading the Bible based on sound patterns and repetitions. But even as its contents lead one into reflections on "biblical poetics, close reading, translation theory, or cultural history. . ., it is above all a passionate, even utopian plea for the revival of the Bible's ability to speak in living words, to renew what Buber called 'the dialogue between heaven and earth.'"[24]

"People Today and the Jewish Bible," the opening piece in the volume, encapsulates what emerges in the whole. It especially sounds the tone, in Michael Fishbane's words,[25] of "a hermeneutical

German see his confession to Hans Urs von Balthasar in a letter dated August 4, 1964; collected in *The School of Charity*, 226-27). I believe he would have had little access to the publication, even in English. The piece was not translated into English until 1963 and that only partially in a relatively minor anthology of Buber's writings (see Olga Marx's translation in Martin Buber, *Israel and the World* [New York: Schocken, 1963], 89-102 and later in Buber's *On the Bible*, ed. N. Glatzer [New York: Schocken, 1968], 1-13).

22 Now translated in English as *Scripture and Translation*, tr. by Lawrence Rosenwald with Everett Fox (Bloomington: Indiana University, 1994).

23 More than most translations of the Bible, the Buber – Rosenzweig translation self-consciously reflects an understanding of a particular construal of the text, its unity and nature – in particular, its awareness of the text's orality. The collection of lectures and articles seeks to make public and clarify the understanding that shapes their translation. Buber and Rosenzweig collaborated on the project from 1925 to 1929 when Rosenzweig met his tragic death. Buber continued the project, bringing it to completion in 1961.

24 Everett Fox, "The Book in its Contexts," in *Scripture and Translation*, xiii.

25 Michael Fishbane, "The Biblical Dialogue of Martin Buber," in Fishbane, *The*

imperative to hear the words of ancient texts and transform them through the power of a personal and engaged receptivity." Or, following Fishbane, it emphasizes that, in the Bible, "the divine speech which calls the world into real being initiates a 'Dialogue between Heaven and Earth' – of which we are the latter-day respondents or speech partners."[26]

"People Today and the Jewish Bible" dates from a November 1926 lecture.[27] As it exhorts each generation of the Bible's readers to engage scripture in terms of the demands of their day – in the "realm of [their] reality" (5) – so does it respond to particular needs of its own time. Buber identifies "people today" as "intellectuals [whose] freedom from real obligation is the signature of our time" (5). With this identification, Buber challenges the contemporary orientation that holds apart *Geist*, i.e., intellect, and life, a mindset that severs the connection of text and world.[28] In this mindset a reader can know no real obligation to the text because he or she has already distanced what is studied from the realm of responsibility, the world. Buber has in mind certain strains of historical criticism whose rationalism and goal of objectivity treat the Bible as a distant artifact and the reader as a detached subject. An Enlightenment legacy, the mindset characterized both Jewish and Christian scholarship on the Bible, but was not simply an intellectual problem.[29] Religion itself, no less than scholarship, embodied the

Garments of Torah (Bloomington: Indiana, 1989), 81.

26 Fishbane, 82.

27 Buber writes in the Foreword to *Scripture and Translation*: "In 1926, the second year of our work, we began to give accounts of what we were doing – to ourselves, and also to both a particular and a general public. During Rosenzweig's lifetime, I myself did this almost exclusively in lectures; only after his death did I begin to make extensive written presentations of the material. Whatever is drawn here from those lectures has been taken from shorthand notes, and for the most part only sparingly revised," page 1.

28 In German "*Geist*" may refer both to "intellect" and "spirit." Buber's usage of the term is fluid and often involves both connotations in a given instance. In this context, the intellectual dimension comes into play in Buber's concern to oppose detached study and reading of the Bible. For discussion of "*Geist*," see Fox's note to Buber's lecture (5).

29 Note Buber's critique of the scholarship of *Wissenschaft des Judentums* in "*Juedische Wissenschaft*," *Die Welt* (October 11 and 25, 1901); translated as "Jewish Scholarship: New Perspectives," in *The Jew and the Modern World. A Documentary History*, ed. P. Mendes-Flohr and J. Reinharz (New York: Oxford,

problem of the "unattached *Geist*" such that it "would itself have to return to reality before it could have a real effect on people today" (5-6). Indeed, as Buber's classic *I and Thou* (1922) amply describes, the tendency to objectify the world and sever the connections of knowers and things known characterizes modern culture, if not the cultural enterprise and human predicament as such. Buber's contemporary "people today" may have been 1926 intellectuals, but the category spills over in his essay to include a wider spectrum that resonates with the broad concern of *I and Thou*.

The timeliness of Buber's lecture shows itself in additional contextual ways. On the one hand, the lecture defends the Jewish Bible in the midst of a German culture whose Marcionite tendencies sought not only to denigrate Hebrew scripture but were escalating into the Nazi attempt to eradicate the culture of Jewish presence per se.[30] On the other hand, Buber addressed particular needs of his modern Jewish contemporaries, many of whom had become alienated from their heritage and were either indifferent or hostile to the notion of biblical revelation.[31] They, like the critical scholar, had no expectation of scripture impinging upon their reality in any significant way and, with regard to the Bible, sought no conjunction of *Geist* and life. For them, like the young Jews of the Prague Bar Kochba group who received Buber's early speeches *On Judaism* (1909-1918), Buber sought to rehabilitate the possibility of a *geistlich* claim upon their existence that required personal receptivity more than religious media, engagement more than expertise. He brings the possibility of a quickening revelation to a group of Jews who find themselves deadened in rootlessness and endangered in political circumstance.

1995), 241-243. See also, Gershom Scholem, "The Science of Judaism – Then and Now," in *The Messianic Idea in Judaism and Other Essays on Jewish Spirituality* (New York: Schocken, 1971), 304- 313.

30 See Fox, "The Book in its Contexts," xiv; and Buber, "The How and Why of our Bible Translation," in *Scripture and Translation*, 209-210.

31 Buber's lecture, I believe, can be considered as part of an effort to continue to challenge those Jews whom modernity had left rootless and alienated, an effort epitomized in the 1909-1918 addresses given to the Bar Kochba group in Prague. See Buber, *On Judaism*, ed. N. Glatzer and tr. E. Jospe (New York: Schocken, 1967), 11-174. On the climate of hostility to biblical revelation in both the contemporary Jewish and Christian communities, see Maurice Friedman, *Martin Buber's Life and Work* (New York: Dutton, 1983), 2:72.

The study of the Bible, for this group, could offer not only personal meaning, but a mode of resistance that upheld identity in the face of destruction. Learning could sustain, but not just any kind of learning would suffice. Only that study that seeks "to penetrate the language of the Bible and to attend to its 'spokenness'" will do. It is this kind of study that Buber emphasizes to the end that the voice of scripture may transform lives to "respond to the demands and decisions of the moment."[32]

Buber's Construal of Scripture: The Book of Encounters

Buber affirms the unity of the Bible by construing it as an anthology of encounters. Its authority lies in the immediacy of its spokenness, its inflection of a living voice that compels personal response and responsibility. He writes that the Bible is in reality One Book. All its stories and songs, all its sayings and prophecies are united by one fundamental theme: the encounter of a group of people with the Nameless Being whom they, hearing his speech and speaking to him in turn, ventured to name; their encounter with him in history, in the course of earthly events. The stories are either explicitly or implicitly accounts of encounters. (4)

As such, the Bible articulates the voice of "the Nameless Being" as a proffer of dialogue. Not the record of a voice that once spoke, but the medium for an ongoing speaking, the Bible encounters the hearing reader in the domain of his or her personal existence, "in history, in the course of earthly events." As in prophetic discourse, the encounter with the vital voice summons response, the reader's "return to the place of encounter [where lies] the restoration of the bond torn asunder" (4).

Buber's construal of scripture as encounter, like Merton's as "breakthrough of the word," resonates with the notion of text as a "living human document." Where the Bible's signature marker is its spokenness, the text's word has a living, dynamic quality. It speaks as Thou and incites the hearing reader to respond in kind. The resulting dialogue – with the full implications of Buber's *I and Thou* relation – is an efficacious exchange: it overcomes isolation and alienation; it bridges distance between the Nameless voice and

32 Fishbane, "The Biblical Dialogue of Martin Buber," 83.

the hearing reader; it repairs "the bond torn asunder." Because the text speaks as Thou, the hearing readers must read and respond with their own full presence. The text as person vitalizes and demands the personhood of the hearing reader.

The implications of Buber's construal, though idiomatic to his own perspective, anticipate Merton's construal as *breakthrough* and expose a close kinship in their understandings of scripture.[33] Some of these implications and their commonplaces with Merton are as follows:

1. The Bible "is in reality One Book" (4). Though the Bible's name signifies "a book that is a book of books" (4), it speaks as one in its presentation of encounters between Israel and the Nameless Being: narrative accounts of their event, "laments over exclusion from the grace of encounter, pleas for the return of it, thanksgivings for the gift of it" (4). As Merton found the Bible's wholeness in the sequence of its word-events, so does Buber set that stage by emphasizing the Bible's encounters as moments of spokenness that confront the hearing reader with the possibility and summons for dialogue. Where the *breakthrough*, for Merton, issued in transformation and liberation, the *encounter*, for Buber, already pointed to the repair of a "bond torn asunder," a restoration of relationship between the Nameless Voice and the hearing reader. Both tie the unity of scripture to its status as a document that lives through the ongoing events of its speaking – its self-expression as Thou – and the efficacy of its speech that consistently challenges and changes those who hear it.[34]

33 Though I do not think Merton intends to allude to Buber's *I and Thou* in his use of the term "breakthrough," one may note with interest Buber's own use of this language as a conceptual correlate to his fundamental category "encounter." Where *I and Thou* affirms that "all actual life is encounter" ("*Alles wirkliche Leben ist Begegnung*"), it also describes the turning to the Thou in encounter – the moment of return – precisely as a "breakthrough" (*Durchbruch*). See Martin Buber, *Ich und Du* in *Die Schriften ueber das dialogische Prinzip* (Heidelberg: Verlag Lambert Schneider, 1954), 15 and 58; and the corresponding English translations of Walter Kaufmann, *I and Thou* (New York: Scribner's, 1970), 62 and 104-5.

34 For Buber, the assertion of the Bible's unity challenges the growing atomism of historical-critical readings. That is, his difficulty with the *Wissenschaft* model

2. <u>In the encounter with Scripture, the hearing reader hears the voice of a "Nameless Being"</u> (4). The voice of scripture speaks with mystery, difference, and otherness. Not the voice of a name among other names, scripture speaks in a way that is fundamental, irreducible, and resistant to the reader's attempts to compartmentalize its claim (6). Our speech, in response, is always a "justified stammering" (12). Where Merton spoke of the word of the Bible as a "non-Word" to emphasize its ultimacy and freedom, its difference from what the reader may expect of it, Buber's use of "Nameless Being" sets the precedent by placing the biblical voice outside the domain of human control, even and especially the attempt to order it through the medium of religion (6). As Merton, too, suggests, scripture's voice addresses the totality of one's existence, not a particular arena within one's life. It speaks fundamentally.

3. <u>The biblical encounter occurs in history</u> (4). Merton noted that the word of scripture broke through in "events and happenings" and set God at the "very center of [human] life." In doing so, Merton echoes Buber's vindication of the worldliness of revelation in a line that runs from Buber's Hasidic writings to *I and Thou* to the biblical writings. For Buber, one finds the distinguishing marker of scripture in the way "event and word take place entirely within the people, within history, within the world. . .In [the Bible] a law speaks

was not simply in its deadening the text as artifact, but in its fragmentation of that which it studied. Buber was scarcely unaware of the Wellhausen model of criticism and was mindful of the biblical text's historical development; nor was his affirmation of the unity of scripture aimed to defend the divine origins of the book. Instead of subscribing to source theory, Buber (and Rosenzweig) emphasized "a model of biblical composition that stressed cumulative addition rather than the pasting together of discrete sources... [Their] approach did not stem from a desire to defend the doctrine of the Torah's divine origin as such, but rather from the perception that, beyond possible earlier stages of composition, the Hebrew Bible is an anthology that frequently cross-references itself, an anthology in which terms and concepts are explained by their complementary use in differing contexts." Fox, "The Book in its Contexts," xix. The unity of the Bible then was stylistic as well as rooted in its ongoing mode of encounter, a recognition that undergirds Buber and Rosenzweig's methodology that focuses upon the "arcs of significant repetition" (14) made by the Bible's *Leitworten* (repeated "leading words").

that concerns the natural life of human beings" (6). Biblical reality has a social and historical character which points to the world – the context of personal existence – as the domain of encounter. Revelation occurs at that place where *Geist* joins life. For Buber, the inseparability of *Geist* and life describes not only what the Bible speaks about, but establishes the foundation of a method of reading scripture that insists upon hearing with obligation and reading in "the realm of reality" – the existential reality that is both the Bible's and one's own.[35] In "the realm of reality" one perceives the evidence of the "bond torn asunder" and the prospect of its restoration.

Buber on Reading, Revelation, and the Self

Buber's dialogical and relational perspective, here extended into the domain of biblical hermeneutics, makes it impossible to separate the encounter of the living voice of scripture from the orientation of the reader who approaches it. As we have already seen, Buber's "People Today and the Jewish Bible" launches a strong critique of the "people today" who read without a sense of obligation to the reality of the texts they read, who encounter their texts out of a false relation of *Geist* and life and thus do not really encounter them at all (5). The detachment of "people today" deadens the living dimension of the text, not robbing it finally of its life, but of its capability of being heard as vital. Subduing the personhood of the reader leads as well to the obscuring of the personal, living dimension of the text.

Buber counters the detachment of "people today" with a contrasting manner of being *present* to the text, a manner of *being there* in the place of encounter with the fullness of one's self in freedom and openness. With confidence, he proclaims that "revelation ... encounters me *if I am there*"(8). Fishbane continues the point: "In a profound and subtle allusion to God's own Name, which he translated as the One who 'is there' (*Ich bin da der Ich bin*), Buber stated that that person will hear the Bible's instruction who

35 Note Buber's exegesis of *ruach elohim* as a *Leitwort* that conjoins spirit and the concreteness of history (14-17). This section of Buber's lecture was omitted in Olga Marx's translation, published in the Buber anthologies, *Israel and the World* and *On the Bible*.

will correspondingly 'be there' before the text – attentive and listening."[36] Following the textual echo, one must be present to the text as God is present in the giving of his name (Exodus 3:14) – freely, irreducibly, and in a way that reveals oneself to the other.[37]

To *be there* before the text takes on specific connotations in Buber's lecture. First, it requires the hearing reader to "face [the text] in the realm of reality" (5). This means, on the one hand, struggling with the text in terms of the contemporary demands of one's own generation, the reality of one's own existential situation and time. Like the manna in the wilderness, the revelation of scripture cannot be saved over from one day to the next, but must be won anew in every present. Its continuity lies in its contemporaneity.[38] *Geist* can join life only in a present moment; to relegate it to the past or future removes it from the realm of life as well. On the other hand, "the realm of reality" also belongs to the biblical text which the reader must enter and heed. One is present to the text when one allows it to speak, free of one's own necessary expectations of it. One must face the text's own situation of spokenness and way of connecting *Geist* and life.[39]

36 Fishbane, "The Biblical Dialogue of Martin Buber," 88.
37 For Buber's exegesis of the tetragrammaton, see *The Prophetic Faith* (New York: Harper & Row, 1949) 27-29 and "The Burning Bush," in Martin Buber, *On the Bible* (New York: Schocken, 1982) 54-62. The elusiveness and freedom implied in this name resonates with Buber's reference to God as a "Nameless Being."
38 On the contemporaneity of revelation, note Emil Fackenheim's discussion of God's presence in history. Where the Exodus functions as a root event in Judaism, it makes central the affirmation that in Israel's history, God reveals himself as present – i.e., present in their immediate present. Accordingly, that affirmation cannot be confined to some past moment in Israel's history without violating its basic conviction. Fackenheim writes: "The Jewish theologian would be ill-advised were he, in an attempt to protect the Jewish faith in the God of history, to ignore contemporary history. For the God of Israel cannot be God of either past or future unless He is still God of the present." *God's Presence in History: Jewish Affirmations and Philosophical Reflections* (New York: New York University, 1970), 31.
39 Envisioning the encounter of scripture in dialogical terms, Buber refuses to collapse the voice of the Bible into the contemporary, though contemporary it must be. As his dialogic perspective suggests, revelation is *between* the voice and the hearer and requires the integrity of both. Thus, he speaks elsewhere that "A Bible course should lead students to the biblical text. . . What matters first, then – and also last – is to teach students to understand what is there. And

Second, being present to the text requires a basic openness to the Bible's speaking. For Buber, readers must take up Scripture as if they had never seen it, had never encountered it in school or afterwards in the light of "religious" or "scientific" certainties; as if they had not learned all their lives all sorts of sham concepts and sham propositions claiming to be based on it. They must place themselves anew before the renewed book, hold back nothing of themselves, let everything happen between themselves and it, whatever may happen. . .They believe nothing *a priori*; they disbelieve nothing *a priori*. They read aloud what is there, they hear the word they speak, and it comes to them; nothing has yet been judged, the river of time flows on, and the contemporaneity of these people becomes itself a receiving vessel. (7)

Such openness does not grow from religious belief – religious certainty may make the text too familiar to be heard in its reality – but is the prerogative of even and especially those who "have little access to sure belief, and cannot be given such access." What matters is not the belief, but the earnest openness: "revelation . . . encounters me *if I am there*" (8).

Third, the readers' presence commits them to being oriented in history in a particular way. Buber's "people today" live in history as if it were either a "muddle, an indiscriminate sequence of processes" (8) or the dooming sway of causality wherein "people determine laws from sequences of events and predict sequences to come, as if the great lines of things were written on a scroll that was just now being unrolled, as if history were not time . . . but a rigid, already present, inescapable space" (8).[40] In contrast, to be present to the text means to approach the time of encounter with an openness to the "secret reciprocity of the lived moment" (9). Neither accident nor fate, human destiny is created in the encounter with the voice of the Nameless One that bids one respond. To approach the text with presence is to know that the give and take of voice and response forges the shape of one's history. The definitive moments of one's biography are times of full

for that, we ourselves must take what is there seriously – its wording, its meaning, its sequences and connections." "A Suggestion for Bible Courses," in *Scripture and Translation*, 176.

40 Note the parallel discussions of causality in *I and Thou* (100-107) and of evolution in *On Judaism* (34-55).

decisiveness, but they are never moments of oneself. They are the moments of one's encounters (9). As evident in the encounter with scripture, history situates us *between* the determinations of our will and the events that shape and summon its intention, its moment of decision.

Buber's "people today" embody a deep resistance to *being there* before the text, open and decisive. The sentence where he introduces the need to *be there* ends in his statement that "with this notion in mind we can understand the resistance of people today as a resistance of their inner-most being" (8). He continues in the next paragraph: "People today resist Scripture because they cannot abide revelation. To abide revelation means to sustain the full decisiveness of the moment, to respond to the moment, to be responsible for it. People today resist Scripture because they are no longer responsive or responsible" (9). The moment of encounter demands all of the self: the commitment to a fundamental openness before the voice of a Nameless Being whose word cannot be controlled, but must be responded to with the full being of one's self. If Buber's "people today" resist with "their inner-most being," it is because revelation puts at stake precisely that being. The encounter reaches deep to touch one's self at its core and to awaken its destiny-creating response. Buber's contemporaries cannot abide revelation because if it fulfills the self – mends the "bond torn asunder" – it costs the self its flight from reality into the seeming ease of passivity, detachment, and banality.

The encounter also costs the self its autonomy and sufficiency. Revelation demands decision, but ever qualifies it as a response to the voice of a nameless other before whom our speech is, at best, "justified stammering" (12). Revelation means that we do not and cannot act alone in history to move from creation to redemption (11). Our intentions are shaped by the very voice that calls them forth, a voice of One who is other. In this lies further ground of the self's resistance to revelation, but also the promise of its hope. History, neither simple muddle nor causal chain, remains the arena of the Nameless Other's speech; scripture, the venue of its personal address. Human complacency may avoid that speaking and obscure its address, but cannot finally deny the presence of its voice that, as other, persists undefined by human response. Even as "openness to belief is not denied" to the skeptical and the indifferent (7), so does the prospect of revelation remain latent in the history of its eclipse, a voice that calls ever and again in the scripture of its speech.[41]

When one encounters the Bible, as Buber describes it, one returns to its primal spokenness. He writes, "Do we mean a book? We mean the voice. Do we mean that people should learn to read it? We mean that people should learn to hear it. . . We want to go straight through to the spokenness, to the being-spoken, of the word" (21).[42] The return to the voice of scripture does not mark a return to the Bible as book, but to a *relation* that unifies one's existence − *Geist* and life − in the "renewal of personhood and response-ability."[43] Encounter brings the self to a point of integrity that holds together its bits of *Geist* and world; but more, in relation, it joins the self to the source of *Geist* and life that speaks in scripture. As such, the Bible's relational word addresses the human predicament of isolation and estrangement; as an existential word, it combats the human tendency toward abstraction and detachment.[44] It reminds the hearing readers that, in the midst of their history, they are neither inevitably alone nor doomed to fate. Revelation says no to the fragmentation of the self and its distance from the Nameless Being who calls it to relation. In the call and response of the reading of scripture the "bonds torn asunder" between the self and its world and the self and its eternal other come to a point of repair. Revelation, the presence of a voice sounding in text and event, maintains the prospect of this repair by its very speaking. Where the voice sounds, history is no closed system, but the invitation to relation and thereby, also, renewal. As such, the revelation of

41 Note the parallel way in which Buber discusses the persistence and ultimate ineradicability of the Eternal Thou in the it-world of causality, use, and objectification. See *I and Thou* (106-7). Note, too, the later, post-holocaust consideration of Buber regarding the eclipse of God. See "The Dialogue Between Heaven and Earth," *On Judaism*, 214-225.

42 On the Bible's spokenness, see Fishbane, "The Biblical Dialogue of Martin Buber," 83.

43 Fishbane, "The Biblical Dialogue of Martin Buber," 83.

44 Buber's critique of abstraction can be seen in his discussion of creation, revelation, and redemption as lived realities (10ff). Buber addresses relation's challenge to the predicament of isolation and detachment as a major concern of *I and Thou*.

encounter cannot reduce to the data of Sinai. It is instead, the "continual possibility of receiving" revelation (8), of *being there* in the encounter of the word.

READING THE BIBLE AS THOU

A turn on Boisen's image of the "living human document" has led us to consider what it might mean to construe texts, the Bible in particular, as Thou. In light of Merton's and Buber's models of reading scripture, we can emphasize four dimensions of a hermeneutic that regards the text as person. First and foremost, as both Merton and Buber stress, to regard the Bible as person – as a speaking voice – commits the reader to a style of reading that requires his or her own personal engagement and presence before the text. The personal dimension of the speaking voice of scripture compels the personal attention of the hearing reader. To suppress personal engagement muffles the personal voice of the text so that it becomes irrelevant if not inaudible. And, in turn, to depersonalize the text only encourages the detachment of readers who, expecting to encounter nothing vital in the reading of scripture, guarantee that outcome.

Second, where the construal of the Bible as person compels the hearing reader's personal engagement, it necessarily involves that reader in a crisis of identity. Speaking as person, the Bible addresses the existential predicament of being human and seeks to bring change to that predicament. For Merton the Bible's *breakthrough* liberates readers from slavishness and falsehood; for Buber, the *encounter* with the voice of scripture brings the prospect of relation to the isolated and estranged, repair to the "bonds torn asunder." Because hearing the Bible summons the person of the hearer to change, it must overcome the reader's resistance to its revelation, the proclivity to hide from its word in detachment and self-deception.

Third, the personal engagement that accompanies the Bible as Thou does not annul critical perspective, but calls for a different mode of critical reading. If Merton and Buber distance their approaches from the historical-critical perspectives that dominated their times, they do not surrender the text's meaning to whatever the subjectivity of a reader would make of it. On the contrary, their model heightens the need for self-critical reading that recognizes the otherness of the Bible's voice and its own resistance to ideological appropriation. As non-word or the voice of a Nameless Being, the Bible's speaking cannot be controlled or co-opted for self-serving purposes, be they personal, religious, or institutional. For Merton, it characteristically collides with the will of the reader and frustrates intentions toward self-assurance. Accordingly, any reading to the contrary would be suspect of robbing scripture of its essential crisis-making character.[45] So, too, for Buber, one cannot appropriate scripture with enthusiasm or surety. Any attempt to speak the word of the Nameless One is always a "justified stammering" (12). The premise for self-critical reading is that our own speaking is provisional and limited before the word of *breakthrough* and *encounter*. Where we can only stammer, we cannot commandeer.

Fourth, the regarding of the Bible as Thou shapes the category of revelation as a dynamic, self-involving process. The Bible is revelatory, not in some inert disclosure of the content of its speech, but in the meaning-effect of its speaking. It reveals not in terms of *what* it says, but through what it *does* as it speaks. For Merton, scripture discloses "the *basic dynamism* of human existence under God, a dynamism of awareness and response, in which lies 'salvation'" (94). For Buber, the "center is not the revelation at Sinai but the continual possibility of receiving it" (8), of knowing the prospect of being addressed and answering in kind. Where the Bible speaks as Thou, revelation confirms the meaningfulness of human hearing and response as such. It confirms the history of persons – the world of human hearing and speaking – as the domain of God's speech, the arena of scripture's revelation of its own non-absurdity.

Jewish and Christian Readers

As we suggested earlier, Buber is Merton's precursor in the construal of text as person. A common tradition unites them in their shared concern for the Bible as "living human document"

---

45 Merton also grounds critical reading in his view of the Bible's unity. Where historical-critical studies often use awareness of the Bible's compositional history to confound ideological assertions of the Bible's unity, Merton appeals to the Bible's canonical unity as a buffer against narrow readings that avoid the critical dialectic of the whole (68).

and its emphasis on the reader's personal engagement of the text. That tradition, as we have understood it, focuses upon the dynamics between text and reader – a phenomenology of reading – and a theological approach to revelation that takes seriously the Bible as the sounding of God's living voice. Do these commonplaces have import for understanding Buber and Merton as Jewish and Christian readers of the Bible?

The significant similarities of Buber's and Merton's perspectives suggest that Jews and Christians not only share a scriptural heritage, but may host a common hermeneutic. Construing the Bible as "living human document," the Jew and the Christian do not necessarily read differently, nor have competing goals for scriptural interpretation. At a basic level, both Jews and Christians may seek to read the Bible with personal presence and anticipate that such reading may transform them. Both read aware of a living, covenantal dialogue that the Bible expresses and mediates.[46]

Recognition of a common hermeneutic provides a framework for fraternal readings and conversation that too may help repair "bonds torn asunder." In their writings on the Bible, Buber and Merton open a window that enables one to see their kindred enterprise and thus the potentially common pursuit of their Jewish and Christian communities. This is no small gain, but should be seen in light of some persisting complications that qualify the shared hermeneutic and its ability to unify. First, to focus upon the Bible as the commonplace may reduce the role of tradition and other authoritative sources that give to both Jews and Christians a strong sense of particularity. As a common denominator, a biblical hermeneutic may establish kinship yet not suffice to preserve or

---

46 Note the similar point made in the second statement of "*Dabru Emet*: A Jewish Statement on Christians and Christianity" (originally appearing in the *New York Times* and in the *Baltimore Sun*; Erev Yom Kippur, September 10, 2000). "*Dabru Emet*" affirms the common authority of the Bible for both Jews and Christians and the common convictions that authority generates regarding God as Creator and the covenant and revelation to Israel. At the same time, it acknowledges persistent differences in interpretation that must be respected. See "*Dabru Emet*," National Jewish Scholars Project, Institute for Christian and Jewish Studies, <www.icjs.org./what/njsp/dabruemet.html>. Note also the tandem volume, *Christianity in Jewish Terms*, ed. Tikva Frymer-Kensky, et al. (Boulder: Westview, 2000).

address the distinctiveness of each religious community which gives to the reading of the Bible its living context.[47]

Second, all similarities notwithstanding, Buber and Merton speak from different vantages and address predicaments that have nuances of their own. Merton's emphasis upon scripture as a critical word, and his concern to validate outsider readings, suggest that he speaks with special attention to the Christian insider whose exercise of religion may generate false securities. Merton assumes a false reader, a reader enslaved to self-deception as a mark of original sin. Scripture, in its *breakthrough* of crisis, answers bondage with the insecurity of freedom, and falsehood with the question of truth. Though Buber's lecture has import for the German cultural community at large, it speaks most directly to the Jewish audience that has become estranged from its own scriptural tradition. His reader is not false as much as deadened in detachment, suffering in the isolation of "bonds torn asunder." Scripture, as *encounter*, provides the prospect of relation more than judgment, though it remains, to be sure, a relation that requires "reality." The predicaments of self that Buber and Merton address do not vary at a fundamental level: Buber's concern for the union of "*Geist* and life" reflects Merton's concern for existential truth; Merton's notion that freedom affirms even when it denies (30), shares Buber's accent on repair. Each, however, has its distinct tonality that reflects something of the persistent Jewish and Christian difference.

Third, Merton's emphasis on the Bible as "everybody's book" (49), begs the question of precisely which Bible belongs to all. For Merton, the unity of the Bible includes both his Old and New Testaments, whereas Buber understandably restricts his concern to the "Jewish Bible" of his title. The issue concerns not simply what

47 In this regard one should note that both Buber and Merton maintained a near-Protestant suspicion of tradition in tandem with their views of the Bible's sufficient address to the individual self. For Buber, the critique of tradition, especially in its rabbinic form, runs deep and derives from the core of his basic distinctions between religion and religiosity (*On Judaism*, 79-94) and between I and Thou generally. One must proceed cautiously in moving from Merton and Buber to generalized Jewish and Christian readers. Though both Buber and Merton write self-consciously as Jew and as Christian, neither may be typical of his respective religious group or representative of its classic styles. Both would remain problematic figures for those readers concerned with normative traditions and the particularities of religious identity that they foster.

texts a biblical canon includes, but the categories through which the texts are organized and labeled as a unity. Even in discussing the texts of Israel's literature that are common to both Jewish and Christian canons, one must be aware of the different ways "Old Testament," "Hebrew Bible," "Jewish Scripture," and "*Tanakh*" construe the significance of the writings.[48] Both Merton and Buber diminish the potential divide by distancing revelation from content and by generalizing the predicaments to which their canons speak. The Bible, for Merton, is "everybody's book" because it addresses the problem of bondage and falsehood that all share; similarly, for Buber, the voice of the Hebrew Bible sounds with broad resonance to the experience of fragmentation and detachment of *Geist* from life in all its many forms.[49] Still, the generalization of human experience that softens division may avoid too easily the scandal of particularity that the question of canon – its nomenclature and content – insists upon.

Read from the later vantage of post-modern culture, both Buber and Merton are vulnerable to the problem of difference.[50] One must remember, however, that, in their own contexts of writing, other questions may have loomed larger and more urgent. The need to overcome alienation in pre-war Germany or cold-war America makes understandable and valuable Buber's and Merton's claim that the Bible's predicament was a fundamentally human one. The threat of their times was not the eclipse of difference, but the assertion of difference in ways that denied basic kinship and relation. It is in this context that their biblical hermeneutic should be read and maintained as a caution against the estranging potential of a politics of difference. Construing scripture as *breakthrough* and *encounter* may not finally establish a hermeneutic that addresses the particularity of Jewish and Christian readers of the Bible. It does, however, speak incisively to the crises of modernity and post-modernity that would

48 "*Dabru Emet*" (statement 2) recognizes the different nomenclatures – "the Bible (what Jews call 'Tanakh' and Christians call the 'Old Testament')" – but does not deal with the implications of naming the Bible one way or the other.
49 Note, e.g., how Buber's *I and Thou* offers a generalized version of the human predicament that he expressed in particular form as the Jewish predicament in the speeches *On Judaism*.
50 For discussion of this problem with respect to Merton and Judaism, see Karl A. Plank, "The Eclipse of Difference: Merton's Encounter with Judaism," *Cistercian Studies* 28/2 (1993): 179-91.

rob both Jewish and Christian readers of confidence in the Bible as a "living human document," a document that reveals and that matters. In their particularity and in their kinship, both Jewish and Christian readers must confront the problem of revelation in a hostile culture, for, apart from the prospect of revelation, the ground of their particularity has already collapsed. For the Jew and the Christian, the writings of Buber and Merton remain pertinent and vital.

"The Bible is *holiness in words*…. It is as if God took these Hebrew words and breathed into them of His power, and the words became a live wire charged with His spirit. To this very day they are hyphens between heaven and earth."

—Abraham Joshua Heschel, *God in Search of Man* (1955), p. 244.

8

WAITING FOR THE MESSIAH: THE SEVENTH DAY

READING TALES WITH BUBER, HESCHEL AND MERTON ON ISRAEL'S HOLY MOUNTAINS

Lucien Miller

My friend and colleague, Dr. Frederick H. Bloom,[1] to whom I wish to dedicate this paper, brought to my attention Pope John XXIII's self-introduction when welcoming a delegation of Jews to the Vatican at Rome: "I am Joseph, your brother." I don't think I dare say to Jewish colleagues that I am Joseph, your brother, but I would like to say it. What I can say is that on the "Judaism" side of our conference, "Merton and Judaism," I feel very much like an *am-ha'aretz*, an ignorant man, an uneducated country bumpkin (what Chinese call a *tu baozi*, a "country bread roll"), among the *lamdanim*, the thoroughly learned. My prayer is that through *ruah hakodesh,* God's Holy Spirit, and the comradeship of the simple with the superior, there may come, in the long run, a *teshuva*, a turning, repentance, and conversion that proves redemptive for us all, Jew and Gentile alike. Probably, it is deeply true that we are all members of what Abraham Joshua Heschel calls "mankind's unfinished symphony," and today, in the presence of one another, we feel "stunned by that which is but cannot be put into words ... The attempt to convey what we see and cannot say."[2] In the mean

1 Dr. Bloom, an optometrist and Director of the Eye Care Program at the University of Massachusetts, guided me through Heschel's writing in a course he gave at the Hillel Foundation in Amherst, Mass., fall, 2001.

2 Heschel, *Man Is Not Alone: A Philosophy of Religion.* (New York: Farrar, Straus, and Giroux, 1972), p. 4. "Unfinished Symphony" is the title of the last chapter of Edward K. Kaplan's *Holiness in Words: Abraham Joshua Heschel's Poetics of Piety* (Albany: State University of New York Press, 1996).

time, in so far as trying to convey what can be put into words, I hope to be a student during our conference in Professor Edward K. Kaplan's "traditional" *yeshiva*, where, he tells us, "students are paired with a partner (*haver*, friend or comrade)," and "can benefit from sharing and listening."[3]

Before any "turning" can occur, personal confession may be in order for this *haver*. There is a need for genuineness. As the wife of another colleague, both Jews, once humorously remarked to me: "Lucien, there are Jews, and there are goddamned Jews." "Ah," I thought to myself, "and there are Catholics, and goddamned Catholics." Of course our insider's view of ourselves may be comical, but the outsider's hostility towards us is not. The suffering of Jews is crystal clear. Much less apparent, yet certain, the Catholic Church is the church people love to hate. Speaking for myself, I never could comprehend bigotry towards Jews until one day I experienced crossing the line. While watching the beginning of "Night and Fog," a French film with footage from Nazi archives of the death camps, I found myself identifying with a man seen in the distance driving a huge tractor. He is wearing a baseball cap, smoking a cigar, and enjoying himself pushing around what appears to be great mountains of earth. As the camera moved closer, suddenly I realized the tractor driver was bulldozing piles of human bodies. For one horrible instant, having identified with the man, I quaked with the experience of being in his place and doing what he did.

What is it that attracts us to Martin Buber, Abraham Heschel, and Thomas Merton? My guess is that it is the need many feel for survival, for energy, for a viable faith, whether we be Jews or Christians. "I am the kind of person who feels at once alien to and intimate with both traditions," writes Edward Kaplan some twenty years ago, in his study of Merton's dialogue with Judaism.[4] In the shadow of September 11, few are strangers to that back-and-forth tug now. Heschel, Buber, and Merton give us reason to believe that our faiths are alive and well, and that it is still possible even for the likes of us – who are so querulous, quarrelsome, skeptical and

3 Kaplan, *Holiness in Words*, p. 31.
4 Kaplan, "Contemplative Inwardness and Prophetic Action: Thomas Merton's Dialogue with Judaism," *Thomas Merton: Pilgrim in Process*, Donald Grayston and Michael W. Higgins, eds. (Toronto: Griffin House, 1983), pp. 85-105.

complaining – to be the Jews and Christians (even Catholics!) we are called to be. Wonder of wonders! As a Trappist monk years ago remarked to me, "the Catholic Church is so big, it's possible even for the likes of you, Lucien, to be in it." Maybe, dear Jewish sisters and brothers, this applies to some of you. Judaism is so big that it is possible to be a Jew, even for the likes of you!

We could do with breaking free from the *Olam-ha-Tohu*, the world of confusion, "the mythical dwelling place of the wandering souls," as Martin Buber confesses he does, when as a young man, he rediscovers Judaism through his encounter with the Baal Shem Tov and Hasidism. Heschel believes that "Jewishness must be felt, must be loved; one should find delight in it."[5] We want that joy. Heschel compares the thought of the "Kotzker," the Hasidic *zaddik*, Reb Menahem Mendl of Kotzk, and that of Kierkegaard, because he thinks the insights of this Jew and this Christian "may help us tap sources for a renewal of faith."[6] We require that renewal today.[7]

Sometimes our need means that we must traverse the bridge to the world of the other in order to be our true self. In a letter to Heschel, Merton speaks of "my latent ambitions to be a true Jew under my Catholic skin."[8] I doubt there is any Jew with a hidden wish to be a true Catholic under his or her Jewish skin, but Merton is a crossroad for many Jews, where Judaism and Christianity meet.

5 Heschel, *A Passion for Truth* (New York: Farrar, Straus, and Giroux, 1973), p. 29.
6 Ibid., p. 320.
7 For an overview of Heschel's Hasidism and contrasts to Buber, see: "Introduction: Heschel as a Hasidic Scholar," Samuel H. Dresner, ed., *Abraham J. Heschel: The Circle of the Baal Shem Tov* (Chicago and London: University of Chicago Press, 1985); Arthur Green, "Abraham Joshua Heschel: Recasting Hasidism for Moderns," *Tikkun* vol. 14, no. 1 (Jan.-Feb., 1999), 63-69; Edward K. Kaplan, *Abraham Joshua Heschel: Prophetic Witness*. New Haven and London: Yale University Press, 1998.
8 Letter to Abraham Heschel dated September 9, 1964. *The Hidden Ground of Love: The Letters of Thomas Merton on Religious Experience and Social Concerns*, William H. Shannon, ed. (New York: Farrar, Straus and Giroux, 1985), p. 434. In "The Eclipse of Difference: Merton's Encounter with Judaism," *Cistercian Studies Quarterly* vol. 28: 2 (1993), 179-193, Karl A. Plank sharply criticizes Merton's understanding of Judaism. While suggesting that other writing by Merton may provide a better base for Jewish-Christian dialogue, his correspondence with Heschel "effaced the Jew he would affirm, allowing a desire for unity to obscure essential difference." "Heschel is rendered invisible in Merton's letter" (pp. 185-186). Merton's Judaism is limited to the Biblical era, overlooking "its historical beginnings in the post-biblical mishnaic period

Especially appealing, notes Shaul Magid, is Merton's vision of his monastic vocation as counter-cultural critique of religion and an alternative path for the irreligious. After all, what is unfamiliar to a Jew about being a monk? "The first monk is really the first Jew, the Patriarch Abraham," writes Magid. Whatever Merton's latent ambitions, Magid concludes, he was one with the *Hasidim*, belonging to a tradition while rebelliously searching for its source. "In this sense, he was far more a disciple of the Hasidic masters than Buber."[9]

I think the secret of the charisma and magnetism of Buber, Heschel, and Merton, is their interiorization of different faiths, the fact that each, to varying degrees, leads others to imagine that it may be all right to have one identity while exploring an hyphenated self, to be not simply a Jew, Catholic, Protestant, Hindu, Buddhist or Muslim, but someone joining the other at the crossroads. In all three, encounter deepens self. One discovers something in the other one lacks, or the other awakens a self-realization that otherwise would never happen. A deeper Jew is born, a fuller Christian. In Merton's case, in this process of exploration, he intends never to eclipse difference, as an eclipse would contradict something that is a matter of principle for him. I believe his inter-faith and ecumenical model is from Jesus' statement in the Gospel of John that Buber celebrates in *I and Thou*: "The Father and I are one."[10] Jesus does not express equivalence of identity. He does not say he is the Father, or the Father is the Son. Rather, the Father and Son are one. That is, they are ever two-in-one and one-in-two. "It [John] is really nothing less than the Gospel of the pure relationship," says Buber.[11]

through the current period of the Shoah [Holocaust] and its aftermath" (p. 188). Merton's concern in his Shoah writings is with the Nazi horror, rather than with the "concrete situation of the Jewish other." Merton's "difficulty in sustaining Jewish difference may derive from his limited and romantic perception of Judaism itself" (p. 187).

9 Shaul Magid, "Monastic Liberation as Counter-Cultural Critique in the Life and Thought of Thomas Merton," *Cross Currents* vol. 49: 4 (Winter, 1999–2000), 447, 452, 456–57.

10 John, 10: 30. *The New Oxford Annotated Bible, New Revised Standard Version*, Bruce M. Metzger, Roland E. Murphy, eds. (New York: Oxford University Press, 1991).

11 Martin Buber, *I and Thou*, Walter Kaufmann, trans. (New York: Charles Scribner's Sons, 1970), p. 133. Buber (not accepting the divinity of the Son)

Analogously, we may say the Jew is not a Christian and the Christian is not a Jew, but there is a chance we Jews and Christians may one day say, not "I am you," but "I and you are one," in Buber's sense of unity-in-difference, forever two, yet "consubstantial." For Christians, there is a certain hope and comfort in Saint Paul's Letter to the Ephesians which says we Gentiles are coheirs and sharers in the promise.[12] For both Jew and Christian, there is a sign of that promise in one of Merton's last letters to Heschel, in which he confides that the solitary life while fruitful is also disconcerting, and he is facing things he has not faced before. Merton concludes: "I would appreciate you remembering me in your prayer before Him whom we both seek and serve. I do not forget you in my own prayer. God be with you always."[13] In sharing prayer and worship, if not theology and history, you and I are one-in-two, and two-in-one.

THE HOLY

Both Heschel and Buber are appalled by a world in crisis following World War II, and proffer Judaism and Hasidism in response. In the late 1940s, Heschel speculates, "Perhaps human beings have never been as much in need of Judaism as they are in our generation. The human species is on its deathbed."[14] "I consider the truth of Hasidism vitally important for Jews, Christians, and other men," Buber declares in1959, writing from Jerusalem, "and at this particular hour more important than ever before. For now is the hour when we are in danger of forgetting for what purpose we are on earth."[15] I suggest that one of the

explicates the "pure relationship" as a divine-human dynamic, emphasizing unity within duality: "There are truer things here than the familiar mystic verse: 'I am you, and you are I.' The father and the son, being consubstantial – we may say: God and man, being consubstantial, are actually and forever Two, the two partners of the primal relationship." *I and Thou*, p. 133.

12 Ephesians, 3: 5-6.

13 Shannon, *The Hidden Ground of Love,* p. 435. Letter dated December 6, 1964.

14 *"Pikuach Neshama*: To Save a Soul," *Moral Grandeur and Spiritual Audacity*, Susannah Heschel, ed. (New York: Farrar, Straus and Giroux, 1996), p. 67. Originally a talk to principals of Day Schools and Yeshivas, first published in 1949. Kaplan, *Holiness in Words*, p. 169, n.19.

15 Buber's "Author's Foreword" to *The Origin and Meaning of Hasidism*, Maurice Friedman editor and translator. (New York: Horizon Press, 1960), p. 22.

truths in Judaism that both Heschel and Buber set forth as an answer to their world's need is the holy (*kadosh*), and that Merton joins them through his intense awareness of the holy, and his lifelong pursuit of holiness in words, drawings, and photography.[16] The celebration of the holy in Heschel, Buber and Merton may be read as a gift offering to our world of crisis, as it was for theirs.

Admitting that the holy "lies beyond the reach of words" and cannot be defined,[17] Heschel invokes it unceasingly, like a lover selecting roses for a nosegay. "Things created in six days He considered *good*, the seventh day He made *holy*," Heschel notes, remarking on what philosophy could learn from the Bible.[18] Throughout his writings, the seventh day seems to be the day Heschel loves to talk about, for it is the embodiment of holiness, "the climax of creation."[19] "I cannot exist without the holy," declares Heschel, addressing an annual convention of American Reform rabbis in 1952.[20] Mindful of biblical commandments, such as, "You shall be holy, for I the Lord your God am holy,"[21] Heschel asserts, "Only in holiness will we *be*."[22] But, while recognizing the call to holiness as central to Jewish identity, Heschel affirms that holiness itself is a universal, divine gift, "rooted in the heart of every cultured person."[23] "All existence stands in the dimension of the holy," Heschel observes, and man cannot escape it.[24] The human task is to initiate holiness in the world, and to reveal the holy.[25]

16 Merton's sense of the holy and holiness is most immediately and unmistakably present in John Howard Griffin's remarkable gathering of Merton's photographs, *A Hidden Wholeness: The Visual World of Thomas Merton*. (Boston: Houghton Mifflin, 1970).

17 Heschel, *God in Search of Man: A Philosophy of Judaism* (New York: Harper and Row, 1955), p. 103. Perhaps the "holy" belongs somewhere between *kavod* (glory) and *Shekhinah* (presence of God's indwelling in the world).

18 *God in Search of Man*, p. 17.

19 Ibid., p. 417.

20 Cited by Dresner, *Abraham J. Heschel: The Circle of the Baal Shem Tov*, p. xxxii.

21 Leviticus 19: 2.

22 "*Pikuach Neshama*: To Save a Soul," *Moral Grandeur and Spiritual Audacity*, pp. 60, 66-67.

23 Ibid., *Moral Grandeur, p. 61.*

24 Heschel, *Man Is Not Alone*, pp. 227, 237-238.

25 Ibid., p. 267; *God In Search of Man*, p. 313. As Edward Kaplan notes, "Heschel's writings call to the Holy Spirit within all readers" (*Holiness in Words*, p.14).

Martin Buber's sense of the holy echoes the dialogic world of *I and Thou*, and seems deeply informed by his understanding of Hasidism. Quoting a Hasidic saying, "God dwells where one lets Him in," Buber explains how the holy becomes holiness: "The hallowing of man means this letting in. Basically, the holy in our world is nothing other than what is open to transcendence."[26] Like Heschel, Buber holds that human beings are responsible for the work of hallowing, of making holy, a work Buber terms sacramental and redemptive. "In the concrete contact with man the world again and again becomes sacramental."[27] Everything "wants to be hallowed, to be brought into the holy ... to become sacrament ... to come to God through us."[28] In the process of letting God in, the world becomes a sacrament, "ready to bear the real happening of redemption."[29]

Without detailing the holy in the whole of Merton's writings, it's obvious that the seventh day, the day the Lord made holy, is Merton's favorite day too, and that his life, like theirs, partly revolves around the quest for and celebration of holiness. Merton wrote voluminously about holiness and the holy, sometimes under specific titles, such as *Life and Holiness*.[30] Based on what we have seen thus far in Heschel and Buber, I should like to speculate about Merton's attraction to the holy in Judaism and Hasidism, and support those conjectures through a brief glimpse at holiness in Heschel's and Buber's Hasidic legends and Merton's *The Way of Chuang Tzu*.[31]

We have some specific information. As noted by William Shannon, Merton's compelling interest in Judaism is obvious in his

26 Buber, *Hasidism and Modern Man*, Maurice Friedman, ed. & trans. (New York: Harper and Row, 1966), p. 30.

27 Buber, *The Origin and Meaning of Hasidism*, Maurice Friedman, ed. and trans. (New York: Horizon Press, 1960), p. 96.

28 Ibid., p.181.

29 Ibid., pp. 96–97. Noting that "in Judaism a tendency to sacramental life has always been powerful," Buber observes: "There is hardly a Christian sacrament that has not had a sacramental or semisacramental Jewish antecedent," ibid., pp. 172–173.

30 *Life and Holiness*. (New York: Herder and Herder, 1963). See "Everything That Is, Is Holy," a signature piece whose title states the underlying theme of Merton's life and work, *New Seeds of Contemplation* (New York: New Directions, 1962), pp. 21–28.

31 Merton, *The Way of Chuang Tzu*. (New York: New Directions, 1965).

correspondence, contemplative writing on Scripture, and essays on the *Shoah*. He joined Heschel in his distress over an early draft of *Nostra Aetate*, which includes the Second Vatican Council's declaration on the relationship of the Church to the Jews, and supported him in helping to bring about its modification. Merton's invitations to Jewish scholars (including Heschel) and conferences with novices and religious sisters, in which he refers to Hasidism and Hasidic tales, further reflect Judaism's significance to Merton.[32] Shannon lists several of Merton's Jewish perspectives: the Jews "were and remain the people especially chosen and loved by God"; the shared heritage of Jews and Christians implies a shared destiny, and the need to seek God's will together; the *Shoah* climaxes centuries of anti-Semitism; the Suffering Servant in *Isaiah* is both Israel and Christ.[33] In regard to Jewish-Christian unity, one of the most telling witnesses of Merton's conviction is his letter to Rabbi Zalman Schachter-Shalomi: "There is one wedding and one wedding feast," he writes, "one bride ... one mystery, and the mystery of Israel and of the Church is ultimately to be revealed as One."[34]

Aside from such direct evidence, I think what opens up our topic, "Merton and Judaism," is what is implied by Merton's life and thought. There is little doubt, given Merton's faith in the Incarnation and his sense of both the presence and transcendence of the divine, he would be deeply drawn to the holy in Judaism and Hasidism, and in Hasidic tales. Indeed, as we shall see in our discussion of tales, Merton shares a kindred holy spirit with Buber and Heschel.

What in particular about holiness in Judaism and Hasidism would speak to Merton? How might he fulfill his "latent

32 Karl A. Plank, "The Eclipse of Difference," pp. 180–181. See Merton's October 29, 1967 conference to novices, Thomas Merton, "*The Mystic Life: Jewish and Christian Existentialism*" (Chappaqua, NY: Electronic Paperbacks, 1976), Series II, Tape 10 Side B, and his May 1968 retreat conference for contemplative sisters, "Asceticism and Results," in *Thomas Merton: The Springs of Contemplation* (Notre Dame, IN: Ave Maria Press, 1997), pp. 151–160. In a letter to Rabbi Zalman Schachter-Shalomi, Merton says: Your gifts were . . . most welcome and I shall continue reading them with great attention and profit. I am very interested in the Hasidim and respond to their fervor very readily." Letter dated Jan. 18, 1961, *Hidden Ground of Love*, p. 533.

33 William H. Shannon, "Thomas Merton and Judaism," *America* (Oct. 6, 1990), pp. 218–222.

34 Letter to Schachter-Shalomi dated Feb. 15, 1962, *Hidden Ground of Love*, p. 535. Shannon cites the letter, "Thomas Merton and Judaism," p. 220.

ambitions to be a true Jew under my Catholic skin"?

Merton, a great lover of nature and sensitive to its holiness, would probably be disappointed by Heschel's intellectual portrait of nature in his book, *God in Search of Man*, a work he wrote in his middle years.[35] "We adore her wealth and tacit wisdom, we tediously decipher her signs, but she never speaks to us," Heschel states flatly.[36] "It is more meaningful for us to believe in the *immanence of God in deeds* [Heschel italics] than in the immanence of God in nature."[37] But Merton would completely empathize with Heschel's youthful Hasidism, where nature does indeed speak to him, especially the moment in Heschel's young life at Vilna, Lithuania, when Heschel puts on his hat when entering a forest. "For me," says Heschel to a friend, astonished by his reverence, "a forest is a holy place (a *makom kodesh*). And a Jew, when he walks into a holy place, covers his head."[38] "Hasidism sings the glories of all Creation, but especially the forest," Arthur Green comments. "This is the forest to which the Baal Shem Tov, as a child, would run away from *kheyder* (school) to be alone with God ...This is also the forest of Heschel."[39]

Another area of the holy in Heschel with which Merton would identify is the tension of belief, the profound awareness of interior contradiction and paradox in the person seeking God, who perceives the holy like a canopy of stars in the heavens or a cloak of grace wrapped around the body of the self, and feels

35 In this work on the philosophy of Judaism, Heschel says Judaism considers the worship of nature absurd, and the Bible warns against it. He finds few biblical songs celebrating nature's beauty. *God in Search of Man*, pp. 88, 90, 95.

36 Ibid., p. 172.

37 Ibid., p. 312.

38 Edward K. Kaplan and Samuel H. Dresner, *Abraham Joshua Heschel: Prophetic Witness* (New Haven and London: Yale University Press, 1998), p. 88.

39 Arthur Green, "Abraham Joshua Heschel: Recasting Hasidism for Moderns," *Tikkun* vol. 14: 1 (Jan.-Feb., 1999), 65. Green points out that the Kabbalists and the Hasidim restored nature to its importance, "a primary testament to the workings of God," after the Talmudic age had lessened its meaning. In the encounter with nature, Heschel, between eighteen and twenty years old, and steeped in his Hasidic upbringing, feels sacred space. Yehudah Mirsky argues that the adult Heschel romanticizes a moribund Hasidism he formerly rejected in his youth, and calls the hat episode, "an unlikely reversal of common practice," and a "stunning pantheistic anecdote." Yehudah Mirsky, "The Rhapsodist," *The New Republic* (April 19, 1999), 39.

unworthy. Heschel experiences this tug most deeply in his inner person in his love for his two mentors, the Baal Shem Tov and the Kotzker Rebbe, Menahem Mendl of Kotzk, two *zaddikim* who were near opposites in personal character and approaches to Hasidism. In his Introduction to *A Passion for Truth*, poignantly entitled, "Why I Had to Write This Book," Heschel recalls the counter-rhythms in his own soul, whose beat is kept by two different maestros:

> I found my soul at home with the Baal Shem but driven by the Kotzker ... my heart torn between the joy of Mezbizh and the anxiety of Kotzk ... my heart was in Mezbizh, my mind in Kotzk ... I was taught about inexhaustible mines of meaning by the Baal Shem, from the Kotzker I learned to detect immense mountains of absurdity. The one taught me song, the other – silence ... The Kotzker restricted me, debunked cherished attitudes. From the Baal Shem I received the gifts of elasticity in adapting to contradictory conditions... The Baal Shem gave me wings; the Kotzker encircled me with chains... I owe intoxication to the Baal Shem, to the Kotzker the blessings of humiliation. [40]

Merton is a man of endless paradox, sometimes bordering on absurdity. When he enters the Trappists, he gives up "the world," including his writing career, only to be asked to write out of obedience. Well aware of his own ironies and inconsistencies, he writes about traveling in the belly of paradox through the metaphor of the whale in *The Sign of Jonas*.[41] Gregarious and social, he longs for solitude and silence. A celibate monk, he falls in love with a nurse during a hospital stay. For years he aspires to be a hermit, and makes plans to join communities of hermits such as the Calmaldolese, and at the same time, he entertains outside proposals to live in active peace and justice communities as a spiritual advisor. Merton would well understand the interior tensions which are part and parcel of a self-aware life yearning for holiness and Holy Being.

40 Heschel, *A Passion for Truth*, pp. xiv-xv.
41 *The Sign of Jonas* (New York: Harcourt, Brace, 1953).

"What can we gain by sailing to the moon," Merton asks, "if we are not able to cross the abyss that separates us from ourselves?"[42]

Merton's tension is more like Buber's "Holy insecurity," than Heschel's doubly placed loyalties. Holy insecurity, Maurice Friedman explains, must be understood in relation to Buber's disquiet over gnosis, and his rejection of any form of Gnosticism that promises salvation through secret knowledge. It "is life lived in the Face of God." It is a principle of living that combines Buber's Hasidism, understanding of biblical Judaism, and his dialogical philosophy. Buber identifies "Holy insecurity" with the stance of the prophets, who shatter all security.[43]

One especially senses Merton's holy tension of living daily "in the Face of God" in his peace writings, where his apprehension towards a "winning" or "end all" strategy or solution is expressed, whether it be coming from a U.S. government or military official regarding Vietnam war policy, or a leading light in the peace and justice movement.[44] His personal example of creative "Holy tension" is explored throughout his contemplative writings as well, particularly in his journals and letters, and objectively described in *New Seeds of Contemplation* as belonging to the life of anyone seeking God, including novices, those living outside the monastery and outside any church, whose loneliness, Merton says, has changed his thinking.[45]

Lastly, I think Merton might be able to see himself as a "true Jew" in love with the holy, in his affinity with the critical stance of both Heschel and Buber towards culture and religious tradition. All three seem to find criticism basic to a life of holiness. Merton's position is somewhere between Heschel and Buber, more like Heschel in his affirmation of orthodoxy and the absolute requirement of a direct, personal response to God, and more like Buber in his impatience with pious hypocrisy and delusion. In their analysis of modern life and faith, Heschel and Merton, and

42 Thomas Merton, trans., *Wisdom of the Desert: Sayings from the Desert Fathers of the Fourth Century* (New York: New Directions, 1970), p. 11.

43 Friedman, Editor's Introduction to Buber, *Origin and Meaning of Hasidism*, pp. 12-13.

44 See Merton's "Letter to a Peace Maker" (Jim Forest), Feb. 21, 1965, *Hidden Ground of Love*, pp. 294-297.

45 See "Union and Division," "A Body of Broken Bones," and "The Wrong Flame" in Merton, *New Seeds of Contemplation*, pp. 47-51, 70-79, 245-249.

to a lesser extent, Buber, create room for contemporary disaffected intellectuals to be believing Jews and Catholics.[46]

THE MESSIAH

In a letter to Rabbi Zalman Schachter-Shalomi, Merton speaks about the two of them waiting for the Messiah (*Meshiah*): "We need to make straight the paths for the coming of the Consoler. And I think the Christian needs to wait with the longing and anguish of the Jew for the Messiah ..." In a subsequent letter to Schachter-Shalomi, Merton continues the theme of waiting:

> And of course it is in no sense a matter of shuttling back and forth institutionally. Each on our side we must prepare for the great eschatological feast on the mountains of Israel. I have sat on the porch of the hermitage and sung chapters and chapters of the Prophets in Latin out over the valley, and it is a hair-raising experience is all I can say.[47]

In Merton's representation, Jewish rabbi and Christian monk join in their expectation while retaining their separation. They are brothers and sisters in exile.[48] In a study of the Hasidim, Buber speaks of a different, but related area of encounter, twice quoting from his earlier writings to emphasis his brotherhood with Jesus:

> I have "felt Jesus from my youth onwards as my great brother." ... the Jews who are such through and through, from the original covenant, the "arch-Jews," among whom I dare to count myself, are "brothers" of Jesus. This too I have expressed before, twenty years earlier: "that we Jews knew him (Jesus) from within, in the impulses and stirrings of his Jewish being, in a way that remains

---

46 See Shaul Magid: "Abraham Joshua Heschel and Thomas Merton: Heretics of Modernity," *Conservative Judaism*, vol. 1: 2-3 (Winter-Spring, 1998), 112-125; "Monastic Liberation as Counter-Cultural Critique in the Life and Thought of Thomas Merton," *Cross Currents* vol. 49: 4 (Winter, 1999-2000), 445-461.
47 First letter dated December 15, 1961, second dated February 15, 1962, *Hidden Ground of Love*, pp. 534-535.
48 I am unaware of Rabbi Schachter-Shalomi's view or his possible response to Merton.

inaccessible to the peoples submissive to him."[49]

For Merton, there is a unity with Jews in awaiting the eschatological feast at the end of time. For Buber, there is a common bond in Jesus, the brother Jew, and insight into his Jewish identity that Christians cannot know.

While Buber is not referring here to Jesus as Messiah, he often does write about Jewish views of the Messiah. Heschel prefers in inter-faith dialogue to avoid fruitless topics: "A rule for Catholics and Protestants would be not to discuss the supremacy of the bishop of Rome or papacy ... a rule for Christians and Jews would be not to discuss Christology."[50] Be that true as it very often is, Heschel, like Buber, frequently talks about Messiah and Jewish Messianism. Merton, as a Christian, believes the Messiah has come and will come again. My view is that the common ground regarding the Messiah in all three writers is the holy and holiness, and that, in the broadest sense, while the fullness of eschatological hope cannot be realized until the end of time, or the fullness of time, they share an unvoiced affinity in encountering the Messiah through history and daily life.

Buber presents Hasidism and its father-founder, the Baal Shem Tov, partly as a correction and a reply to the agnosticism or atheism of Baruch Spinoza (Jewish rationalist philosopher), and the pseudo-Messianism of Shabbatai Zvi – a "process," Buber says, which began with "a single historical manifestation, with Jesus."[51] Buber finds important similarities between Hasidism and Jesus' teachings, but differentiates "the Christianity which sees in Jesus the Christ, the Messiah Come,"[52] from Hasidism, which sees many "meshihim" down through the generations, hidden "suffering servants" whose common epithet is "Messiah son of Joseph," each of whom is "the suffering Messiah who ever again endures mortal agony for the sake

---

49 Buber, *Origin and Meaning of the Hasidim*, p. 251. Buber's first quotation of his earlier writing is from *Two Types of Faith*, Norman P. Goldhawk, trans. (London: Routledge and Paul, 1951), p. 12; the second is from *Between Man and Man*, Ronald G. Smith, trans. (Beacon Paperback, 1955), "Dialogue," p. 5f.

50 "What We Might Do Together," *Moral Grandeur*, p. 300.

51 *Origin and Meaning of Hasidism*, pp. 90-91. Shabbateanism was a "pseudo-Messianic movement of the seventeenth and eighteenth centuries," Friedman, "Editor's Introduction," ibid., p. 9.

52 Friedman, ibid., p. 12.

of God." "The Messiahship of the end of time is preceded by one of all times ... and without this the fallen world could not continue to exist." The *meshihim* are "forerunners" who share the Messianic power, and whose work of suffering is hidden and secret. "Messianic self-disclosure is the bursting of Messiahship," Buber declares.[53] Buber favors "Jesus of Nazareth" as the "Jewish Christ,"[54] "the first in the series," who "was incomparably the purest, the most legitimate, the most endowed with real Messianic power – as I experience ever again when those personal words that ring true to me merge for me into a unity whose speaker becomes visible to me."[55]

Like Buber, Heschel sees the Messiah at work in history, and in particular individuals: "History is a circuitous way for the steps of the Messiah," he writes.[56] Rallying to the Baal Shem Tov, the Jews of Eastern Europe see "the light of the Messiah shining overhead."[57] Indeed, every person is a potential redeemer, needed by God to share the Lord's daily work of redeeming the world and revealing the holy.[58] As Edward Kaplan notes, according to Heschel, "We can help fulfill God's messianic dreams."[59] Still, Heschel states, Judaism insists on "the promise of messianic redemption," for messianism implies human effort "must fail in redeeming the world," and history "is not sufficient to itself."[60]

In a powerful Hasidic tale of awe, fear, and joy, "The Call," re-told by Buber, the Baal Shem Tov reprimands one Rabbi David Dirkes, who wants to call down the Messiah:

> O Rabbi David . . .do you imagine that your power can grasp the ungraspable? And even were it to press forward to the innermost heaven and clasp the throne of the Messiah,

53 Ibid., pp. 108-109.
54 Ibid., pp. 246-247. In his "Introduction" to an early work, *The Legend of the Baal-Shem*, p. 11, Buber speaks of "the great Nazarene," who was supported by a circle of men descended from the Essenes, who created the legend of Jesus, "the greatest triumph of myth."
55 Ibid., p. 110.
56 *God in Search of Man*, p. 238.
57 Heschel, *A Passion for Truth*, p. 7.
58 Heschel, *God In Search of Man*, pp. 50, 156, 313.
59 Kaplan, *Holiness in Words*, p. 123.
60 Heschel, *God in Search of Man*, p. 379.

do you imagine that you could hold him as my hand grips your shoulder? Above the suns, above the earths Messiah changes into a thousand and a thousand forms, and the suns and earths ripen in face of him. Concentrated in his higher form, scattered in unspeakable distances, he everywhere guards the growth of the souls, from out of all depths he lifts up the fallen sparks. Daily he dies silent deaths, daily he springs up in silent births, daily he ascends and descends. When once the soul, slender and perfected, treads pure ground with pure feet, then his hour will throb in his heart, then he will divest himself of all manifestations and will sit on the throne, lord of the flames of heaven that have blazed up from the redeemed sparks, and he will descend and come and live and will bestow on the souls their kingdom.[61]

Rabbi David is reduced to redemptive tears, which the Baal Shem Tov says came to the disciple with his giving up of his will:

When your weeping overcame you, the suffering of Israel took fire from your suffering. Each stood before God in the refining fire of his heart's suffering, each became pure in the stream of his tears. How many fallen sparks you have thereby elevated![62]

This is the purification that Merton calls for in his appeal that Christians need "to wait with the longing and anguish of the Jew for the Messiah." Merton's point is not mere empathy. We Christians must weep and suffer together with Jews, to call forth the Messiah. The Messiah's coming is delayed only because each person has not yet fulfilled his or her unique potentiality.[63] A quotation Buber cites from an unnamed Hasidic source, may remind us Christians of our mother, Jerusalem, and our communal role as children of Israel: "This is a very great thing and a very great faith – that every one of Israel, by the faith in his heart, will hasten the coming of the

61 Buber, *Legend of the Baal-Shem*, pp. 199-200.
62 Ibid., p. 201.
63 Buber, *The Way of Man According to the Teaching of Hasidism* (Secaucus, New Jersey: Citadel Press, 1976), p. 16.

172 · Lucien Miller

redeemer."[64] And why should Jews and Christians together want to hasten the coming? Because, writes Buber, when the Messiah comes the Great Shofar (ram's horn) will be blown, and it will "awaken and call together 'the exiles from the four corners of the earth.'" [65] "In the messianic world all shall be holy,"[66] because there will no longer be a distinction between sacred and profane,[67] for the Messiah will make "all beings free."[68]

There is a grave question of fairness regarding Jew and Christian Gentile waiting together for the Messiah. Heschel points out that Jewish authorities, including Yehudah Halevi and Maimonides, acknowledge Christianity "to be *preparatio messianica*, while the Church regarded ancient Judaism as having been a *preparatio evangelica*." The Jewish view, writes Heschel, sees Christianity's role in the divine plan for redemption, but Church doctrine has commonly seen Jews as "candidates for conversion."[69] Despite this painful awareness, Heschel generously points forward with hope to the promise: "The goal of all efforts is to bring about the restitution of the unity of God and world. The restoration of that unity is a constant process and its accomplishment will be the essence of Messianic redemption."[70]

HOLINESS IN WORDS

One might say, given the previous discussion of Heschel, Buber, and Merton, that a basic difference and a basic likeness between Jews and Christians are in relation to the Messiah and the holy. Christians commonly, and erroneously, think that, for the Jew, the Messiah has not come. Jews assume that for the Christian, the Messiah came and is coming – which is correct for Christians, but is not their complete doctrine.[71] One common ground we have seen in Heschel, Buber,

64 Buber, *Origin and Meaning of Hasidism*, p. 208.
65 Buber, *Legends of the Baal-Shem*, Glossary, "Shofar," p. 221.
66 Buber, *Hasidism and Modern Man*, p. 29.
67 Buber, *Origin and Meaning of Hasidism*, p. 51; Buber quotes an anonymous *zaddik*.
68 Buber, *Legends of the Baal-Shem*, p. 33.
69 Heschel, "No Religion Is an Island," *Moral Grandeur*, p. 248. [For a recent shift see Appendix C.-Ed.]
70 Heschel, *Man Is Not Alone*, p. 112. Cited by Kaplan, *Holiness in Words*, p. 153.
71 The basic Christian teaching is: Jesus is the Christ, the "anointed" one, not

and Merton is the waiting for the Messiah, what we might call looking forward to the pleroma or fullness of the coming of the Messiah. As we have remarked in addition, another overlapping vision is one in which the Messiah is always here, has come and is coming. For Heschel, Buber, and Merton, such elemental likenesses and contrasts may originate in personal erudition and interpretation. Generally, Jew and Catholic Christian seem ignorant of the other's history and textual tradition of the past two thousand years. The average Jew (but there is no average Jew) may well religiously ignore the Gospels, the Christian churches, and the Christian tradition. Speaking for myself, the average Catholic knows little or nothing of the Talmud, Mishnah, and oral tradition. We are well aware of the sufferings of the Jews, and more aware than we used to be of our ancestors' role in that suffering.

However, in spite of history, and the chasm between traditions, intermingling and encounter may take place through folk literature, written tales, and oral art. Again in my speculative mode, this is where I think Heschel, Buber, and Merton meet most profoundly. For them, the presence of the Jewish and Christian Holy Other occurs in telling, reading, and interpreting both Hasidic and Chinese tales (both Buber and Merton translated Chuang Tzu). If Jews and Christians cannot come together in synagogue or church for prayer, or engage holiness in Gospel or Torah, they might find one another in a tale. The reason why my imaginary encounter works for Heschel, Buber, and Merton is that, in story, all three stumble upon Holy Being, the eternal one, the light of lights. Awareness of this meeting may encourage readers to discover divine sparks in our three mentors' tales too, and provide grounds for Twenty-First Century hope of healing the divisions which wound us.

Welcome, *Olam-ha-ba*! Welcome, world to come.[72]

The appreciation of legends and tales by Heschel, Buber, and Merton promises to move the reader or hearer up the ladder of

---

simply in the sense of being a holy man, or divinized human being, but God, the Second Person of the Trinity, the Word, "the only Son," through whom "all things came into being." Gospel of John 1: 1-3.

72 *Olam-ha-ba*: "The age inaugurated by the coming of the Messiah." Glossary, *Legend of the Baal-Shem*, p. 223.

spiritual awareness, from the level of *katnut*, or constricted consciousness, to the rung of *gadlut*, or expanded consciousness. Of course one needs to spend time with hundreds, if not, thousands, of tales the authors tell or compile. Here we will look at a handful. What is it about these stories that is inviting to Jew and Gentile, rabbi and monk? I believe it is the experience of holiness in words, or "Word-Event."

"Word-Idea" and "Word-Event" are phrases coined by Shigeto Oshida, O.P., Dominican priest, and head of the Takamori contemplative community in the Japanese mountains above Nagano, Japan.[73] Word-Idea refers to language that is analytical and discursive. It is the language of logic and syllogism, the language of education, in which we talk about a topic or problem. Father Oshida calls it "about talk." Word-event is the language we use in which we respond with the whole of our being: the cry of a baby, a prophet's "Ah" encountering God. Typically rich in imagery and metaphor, Word-Event is the language of Scripture through which we experience God, directly and unmistakably.[74]

"The Bible is *holiness in words*," says Heschel, and the words are "a live wire charged with His spirit . . . hyphens between heaven and earth."[75] Buber speaks of Hasidic tales as "a literature of legends, the like of which in compass, many-sidedness, vitality, and popular wild charm I do not know."[76] He notes that a legend, ordinary in its everyday content, is like sacred scripture to the *hasidim*, and often appears as the centerpiece in a *zaddik's* sermon, "spoken slowly and solemnly as if it were the mystery of the *kedusha*, and the people listened to it as if it continued the revelation on Sinai."[77] Buber also stresses something Merton would appreciate – that in Zen stories and the Taoist Chuang Tzu he finds materials kindred to Hasidic

---

73 Shigeto Vincent Oshida, O.P., unpublished essay, "Zenna," Article for the International Mission Congress, Manila, Philippines, December 2-6, 1979.

74 Oshida's "word-event" echoes Heschel's understanding of prophetic, biblical language, in which the actuality of God is communicated through the prophet. For Heschel's critique of Buber's "atheism" and Buber's notion that scriptural language is symbolic rather than experiential, see Kaplan, *Holiness in Words*, p. 82-84; "Sacred versus Symbolic Religion: Heschel versus Buber," *Modern Judaism* vol. 14: 3 (Fall, 1994), 213-231.

75 Heschel, *God in Search of Man*, 244.

76 Buber, *Origin and Meaning of Hasidism*, p. 174.

77 Buber, *Legend of the Baal-Shem*, p. 150.

legends in spirit and content.[78] In his analysis of Heschel's own rapturous literary style, Edward Kaplan remarks how it "pulses with the holy," and how reading Heschel is an existential process that leads to a "turning to God."[79]

Merton hears the premonitions of God's wisdom in the Taoist humanist, Chuang Tzu,[80] and in the *Zhuangzi*, the Chinese text attributed to him, and thinks his project of creating an English version, *The Way of Chuang Tzu*, "has the marks of the Holy Spirit's action upon it."[81] He encourages his mentor and friend, sinologist John C. H. Wu, to listen to the Holy Spirit with "the gaiety and childlike joy of Chuang Tzu," whose spirit Merton sees in St. John and St. Paul in the New Testament,[82] reminding him of the Sermon on the Mount, the Discourse of the Last Supper, Christ in the manger, the cross, and the resurrection.[83] Rejoicing in his personal understanding of Taoism, imbibed through study of Chuang Tzu and other Chinese texts, Merton writes Wu, "Now I enjoy the quiet of the woods and the song of the birds and the presence of the Lord in silence. Here is Nameless Tao, revealed as Jesus, the brightness of the hidden Father, our joy and our life."[84] In a word, for Merton the Chinese *Chuang Tzu* is the Chinese Gospel. This sense of "holiness in words" – in Scripture, Hasidic tale, Heschel, Buber, and Chuang Tzu – of vitality and wild charm, and of turning or conversion (*teshuva*), is what makes legend and story word-event.[85]

78 Buber, *Origin and Meaning of Hasidism*, pp. 234, 237. Buber's German translation of Chuang Tzu is entitled, *Nanhua jing* [Chuang Tzu], 1910. For an English translation of Buber's version, see *Chinese Tales*, Alex Page, trans. (Atlantic Highlands, NJ, and London: Humanities Press International, Inc., 1991).

79 Kaplan, *Holiness in Words*, p. 133. "Its verbal grace ushers us beyond the beautiful to the holy." Ibid., p. 43. "Even considered as 'fictional' narratives, his [Heschel's] writings convey 'holiness in words,'" (ibid., p. 148).

80 *Turning Toward the World: the Pivotal Years*, The Journals of Thomas Merton, vol. 4. Victor A. Kramer, ed. (HarperSanFrancisco: 1996), p. 102. Entry dated March 24, 1961.

81 Letter to John C. H. Wu, April 1, 1961, *Hidden Ground of Love*, p. 613. The *Zhuangzi* is an anthology of contending schools of Chinese thought, mainly Taoist, compiled by various authors, and traditionally ascribed to "Chuang Tzu."

82 Merton, Letter to Wu, April 11, 1961. ibid., p. 615.

83 Ibid., Dec. 20, 1962. Ibid., pp. 623-624.

84 Ibid., May 19, 1961. Ibid., p. 617.

85 Merton expresses his desire to understand Jewish metanoia in words that sound like a Hasid releasing sparks: "I wish I knew more about doing T'shuvah

Teshuva: TELLING AND LISTENING TO TALES

As storytellers and narrators of legends, Heschel, Buber, and Merton are creative interpreters of "holiness in words," who identify with their sources. Samuel H. Dresner observes that Heschel closely paraphrases the original, using quotation marks "only for exact quotations," and retells the original "in a more felicitous style."[86] Heschel's inventive approach is mirrored in his rendition of a tale by Rabbi Isaac of Drohobycz, who stresses the importance of hiding intentions:

> Each time I plan a journey during which to reprove the children of Israel and uplift straying souls, the *yetzer hara* [Evil Impulse] pounces upon me, arguing: "Isaac, stay home and continue with your study of Torah. Why trouble yourself to travel from place to place? Why interrupt your studies?"

> So I say to him: "But my travels and lectures are intended only to earn a little money, which I am badly in need of."

> "Oh," replies the Evil Impulse, now encouraging me. "If it is only money that you're after," he says, "then go in peace."

> And he no longer troubles me.

> However, once I reach the place where I am to preach, I put aside all thoughts of reward. I preach and reprove only for the sake of Heaven.

> ... For no great *mitzvah* [divine commandment, good deed] is without an admixture of *yetzer hara* at its inception. For when an individual intends to perform a *mitzvah* for its own sake, he is always set upon by the *yetzer* and consequently frustrated from implementing the act. But, if one embarks on his mission with a selfish motive in mind,

[metanoia or penance]. It is the only thing that seems to make much sense in these days. And in the political dark I light small, frail lights about peace and hold them up in the whirlwind." Letter to Zalman Schachter-Shalomi, December 15, 1961, *Hidden Ground of Love*, p. 534.
86 Heschel, *Circle of the Baal Shem Tov*, p. 47n14, p. 61n67.

the *yetzer* is outwitted and is no longer an obstacle. One can rid himself of his apparent selfish purpose while performing the deed and execute his mission with only Heaven's will in mind. In short, a person must conceal his true intentions from the *yetzer hara*.[87]

If one is too literal or direct in intention in translating, the *yetzer* may get you.

Buber's self-sense of himself as creative translator is more intense and convoluted, due to personal identification with the originators, the *zaddikim* who told and the *hasidim* who re-told and recorded. Speaking in 1907 of his role in telling the Hasidic legend, Buber says:

> I have received it and have told it anew. I have not transcribed it like some piece of literature; I have not elaborated it like some fabulous material. I have told it anew as one who was born later. I bear in me the blood and the spirit of those who created it, and out of my blood and spirit it has become new. I stand in the chain of narrators, a link between links; I tell once again the old stories, and if they sound new, it is because the new already lay dormant in them when they were told for the first time.[88]

Following the model of his forebears, who reconstructed pure events from legendary anecdotes that were "handed down in crude formlessness,"[89] Buber rejects close translation which he says distorts the spirit and form of the original, and tells the stories "that I had taken into myself from out of myself," discovering that even in completely new sections he inserts, he has found true faithfulness even "more adequately than the direct disciples." "I came to my own narrating in growing independence; but the greater the independence became, so much the more deeply I experienced the faithfulness."[90]

---

87 Ibid., pp. 175-176.
88 Buber, Introduction, *Legend of the Baal Shem*, p. 10.
89 Buber, *Hasidism and Modern Man*, p. 26.
90 Ibid., pp. 61-63. Interestingly, on p. 63 Buber mentions that, subsequent to his Hasidic books, he has discovered another method of faithfulness, but does not discuss it.

Buber speaks of his oneness with the "blood and spirit" of his
Hasidic ancestors. John C. H. Wu writes to Merton: "I have come to
the conclusion that you and Chuang Tzu are one. It is Chuang Tzu
himself who writes his thoughts in the English of Thomas
Merton."[91] As in the case of Heschel and Buber, this deep
interiorization of ancestral spirit is what enables Merton to recreate
Chuang Tzu's "holiness in words." Merton's versions are akin to
musical variations, new creations in which one hears the original
and the recreation simultaneously. While rich in interpolation,
contemporary political and cultural associations, and Christian
theological underlayers, their amazing closeness to the style and
spirit of the original *Zhuangzi* has been singled out by sinologists.[92]

Besides identifying with their sources, Buber, Heschel and
Merton experience a personal turning or *teshuva* as they listen to or
retell folktales and legends, and they invoke that *teshuva* spirit of
conversion, repentance and forgiveness in their audience. Heschel
and Merton would doubtlessly agree with Buber that the spiritual
state of the listener to "holiness in words" is paramount. As in
reading and responding to sacred Scripture, where the pilgrim is on
his or her pilgrimage determines what is heard and absorbed.
Buber's retelling of a Hasidic tale about fasting makes his point well:

> A hasid of the Rabbi of Lublin once fasted from one
> Sabbath to the next. On Friday afternoon he began to
> suffer such cruel thirst that he thought he would die. He
> saw a well, went up to it, and prepared to drink. But
> instantly he realized that because of the one brief hour he
> had still to endure, he was about to destroy the work of
> the entire week. He did not drink and went away from
> the well. Then he was touched by a feeling of pride for
> having passed this difficult test. When he became aware of
> it, he said to himself, "Better I go and drink than let my

91 Wu letter to Merton, Nov. 24, 1965, *Hidden Ground of Love*, p. 631.
92 Besides Wu, see Burton Watson, trans., Introduction, *The Complete Works of
Chuang Tzu* (New York and London: Columbia University Press, 1968), p. 28.
For a close comparison of Merton's *Way of Chuang Tzu* with the original
Chinese text, see my unpublished "Merton's *Chuang Tzu*," available through
the Thomas Merton Center, Bellarmine University, Louisville, Kentucky.

heart fall prey to pride." He went back to the well, but just as he was going to bend down to draw water, he noticed that his thirst had disappeared. When the Sabbath had begun, he entered his teacher's house. "Patchwork!" the rabbi called to him, as he crossed the threshold.[93]

Buber comments that the story is both a critique of egoistic asceticism and the disciple's self-conscious dithering about. How does the man's "patchwork" become "all of a piece"? asks Buber. "Only with a united soul," he answers.[94]

There is a parallel tale in Merton's *Way of Chuang Tzu* that illustrates a similar point, "The Fasting of the Heart." Yen Hui, a favorite disciple of Confucius, comes to take leave of his Master, as he is on his way to instruct the Prince of Wei, a corrupt official, in the proper ways of government. Like the Rabbi of Lublin, Confucius censures his disciple, saying he has too many plans. "You must *fast!*" says Confucius, emphasizing the need for interior unity:

> The goal of fasting is inner unity. This means hearing, but not with the ear; hearing, but not with the understanding; hearing with the spirit, with your whole being. . . Fasting of the heart empties the faculties, frees you from limitation and from preoccupation. Fasting of the heart begets unity and freedom.[95]

The theme of many passages from Buber, Heschel and Merton is *teshuva*, in the sense of turning from external distraction to interior freedom, a conversion. In Chuang Tzu, *teshuva* is found in the realization of "no self":

> If a man is crossing a river
> And an empty boat collides with his own skiff,
> Even though he be a bad-tempered man

93 Buber, *The Way of Man*, p. 21.
94 Ibid., p. 22.
95 Merton, "The Fasting of the Heart," *Way of Chuang Tzu*, pp. 52-53.

He will not become very angry.
But if he sees a man in the boat,
He will shout at him to steer clear.
If the shout is not heard, he will shout again,
And yet again, and begin cursing.
And all because there is somebody in the boat.
Yet if the boat were empty,
He would not be shouting, and not angry.

If you can empty your own boat
Crossing the river of the world,
No one will oppose you,
No one will seek to harm you.[96]

Merton would probably say to us Jewish and Christian intellectuals, such a conversion, a real change of heart, is pretty difficult for you. As the Ocean God asks in another passage from *The Way of Chuang Tzu*, "Can you talk about the way of Life / To a doctor of philosophy?"[97]

Actually, according to both Buber and Merton, what blocks turning is interior conflict and contradiction, symptoms of the reality that the modern self does not know where it is. Buber quotes a tale told by Rabbi Hanokh:

There was once a man who was very stupid. When he got up in the morning it was so hard for him to find his clothes that at night he almost hesitated to go to bed for thinking of the trouble he would have on waking. One evening he finally made a great effort, took paper and pencil and as he undressed noted down exactly where he put everything he had on. The next morning, very well pleased with himself, he took the slip of paper in his hand and read: "cap" – there it was, he set it on his head; "pants" – there they lay, he got into them and so it went until he was fully dressed. "That's all very well, but now where am I myself?" he asked in great consternation. "Where in the world am I?" He looked and

96 Merton, "The Empty Boat," ibid., pp. 114–115.
97 Merton, "Autumn Floods," ibid., p. 84.

looked, but it was a vain search; he could not find himself. "And that is how it is with us," said the rabbi.[98]

Merton adds to the paradigm in "Keng's Disciple," a story about a man who does not get it – "Tao is only a word in my ear. / It does not ring any bells inside." Master Keng gives up, saying "Bantams do not hatch goose eggs," and sends his hopeless disciple to Lao Tzu, the grand father-figure of Taoists. Lao Tzu asks:

"Who are all those people you have brought with you?"
The disciple whirled around to look.
Nobody there. Panic!
Lao said: "Don't you understand?"
The disciple hung his head. Confusion!
Then a sigh. "Alas, I have forgotten my answer."
(More confusion!) "I have also forgotten my question."

In his pursuit of Tao, the disciple carries many other people with him, anxieties and interior contradictions, counter views and philosophies, what ifs and whatevers, probably similar to those immersed in the study of Merton and Judaism. Lao Tzu concludes with a critique of human willfulness:

"If you persist in trying
To attain what is never attained
(It is Tao's gift!)
If you persist in making effort
To obtain what effort cannot get;
If you persist in reasoning
About what cannot be understood,
You will be destroyed
By the very thing you seek.

"To know when to stop
To know when you can get no further
By your own action,
This is the right beginning!"[99]

98 Buber, *The Way of Man*, p. 30.
99 Merton, "Keng's Disciple," *Way of Chuang Tzu*, pp. 128-129.

The moral of the tale seems right for us who are involved in Jewish-Christian encounter. Receptivity to the gift of grace is more needed than exercising limited will and reason. Even if the question is remembered, even if Tao's gift is received, Buber emphasizes that ultimately, the direction of all *teshuva* is not remaining in self-discovery or interior conversion, but turning to the world:

> Rabbi Hayyim of Zans had married his son to the daughter of Rabbi Eliezer. The day after the wedding he visited the father of the bride and said: "Now that we are related I feel close to you and can tell you what is eating at my heart. Look! My hair and beard have grown white, and I have not yet atoned!"
>
> "O my friend," replied Rabbi Eliezer, "you are thinking only of yourself. How about forgetting yourself and thinking of the world?"[100]

Buber explains that the Jewish conception of turning stressed in this Hasidic tale is something much more significant than mere penance. "Turning is capable of renewing a man from within and changing his position in God's world . . . it means that by a reversal of his whole being, a man who had been lost in the maze of selfishness . . . finds a way to God, that is, a way to the fulfillment of the particular task for which he . . . has been destined by God."[101]

One way out of the maze of selfishness is Heschel's sense of "indicative" words. Whether they appear in Scripture, legend or tale, indicative words can communicate what is ineffable, and lead to conversion:

> *indicative words* ... stand in a fluid relation to ineffable meanings and, instead of describing, merely intimate something which we intuit but cannot fully comprehend. The content of words such as God, time, beauty, eternity cannot be faithfully imagined or reproduced in our minds.

100 Buber, *The Way of Man*, p. 31.
101 Ibid., p. 32.

Still they convey a wealth of meaning to our sense of the
ineffable. Their function is not to call up a definition in our
minds but to introduce us to a reality which they signify.[102]

An example of this fluid relation between words and ineffable
meaning may be seen in the following tale Heschel tells, which I
should like to title, "Wrong Baby":

> It is related that R. Isaac was accustomed at the birth of
> each of his sons to hasten immediately to view the
> newborn child. After scrutinizing the infant, he would
> conclude: "This is not what I had in mind" (*Nisht dos hob
> ikh gemeint*), and would go up to his room, as was his wont.
> Whereupon the child would fall into a coma and then die.
>
> This occurred many times – whenever his wife gave birth –
> and many souls thus departed this world. When the holy
> rav, R. Yehiel Mikhel, was born, R. Isaac's wife became
> furious with him and absolutely refused to show him the
> baby until he had given her his most solemn assurance that
> he would not say what he always said. When he came to
> gaze upon the infant's holy countenance, he said, "Alas!
> Many more beautiful souls than this were let go! (*O va
> asakh sheynere neshomos avek gelost!*)"[103]

What is ineffable here? What is intimated that is not described
nor fully understood? I think we can intuit that the reality
signified here is the mysterious power of the Rabbi's words, the
satire directed against the vanity of his paradoxical character, and
above all, the mystery of the father-son relation, which may be
read as a metaphor for the search for the true self and for God.

This latter possibility is exemplified in a wonderfully parallel
tale from the *Way of Chuang Tzu*, which Merton calls, "When a
Hideous Man ...":

102 Heschel, *God in Search of Man*, pp. 182-183. Cited by Kaplan, ibid., pp. 51-52.
103 Heschel, *The Circle of the Baal Shem Tov*, p. 175.

When a hideous man becomes a father
And a son is born to him
In the middle of the night
He trembles and lights a lamp
And runs to look in anguish
On that child's face
To see whom he resembles.[104]

For Heschel, "religious assertion functions as *understatement*."[105] Merton's "When a Hideous Man" epitomizes understatement and paradox, marks of holiness in words. The parent wonders whom the son looks like. Is it my child? He wants the child to be an extension of himself, yet dreads it too. Who wants an ugly child, a child who reminds one of his own ugliness? Identity is sought in secret – one's paternity may need to be kept hidden. Again, like Heschel's "Wrong Baby," Merton's "Hideous Man" is Word-Event, or holiness in words, showing the paradoxical desire to reveal what is buried, and to keep it out of sight.

Conclusion

Heschel, Buber, and Merton meet in the indicative words of legend and tale, and in the redemptive turning that reading inspires. Merton seems most at home with them in waiting and looking forward, and at the same time, knowing that "every thing that is, is holy." Of course, like them, we Jews and Christians are part of an unfinished symphony. Buber cautions against comparison of religions, because one can know only one's own temple from the inside, and the other's from the outside, and the latter's relation to the Holy is concealed.[106] We might do well to bear this in mind. Still, Heschel's universalism, his special contribution of which Arthur Green reminds us, argues that any person can do a *mitzvah*, a deed that fulfills God's will and brings blessings to God and this world.[107] My suggestion is that one *mitzvah*, one holy deed, that we might all share is telling, reading, and interpreting tales.

104 Merton, "When a Hideous Man . . .", *The Way of Chuang Tzu*, p. 77.
105 Kaplan, *Holiness in Words*, p. 56.
106 Buber, *Origin and Meaning of Hasidism*, p. 243.
107 Green, "Abraham Joshua Heschel: Recasting Hasidism for Moderns," p. 69.

9

COME TO THE WEDDING:

SOME HASIDIC THEMES IN SELECTED LETTERS
TO MERTON FROM JEWISH CORRESPONDENTS

Mary Heléne P. Rosenbaum

There is a story told of Hasidic founder and sage R. Israel b. Eliezer, the Ba'al Shem Tov, or BeSHT, that during his lifetime in 18th century Poland, he would take his disciples to a holy spot in the forest where he would light a fire and lead them in ecstatic prayer. After his death, his heir Dov Baer advised against lighting the fire for fear of the Cossacks, so they only went to the forest and said the prayer. The next generation forgot the location, so his followers merely said the prayer. More time passed, and the prayer was forgotten. But still, says the tale, we tell the story – and there is merit in that alone.

The previously unpublished other side of Merton's conversations with some of his Jewish correspondents, particularly as they touch on the mystical spirituality connected in Jewish tradition with hasidism, illuminates this principle.

Of course, it is in the search for the Divine Light, the ideal of *hitlahavut* or burning enthusiasm of the soul, that Merton and those who seek enlightenment from hasidic tradition are most united. This search is explicit in Abraham Joshua Heschel's letters to Merton. [See the Heschel Correspondence.] But it is also evident in Merton's correspondence from two very different Jewish thinkers who both found areas of sympathy with him: Erich Fromm and Zalman Schachter-Shalomi.

Two social influences are paramount during the time that the bulk of the correspondence took place, the late 50s through the mid 60s: the growing concern that the stresses of the Cold War might lead to nuclear holocaust, and the impact of the statements coming out of the Second Vatican Council, especially as regards Jews and Judaism in the plan of salvation. Both these strains have as their background the awareness, on the part of both Merton and his correspondents, of that other "holocaust" just past, the *Shoa*.

Others have explored these themes in detail elsewhere in this volume. I bring them up only to observe that the tension or dialectic they set up in the correspondence in some ways echoes an underlying strain in classic hasidism: that between the emphasis on *mitzvot* (good works) in society, or what Christians call the Social Gospel, on the one hand and the desire for mystic union or *devekut* that is a hallmark both of hasidism and of the monastic contemplative life.

There are other similarities between Merton's situation and the forces that impelled the growth of hasidism in the 18th and 19th centuries, and a reawakening of interest in it in the mid 20th century. In both cases, a perception of evil or threatening forces in society led to a conviction that resistance to or even withdrawal from it is both prudent and virtuous. And both hasidic communities and monastic ones, with their emphasis on holiness through communal discipline and characteristic liturgical patterns – and, one may say, their tendency to draw young men away from their cradle communities – are the object of some suspicion and lack of regard by the larger society.

In Fromm's case, the combination of his religious training and education with his development as a pioneering secular psychologist and social philosopher brought him to investigate a dichotomy very close to Merton's concerns: that between authoritarian and humanistic religion. The correspondence with Fromm also involved their mutual antipathy to the "bellicist" attitudes and inhumane policies of modern industrial/capitalist society. Fromm's recurring theme of the "non-theistic form of mysticism" he sees in Marx's writing makes even more explicit the interaction of the political and the spiritual in his thought. In speaking of his own spiritual development, Fromm even alludes to "veils and blindfolds" – reminiscent of the hasidic notion of *kelipot*, shells of personality and worldly accidence, to be sloughed off in order to release the inner divine spark – as relating to Fromm's own meditative experience.

This seems an appropriate note on which to turn to the letters from Rabbi Zalman Schachter-Shalomi, whose interest in mysticism and spiritual renewal made him a congenial correspondent for Merton. If, in their letters to Merton, Heschel's social concerns arise out of his spiritual awareness, and Fromm's perhaps the converse, Reb Zalman touches intermittently on both ends of the continuum. One has the impression of a soul ironically hindered in exploring its most passionately felt necessity precisely because the person has become the locus for others who hunger after the very insights and illumination that exploration has produced.

This, of course, was very much Merton's case as well: in letters to one obviously troubled soul during the mid-60s, Merton repeatedly, and with an ever-greater degree of exasperation, insists that he is not a "guru" and does not wish to be one. The reader even senses, in this one case, a certain undertone of relief when the increasing constriction on the part of his superiors of Merton's contacts with the outside world force him to curtail this particular correspondence.

Schachter, however, had not the monastic structure to constrain – or protect – him from constant involvement with would-be followers, genuine disciples, the demands of academe, and other calls on his time and energy. Several of his letters are concerned with practical, ephemeral details such as plans for visits and complaints about traffic and the like; one has the impression that Reb Zalman preferred and prefers to express himself orally rather than in writing. But when his letters do address more fundamental themes, they go to the deepest level.

Where Reb Zalman sees no problem with using christological terms to express Jewish mysticism, Father Louis perceives the underlying oneness in the vision. We see the following comments from Merton (again in *The Hidden Ground of Love*) made in February. 1962, crystallizing Merton's vision of the spiritual essence of the relationship between Christianity and Judaism.

"Guess what, I just got through reading *The Last of the Just* [a novel by Andre Schwarzbart joining the Jewish legend of the 36 Just Ones who bear the suffering of the world to the suffering of a child in the *Shoa*]. I think it is a really great book. It has helped crystallize out a whole lot of things I am thinking about."

"Chief of these is of course no news to anyone: that the Jews have been the great eschatological sign of the twentieth century. That everything comes to depend on people understanding this fact, not just reacting to it with a little appropriate feeling, but seeing the whole thing as a sign from God, *telling* us. Telling us what? Among other things, telling Christians that if they don't look out they are going to miss the boat or fall out of it, because the antinomy they have unconsciously and complacently supposed between the Jews and Christ is not even a very good figment of the imagination. The suffering Servant is One: Christ, Israel. There is one wedding and one wedding feast, not two or five or six. There is one bride. There is one mystery, and the mystery of Israel and of the Church is ultimately to be revealed as One. As one great scandal maybe to a lot of people on both sides who have better things to do than come to the wedding."

By February of 1964, their relationship had deepened to the point where Reb Zalman could share some of his more intimate concerns, finding time for a spiritual life in a life of activity. The extraordinary meditation on what has been called the dark night of the soul written in that month, evidently evoked by some copy of Merton's published or mimeographed writing, illuminates Schachter's inner struggle, reflects his confidence in Merton's understanding, expresses the essence of mystical experience, and is an extraordinary passage in itself.

The remainder of this Jewish correspondence engages both the social and the spiritual aspects of Merton's concerns. Rabbi Steven Schwarzschild adds insight to Merton's involvement in the anti-war movement; Dr. R. J. Zwi Werblowsky primarily engages his interest in Jewish mysticism. Both are vital to Merton's "wedding" of Christians and Jews. Finally, as an addendum to the letters, Rabbi Lou Silberman shares reminiscences of his two visits to Gethsemani.

A chronological chart of the correspondence concludes this chapter.

SELECTED LETTERS TO THOMAS MERTON
FROM JEWISH CORRESPONDENTS

In the correspondence below, only letters or passages of letters from Merton that bear so directly on the topics of his correspondents' letters as to be necessary in understanding them are included. For the reader's convenience, references to previously published letters are otherwise included as notations in their chronological places. The texts have been modestly edited with respect to spelling and punctuation.

Erich Fromm

Dr. Erich Fromm (1900-1980), German-born psychoanalyst, philosopher, and social critic, was described by Merton as an atheistic mystic. After moving to New York City, he encountered such other seminal thinkers as psychologist and social theorist Karen Horney. Fromm's own theories, developed under the influence of both Freud and Marx, are notable for their departure from the deterministic bent of both older thinkers. His emphasis on the freedom of the human spirit and the necessity to connect with one's society in a non-authoritarian relationship formed the basis of his common ground with Merton. (Biographical notes from Dr. C. George Boeree, copyright © 1997, used with permission.)

We were unfortunate in not being able to obtain permission to publish the letters from Erich Fromm, with whom Thomas Merton had a lively, full, and moving correspondence over a period of twelve years (1954-1966). However, from the Merton side of the exchange, published in *Hidden Ground of Love*, we can get some sense of the topics they discussed. In general, they seem to have found common ground in their belief that all people could come together in terms of a sense of the value of the human person and the conviction that mysticism is not antithetical to humanism, in spite of the fact that Merton's thought grew from a theistic position that Fromm did not share.

Merton, who had been reading Fromm's books and finding parallels between his own experience as priest and the vocation of the psychotherapist, initiated the correspondence. The two thinkers explored issues in philosophical anthropology, such questions as whether one can be self-seeking even in self-sacrifice, and the spiritual dissonance created by the note of commercialism in some popular religious movements.

In 1955, Albert Einstein and Bertrand Russell, supported by such people as Lewis Mumford, Reinhold Niebuhr, and Fromm himself, issued a Manifesto warning of the dangers of continuing the nuclear arms race and stating that "nuclear weapons threaten the continued existence of mankind." Merton discussed this declaration with Fromm with sympathy for its aims, but as a cloistered monk could not sign it. (He and Fromm both supported SANE, The Committee for a Sane Nuclear Policy, an organization of private citizens seeking to alter official nuclear policies, formed in 1957.)

The conversation then moved to thirteenth-century Sufi poet Rumi, twentieth-century Catholic political philosopher Simone Weil, the myth of Prometheus, and Zen Buddhism.

There is a gap of several years; the correspondence resumed in 1959, when Merton sent Fromm his recent publication, *Prometheus, A Meditation* (U. of Ky: 1959, Ltd. Ed.). Apparently Fromm had also been sending his works to Merton, who had been studying Chinese philosophy and appreciating Fromm's interest in Zen. Merton proposed their writing something together with Daisetz Teitaro Suzuki, but the Buddhist scholar and philosopher of religion was 91 years old by then and the project never developed. (Merton did publish an essay, "Wisdom in Emptiness, A Dialogue: D.T. Suzuki and Thomas Merton," in *Zen and the Birds of Appetite,* New Directions, 1961.)

Both correspondents remained deeply concerned about government policies on nuclear armaments. Merton had published a piece on the atom bomb. Fromm had written an introduction to an English translation of some of Karl Marx's previously unpublished philosophical work, which Merton read and commented on in a letter of 1961. Fromm's comparison of Marx's concept of the unalienated human being to Zen as a non-theistic way to human integration especially struck Merton as significant.

Merton expressed his appreciation of Fromm's *May Man Prevail* (late 1961) and the possibility of a Catholic peace movement became a topic of correspondence. Catholics, Merton felt, were not being very forward in the more outspoken pacifist/disarmament proposals of the time. Merton was interested in Fromm's writing appearing in various symposia and journals concerned with peace issues, civil defense, and the highly distressing suggestion that a nuclear war killing "mere" millions would be survivable and acceptable. Merton was moved by the poem Fromm sent him, Yevgeny Yevtushenko's "Babi Yar," about the Russian ravine where the Nazis slaughtered thousands of Jews.

In 1962-1963, humanism as a spiritual necessity became a topic. Merton received an honorary LLD degree from the University of Kentucky and was presented with the PAX Medal for his outstanding contributions to the cause of world peace in 1963 – a year after the Cistercian Abbot General had instructed Merton's superior Dom James that Merton was to cease his publications on such issues.

Merton resumed the regular correspondence in 1966 as Fromm was finishing his work on *You Shall Be as Gods*. The book undertakes to demonstrate that the Hebrew Bible is revolutionary in character and has human liberation as its primary theme. In the mid-60s, a number of people were beginning to say that the phenomenon of the religious experience itself was not entirely dependent on its theological background, and that various traditions could understand one another at this level, even if they were deeply divided in terms of theology. Thus, even a tradition such as Zen, which has no theology, nevertheless promotes religious experience. Merton commented on this.

By late summer of 1966 the idea had come up of asking the Pope to convene a conference on solutions to present dangers to human survival, and Merton expressed enthusiasm about it, which Fromm shared. All sorts of people should be involved, some with a religious point of view, but also secular humanists and those working from political concerns. Threats to survival include thermonuclear warfare, environmental degradation, global poverty, and severe economic disparity. Merton felt that this would be a fitting sequel to the Second Vatican Council and to Pope Paul VI's recent encyclical, *Christi Matri Rosarii,* which called on nations to "come together and work out concrete plans" for living peacefully and justly together. Fromm responded with an extensive memorandum addressed to the Pope, making recommendations about the conference. The last letter we have from Merton to

Fromm is dated October 13, 1966, and ends with a plea to Fromm
to "keep [him] posted."

*Note: The letters of Erich Fromm to Thomas Merton are in the
possession of, and may be seen by application to, the University of
Kentucky Libraries Special Collections, Lexington, KY. For permission to
reprint, contact Dr. Rainer Funk, The Erich Fromm Archives, Ursrainer
Ring 24, D-72076 Tübingen, Germany. Some of Merton's side of the
correspondence is reprinted below; the dates of Fromm's letters are included
for ease of reference for researchers.*

October 2, 1954 Merton to Fromm

From The Hidden Ground of Love: The Letters of Thomas
Merton on Religious and Social Concerns, *William H. Shannon, ed.
(NY: Farrar, Straus, Giroux, 1985) pp. 308-311. Copyright © 1985 by
the Merton Legacy Trust. Reprinted by permission; all rights reserved.*

Some time ago when I was reading your *Psychoanalysis and
Religion* I thought I would write you a letter. Now that I am in the
middle of *Man for Himself* and am hoping to get *Escape from
Freedom,* I think I shall put a few of my thoughts on paper and
send them to you.

The chief reason for my writing is that since discovering Karen
Horney I have been revaluating my originally rather premature
judgment of psychoanalysis. Now that I am in contact with what is
best in the field at the moment, I would like to say that I notice a
profound agreement between the psychoanalyst and the Catholic
priest on some very fundamental points. I believe that this
agreement ought to be noticed and emphasized, because I feel that
our two vocations in a sense complete and assist one another. I also
feel that there is much in Christian tradition that fits in very well
with the general tendency of writers like Horney and yourself.

The reason for this is that Christianity is fundamentally
humanistic in the sense that its chief task is to enable man to achieve
his destiny, to find himself, to be himself: to be the person he is made
to become. Man is supposed to be God's helper in the work of
creating himself. *Dei adjutores sumus.* Salvation is no passive thing.
Nor is it an absorption of man into a kind of nonentity before the
face of God. It is the elevation and divinization of man's freedom.

And the Christian life demands that man be fully conscious of his freedom and of the responsibility it implies. I am in full agreement with your basic thesis on the humanistic conscience. I also observe with satisfaction that you emphasize the mystical element in religion. In fact, Christian humanism and Christian mysticism coincide. "Where the Spirit of the Lord is, there is liberty."

At a time like the present, when over vast areas of the earth systems of thought and government are tending to the complete debasement of man's fundamental dignity as the image of God, it seems to me important that all who take to heart the value and the nobility of the human spirit should realize their solidarity with one another, and should be able to communicate with one another in every way, in spite of perhaps grave doctrinal divergences. I know indeed that in France Catholicism and psychoanalysis are not now considered to be in any way mutually exclusive. In fact there are priests who are practicing psychoanalysts – though this should not be regarded as normal. There are congresses in which the priest and the analyst join in giving papers and conducting discussions that further the spiritual life of Christians. I believe that there is an association of priests in this country interested in psychiatry, but I do not know any of them.

As spiritual director of some thirty young monks in this Trappist monastery – monks in the crucial period of their formation, who have been in the monastery between two and six years, – I fully realize the wisdom of what you have to say about types of conscience and modes of conscience formation and malformation. You can well realize that I run into all kinds of difficulties and problems precisely where an "authoritarian" conscience is allowed to have its way. It is pitiful to see the harm that can be done in potentially fine monks by the pettiness and formalism they can get into as a result of making their whole life depend entirely on the approval of another.

If you have read the Rule of St. Benedict, you can realize that I seem to be faced with an insoluble problem. But I do not think the position is as bad as that. It is true that the Rule of St. Benedict presupposes a long period of formation in which the whole spiritual life is summed up in the two words "obedience" and "humility." I know that it is also true that men who are, in your terminology, "authoritarians" can wreak havoc on themselves and others by a narrow and absolute view of what St. Benedict means. Obedience for its own sake, humility for its own sake.

However, familiar as I am with ancient monastic tradition, I am convinced that it is possible to take the true Benedictine idea just as it stands and make it the foundation of a life of spiritual freedom and "humanism" and "mysticism" in the best sense. I am sure that is what St. Benedict intended. The function of obedience, in his context, is not merely to bring the monk into submission to authority as if the authority were everything. It simply presupposes that in the beginning he does not know how to go about living the monastic life and needs to be told, and that the more he is willing to be open to suggestion and formation, the better off he will be. But if we consider the Rule closely we find that the mature monk is a very capable and many-sided person, completely integrated, leading a life of freedom and joy under the guidance of the Holy Spirit rather than out of servile fear. In fact, servility is the exact opposite of the Christian and monastic spirit.

I think that in your treatment of obedience and authority you are perhaps too absolute – but this is quite natural, since you have in mind Nazi authoritarianism, than which I can think of nothing more abominable. But in the monastic life I think we are quite entitled to "escape" from certain responsibilities – those of worrying about how to plan meals, what to wear, when to get up, when to go to bed, how to plan our social life etc. – in order to be free for something better.

Finally on one point I think you are definitely wrong. I do not see how you can consider that mystical religion is indifferent on the question of the objective existence of God. Jnana yoga and perhaps Buddhism are more or less atheistic, but the majority of true mystics stand or fall with the existence or non-existence of God. Besides there is, it seems to me, the absolute ontological impossibility of anything existing if God does not exist. However, I have argued on that point long and uselessly enough not to start it again. I think what you are really saying is that true mysticism does not know God after the manner of an object, and that is perfectly true. God is not experienced as an object outside ourselves, as "another being" capable of being enclosed in some human concept. Yet though He be known as the source of our own being, He is still *das ganz Anders*. Surely you know Rudolph Otto's work. And do you think God was not real to the Prophets?

However, I did not write to emphasize our differences. I simply want to take this opportunity to express my appreciation of your work, and to thank you for the thoughts you have suggested, which have been of great value in my own work. I hope I can someday do the same for you.

December 8, 1954 Fromm to Merton

March 18, 1955 Merton to Fromm in Hidden Ground of Love, *p. 311*

April 13, 1955 Fromm to Merton

September 12, 1955 Merton to Fromm in Hidden Ground of Love, *p. 313*

October 28, 1955 Fromm to Merton

October 30, 1958 Fromm to Merton

September 26, 1961 Merton to Fromm in The Hidden Ground of Love, *p. 315*

October 9, 1961 Fromm to Merton

November 14, 1961 Merton to Fromm in The Hidden Ground of Love, *p. 316*

November 23, 1961 Fromm to Merton

[Enc: "Babi Yar" by Yevgeny Yevtushenko, headed "Yevtushenko's Poem about Babi Yar and Anti-Semites"]

December 1961 Merton to Fromm in The Hidden Ground of Love, *p. 317*

January 30, 1962 Fromm to Merton

February 16, 1962 Merton to Fromm in The Hidden Ground of Love, *p. 319*

February 26, 1962 Fromm to Merton

September 10, 1963 Fromm to Merton

October 8, 1963 Merton to Fromm in The Hidden Ground of Love, *p. 320*

January 15, 1966 Merton to Fromm in The Hidden Ground of Love, *p. 321*

February 7, 1966 Fromm to Merton

April 27, 1966 Merton to Fromm in The Hidden Ground of Love, *p. 327*

August 25, 1966 Fromm to Merton

September 16, 1966 Memo Enclosure, Fromm to Merton:

Memorandum
Re: Papal Conference on Solutions to the Present Dangers to the Survival of Mankind.

October 13, 1966, Merton to Fromm in
The Hidden Ground of Love, p. 322:

...The idea is a splendid one and I am sure Pope Paul would consider it very seriously. My own reactions are these. First of all I think it would be better in ways if it were not in Rome. But that all depends. To my mind it ought to be in Latin America perhaps, say Mexico City itself. This would be impressive and would perhaps serve to underline the fact that the conference would be entirely free of the influence of any great power bloc. But of course there may be reasons for having it in Rome. But does Rome mean to everyone just what we would like this conference to mean?

I think too your title – a conference "on solutions to the present dangers to the survival of mankind" is very telling. It could almost be a kind of secular "Council" following up and implementing what the Vatican Council barely suggested in some lines; and if we consider *all* the dangers to the very great and immediate danger of global war. I would say by the way that it is not just a question of *thermonuclear* war. It is possible that we may see an entirely savage and barbarous war in China soon, waged without nuclear weapons – but with just about everything else under the sun! I know that your prospectus as it stands allows for all this. Certainly it is a matter of very great urgency. The total war seems to be more and more imminent in Asia. I doubt if there remains another year.

In any event, I am heartily in agreement that it would be very effective indeed for the Pope to call this conference, and I think this should somehow [be] done with such authority and force (moral not juridical) that the U.S. would be shamed into slowing down its escalation and holding back from an invasion of North Vietnam and China. This in itself would be an achievement. Then perhaps the conference might be able to bring the whole affair to the point of negotiation and the next World War be averted. It would be a tremendous thing, and I think there is a very real hope. Do keep me posted (actually I suppose that having it at Rome would be more practical for quick planning. The Pope would have a hard time calling it somewhere else maybe.)...

Abraham Joshua Heschel

The letters of Rabbi Dr. Abraham Heschel to Thomas Merton are contained in "The Merton–Heschel Correspondence" in this volume. A chronology of the correspondence is below.

October 23, 1960 Heschel to Merton

January 26, 1963 Merton to Heschel in The Hidden Ground of Love, *p. 431*

On July 13, 1964, Heschel visited Merton at Gethsemani to discuss the Vatican Declaration on Christian-Jewish Relations

July 27, 1964 Merton to Heschel in The Hidden Ground of Love, *p. 432, with enclosed copy of Merton's letter to Cardinal Augustin Bea of July 14 (*The Hidden Ground of Love, *p. 433)*

September 3, 1964 Heschel to Merton, Enclosure of Heschel's Memorandum to the Council Fathers.

Zalman Schachter-Shalomi

Born in Vienna in 1930 and raised in the Orthodox Jewish Lubavitch branch of the Hasidic tradition, Rabbi Dr. Zalman Schachter in 1962 founded P'nai Or (Faces of Light) Religious Fellowship. Now called ALEPH: the Alliance for Jewish Renewal, the movement is characterized by egalitarian liturgy and Hasidic-style ecstatic prayer. He has written and spoken widely on Jewish mysticism and related topics. He added the hyphen and "Shalomi" (my peace) to his name after the Camp David peace accords were signed; he has said he will drop the "Schachter" altogether if peace is ever actually achieved in the Middle East. Currently at Naropa University in Boulder, CO, he was at the time of his correspondence with Merton director of B'nai B'rith Hillel at the University of Manitoba in Winnipeg, Canada.

December 12, 1960 Schachter to Merton

Xmas continues through the feast of the *b'rith* ["covenant," written in Hebrew in the original] the circumcision on to Epiphany. So a very Merry Xmas to you and your brothers. Jerry Steinberg told me of his visit and asked that I send to you the "step" and some other materials – it is on the way via surface mail. Please pray for my intention – you and all your other religious problems have been on my intercession list for a while. We'll visit with Dom Fulgence for Matins soon.

January 18, 1961 Merton to Schachter in The Hidden Ground of Love, p. 533

April 2, 1961 Merton to Schachter in The Hidden Ground of Love, p. 534

December 15, 1961 Merton to Schachter in The Hidden Ground of Love, p. 534

January 29, 1962 Schachter to Merton

Allow me to thank you for the two books. I like *The New Man* a whole lot and am, when reading your work, involved in a very curious, almost unconscious process. You see, all the christological references are now almost without effort translated into their Hasidic counterparts, so that I am not really very conscious of its

Christian origin. This gets me into some incongruous situations. At a seminar on existentialism I started reading some of the things you had to say and did not notice for the first ten minutes how the countenances of my good flock began to be clouded. I asked them if anything was wrong and they told me that they could not understand how I could read the materials without an apology for the christological terms. We had a ball afterwards.

I liked what you did to Buber, unmasking the I of man in the confrontation. As a constantly grace-given being, I started marking up your book with a number of Aha's and parallels, atta-boys, etc. It is the sort of thing that is difficult to put into a letter and is best done in conversation. With G-d's help, this may happen in August, when D.V. I get through with the B'nai B'rith Institute in Tennessee. I have already marked August 8th, 9th and 10th in my calendar for Gethsemani.

Steven Schwarzschild has asked me to ask you for your articles. I am sending my copies to him so send me others — of the 3 on the war and the CW [Cold War]. Chances are that he will use it not directly and this would be more comfortable for you, but rather review it as part of his quarterly review of modern theological literature. He has mentioned you already in his discussion of the liturgical movement and I will ask him to send you an off-print of that. His warning not to mess around with too much vernacularisation ought to be heeded....

February 1, 1962 Schachter to Merton

Enclosed you will find a copy of a letter to Mr. Joseph Manella who is the head of the Kibbutz of the Jubalites. They are described in Herbert Weiner's *Wild Goats of Ein Gedi*. (If you don't have a copy in any of your libraries, I will ask Herb to send you one.) He also translated *The First Step* into Hebrew, and, honestly, it makes better reading in Hebrew than in English.

In short, they are a group who have organized kibbutz fashion to live a religious life, though they find their way to tradition at this point blocked.

Manella has been in Europe just now, visiting various communities with special emphasis on the French Protestant monks [Taizé] and the oekumenische Marienswesternschaft in Halberstadt, as well as the Michaelsbrueder. I sent him the enclosed letter. Will you please send him *Spiritual Direction and Meditation*, as well as *The Silent Life* and some of the smaller pamphlets.

Your "Target Equals City" I read and the horror of this thing is continually increasing. I sent it to Steve Schwarzschild for his Current Theological Review in *Judaism*.

February 2, 1962 Enclosure, copy of letter from Schachter to Joseph Manella

...You ask if I can send you some of the books of Thomas Merton. There are a number of books that you should have...

To me it seems that the most important books by Thomas Merton are: *New Seeds of Contemplation* (try also to get a copy of the first edition of *Seeds of Contemplation*, which is inexpensive in its pocket book form); *Bread in the Wilderness, The New Man, No Man Is an Island, The Sign of Jonas, The Silent Life, Spiritual Direction and Meditation, Wisdom of the Desert, Ascent to Truth, The Waters of Siloe*, and *The Secular Journals of Thomas Merton* (also available in pocketbook form). As you see there will be quite a Heshbon [Hebrew for bill for expenses]. I will ask Thomas Merton to send you in the meantime and bill to me *The Silent Life* and *Spiritual Direction and Meditation* and then he has a number of smaller pamphlets on the Monastic Vocation n.f.s. which I will ask him to send to you.... These books, I think, are very, very important to you, because they deal with the spiritual life in the monastic setting in an indirect way....

Handwritten notation to Merton

If you have the chance, a little word of encouragement to them will be appreciated....

February 24, 1962 Merton to Schachter in The Hidden Ground of Love, *p. 536*

May 21, 1962 Merton to Schachter in The Hidden Ground of Love, *p. 533*

September 11, 1962 Merton to Schachter in The Hidden Ground of Love, *p. 533*

October 15, 1962 Merton to Schachter in The Hidden

Ground of Love, *p. 536*

January 11, 1963 Merton to Schachter in The Hidden
Ground of Love, *p. 537*

August 3, 1963 Merton to Schachter in The Hidden
Ground of Love, *p. 537*

November 24, 1963 Schachter to Merton

I have already sent you, by surface mail, the book by Lou
Jacobs – *Tract on Ecstasy.* I would greatly appreciate it if after you
read through it, you would send it on to Gerald Heard…. Before I
could get the copy for you, I had written out a long letter all about
apophatic mysticism and how Rabbi Dov Baer can be compared to
so-and-so, but now that you have the book you can draw your own
conclusions. If you have managed to have gotten a copy, then please
send this right on to Gerald Heard. If not, then would you please
(this is one of the conditions of the loan) as you read it, mark it with
pencil as to comparisons and so forth. That will make the reading of
the book, for me, a great delight. I will then ask Gerald to do the
same thing. I know your handwritings apart. By the way, you must
get also a copy of Gerald's *Five Ages of Man.* In fact, the parallels that
suggest themselves between these two books and Juan de la Cruz –
anyhow, read the book yourself and enjoy it. I still have not heard
from Tom Glover and I still have not yet written to him a third
letter. Margaret Bradbury, his friend in Detroit, asked me to write to
him. I have been waiting for an order. I have not yet received it. I
hope that at the right moment I may deserve to be an instrument
of grace for Tom.

   The local monks have promised to badger Father Abbot to
request your release for a retreat. My hope, of course, is that you
would still be in transit on Friday night and Saturday so that you
could spend a Sabbath with me. Even better would be if it would
turn out to be Passover. So, I say to myself, "Zalman, stop
dreaming. What will you leave for the feast?"

   In case I have not yet sent the enclosed picture, I am sending
it to you now. It is from the monastery and school (not reformed
and are strict observants) at Oconomowoc, Wisc. Which most
probably is of Austrian or German foundation. The icon quality and

the gold inlay, the way in which the crucifix received more light below, makes it a very lovely picture to inspire you with great fervor and intensity on behalf of east and west union.

Handwritten note: The girl typed this today – Sunday. This was dictated Thurs – before Kennedy's assassination. And I am afraid of the eschaton.

December 24, 1963 Merton to Schachter in The Hidden Ground of Love, *p. 538*

February 1, 1964 Merton to Schachter in The Hidden Ground of Love, *p. 538*

February 6, 1964 Schachter to Merton

...It is so difficult to think about G-d, always being His errand boy, then I say to myself: "I didn't ask for the errand. It was sent to me. Maybe He wants my errands more than my meditations." Even the time I used to have for intercession, while driving to and from Campus, which is thirteen miles out of town, on my windshield visor there being a long list of people and I would glance up from time to time, and wherever I would feel for a moment arrested, I would take that name and offer a few rounds of favorite psalms or something for them, as well as make up my mind to offer charity on their behalf; but even this has been taken away from me. This little letter that I am dictating, is being done while I am driving. So, I will pray for you and please do pray for me, and we will keep in mind, won't we, that whatever curve we get pitched, we will try to bat. And after all, what is that business of the cross all about if not that.

I am sending you a transcript of a talk I gave on *LSD and the Ascent of the Soul of the Ba'al Shem Tov* to a group of colleagues at Oconomowoc, Wisconsin. There are so many Hebrew words, and I could not just clean the thing up, yet I think you will glance through this thing.

Just send the book on. Don't answer this as I won't expect any mail from you until a week after Easter.

And grit or no grit, Palm Sunday is a joke and Good Friday is not. I'm just reading the *Exemplar* of Henry Suso. (Don't take the word reading too seriously; there may be the off-quarter hour someplace). He has done me a great favor the other day by giving me back my table manners. Light a candle for him or something. Since he is not a saint, I don't know where in the calendar he fits, but there is also the story about his balk.

What you say about the Order, the reforms that they will want, I hope that wisdom will prevail over understanding and that the special vocation of Citaux remain what it is intended to be.

All the prayers of the next Sabbath I will offer for you and for your intentions and for your wellbeing, whatever they* be worth. (*My prayers)

February 13, 1964 Schachter to Merton

Your latest thing on dread coincides with much that has been happening to me lately, and if you would not be at Gethsemani, that is to say, at a monastery in which silence is important, I would want to send you a tape in which I could express myself to you, without the medium of a secretary transcribing things (as usual I am dictating this on my way to Campus in the morning), because it takes something less anchored down than the written word to convey some of the echoes and reactions to that paper. This may seem to be a trite reaction but I thought that [Morris] West did very well in *The Shoes of the Fisherman,* portraying just this aspect of dread. It is interesting that for most modern men the angels are less important than they used to be at one time. Perhaps one of the sources of dread and awe in the past, was the angelic choir. It was easier to think of the angels and of their fervor and of their being lost in the presence of G-d, and what we got was a secondary reaction of the dread from the angels. In fact, it still is in our liturgy and in yours, and yet, you demand and rightfully so, a much stronger discipline; now that was a bad word, but I don't know what other word you can give it.

Of late, in writing some of my friends who reacted to [Reform] Rabbi [and Union of American Hebrew Congregations President Maurice] Eisendrath's statement in one way or another, I felt that our problem is not so much to come to terms with the Jesus of the Gospels – that is easy. Midrash and the early fathers of the Jewish faith parallel the Gospels so closely that we have no problem whatsoever in that. At one time I thought that the epistles were the farthest away from Judaism, but even this is not quite so. There is enough of the antinomian demand not to seek in the fulfillment of the commandments a defence against the true belonging to G-d that comes out of a committed faith. This, too, is not a problem; and the problem that remains a problem is not something that we can handle conceptually. That is, to come to terms with the Passion, and of this, I am personally convinced, having had some experiences in that direction. (This I did not write out in that LSD report that I sent you.) If the Passion would merely stand for physical suffering then it is nothing; Policarp too, and Steven and countless other martyrs were able to do this, being sent on their martyr voyage amidst certitudes and harmonies and glories it is all together different; when, in taking upon oneself peccata mundi he takes upon himself also the alienation of peccata mundi, where there is no support. In fact, there is not even the momentary support that a Kierkegaardian begins [with], and in this you are close to Kierkegaard but not that close, and surely not identical. In Kierkegaard at least you have the security that comes from committing oneself to leap, and so the initial impetus comes from man's own leaping. What you are describing is a falling in which suddenly the ground from one's feet has been ripped and one falls into a vertigo in which not a single coordinate remains where it is, where every bit of security and sureness is gone, and one falls, falls, falls, if only one were sure, into the hands of the living G-d. At the moment one falls one is under no assurance that underneath there are the Eternal Arms. How gladly one would exchange this for the greatest awe that comes from certitude.

The story is told of how Reb Zusheh of Anipoli loved G-d and said: "Dear L-rd, grant me some of the awe that your angels experience," which G-d granted him, whereupon Reb Zusheh crawled underneath the bed; unable to take any more of this, he implored G-d: "Please give me back the love that Zusheh has, and take away the angels' awe." But this kind of awe and here, look who is talking, as if I had enjoyed or been threatened by it, sure it must be something holy and tremendous, but this is not what you are talking about, because this too would be welcome, and much more easily endured than the dread of utter emptiness which you describe. In Reb Zusheh's awe, you have at least the consensus of the angels, you have a radiance of light and not a darkness.

The dread which you describe would also find a very real relief in death, if death were oblivion. Almost to a point where the soul under dread would welcome any kind of non-being [rather] than being where there are no coordinates with one's own falling, and yet in this falling one refuses to die, because perhaps this is the grace which allows man to die to himself, and thus find a ground in his being. But all kinds of holy schemes present themselves in the middle of this falling, hoping to have heard even the impact with the ground or to prolong one moment of the fall that could turn into a life, and then to build a theology out of askewness, but the fall is a tumbling, and while there may be a moment of quiet in the falling there surely is not a lifetime and a theology of it.

And there may be another moment of being a wheel in the gigantic clock, but even that can't be arrested, and so every time a death presents itself, or sneaks in between death and oneself, or between G-d and oneself, a little bit of a bargain [appears], who wants to say, all right, I'm glad, I'll die, but give me this assurance or that assurance, or I will be glad to die as long as...., or I will be glad to die providing that..., and even if this has to be rejected, as it certainly must at the end, the joy to expand that moment of the deal with all the warm, womby security it seems to give.

Or there may be something that is happening between you and me, right now, or that is happening between countless lovers. Lovers may cling to each other in the fall in order to have at least one coordinate of warmth and assuredness as it is in the tumble of love. There is a mighty pull to build around that moment of love so that I, too, will not be alone but with you, and maybe in my tumbling, I'm like Dismas looking for assurance in the last moment of dying, and even if you were to give it to me, or if I were to give this to others, in the last moment, you and I would have to bear our own total abandonment, being unprotected by *our* G-d, in fact, being completely unsure of [there] ever existing a covenant between us and G-d, so that we frantically can look for the covenant policy so that we can put in a claim, can't find it and must yield, and then to come with the poor ones, the word faqir, the whirling, tumbling dervishes who chant the beloved name of Allah, and find themselves in joy which can only be innocent because of the truth behind their tumbling.

Tom, I thank you very much for what you have done for me, and I would like to ask you for about fifteen copies of each as I would like to be able to share them with others. If there is anything that I can send you, don't hesitate to say it. At this moment, I am even ashamed for offering you a bargain, and a covenant of this sort, and I suppose that grit is a whipping and a lashing not with one whip, but with a host of tiny, tiny ones, and your beating the air is not your beating but your being lashed by the countless molecules of air. It is not a big heroic kind of mortification.

April 7, 1964 Merton to Schachter in The Hidden Ground of Love, *p. 539*

April 25, 1964 Merton to Schachter in The Hidden Ground of Love, *p. 539*

May 6, 1964 Merton to Schachter in The Hidden Ground of Love, *p. 540*

November 28, 1964 Merton to Schachter in The Hidden Ground of Love, *p. 540*

December 1, 1966 Schachter to Merton, taped communication

Shalom – Pax – Enchanté – Om – "tah-tah" – and all the good!

Today is a day. Yesterday was freezing rain and a blizzard. Driving is really terrible. I'm not quite with you then, so have to watch driving a bit. This week is loused up something terrible. Because of the freezing rain, I couldn't get back to meet two classes of mine. They wouldn't land in Winnipeg. I needed that day like a breath of air. Have to leave on Thursday again which means canceling a couple of classes. Everything is so compact that it's terrible.

And I want to say I love you! How's your back and the bones and everything else that goes with it? So, just in case you might think that a vocation in the world is nicer, I just told you...

I was in Montreal, talked to some of the people of the Bucke Memorial Society. One in particular sends regards and regrets the embargo on communications. This being also the cause of my concern for your health. I mean – you know – all that jazz, but the Abbey of the Prairies here would be a nice exile where one could relax, come to one's strength, not be bugged, and so forth.

But anyhow... I talked to a group of kids in Montreal under the auspices of Hillel on the question of the war. I wanted them to share with me my struggles of the difficulty of making any kind of "pronunciamento" especially that they felt the basic unsaved exilic condition in which we are and the conviction that says that, before the Messias, the body of the world has to bleed a little some place. Maybe that all the peace efforts ought to be directed to keep the bleeding down to a minimum.

I can see where we, sooner or later, will get to the point where we will send one man to the moon, the Russians will send another man to the moon, and between the two men there will be a battle. We would be able to call on volunteers who'd be willing to be the sacrifice for the rest of mankind so there wouldn't be any war elsewhere. This could keep the whole machinery going in an economy that's built on very heavy hardware and so forth. Standard of living. In every year we'd have a few more peaceniks volunteer. I suppose I'd volunteer too if I knew that this would stop the rest of the stuff. And we'll have big bonfires every night – you know – when there's a new moon and the moon will burn up all the napalms so it can be seen all the way to the earth.

Will you tell someone to mail me a copy of *Conjectures of a Guilty Bystander*, and enclose a bill. I'll send a check in when I get it. I'd like to have a word inside there from you...You never answered me since I sent you that thing on *Life* magazine. I'd like to get a word, just hello, or goodbye, or "go to hell," or something from you. So at least I know you're alive. Otherwise I get all kinds of schemes in my head – like Thomas Merton is a prisoner in a Catholic cookie factory or cheese and every noble impulse wants me to come down to Kentucky and pull you out. At the same time, I know that you have no such problem and you are there because you want to be there and it was part of your life struggle and what have you. But, just a word would always be good. For the time being I have nothing more to say, so I'm sending you only this one thought – Just, I love you!

Rabbi Dr. Steven S. Schwarzschild

Rabbi Dr. Steven S. Schwarzschild, 1924-1989, editor of the scholarly journal Judaism, *would be appointed the first professor of Jewish studies at Washington University, St. Louis, in 1965. At the time of his correspondence with Merton, he was a professor at Brown University.*

February 1, 1962 Schwarzschild to Merton

Zalman Schachter has just sent me several of your recent essays. I had seen the one in *The Catholic Worker* earlier.

I read "Christian Ethics and Nuclear War" and was much relieved by it. It gave me a lift after the gravely depressing experience of reading Paul Ramsey's *War and the Christian Conscience.* You may have seen the booklet put out by the Church Peace Vision in which mine is the only pacifist reaction to Fr. J. C. Murray.

The essays Zalman sent me I cannot, of course, use in *Judaism* because they are specifically Christian. (I have discontinued my theological review column in the journal since taking over its editorship.) But I would be very eager to publish something from your pen. Is there anything you would want to say re Judaism, Israel, the mystical tenor and task in our time, etc.? I should be happy to hear from you.

I take the liberty of enclosing a few diverse reprints of my column now taken over by someone else.

February 7, 1962 Schwarzschild to Merton

As an addendum to my recent note: I have just read your essay "Target Equals City."

You are, of course, entirely and significantly right. But I want to make one additional point in this connection (it is a theoretical point which does not detract in the slightest from the practical validity of what you say): upon consideration, must not your "nuclear pacifism" yield to "absolute pacifism"? Who can argue—or prove—that an invasion of Japan might not have cost more American and Japanese lives than the Hiroshima bomb? And this unanswerable question can equally be applied to the alternative "target-bombing *vs.* obliteration-bombing," etc. From this the bellicists invariably conclude that they may proceed from the latter to the former. Must we not teach the opposite – that the two are, indeed, in the last analysis indistinguishable and must, therefore, both be outlawed? (This, of course, would have to lead to a retrospective reconsideration of the entire doctrine of "just war." Think of the effect of *homo religiosus*, not to say "the Church," doing public penance for 2,000 years of un-Biblical, Greek-pagan doctrine and practice!)

One other thing: we have to yell louder! How about a public declaration of some religious leaders, you, Zalman, Uphaus, etc. – *à la* Bertrand Russell – of complete non-cooperation with the government (and not because we are anarchists like Dorothy Day, may G'd bless her, but precisely because we are parts of the religious Establishment)?

February 24, 1962 Merton to Schwarzschild in

From Witness to Freedom: Letters in Times of Crisis, *William H. Shannon, ed. (NY: Harcourt, Brace & Co., 1994) p. 35. Reprinted by permission.*

Thanks for your two very good letters. I am happy that Zalman sent you my texts on peace, for they have brought us into contact and have brought me your fine offprints, which I have very much enjoyed. The one on "Speech and Silence before God" is wonderful and very close to my own heart. Thank you for it.

As a matter of fact, I had also read your essay in *Worldview,* the collection of essays on nuclear war, gathered around the rather dubious witness of good Fr. [John Courtney] Murray [S.J.]. I felt that yours was the only voice that really spoke with a full and unequivocally religious note and really was loyal to the holiness of Him who is All Holy. It seemed to me that the others were not listening to His demands, and that from the book as a whole He was absent.

God's absence among religious people, among religious groups, His absence where it is claimed that He is worshipped, is something terrifying today. Or sad in the utter extreme, because it is not His wrath, exactly, it is His loneliness, His lostness among us. That He waits among us unknown and silent, patiently, for the moment when we will finally destroy Him utterly in His image ... And leave Him alone again in the empty cosmos.

It is the terrible power that He has given to man, that man can isolate himself and blast himself irrevocably into an outer darkness

210 · *Mary Heléne P. Rosenbaum*

where he is separated from Him Who is nevertheless everywhere. I cannot believe that this is designed to be irrevocable, but so we are told and so perhaps it is. How can it be? There are dimensions that we are not capable of investigating.

But at any rate let us finally have pity on Him, that we may return to ourselves and have pity on one another.

Certainly I think the unutterable pity of the fate of the Jews in our time is eschatological, and is a manifestation of the loneliness and dejection of God, that He should bring upon Himself so much sorrow and suffer it in His Beloved People. In this He is speaking to us who believe ourselves, in His mercy, to have been adopted into His Chosen People and given, without any merit, the salvation and the joy promised to the Sons of Abraham. But we on the other hand have been without understanding and without pity and have not known that we were only guests invited to the banquet at the last minute.

We have not lived up to our share in the promise and we have not been to Israel, as we were meant to have been, a consolation. It is terrible to see how little we have been that, so little that the irony is almost unbearable. Who notices this?

I am not worthy yet to write about the mystery of Judaism in our world. It is too vast a subject. I wish I could. Maybe someday. If there is anything I say en passant that happens to make sense to you, you can quote it if you like. The article will have to be a thing of the future, if God wills us to have a future on this earth. (I do not doubt that He does, but sometimes the chances are a little disconcerting.)

March 1, 1962 Schwarzschild to Merton

I think you are probably right. There are too many "statements" around these days anyway. Perhaps we ought to wait until soon, G.w., some of us can take action together. I imagine, *e.g.,* that you, Zalman, my friend Markus Barth of McCormick Seminary (Karl Barth's son), and perhaps I – and others of whom we might be able to think, if we were to keep a prayer-vigil together somewhere, perhaps at the White House, – perhaps G'd would listen to us.

R. J. Zwi Werblowsky

Dr. R. J. Zwi Werblowsky is professor of comparative religion at the Hebrew University of Jerusalem. He corresponded with Merton from Brown University, Providence, R.I.

July 11, 1963 Werblowsky to Merton

I take the liberty of writing to you, having been strongly urged to do so by our mutual friend, Rabbi Zalman Schachter of Winnipeg. Zalman came over from Camp Ramah, where he and his family are for the summer vacation, to Providence and we had one brief day together. He repeatedly urged me to spend a few days at Gethsemani, and actually asserted that you would not mind this imposition. ...

I am sending you, under separate cover, a small article on "Mystical and Magical Contemplation" among the 16th century kabbalists. It is the only offprint in English I have with me here. Unfortunately my paper on "The non-cognitive mysticism of St. John of the Cross" is in Hebrew.

It would be nice to spend a few days at a Trappist house. The prospect reminds me of the complaint of one of my friends in Jerusalem, Fr. Stiasny of N-D de Sion: the one thing he will never forgive the Israeli army is that they did not conquer Latrun! Indeed we have no Trappist house on the Israeli side of the Holy Land.

July 16, 1963 Merton to Werblowsky in The Hidden Ground of Love, *p. 586*

July 22, 1963 Werblowsky to Merton

Thank you for your good letter of 16th inst. And your kind invitation.

I was at the travel office today, and booked a flight to Louisville, scheduled to arrive on Thursday, 1 August....

A little talk on Hasidism will present no major difficulty, though it seems strange that I should find myself doing more talking even when visiting a Trappist house!

With all good wishes, and au revoir -D.v.- next week,

October 11, 1963 Werblowsky to Merton

... One request. When I was in Vermont, Abbot Leo asked me to talk to his monks. On one occasion I gave them my paper on St. John of the Cross, but in subsequent private talks I had with the monks I noticed that they were slightly disturbed by what I had said, particularly as they could not square it with their ideas about the Sacred Humanity as an object of meditation, etc. I told them that I didn't feel competent to discuss this point with them, but that Thomas Merton had said some very pertinent things on the subject. I also promised them to ask you to send them a copy of your stencil – I am sure that reading your talk on the subject may help them a great deal....

P.S. I had mentioned to Father Francis of Assisi that Buber had written a rejoinder to Scholem's criticism of his interpretation of Hasidism. At the time I only knew of a German version of Buber's reply (publ. in the *Neue Zurcher Zeitung*, literary supplement). I just phoned Buber to ask him about an English version, and he told me that a recent number of *Commentary* (vol. 36, no. 3, i.e. September 1963) carried his article "Interpreting Hasidism."

January 1, 1964 Merton to Werblowsky in The Hidden Ground of Love, *p. 586*

Lou H. Silberman

Lou Hackett Silberman was born in San Francisco, California on June 23, 1914. He attended Hebrew Union College in Cincinnati, Ohio, earning a B.H.L. degree in 1939, and M.H.L. degree and ordination as a rabbi in 1941, and a D.H.L. degree in 1943. Silberman served as a rabbi until 1952, when he left the rabbinate to become a professor of Jewish literature and thought at Vanderbilt University in Nashville, Tennessee. In 1955 Silberman was promoted from associate professor to the position of Hillel Professor of Jewish Literature and Thought. He has authored numerous publications dealing with such topics as the Dead Sea Scrolls, rabbinic literature, and contemporary theology.

RECOLLECTIONS OF THOMAS MERTON'S GETHSEMANI

My first meeting with Thomas Merton took place in 1949 at Matthew's Bookstore in Omaha, Nebraska, when Miss O'Leary handed me a book bound in what seemed to be burlap with green and white labels, saying, "I think you will find this interesting." It was a copy of *Seeds of Contemplation,* and indeed I found it more than interesting. My undergraduate degree had been in philosophy centered on medieval thought, primarily Thomistic, so that Merton's meditations pointed toward an unfamiliar avenue of Roman Catholic thought. Yet more important than the thought was the man shining through. That sometime in the future I would meet him never entered my mind.

Some years later – I was living in Nashville and teaching at Vanderbilt University – the unexpected opportunity arrived. Rabbi Zalman Schachter [-Shalomi], whom I knew through the Hillel Foundation, called me to inquire whether I would be interested in visiting the Abbey of Gethsemani in Kentucky. He had been in touch with Thomas Merton and had been invited to visit. I understand that he has described the visit and, lacking clear memory of the trip other than that we drove up through Tennessee and Kentucky to the Abbey near Bardstown, I am more than ready to accept his narrative.

My first clear recollection of the visit is of being in the tribune, the balcony at the rear of the nave of the monastery church, gazing out into the dim light of flickering candles, listening to the monks reciting the liturgies of matins and lauds. I felt transported to an utterly strange world, the world of Merton's meditations. Later on in the morning but still quite early, when Zalman and I were back in the tribune to attend the conventual mass, the abbot sent a lay brother up to invite us to come down into the nave. Looking around, I wondered which of the monks was Thomas Merton. The answer came quickly enough when I saw him coming toward us still wearing his choir robe – his angel wings – and a shining face with such an expression of joy as one seldom sees. It was Thomas Merton with all of his warmth, all his friendliness, his goodness shining forth.

Since Trappists have the discipline but not the vow of silence, our opportunity to meet with him was made possible because he was novice master. He invited Zalman and me to speak to the novices. Since the offices recited throughout the day contain many Psalms, I decided to share some thoughts about what I was teaching in the Vanderbilt Divinity School. I spoke about the contemporary scholarly approach to Psalms, particularly the new insights into their structure. One of the monks, Father Romano, was a scholar completely at home in contemporary biblical scholarship, so that we carried on a lively discussion. At one point, Zalman asked one of the monks about the problem of intention and attention: the question, in Jewish thought, of *kavana*. Did it ever happen that, surrounded by one's fellows, one's recitation became automatic, one's attention was diverted? "Yes," came the answer, "one is not always there."

Thomas had introduced us to each of the novices, so that we were involved with persons not abstractions. One of them had recently arrived from Canada, where he had been a member of a less restrictive order. (On a subsequent visit, I saw that he was gone. I asked Thomas what had happened, and he replied that the Trappists were not strict enough for him; he had become a Carthusian.)

We left the following day, grateful for the experience – most particularly for having been with Thomas Merton.

The following year, I received a letter from him inviting me to come to Gethsemani to talk to the novices about the Dead Sea Scrolls. I had mentioned that I had been working on some of them since their appearance in the early 50s, and he thought they – apparently the writings of a "monastic" group – would be of interest. He was correct. The discussion was animated, and exciting for me, reflecting as it did the novices' view of Qumran from a novel perspective.

By this time Thomas had been permitted to move out of the abbey proper into a hermitage on the grounds. This reflected his sense that his contemplative life was being overwhelmed both by his duties as novice master and by his urge to keep on writing. It seems to me, on reflection, that the move was self-defeating, for it made it more possible for an outsider such as I to impinge upon his time.

On the occasion of this visit, his other guests were the well-known Berrigan brothers, whose social action position was raising quite a stir. The conversation was more than lively. In the course of it, Thomas spoke of the way in which the Trappists were victims of capitalism. They originally came out into the wild forest of Kentucky to live a life of contemplation. In order to support themselves (they are not a mendicant order), they established a dairy farm. Over the years it became more and more successful, so that the Abbey became quite wealthy. There was, however, no way of spending the money; the Rule of the order had never anticipated this situation and so provided no way of dispersing wealth other than by establishing a daughter house in some remote place where it would require support until it could manage on its own. So periodically, a cadre of monks and lay brothers would be chosen, endowed, and sent off. That is what had happened to Father Romano. He had gone off to a remote region of Peru.

I never returned to Gethsemani after that second visit in 1963, but Thomas Merton has remained with me in a sheaf of poems he sent and in ten volumes on a shelf. Knowing him was a gift for which I have ever been grateful. I shall never forget the shining face of joy I saw one morning in a corridor at Gethsemani.

Lou H. Silberman February 15, 2002

CHRONOLOGY OF MERTON'S CONTACTS
WITH CORRESPONDENTS INCLUDED ABOVE

Fromm	Heschel	Schachter	Schwarzschild
3/18/55			
9/12/55			
9/30/60			
	12/17/60		
		1/18/61	
		4/2/61	
9/26/61			
11/14/61			
12/61		12/15/61	
2/16/62			
2/24/62		2/24/62	2/24/62
		5/21/62	
		9/11/62	
		10/15/62	
		1/11/63	**Werblowsky**
			7/16/63
		8/3/63	
10/8/63			
		12/24/63	
			1/1/64
		2/1/64	
		4/7/64	
		4/25/64	
	visit 7/13/64	5/6/64	
	7/27/64		
	9/9/64		
	10/28/64		
	12/6/65	11/28/64	
1/15/66			
4/27/66			
10/13/66	12/12/66		

MERTON–HESCHEL CORRESPONDENCE

Rabbi Dr. Abraham Heschel, 1907-1972, was professor of Jewish Ethics and Mysticism at the Jewish Theological Seminary of America from 1945 to 1972. A descendent of hasidic sage Dov Baer of Mezhirech, he was author of books on theology, medieval Jewish philosophy, and Jewish mysticism. His highly influential writing was complemented by his active engagement in the social issues of the day, particularly the cause of civil rights. He had a prominent role at the National Conference of Religion and Race in Chicago, 1953, which led to the march on Washington later that year, at which he delivered a major address; he marched with Dr. Martin Luther King, Jr. at Selma. Another cause with which he and Merton were in sympathy was that of peace: he helped organize and served as co-chair of Clergy and Laity Concerned About Vietnam.

Incomplete correspondence of Abraham Heschel and Thomas Merton preserved by the Merton Collection at Bellarmine College Louisville, Kentucky, and reproduced by the kind permission of Mrs. Abraham Heschel and The Thomas Merton Legacy Trust.

The Jewish Theological Seminary of America
Northeast Corner, Broadway and 122nd Street
New York, N.Y. 10027

October 23, 1960

Dear Father Merton:
   Your kind letter came as a precious affirmation of

what I have known for a long time: of how much there is we share in the ways of trying to sense what is given in the Word, in the things created, in the moments He continues to create; in the effort to counteract the desecration of stillness. For many good hours in reading some of your writings, I am indebted to you.

I am a very poor letter writer, and am ashamed of it. It certainly would be good to meet you. Near what city is Trappist?

I am sending you some books of mine. At the moment I am trying to complete a book on the prophets – a humiliating undertaking.

I cherish your statement: "How absurd it is ... to attach such overweening importance to our reflections and so little to the revelation itself." And still, reflect we must, only that all reflection fades when we get close to the light.

I hope very much to remain in touch with you with the request for forgiveness of the brevity and inadequacy of my letter.

Cordially,
Abraham J. Heschel

January 26, 1963
Dear Dr. Heschel:

It is a great pleasure to have received your fine book on the PROPHETS. I have been anticipating this for a long time, and my anticipation is not disappointed. It is a fine book, perhaps your very best. Or at least it is one that says a great deal to me. You take exactly the kind of reflective approach that seems to me most significant and spiritually fruitful, for after all it is not the prophets we study but the word of God revealed in and through them. They offer us examples of fidelity to Him and patterns of suffering and faith which we must take into account if we are to live as religious men in any sense of the word. The book is in many ways just the kind of reflection germane to monks, and I hope to be able to use it in conferences with the novices.

In any case it is a privilege to be able to share your own meditations on the prophets and indeed to find very little in those pages that I would not myself want to express in much the same way. Some day perhaps I will muster up courage to try the difficult task of saying what the Prophets must mean to a Christian: difficult because of the heritage of past interpretations and allegories. We have had the bad habit of thinking that because we believe the prophecies are fulfilled, we can consider them to be fulfilled in any way we please, that is to say that we are too confident of understanding this "fulfilment." Consequently the medieval facility with which the Kingdom of God was assumed to be the society inherited from Charlemagne. And consequently the even more portentous facility with which Christians did exactly what they accused the Jews of having done: finding an earthly fulfillment of prophecy in political institutions dressed up as theocracy.

The twentieth century makes it impossible seriously to do this any more, so perhaps we will be humble enough to dig down to a deeper and more burning truth. In so doing, we may perhaps get closer to you, whom the Lord has not allowed to find so many specious arguments in favor of complacent readings.

> With very best wishes,
> Most cordially yours,
> [Thomas Merton]

On July 13, 1964, Heschel visited Merton at Gethsemani to discuss the Vatican Declaration on Christian-Jewish Relations.

July 27, 1964

Dear Dr. Heschel:

Shortly after your visit, that warm and memorable occasion, which was a real and providential gift, I wrote this letter to Cardinal Bea. I have been meaning to send you a copy, and am only just getting around to it. Every time I approach any such statement, I am more deeply convinced of the futility of statements. But statements are easy. And the fact of not having made one when it was required can be a terrible and irreparable omission.

Your books and offprints arrived promptly. I am at the moment most involved in "The Earth is the Lord's" and "The Sabbath." I note that your preoccupation with the sanctification of time runs parallel to some ideas of my own in a recent ms I have sent to the publisher on Liturgy. But I am not at all satisfied with my book.

Fortunately I have received permission to publish the material on peace that was still swinging in the balance, I think, when you were here. That is a relief.

Please think of us when you are in this area again. The door is always open to you, if you let us know when you are coming. Also I would always be glad to hear any news, especially anything that may affect the Jewish Chapter in the Council, and other such things.

With best wishes and cordial friendship always, in the peace of the Lord.

[Thomas Merton]

Letter of Thomas Merton to Cardinal Bea

July 14, 1964
His Eminence, Augustin, Cardinal Bea
Secretariat for Christian Unity
Vatican City

Your Eminence:

Yesterday I had the very great pleasure of speaking at some length with Rabbi Abraham Heschel who visited us briefly here at the monastery. He spoke much of his hopes and fears for the Council and of course spoke very much of your Eminence and of the Jewish Chapter, which we all have so closely at heart, and concerning which we share a certain sadness, not devoid of hope.

Naturally, one such as I, who am very far from the scene, can offer no constructive help save that of prayer. But this may turn out in the end to be more efficacious than other means. In any event, the purpose of this letter is to assure your Eminence that I and my brothers here will certainly be praying that God may see fit to grant His Church the very great favor and grace of understanding the true meaning of this opportunity for repentance and truth which is being offered her and which so many are ready to reject and refuse. It is true that the Chapter can do much for the Jews, but there is no question that the Church herself stands to benefit by it spiritually in incalculable ways. I am personally convinced that the grace to truly see the Church as she is in her humility and in her splendor may perhaps not be granted to the Council Fathers if they fail to take account of her relation to the anguished Synagogue. This is not just a matter of a gesture of magnanimity. The deepest truths are in question. The very words themselves should suggest that the *ekklesia* is not altogether alien from the *synagogue* and that she should be able to see herself to some extent, though darkly, in this antitypical mirror. But if she looks at the picture, what she sees is not consoling. Yet she has the power to bring mercy and consolation into this mirror image, and thus to experience in herself the beatitude promised to the merciful. If she forgoes this opportunity out of temporal and political motives (in exactly the same way that a recent Pontiff is accused of having done) will she not by that very fact manifest that she is perhaps in danger of forgetting her own true identity? Is not then the whole meaning and purpose of the Council at stake?

These are some of the thoughts that run through my mind as I reflect on the present situation in the Church of God. I dare to confide them to your Eminence as a son to a Father.

Would it not perhaps be possible, theologically as well as "diplomatically," to meet the objections raised by those who fear to alienate the Moslems? This too is a theological question, in view of the fact that Mohammed, before the decision which led to the beginning of Islam, stood face to face with the Christianity that existed in Arabia at that time, so that there was for a moment question, in his mind, of embracing the Christian faith. In any event Christians and Jews together in the Koran occupy a privileged position as "people of the Book" and as spiritual descendents of Abraham. Perhaps this common theological root in the promises made to Abraham might bear fruit in a Chapter on antisemitism oriented to peace with *all* Semites and then with special emphasis on the relation of the Church and Synagogue and at least an implicit recognition of the long-standing sin of anti-Jewish hatred among Catholics.

In conclusion, turning to a more consoling topic, I can assure your Eminence that the possibilities of ecumenical contact afforded by the monastic Orders are great and in some ways unique. Here at this Abbey, already for many years, we have been receiving visits from groups of seminarians and ministers of various Protestant denominations, and of course these visits are now more frequent and more significant. The fruits, to say the least, are most encouraging. I thought your Eminence would be pleased to know this.

Begging the paternal blessing of your Eminence and assuring you once again of my humble and persistent prayers for these great intentions and for your Eminence personally,

I remain,
Your Eminence's most humble servant in Christ,

Abraham Heschel's Mimeographed Statement to the Second Vatican Council, [See Appendix A, Text I, p.341, and Text II, p.343] Sept. 3, 1964:

Chapter Four of the Schema on Ecumenism printed and distributed in November, 1963, to the Council Fathers, dealing with the "Attitudes of the Catholics ... toward the Jews," made special headlines around the world. Except for a few words, troublesome to the Jewish conscience, it represented a momentous declaration and was hailed as an event of historic importance.

Subsequently, this Chapter has been rewritten and the version now distributed to the Council Fathers as publicly reported is not only ineffective, but also profoundly injurious.

The omissions, attenuations and additions are so serious that, if adopted, the new document will be interpreted as a solemn repudiation of the desire which, to quote a distinguished American Archbishop, intended "to right the wrongs of a thousand years."

The new document proclaims that "the Church expects in unshakable faith and with ardent desire ... the union of the Jewish people with the Church."

Since this present draft document calls for "reciprocal understanding and appreciation, to be attained by theological study and fraternal discussion," between Jews and Catholics, it must be stated that *spiritual fratricide* is hardly a means for the attainment of "fraternal discussion" or "reciprocal understanding."

A message that regards the Jew as a candidate for conversion and proclaims that the destiny of Judaism is to disappear will be abhorred by the Jews all over the world and is bound to foster reciprocal distrust as well as bitterness and resentment.

Throughout the centuries our people have paid such a high price in suffering and martyrdom for preserving the Covenant and the legacy of holiness, faith and devotion to the sacred Jewish tradition. To this day we labor devotedly to educate our children in the ways of the Torah.

As I have repeatedly stated to leading personalities of the Vatican, I am ready to go to Auschwitz any time, if faced with the alternative of conversion or death.

Jews throughout the world will be dismayed by a call from the Vatican to abandon their faith in a generation which witnessed the massacre of six million Jews and the destruction of thousands of synagogues on a continent where the dominant religion was not Islam, Buddhism or Shintoism.

It is noteworthy that the Vatican document on Mohammedans makes no reference to the expectation of the Church for their conversion to the Christian faith. Is one to deduce from that that Islam offers a more acceptable way to salvation than Judaism?

Our world which is full of cynicism, frustration and despair, received a flash of inspiration in the ecumenical work of Pope John XXIII. For a few years all men of good will marvelled at the spiritual magnificence which he disclosed, and were touched by his reverence for the humanity of man. At a time of decay of conscience, he tried to revive it and to teach how to respect it. Mutual reverence between Christians and Jews began to fill the hearts. We ardently pray that this great blessing may not vanish.

It is our profound hope that during the course of the forthcoming third session of the Vatican Council, the overwhelming majority of the Council Fathers who have courageously expressed their desire to eradicate sources of tension between Catholics and Jews, will have an opportunity to vote on a statement which will express this sacred aspiration.

Abraham Joshua Heschel

September 9, 1964

Dear Dr. Heschel:

Your mimeographed bulletin referring to the revised Jewish chapter has just reached me.

It is simply incredible. I don't know what to say about it.

This much I will say: my latent ambitions to be a true Jew under my Catholic skin will surely be realized if I continue to go through experiences like this, being spiritually slapped in the face by these blind and complacent people of whom I am nevertheless a "collaborator." If I were not "working with" the Catholic movement for ecumenical understanding it would not be such a shock to take the three steps backward after each timid step forward.

I must however think more of people like Cardinal Bea who must certainly be crushed by this development.

The Psalms have said all that need to be said about this sort of thing, and you and I both pray them. In them we are one, in their truth, in their silence. *Haec fecisti et tacui,* says the Lord, of such events.

With warm and cordial brotherhood
[Thomas Merton]

September 10, 1964 in Dancing in the Water of Life: The Journals of Thomas Merton (Journals Vol. 5, *Harper Collins, 1997), pp. 142-143; reprinted by permission* [There are two (slightly different) versions of this text. The one printed here is the original as written in the Journal itself. The other, published in *A Vow of Conversation,* is Merton's own edited version. See Ron Miller's piece in this collection, p. 293. – Ed.].

...Abraham Heschel sent a memo on the new Jewish chapter. It is incredibly bad. All the sense has been taken out of it, all the originality, all the light, and it has become a stuffy and pointless piece of formalism, with the *incredibly* stupid addition that the Church is looking forward with hope to the union of the Jews to herself. As a humble theological and eschatological desire, yes, maybe; but that was not what was meant. It is this lack of eschatological and spiritual sense, this unawareness of the real need for *profound* change that makes such statements pitiable. Total lack of prophetic insight and even elementary compunction.

It is precisely in prophetic and therefore deeply humiliated and humanly impoverished thirst for light that Christians and Jews can begin to find a kind of unity in seeking God's will together. For Rome simply to declare itself, as it now is, the mouthpiece of God and perfect interpreter of His will for Jews (with the implication that He in no way speaks to them directly) is simply monstrous. It is perfectly true that the Church in the highest sense can indeed speak a message of prophecy and salvation to the Jews. But to say that the few blind juridical niceties of curial officials and well-meaning Council Fathers are the *only* source of light for the Jews today – this is absurd misunderstanding of the Church's mission. Reflect that the church in this rather imperfect sense (of Bishops, etc. Speaking more or less humanly and politically) delivered the Jews over to Hitler without a murmur (here and there helping a few individuals to escape, to make it less intolerable to conscience).

The Jewish Theological Seminary of America
September 18, 1964

Dear Friend,

My profound gratitude for your letter of Sep. 9. It moved me deeply. It was comfort at a very difficult moment.

There still is some hope left.

Affectionately,
A. J. Heschel

[Telegram to A. Heschel, by permission of the Merton Legacy Trust]

October 28, 1964

Gladly join you in interfaith statement and protest against hypocritical distortion of morality in this campaign; it is nauseating.

Merton

Jewish Theological Seminary
October 30, 1964

Dear Friend:
    Doctor Bennett and I were delighted to receive your telegram which was read at the news conference held yesterday afternoon at the Overseas Press Club.
    I am sure you know how often you are in my thoughts. Regretfully, I am a very poor letter writer.
    The overall picture in Rome is highly ambiguous. I would also like to call your attention to the editorial in the magazine AMERICA of October 31.★ I am sure that your reaction to the tone and content of that editorial will be the same as mine. I feel like crying.

In deep affection,
Abraham J. Heschel
Just received encouraging
words from Rome.

★"**Letter from the Council**"
America, October 31, 1964
By Donald R. Campion, S.J.
[Excerpt relevant to the Statement on the Jews]

Journalists took a new lease on life during our fifth week here. Actually, the affair began on Friday evening, October 9. That night and all of Saturday, Rome's unique tomtoms beat out a rumor that the declaration on religious liberty and on the Jews had hit a snag once more. The Secretariat for Promoting Christian Unity, one heard, had taken it on the chin from some undetermined power "higher up." This was on my mind in my last letter, when I wrote of "an affair that could eventually provoke a spreading crisis of confidence in the Council."

    Sunday, October 11, the story broke in Milan's *Corriere della Sera*, a daily with inner Vatican contacts. In brief, it reported that Cardinal Bea, head of the Unity Secretariat, had received two letters on Friday to the effect that "by higher command" the statement on the Jews should be reworked by a mixed commission and inserted into chapter 2 of the schema On the Church; that the religious liberty declaration be completely revised by a second mixed commission. Next came a report that the second body had to include Cardinal Michael Browne, Archbishop Marcel Lefebvre (superior general of the Spiritans), Fr. Aniceto Fernandez (master general of the Dominicans) and Bishop Carlo Colombo. Since three out of these four were publicly known as the staunchest opponents of the whole declaration, many inevitably felt uneasy.

Unlike some of last year's cliffhangers, this little drama seemed to end swiftly, quietly and reassuringly – at least for those concerned about the fate of two Council documents. On Monday, *Il Messaggero* told about a meeting of some European and American cardinals on Sunday. It resulted in a joint letter to Pope Paul expressing regret over innovations in the procedure that might threaten the conciliar spirit. Subsequently, the usually well-informed *L'Avvenire d'Italia* corrected some minor errors in the story and added names to the list of cardinals said to have signed the letter. (For the books, the full list now seems to have included: Frings, Liénart, Döpfner, Lercaro, Alfrink, Léger, Meyer, Ritter, Lefebvre, Silva, Henriquez, Landazzuri, Ricketts, Quintero, Koenig, Suenens, Rugambwa, Richaud and Feltin – quite a lineup, however you may look at it.)

Next came word that Cardinal Frings had an hour-long audience with the Holy Father on Tuesday evening, October 13. On Wednesday, no public announcement of any sort. But calm returned to the press hall and a certain indicative serenity ruled the ranks friendly to strong texts on religious liberty and the Jews. Thursday, all talk turned to news from Moscow of Khrushchev's dismissal for "hare-brained scheming." Gone was worry over such puzzles as how the letters to Cardinal Bea came to be written in the first place; what they really aimed to do; what could be done to insure that similar episodes did not trouble the Council again. There remained the lesson that prompt action by prominent Council figures could serve to alert the Pope and nip one more crisis in the bud. A felicitous outcome.

Dec. 6, 1965

Dear Rabbi Heschel:

This matter of business gives me opportunity to say "hello" and to hope you are well. Also to say how distressed I was about Dan Berrigan, and how thankful to you for your support of him. I don't suppose much has been done about it, but I do not get much news. If he is back in New York, by any chance, I wish you would let me know.

As to the business: it [...]. He wrote me telling me that he wanted to come down and converse with me about his dissertation [...]. Yet I have had to answer "No" because now I have been allowed to retire to a life of greater solitude and my Superiors have rightly required me to discontinue visits, at least of this kind, to give the experiment a good try.

[Paragraph omitted]

The solitary life I find very fruitful and in some ways disconcerting. It has brought me face to face with things I had never had to consider before, and I find that some pretty drastic revaluations have to be made in my own life. This keeps me busy. I would appreciate you remembering me in your prayer before Him whom we both seek and serve. I do not forget you in my own prayer. God be with you always.

Most cordially in His Spirit,
[Thomas Merton]

Dec. 6, 1966

Dear Dr. Heschel:

Father Abbot spoke to me of your phone call, something about an article on the Bible for *Life*? Or is it for a book in a series to be put out by *Life*? The project is not totally clear. Though I am not too happy with big fancy projects organized by the mass-media, I don't say "no" on principle: there is still room for "yes" if I can get a clearer idea of what is involved. Can you please tell me what it is? Fr. Abbot said you might drop by here and explain personally. That would be marvelous. But in any case, I need to know what the project is before I can commit myself finally. I sincerely doubt my capacity to write anything worth while on the Bible. I am not a pro. But if it is something within my powers I can at least think about attempting it.

I have still to thank you for a couple of books of yours which came in during the past months. I appreciate them very much though I have not yet finished both of them. I have found much that is very stimulating indeed in *The Insecurity of Freedom* and have been reserving *Who Is Man?* for a time of freedom and thoughtfulness. I should of course be always free and thoughtful but I get myself reading and thinking in terms of current work a lot of the time, and cannot always fit other things in.

In any case it is good to hear from you again however indirectly. I am as you know happily holed away in the woods where I belong and find the existence perfectly congenial. I could not ask for anything better, and in snow it is even quieter still.

I asked my publisher to send you a copy of my latest book and I hope they did so.

> With all my very best wishes
> and warm fraternal regards.
> [Thomas Merton]

The Jewish Theological Seminary of America
December 15, 1966

Dear Friend,

I had certainly hoped when I called to have the pleasure of hearing your voice. You are so often in my thoughts. There are concerns which I would love to share with you but Father Abbot explained to me how difficult it is for you to come to the phone.

I am very happy to know that you are finding your present way congenial. There are many moments when I too long for complete solitude.

By now Mr. Russell Bourne's letter must have reached you and described the project he has in mind. I have consented to serve as consultant because I believe that the work will be carried out with dignity and should help a great many people to find access to the Bible.

I was deeply moved by your piece on Thich Nhat Hanh. I look forward to receiving your new book; I will certainly cherish it. I am enclosing a short piece on Viet Nam.

> With warmest regards and
> best wishes, I am,
> Cordially yours,
> Abraham J. Heschel

"Worship is the climax of living. There is no knowledge without love, no truth without praise. At the beginning was the song, and praise is man's response to the never-ending beginning."

—Heschel, *On Prayer*

II

ABRAHAM JOSHUA HESCHEL AND THOMAS MERTON HERETICS OF MODERNITY*

Shaul Magid

"... do not concern yourself with being modern. It is the only thing, unfortunately, no matter what you do, that you cannot avoid being."

— Salvador Dali

I

Abraham Joshua Heschel and Thomas Merton are anomalies as twentieth-century religious figures.[1] They are simultaneously staunch defenders *of* tradition and sources of inspiration for those

*An earlier version of this paper was delivered at a conference entitled *Thomas Merton's Prophetic Stance* at the Corpus Christi Church, New York City, November 16, 1997. I'd like to thank Brenda Fitch Fairaday for giving me the opportunity to participate. This essay first appeared in *Conservative Judaism* L, 2-3 (Winter-Spring, 1998), pp. 112-125.
1 Thomas Merton (1915-1968), Trappist monk, political activist, writer and poet, was an inspiration for a whole generation of Christians seeking spiritual meaning in Catholicism, particularly in the monastic tradition. His autobiography, *The Seven Storey Mountain*, tells the story of a spiritual journey almost unparalleled in twentieth-century literature. He corresponded with Heschel during the 1960s on the issues of civil rights, spiritual renewal and ecumenical dialogue. Some of that correspondence was printed in the multi-volume collection of Merton's letters. See also Edward Kaplan, "Contemplative Inwardness and Prophetic Action: Thomas Merton's Dialogue with Judaism" in *Thomas Merton: Pilgrim in Process*, eds. Donald Grayston and Michael W. Higgins (Toronto, 1983), pp. 85-105.

alienated *from* tradition. Their writings have become the subject of studies among scholars of religion yet the nature of their discourse does not easily lend itself to precise academic analysis.[2] They refused to abandon the popular audience of the contemporary "marketplace" even as each had the training and intellectual acumen to succeed in the elitist academy. As a result both remain, to a large degree, misunderstood. In this brief essay, I will offer a preliminary analysis as to why these two spiritual icons remain largely misunderstood and why they have defied categorization and definition.

Peter Berger, well-known sociologist of religion and astute observer of the interface between tradition and modernity, divides modern religious ideologies into three major categories: modern, counter-modern and demodernizing.[3] The first embraces modernity and views the progressive orientation of modern thought as redemptive. The second rejects modernity and sees it as "heretical." The third uses modernity against itself, presenting tradition as a "liberation from the many discontents of modernity."[4] This demodernizing consciousness uses modern modes of communication and discourse as tools to deconstruct the edifice of modern ideology. Heschel and Merton defy all three of these categories, which is what makes their contributions so intriguing. They are simultaneously post-traditional defenders of tradition and modern critics of modernity.

In spite of their respective traditionalist critiques of the ills of modernity, they remained active participants in modern society, celebrating that fact throughout their lives, never intending that their pietistic religious critiques of modernity would be read as anti-modern, counter-modern or de-modernizing. This fact is particularly intriguing regarding Merton, whose secluded life as a monk and then a hermit never weakened his commitment to the contemporary issues outside the monastery. This can be readily seen in his voluminous correspondence throughout his years at Gethsemani.[5] Merton

2 For a recent study which illuminates various methods of reading Heschel, see Edward Kaplan, *Holiness in Words: Abraham Joshua Heschel's Poetics of Piety* (Albany: SUNY Press, 1996), esp. pp. 19-32.
3 Peter Berger, *Homeless Mind* (New York: Vantage Books, 1973), pp. 159-178.
4 *Ibid.*, p. 196.
5 See, for example, *Thomas Merton, The Hidden Ground of Love: Letters I,* ed. William H. Shannon (New York: Farrar, Straus & Giroux, 1985).

described, criticized and even admonished modern civilization
without abandoning his positive views of its potentiality. He described
modernity as containing the "possibilities of an unexpected and
almost unbelievable solution, the creation of a new world and a new
civilization the like of which has never been seen."[6] Merton did not
advocate the monastic perspective as an attempt to retrieve some
distant romantic past but as a wholly modern alternative.[7] The monk
contributes to this possibility of "new world" by simultaneously
remaining the bulwark of an unchanging Church and being intensely
involved in contemporary social issues, serving as what Merton
defines as "the representative of God in the world."[8] His assessment of
modernity is not apocalyptic – he doesn't see modernity as the
darkness which precedes the eschatological dawn. Rather, he sees the
awakened sparks of holiness around him, in civil rights and anti-
Vietnam War movements, in democracy, in the counter-culture of
Haight Ashbury and Greenwich Village and in the spiritual
renaissance from the East as all bearing the potential of a new era.[9]
Piety and monastic vocation were never meant to liberate the
individual from the modern dilemma. Rather, they offered ways in
which the modern person could live *in* modernity, surviving and
transforming a misguided culture dedicated to the proliferation of

6 Thomas Merton, *The Silent Life* (New York: Farrar, Straus & Giroux, 1957),
   p.173.
7 See Thomas F. McKenna, C.M., "A Voice in the Postmodern Wilderness:
   Merton on Monastic Renewal" in *The Merton Annual: Studies in Culture,
   Spirituality and Social Concerns*, 8 (1995), pp. 122-137.
8 The *Silent Life*, "Epilogue," pp. 172-176.
9 On Merton's sustained argument for civil rights, see the collection of essays in
   Thomas Merton, *Faith and Violence* (1968) and idem. *Thomas Merton on Peace*,
   ed. Gordon Zahn (1971). Cf. *Conjectures of a Guilty Bystander* (Garden City, NY:
   Doubleday, 1968) and the recent publication, *Passion for Peace: The Social Essays
   of Thomas Merton*, William H. Shannon, ed. and Introduction (New York, 1995).
   His three books on religions of the East are *Mystics and the Zen Masters* (New
   York: Farrar, Straus & Giroux, 1961), *Zen and the Birds of Appetite* (New York:
   New Directions, 1968); and *The Asian Journal of Thomas Merton*, eds. Naomi
   Burton, Patrick Hart, and James Loughlin (New York: New Directions, 1973).
   Cf. Thomas Merton, "Christian Culture Needs Oriental Wisdom" in *A Thomas
   Merton Reader* (New York: Image Books, 1974), pp. 295-303, William F. Healy,
   "Thomas Merton's Evaluation of Zen," *Angelicum* 52 (1975), pp. 385-409; Anne
   E. Carr, *A Search for Wisdom and Spirit* (Notre Dame: Notre Dame University
   Press, 1988), pp. 75-95; and Robert Faricy, "Thomas Merton and Zen," *The
   Thomas Merton Annual* 9 (1997), pp. 142-151.

leisure as opposed to contemplation.[10]

This vision is encapsulated in Heschel's thinking as well. His general commitment to social concerns is exemplified in his active vocal support for civil rights and the anti-war movement.[11] Referring to the American counter-culture of the 'sixties, Heschel stated:

> Young people are being driven into the inferno of the drug culture in search of high moments. Add to this the tremendous discontent of youth and its cry for justice for the disadvantaged, its disgust with half-hearted commitments and hypocrisies, and we may have the beginning of a thirst for the noble and the spiritual . . . this is the challenge. The new witnesses for a revival of the spirit in America may well be those poor miserable young men and women who are victims of the narcotic epidemic. If we will but heed the warning and try to understand their misguided search for exaltation, we can begin the task of turning curse into blessing.[12]

Heschel identified with the counter-culture because he viewed Hasidism in a similar vein. Hasidism was, for Heschel, a form of religious reform.[13] The Baal Shem Tov, in Heschel's estimation, was a religious rebel against the injustice and

10 See Thomas Merton, *Contemplation in a World of Action* (New York: Image books, 1973), p. 178.

11 See Heschel, "The Reasons for My Involvement in the Peace Movement," reprinted in *Moral Grandeur and Spiritual Audacity*, ed. Susannah Heschel (New York: Farrar, Straus & Giroux, 1996), pp. 224-226. Heschel made numerous comments about the drug culture which were quite unorthodox for a "neo-traditionalist." Cf. "In Search of Exaltation" in *Moral Grandeur*, pp. 227-229. For Merton's view of this phenomenon, see "Mysticism in Man's Life" in *The Ascent to Truth* (New York: Harcourt, Brace and World, 1951), pp. 3-18.

12 Ibid., p. 229.

13 Heschel was not the first to see Hasidism in that light. Buber presented Hasidism as religious reform in the early part of the century. Even as Buber was justifiably criticized for his overtly romantic view of Hasidism and his use of Hasidic sources to support his rejection of tradition, his influence was far-reaching. Heschel, who knew Hasidism from the inside, came to similar conclusions. See Martin Buber, *Die Chassidischen Bucchler* (Berlin: 1921), pp. 130 ff; *The Origin and Meaning of Hasidism* (Atlantic Highlands, NJ: Humanities Press International, 1988), pp. 89-112; and Samuel Abba Horodetzky, *Rabbi Nachman von Bratzlaw*

complacency of Eastern European rabbinic culture.[14] The historical veracity of such a claim is not at stake here. Heschel's interest in Hasidism was not merely academic.[15]

Hasidism was, for Heschel, the foundation of a contemporary theology of Judaism. By giving us a "Hasidic" interpretation of Judaism for twentieth-century America, Heschel was not giving us a "traditional" interpretation, as he thought Hasidism was itself quite unconventional in its interpretation of tradition. In some ways, the early Hasidic masters, at least in the way they are depicted in the literature of Heschel's time, bordered on being anti-traditional.[16]

(Berlin, 1910). Samuel Dresner, the most celebrated proponent of Heschel's Hasidic scholarship and influence, summed up Heschel's view as follows: "Hasidic teaching in its authentic form must be made available now in order to bring about the renaissance of modern Judaism for which our time and our people wait." Samuel Dresner, *The Zaddik* (London and New York: Abelard Schuman, 1960), p. 18. Dresner also says that, "For Heschel, Hasidism was neither romanticism, rebellion, nor an affirmation of Orthodoxy." See his "Heschel as a Hasidic Scholar" in *Circle of the Baal Shem Tov* (Chicago: University of Chicago Press, 1985), p. xxiv. I would maintain, however, that Heschel did indeed view Hasidism as critique and moderate reform. See also the fascinating essay by Emil Fackenheim, "Two Types of Reform: Reflections Occasioned by Hasidism: in *CCAR Yearbook LXXI* (1961), pp. 208-228, esp. p. 217: "Whereas the Western rationalist reform seeks to free the life of the human intellect, the Eastern Hasidic reform seeks to free the life between man and God." Although this is largely a Buberian formulation, Heschel's thinking on this matter is quite similar yet far more textually nuanced.

14 See his scholarly studies collected and translated in Samuel Dresner, *Circle of the Baal Shem Tov* (Chicago: The University of Chicago Press). Cf. Heschel, "Hasidism as a New Approach to Torah," *Jewish Heritage 14-3* (Fall-Winter 1972), pp. 4-21 reprinted in *Moral Grandeur*, pp. 33-39. Cf. Steven T. Katz, "Abraham Joshua Heschel and Hasidism" in *The Journal of Religion 54-3* (July 1974), pp. 185-198.

15 See Samuel Dresner, "Heschel as a Scholar of Hasidism" in *Circle of the Baal Shem Tov*, pp. vii.

16 We must take into account Moshe Rosman's new study, *The Baal Shem Tov: The Founder of Hasidism* (Berkeley, CA: University of California Press, 1996) and various other studies which question the historical depiction of the radical and religious nature of the early masters. Cf. Ada Rapaport-Albert, "Hagiography with Footnotes: Edifying Tales and the Writing of History in Hasidism" in *Essays in Jewish Hagiography*, A. Rapaport-Albert ed. (Atlanta, GA: Scholars Press, 1991), pp. 119-159; and idem. "Hasidism After 1772: Structural Continuity and Change" in Ada Rapaport-Albert, *Hasidism Reappraised* (London: Valentine Mitchell, 1997), pp. 70-140. Be that as it may, Heschel used Hasidism to justify many of his personal responses to the culture around him.

In this light, I respectfully disagree with Eugene Borowitz's depiction of Heschel as a neo-traditionalist. Borowitz claims that Heschel "used the intellectual tools of modernity to move beyond his predecessor's procedures to a contemporary justification of traditional Jewish belief."[17] Although Borowitz praises Heschel's creative contribution to contemporary theological discourse, he feels ultimately that he fails as a modern Jewish thinker because he was unwilling to accept the full weight of the modern dilemma. "Again and again he begins an insightful discussion of a modern problem, shows its implications, and, just as one expects that he will respond to them, he says instead that from the standpoint of faith that is not the real question at all."[18] Borowitz's reading of Heschel would most accurately fit into Berger's demodernizing camp (albeit in a unique manner) of one who uses the outer trappings of modernity to invalidate the modern experiment.

I would suggest a subtler reading of Heschel's theological project which I believe emerges from a more intimate knowledge of the ways in which he integrates Hasidism as the basis of his radical "anti-traditionalist traditionalism." For example, Heschel's invalidation of a question from "the standpoint of faith" (citing Borowitz above) has a long history in Hasidism, from the Baal Shem Tov to R. Nachman of Bratzlav to Rabbi Menachem Mendel of Kotzk.[19] We find many instances, apocryphal as they may be, in which the Kotzker responds to a question by showing that the question itself rests on mistaken assumptions. Emil Fackenheim, in an essay entitled "Two Types of Reform: Reflections Occasioned by

---

17 Eugene Borowitz, *Choices in Modern Jewish Thought* (New York: Behrman House, 1983), p. 167.

18 Ibid., p. 180. Borowitz's critique of Heschel echoes many other Jewish "philosophers" who could not accept the decidedly un-philosophical nature of Heschelian discourse. For perhaps the most severe critique, see Arthur Cohen, *The Natural and Supernatural Jew* (New York: Pantheon Books, 1962), pp. 234–259. I'd like to thank Shai Held for bringing this chapter to my attention. One of the more subtle and philosophically sophisticated, albeit quite harsh, critiques of Heschel's argumentation can be found in Emil Fackenheim's review of *Man Is Not Alone* in *Judaism* (January 1952), pp. 85-89.

19 The most sustained presentation of this phenomenon can be found in R. Nachman of Brazlav's tale, "The Wise Man and the Simpleton." Cf. Heschel, *A Passion for Truth* (New York: Farrar, Straus & Giroux, 1973) and his two-volume Yiddish study, *Kotzk: In Gerangel far Emesdikeit* (Tel Aviv, 1973).

Hasidism," seems to have a similar point in mind when he says ." . .
the liberal Jew who faces the Hasidic challenge must at this point
turn from a problem of modern thought to a problem of modern
life. Philosophical analysis shows that a religious effort to reopen
communications with God is no offense to modern critical reason.
The question still remains – and it is the vastly more complex and
more difficult one – whether such an effort is a concrete possibility
of modern life, as well as compatible with modern thought."[20]
Instead of responding to a question built on the assumptions of
"modern thought," Heschel may have responded by questioning
those very assumptions, not by rejecting modernity but by turning
the inquiry to a question of modern life. Be that as it may, Borowitz's
reading is partially correct in that Heschel does serve as a translator
of traditional ideas to late twentieth-century American Jewry, largely
but not exclusively through the prism of Hasidism. However, I
would maintain that Heschel's relationship to modernity (as was
Merton's) was far more complex than merely a tool for translation.

The claim Borowitz's critical appraisal of Heschel as a "neo-traditionalist"
implies a kind of intellectual deception that I believe is overstated.
Merton, who claimed merely to be "a mouthpiece of a tradition
centuries old,"[21] may have also been wrongly accused of neo-
traditionalism. Both were unwilling to submit to the conventional
"modern" assumption that faith is an illegitimate response to the
modern dilemma. However, as we will see, their respective
definitions of faith are far from conventional. Faith was not depicted
as submission to a doctrine or truth-claim but as orientation toward
the world, a celebration of the mystery of creation, becoming open
to the experience of that which lies beyond reason. In Heschel's
words, faith is the "act of believing" as opposed to "creed," or that
which we believe in. "The act of faith is an act of spiritual audacity
not traditional conservatism."[22]

The claim that both Heschel and Merton are merely defenders
of tradition cloaked in modern theological language misses the core
of their contribution to modern religious discourse because it
misunderstands their critical/heretical call for a return to tradition as

20 Emil Fackenheim, "Two Types of Reform," pp. 221, 222.
21 *The Silent Life*, "Prologue," pp. vii, xiv.
22 Heschel, *Man Is Not Alone* (New York: Farrar, Straus, Giroux, 1951), p. 167.

a position of retreat as opposed to internal critique. In religious discourse we often define defenders of tradition as those who take a stance against an outside threat to their system of belief or practice. These defenders often, but not always, fall into two general categories: "rejectionists," i.e., those who refuse to acknowledge any legitimacy in an ideological position which threatens their ideology or way of life, or "apologists," those who attempt to present their tradition in the garments of modern language or ideas in order to defend the core of tradition against the onslaught of heretical belief.[23] Neither Heschel nor Merton fits into those categories, even in their widest interpretation, because their defense of tradition emerges from an internal critique of the tradition itself and their relationship to modernity was more than nominally tolerant or even positive; it is almost celebratory.

Heschel is a defender of tradition, yes, but not an apologist for it. He is a harsh critic of modernity, yes, but not one of its detractors. Heschel's "Pious One" and Merton's "Monk" are *responses* and not *solutions* to modernity.[24] Therefore, I would prefer to call both "heretics of modernity." By this I mean that both question and deeply criticize basic tenets of modernity but remain devoted to modern culture. Karl Rahner's distinction between the heretic, who remains a Christian, and the apostate who abandons the Church, is perhaps useful here.[25]

---

23 I present these two categories only to suggest two general orientations. These two approaches do not encompasss the entirety of traditionalist responses to modernity. For a wide-ranging study of this phenomenon see Mordechai Breuer, *Modernity within Tradition: The Social History of Orthodox Jewry in Imperial Germany*, translated by Elizabeth Petuchowski (New York: Columbia University Press, 1978), esp. pp. 19-61.

24 The chapter, "The Pious One" is the final chaper in Heschel's *Man Is Not Alone*, pp. 273-296. The chapter appeared in a slightly different form as "An Analysis of Piety" in *The Review of Religion* 6-3 (March 1942), pp. 293-307 and reprinted in *Moral Grandeur*, pp. 305-317. Cf. ibid., "The Holy Dimension," pp. 318-328. Merton speaks of the vocation of the monk in numerous books. See, for example, *The Silent Life* and *Monastic Journal* (Garden City, NY: Doubleday, 1978).

25 Karl Rahner, *On Heresy* (London: Burns and Oates, 1964), pp. 26-27. For earlier studies on this matter, which illuminate the complexities of the relationship between orthodoxy and heresy, see Walter Bauer, *Orthodoxy and Heresy in Earliest Christianity*, translated by Robert Craft (Philadelphia: Fortress Press, 1971) and Walter L. Wakefield and Austin P. Evans, *Heresies of the Middle Ages* (New York: Columbia University Press, 1969), esp. pp. 1-67.

Rahner argues that the heretic (as opposed to the apostate) still maintains the one saving reality which is "signified both by the truths that are maintained as well as by those that are denied."[26] For Rahner, heretical discourse lies within and not beyond the perimeters of the ideology under scrutiny. Heresy, or that which is initially labeled as such, carries the potential to widen the boundaries of the tradition it scrutinizes. If it is successful in doing so, the label of heresy falls away and the critique becomes normalized into the tradition.[27] If it is unsuccessful, it dissolves or results in apostasy.

The formulation of "defense as retreat," embodied in the rejectionist position suggested above, would represent, perhaps, an apostate of modernity, one who abandons modernity in favor of what he determines is a pre-modern and thus more pristine ideology. Alternatively "defense as critique," which I believe more accurately represents Heschel and Merton, is heretical in the most positive sense in that the individual protests yet remains devoted to the culture under scrutiny. Yet, Heschel and Merton were not only heretics of modernity. As defenders of and adherents to traditional society coupled with their devotion and commitment to modernity, they became quasi-heretics of the tradition they sought to defend. Their re-formation and re-presentation of Jewish pietism and Christian monasticism placed them on the margins of their respective traditions because these traditional ideologies were set within and not against modernity. It is thus not surprising that both were viewed suspiciously by the mainstream traditionalists in their time.

Both were pietistic critics of tradition, not unlike the way that the Prophets and the Desert Fathers were critics of First Temple Israelitic society and of early Christianity. As was common in deeply spiritualistic critiques of a particular religion, the critic bases his/her critique on princples which are deeply rooted (albeit abandoned or marginalized) in the tradition itself, accompanied by an experience which allows for these subterranean strains to emerge. The individual's experience, which serves as a catalyst for lost ideals, is realized and accomplished in the form of what tradition may call an "error."[28] Concomitant with their attempts to build a foundation for

26 Ibid., p. 29.
27 On this see Menahem Kellner, "What is Jewish Heresy?" *Studies in Jewish Philosophy III*, ed. Norbert Samuelson (New York: 1983), pp. 55-70.
28 Both Heschel and Merton subtly attempt to re-introduce traditional ideas

modern pietism, Heschel and Merton attempted to uncover lost elements in their respective traditions buried deep beneath the blankets of religious institutionalization and convention.

Both Heschel and Merton achieved at least moderate success in the modern religious communities and the traditional world, yet both defied categorization precisely because each succeeded in widening the intellectual boundaries of both the modern and traditional communities simultaneously. As critics (yet defenders) of tradition and critics (yet participants) in modernity, they lived on the margins of both worlds and, by exposing the weaknesses of both they created a bridge over which individuals in both communities have begun to travel.

One of the salient characteristics of both Heschel and Merton is that each used various aspects of tradition to criticize the contemporary society in which they lived without arguing that the entirety of the tradition should eclipse the world it challenged. Both thinkers wrote for moderns, not for detractors.[29] Merton spoke of contemplative prayer as a "modern problem." He wrote about "the monk and the world"[30] and the monastic vocation as a "modern choice." Heschel faced modernity with a similar orientation. He presented the religious category of piety as that which speaks to the modern dilemma of apathy and the illegitimacy of faith. He did so by drawing a distinction between faith and piety that opens us to the possibility of viewing piety as an orientation and posture toward the world and not a requirement to believe:

which they claim have been discarded by their respective religions. Heschel's "theology of pathos" which serves as the foundation of *Man Is Not Alone* and *God in Search of Man* is founded on what he determines as the prophetic message first presented in his doctoral dissertation *Die Prophetie* (Cracow, 1926), later revised and translated as *The Prophets* (New York: Harper and Row, 1962). Merton sought out the early Christian Egyptian desert dwellers as his model of the authentic monastic life which was used as a critique of his contemporary monastic orders which he felt had become institutionalized and overly secure. See Thomas Merton, *The Wisdom of the Desert* (New York: New Directions, 1960) and McKenna, pp. 126-127.

29 Even as Merton composed various works specifically for the monks at Gethsemani, his language was contemporary and one could argue that these works were attempts to reform the monastic life from the inside. See *The Monastic Journey* as an example of such a book.

30 See *The Silent Life,* "Epilogue."

> Faith is a way of thinking, and thus a matter of the mind; piety is a matter of life. Faith is a sense for the reality of the transcendent; piety is the taking of an adequate attitude toward it. Faith is vision, knowledge, belief; piety is relation, judgment, an answer to a call, a mode of life. Faith belongs to the objective realm; piety stands entirely within the subjective and originates in human initiative ... It is through piety that there comes the real revelation of the self, the disclosure of what is most delicate in the human soul, the unfolding of the purest elements in the human venture.[31]

Piety as an orientation toward the world as opposed to submission to doctrine is not something confined to any historical epoch. Heschel begins with the assumption that human beings are always forced to orient themselves to the world around them and must take stock of the numerous truth theories and ideologies that the modern world presents. Piety is presented in his essay as alternative, admittedly one among many, but one that Heschel maintains speaks to the despair and meaninglessness so prevalent in modern society.[32]

A second distinction Heschel suggested which he believed "corrected" conventional misunderstandings of piety is between faith and belief.

> Belief is the mental acceptance of a proposition or a fact as true on the ground of the authority or evidence; the conviction of the truth of a given proposition or an alleged fact ... [f]aith, on the other hand, is not only the assent to a proposition, but the staking of a whole life on the truth of an invisible reality.[33]

Belief is problematic for two reasons. First, belief has an object,

---

31 Heschel, "An Analysis of Piety" in *Moral Grandeur*, p. 310. Cf. his discussion on faith in *Man Is Not Alone*, pp. 159–176. For a simular formulation in an apologetic context, see Leo Baeck, *The Essence of Judaism* (New York: Schocken Books, 1948), pp. 118–119.

32 Ibid., p. 313.

33 See *Man Is Not Alone*, pp. 166,167.

244 · *Shaul Magid*

be it a idea, dogma or proposition. As a conviction, belief closes rather than opens the possibility of experiencing the ineffable. Second, belief, Heschel argued, is centered on the self, the personal conviction of a truth claim.[34] Alternatively, faith begins and ends with uncertainty. Faith has no object but is "the staking of a whole life on the *truth of an invisible event*."[35] It is faith and not belief that challenges the certainty implicit in the scientific world-view which Heschel so passionately railed against. The ineffable event, which Heschel held was the foundation of Prophetic Judaism, is only possible when we "come to terms with our desire for intellectual security . . ."[36] By this he means that we must submit to the limits of knowledge before we can become open to the vistas of religion. Insecurity, and not certainty, is the foundation of Heschel's theology of Judaism.

II

Both Heschel and Merton present prayer, in its widest sense, as the apex of the pious life.[37] Yet they argue that prayer is an act which is widely misunderstood. The misunderstanding and diminished value of prayer is viewed as one of the great tragedies of modern religion. Heschel and Merton each devote a separate volume to prayer in an attempt to re-present prayer to the modern reader in a new way which maintains its traditional valence and form but sheds new light on prayer as a response to the human being's experience of the world. Both independently speak of prayer as poetry, about the need for the aesthetic to precede the ascetic, for the appreciation, beauty and wonder of creation to become part of one's choice to abstain from it.[38] Prayer is essentially

34 For a study of the place of "self" in the Jewish mystical tradition which enlightens some of Heschel's more opaque comments, see Alexander Altmann, "'God and Self' ... in Jewish Mysticism," *Judaism* 3 (1954), pp. 1-5.

35 Ibid., p. 167.

36 Ibid.

37 Heschel's book-length study of prayer entitled *Quest for God* [originally published as *Man's Quest for God*] (New York: Scribner, 1954) was augmented by various other essays and lectures Heschel gave on other dimensions of prayer. See, for example in *Moral Grandeur*, "The Spirit of Jewish Prayer," pp. 100-126, and "Prayer," pp. 257-267.

38 On this see Thomas Merton, *Contemplative Prayer* (New York: Image Books,

an ascetic act precisely because it demands a posture which fosters an appreciation of the inner life as the mystery of the divine and not as the reflection of the self. In a sense, the ascetic nature of prayer is that it denies the modern assumption that the inner life is "dominated by the spirit reflection of self-consciousness."[39] It is only the ascetic denial of the all-encompassing nature of self and subjectivity that makes true love of the world, i.e., the aesthetic, possible. Yet the ascetic without the aesthetic is destructive.

> [If one begins with the] pretext that what is within is in fact real, spiritual, supernatural, etc., one cultivates neglect and contempt for the external as worldly, sensual, material and opposed to grace. This is bad theology and bad asceticism. In fact, it is bad in every respect, because instead of accepting reality as it is, we reject it in order to explore some perfect realm of abstract ideals which in fact has no reality at all . . . Meditation has no point unless it is firmly rooted in life. Without such roots, it can produce nothing but the ashen fruits of disgust, *acedia*, and even morbid and degenerative introversion, masochism, dolorism, and negation.[40]

For Merton prayer aids the modern attempt to balance between a denial of the world via asceticism, seeing the world as evil; and a denial of the world via radical subjectivism, seeing the entirety of the real as a reflection of subjective reflection.

Underlying Heschel's discussion on prayer is the classical Jewish correlation between prayer and sacrifice, seeing both as expressing an abandonment of self to facilitate self-discovery. Self-discovery for Heschel is not the discovery of the unconscious or one's inner-self,

1971); this work is a composite of two manuscripts, "The Climate of Monastic Prayer" written for the monks at Gethsemani and circulated privately, and "Prayer as Worship and Experience," written for a general audience, published for the first time in *Contemplative Prayer*. For a thorough discussion of the complex construction of this book see William Shannon, *Thomas Merton's Dark Path* (New York: Farrar, Straus & Giroux, 1987), Chapter 7.

39 See Emil Fackenheim, "Two Types of Reform," p. 222. For another non-traditional formulation of asceticism as a necessary component of the religious life, see Leo Baeck, *The Essence of Judaism*, p. 269.

40 Merton, *Contemplative Prayer*, p. 38.

but the discovery of the mystery of God, the part of oneself that is beyond the self.

> The focus of prayer is not the self ... Prayer comes to pass in a complete turning of the heart toward God, toward His goodness and power. It is the momentary disregard for our personal concerns, the absence of self-centered thoughts, which constitute the act of prayer. Feeling becomes prayer in the moment we forget ourselves and become aware of God.[41]

Heschel attempts to correct the misconception of prayer and asceticism as negation of the world by stressing the poetic power of the liturgy, seeing the poetic as a deep appreciation of nature which serves as a foundation for asceticism in general and prayer in particular. Just as prayer is a "sacrificial offering," the ascetic life is envisioned as "gift-giving." "True asceticism is not merely depriving ourselves but is giving God what was precious to us."[42] For Heschel the aesthetic appreciation of the beauty of nature requires an offering to the Master of Creation, a turning from the world to God and only then a turning back to the world.

Merton also equates prayer with poetry. Prayer releases the spiritual potency in creation and enables the worshiper to share in the relationship between God and the world.

> The words of a poem are not merely the signs of concepts; they are also rich in affective and spiritual associations ... [The poet] seeks above all to put words together in such a way that they exercise a mysterious and vital reactivity among themselves, and so release their secret content of associations to produce in the reader an experience that enriches the depths of the spirit in a manner quite unique.[43]

41 "Prayer" in *Moral Grandeur*, pp. 348-349. A similar formulation is made by Emil Fackenheim in "Two Types of Reform," pp. 215, 216: ." . . Jewish prayer, once between a 'subjective' self and an 'objective' God, is viewed [in modern discourse] as the self's disport within its own feelings, conducive to aesthetic or therapeutic benefit."

42 "An Analysis of Piety", ibid., p. 315.

43 Thomas Merton, *Bread in the Wilderness*, cited in *A Merton Reader*, ed. Thomas P. McDonnell (New York: Harcourt Brace and World, 1962), p. 388.

His discussion of poetry in general leads to an understanding of the Psalms as religious poetry which contains unique characteristics but never transcends the purely poetic. "The real content of the Psalter," says Merton, "is poetic."[44] Merton continues, "Since the inspired writer [of the Psalms] is an instrument of the Holy Spirit, what is revealed ... is the poetry of the Psalter and is only fully apprehended in the poetic experience of the inspired writer.

Prayer, like poetry, is presented as an expression of love. Merton's description of the monk is one who is madly in love with God. Hence for the monk, prayer is the embodiment of his entire vocation. The monk's love of God is such that he cannot bear to be apart from Him. To illustrate this point Merton offers an interesting midrashic rendition of Exodus 33:20 and 33:13 by reversing the order of the verses, putting Moses' request for divine presence, "Show me Thy face," as a response to God saying, "No one shall see My face and live,"[45] instead of the request being that which evokes God's response. The monk persists in crying out with Moses; "Show me Thy face"[46] even after, or precisely after, God denies His presence. Moses' (and the monk's) protest is based on the fact that they are both madly in love and as such, cannot bear divine absence, even as such an absence is decreed by God Himself.

Whereas Merton uses the early Christian Egyptian Desert Fathers as a source for his "reform" of monastic life and presentation of the monastic journey as a modern alternative,[47] Heschel uses Hasidism. Describing the contribution of Hasidism, which largely served as the wellspring of tradition from which Heschel drank, he says, "To be a Hasid is to be in love, to be in love with God and with what He has created . . . he who has never been in love will not understand and may consider it madness."[48] Prayer as sacrifice is, for Heschel, "man's gift to God, it is a love offering that heals the break between God and the world."[49] The traditional liturgy of prayer is the love poetry between the Jew and God. "Worship is the climax

44 Ibid., p. 389.
45 *The Silent Life*, p. x.
46 Ibid.
47 See McKenna, "A Voice in the Postmodern Wilderness," pp. 126-127 and Merton, *Wisdom of the Desert* (New York: New Directions, 1960).
48 Heschel, "Hasidism as a New Approach to Torah," reprinted in *Moral Grandeur*, pp. 33-39.
49 Heschel, "On Prayer," reprinted in *Moral Grandeur*, p. 259.

of living. There is no knowledge without love, no truth without praise. At the beginning was the song, and praise is man's response to the never-ending beginning."[50] But the Hasid's love for God, even as it is understood as a sacrifice, is not expressed as making translucent the opaque walls that conceal the divine dimension *in* creation. Worship does not transcend the world – it transforms it.

Both attempt to lift the sacred core of ancient notions of devotion and sacrifice from their cultural contexts and present them as models which have relevance in the contemporary world. Both share the prophetic sensitivity which enables them to see the divinity that lies buried in the externals of tradition and secularism. Therefore, they do not see a contradiction in their defending the Church Fathers or Hasidic Masters in the public square of American secular culture. They do not defend tradition from the onslaught of modernity. Rather, they suggest that modernity too can become holy precisely because holiness demands self-reflection and a recognition of the vitality of the inner-life, both of which, being innately human and not merely cultural categories, find expression in these premodern spiritual models.

Prayer and the larger devotional life are not subsumed in the structures of ritual, even as ritual remains the centerpiece of the devotional life. Both see devotion as an orientation and posture toward the world. Ritual may symbolize and externalize that posture but not encompass it. Moreover, the broader definition of devotion as an orientation toward life and not merely the performance of prescribed rituals cannot be solely the inheritance of one historical epoch (i.e., rabbinic Judaism or the medieval Catholic Church) – it is a natural and healthy externalization of the human experience. Answering the rhetorical question as to "Why do we pray?" Heschel responds, "We pray because we are human!" or "We pray in order to pray."[51] He is simultaneously not willing to relegate prayer to commandment, yet not willing to abandon the obligatory nature of prayer. Heschel's model of piety is not a commitment to a particular "deed" but a commitment to "the way,"

---

50 Ibid, p. 263.

51 The first definition was suggested by Samuel Dresner in a private conversation, the second can be found in Heschel's "On Prayer," in *Moral Grandeur*, p. 259.

to the process of self-discovery and discovery of God.[52]

A similar re-formulation of a life of devotion and worship enables Merton to speak of "bad asceticism" as that which negates the world, as opposed to an asceticism that ultimately appreciates and loves the world. Merton is in agreement with Heschel's prophetic lamentation of the proliferation of empty ritual in contemporary Jewish religiosity.[53] We have abandoned ritual, both intimate, because we have refused to see beneath the outer garments of ritual as mere obedience. The actual form that piety takes is dynamic even though both defend, adopt, and integrate classical forms of piety into their own spiritual lives. In this light I believe that they offer a highly un-traditional defense of tradition, perhaps even an anti-traditionalist defense of tradition, which makes them simultaneously marginal in the world they are defending[54] and the world they seek to heal. They are both misunderstood and important precisely because they live deeply in the world they critique and thus defy the sharp lines of sociological classification.

Both celebrate sacrifice as the ladder which allows one to ascend the stone wall of false autonomy and recognize that certainty is not a religious posture. One needs to enter into the darkness of mystery in order to discover the divine light concealed under the veil of absence. Radical autonomy is the false idol of modernity; yet both attempt to deconstruct the idol while remaining members of the culture that constructed it.[55] For example, the foundation of prayer for Heschel is despair and the unwillingness to succumb to that despair. In concert with Hasidic doctrine, prayer for Heschel is the radical rejection of destiny, the recognition of the frailty of the human condition and the unwillingness to accept one's fallen state as final. Deeply embedded in Heschel's Jewish theology is the

52 On this see Heschel, *Man Is Not Alone*, pp. 257-270.

53 On Heschel's "pan-halakhic" view see his "Toward an Understanding of Halakha" reprinted in *Moral Grandeur* p. 127-145. For a critical appraisal of Heschel's attitude toward halakha see Marvin Fox, "Heschel, Intuition and Halakha" *Tradition* 3-1 (Fall 1960), pp. 5-15.

54 In a letter to Rosemary Radford Ruether on May 5, 1967, Merton wrote, "I am now convinced that the first way to be a decent monk is to be a non-monk and an anti-monk, so far as the image goes." See Thomas Merton, *The Hidden Ground of Love*, p. vii.

55 See Thomas Merton, *Thomas Merton in Alaska: Prelude to the Asian Journal* (New York: New Directions, 1988), pp. 76-78.

Hasidic dialectic between the pietistic notion of one's utter dependence on God and the kabbalistic notion of *tikkun*, the individual's ability to overcome adversity and redeem the world. Yet the very rejection of human frailty must first confront the despair and apparent emptiness of existence.

Another dimension of their thought which seeks to deepen the symbiosis between tradition and modernity is that neither seeks to counter modernity by retrieving a romanticized vision of a forgotten past. Even as Heschel may romanticize Eastern European shtetl life before the First World War in *The Earth Is the Lord's*, he does so as a eulogizer, lamenting the loss of a great period in Jewish history. Heschel may be implying that the shtetl may have something to teach us, but he does not in my view seek to retrieve it. Rather, both he and Merton seek to heal modernity, to awaken the inner-life within us, to ask us to re-consider piety and the contemplative life as more than a relic of an unenlightened society. Both recognize the "heretical imperative"[56] of modernity as much as they both acknowledge the necessity of such heresy. As traditionalists they deeply understood the ways in which modernity has moved beyond the perimeters of traditional theological and philosophical categories. Rather than lamenting this rupture and mourning the loss of innocence and purity of spirit, they celebrate the potential that lies beneath the modern project. Hence, as moderns they raise their voices in protest against the society in which they live, challenging us to look beyond ourselves by looking into ourselves.

It is not insignificant that Heschel never returned to the ultra-Orthodox world from which he came, and Merton's spiritual development marginalized him from the monastic community in which he lived. The spiritual sustenance each found in their respective traditions never diminished their intellectual curiosity. Piety never led to isolation. In the spirit of true heretics they never abandoned the world they challenged. Instead, their heresy of modernity simultaneously became our convention and inspiration. Heschel taught us what it is to be a Hasid in a world where

56 The phrase is taken from Peter Berger's *Heretical Imperative* (New York: Doubleday, 1979), pp. 1-30, which argues that modernity begins with what its antecedents would determine as heresy and then continues to build the edifice of modernity on those foundations.

Hasidism is anathema and Merton tuaght us how to appreciate the monk which conventional modern intuition slights as "non-productive" and thus a parasite of our society.[57] Like spiritual Zarathustras they made us see the extent to which our productive lives are missing a center; that life is like a cone where the center simultaneously hovers above and within the circumference of the circle. The center is silence, contemplation, devotion, and sacrifice. The center is realization that the goal of existence is the exaltation and not conquest of the world around us. Activism remains; modernity survives. But it does so with a gentle whisper and not a bellowing horn. Their contribution is that they have taught us to be modern and yet remain human, while teaching us that becoming God-like *is* becoming human.

These two contemporary spiritual voices of faith sought to re-formulate the tradition they loved and lovingly criticize the world they lived in. They simultaneously accepted and challenged the heretical imperative of modernity by becoming "heretics of modernity." The tradition which was abandoned in a modern society was abandoned for good reason. But, they argue, embedded in the essence of those respective traditions lies the secret meaning of being human. In both we see the daring life of the "double-critic," the one who criticizes tradition yet uses tradition to criticize modernity. Abraham Joshua Heschel and Thomas Merton: inspiring, confusing, playing both sides against the other. We have only begun to understand what it was they were all about.

57 *The Silent Life*, p. viii.

"Catholic-Jewish dialogue can become a sign of hope and inspiration to other religions, races, and ethnic groups to turn away from contempt, toward realizing authentic human fraternity. This new spirit of friendship and caring for one another may be the most important symbol we have to offer to our troubled world."

—Pope John Paul II from "The Prague Statement"

12

CONTEMPLATIVE INWARDNESS AND PROPHETIC ACTION:

THOMAS MERTON'S DIALOGUE WITH ABRAHAM JOSHUA HESCHEL

Edward K. Kaplan

As secularized academic I have been fascinated and challenged by Merton's integration of mystical inwardness and social commitment. My professional interest in poetic imagination has allowed me some access to the living flame of Christian devotion, despite, or perhaps because of the fact that I am a Jew. But I am the kind of person who feels at once alien to and intimate with both traditions. The fellowship of Merton and the contemporary Jewish philosopher, Abraham Joshua Heschel (1907-1972), who also revitalized prayer and prophetic ethics, responds to my discomfort. Merton's and Heschel's spiritual dissatisfaction echoes mine.

Thomas Merton believed that contemplative religion nurtures more openness than does a strictly ethical or theological approach. The experience of God's presence or absence, while interpreted variously, can be shared. Merton wanted contemplatives to become more receptive to "modern thought" (e.g., atheism, Marxism, psychology) and its perceptions of today's realities. In cooperation with other progressive forces, people of prayer could help transform human life in accordance with spiritual values.

Thomas Merton and Abraham Heschel, both born in Europe, matured and fulfilled their missions in the United States, motivated by a similar love of their adopted homeland combined with militant spiritual criticism. In contrast to most members of their orthodox communities, they harmonized personal piety and radical moral involvement. Thomas Merton expressed his pacifism and progressive social views in numerous articles and speeches (collected mainly in *Faith and Violence* [1968] and *Thomas Merton on Peace,* ed. Gordon Zahn [1971]). Abraham Heschel also strongly opposed the Vietnam War and marched beside Martin Luther King during the Selma-Montgomery protest (see *The Insecurity of Freedom, 1966*). Both started their professional careers as proponents of mysticism: Merton in *The Seven Storey Mountain* (1948) and in *The Ascent to Truth* (1951); and Heschel in a seminal article, "The Mystical Element in Judaism" (1949), *The Sabbath* (1951), and *Man's Quest for God* (1954). Both were poets who savored language and the richness of imagination. They speak to our opposing demands of history and tranquility, or anger at or love of God; and they question the very foundations of religion today.

THE PREMISE OF WORLDLINESS

From the very first, Thomas Merton presents his story as inseparable from that of society: "On the last day of January 1915, under the sign of the Water Bearer, in a year of great war, and down in the shadow of some French mountains on the borders of Spain, I came into the world. Free by nature, in the image of God, I was nevertheless the prisoner of my own violence and my own selfishness, in the image of the world into which I was born."[1] The autobiography, in spite of its negative view of the world which the mature Merton embarrassedly deplored, clearly places his personal struggle within a context of social and moral responsibility. Yet the book also exemplifies an unresolved conflict not entirely acknowledged or understood, to which the opening lines of *The Ascent to Truth* give voice:

> The only thing that can save the world from complete moral collapse is a spiritual revolution. Christianity, by its very nature, demands such a revolution. If Christians would all live up to what they profess to believe, the revolution would happen. The desire for unworldliness, detachment, and union with God is the most fundamental expression of this revolutionary spirit. The one thing that

1 *The Seven Storey Mountain* (Doubleday Image Books, 1948), p. 11.

remains is for Christians to affirm their Christianity by that full and unequivocal rejection of the world which their Baptismal vocation demands of them. This will certainly not incapacitate them for social action in the world, since it is the one essential condition for a really fruitful Christian apostolate.[2]

Merton's repetition of the word "revolution" and his defensive stance against social indifference betray an ambiguous definition of moral action. More firm was his lifelong exploration of mysticism as the most radical solution to spiritual corruption. We know that Merton's understanding of "the world" completely altered. In 1966 he wrote: "I am ... a man in the modern world. In fact, I am the world just as you are! Where am I going to look for the world first of all if not in myself?"[3] Contemplation reoriented his appreciation of the secular.

Abraham Heschel traces a parallel path from mysticism to prophetic activism in Jewish terms. He introduced himself to the Union Theological Seminary in a way which recalls Merton:

> I speak as a member of a congregation whose founder was Abraham, and the name of my rabbi is Moses.
>
> I speak as a person who was able to leave Warsaw, the city in which I was born, just six weeks before the disaster began. My destination was New York. It could have been Auschwitz or Treblinka. I am a brand plucked from the fire in which my people was burned to death. I am a brand plucked from the fire of an altar of Satan on which millions of human lives were exterminated to evil's greater glory, and on which so much else was consumed: the divine image of so many human beings, many people's faith in the God of justice and compassion, and much of the secret and power of attachment to the Bible bred and cherished in the heart of men for nearly two thousand years.[4]

2 *The Ascent to Truth* (London: Hollis and Carter, 1951), p. 3.
3 "Is the World a Problem?" in *Contemplation in a World of Action* (Doubleday Image Books, 1973), p. 117; cited hereafter as CWA.
4 Abraham J. Heschel, " No Religion Is an Island," *Union Seminary Quarterly*

Heschel shares with Merton this double premise: the ultimate preciousness of human life and the devastation of faith by recent history. Merton and Heschel repudiate the conspiracy to destroy the ideal that humanity is an image of God. Heschel's activist and scholarly career defies the Nazi holocaust; as a theologian he strove to save Judaism and its vision of justice from the furnaces of modern warfare and callousness. Heschel begins with a prophetic task.

Merton's public appreciation of the prophets was not extensive. His early approach to the Hebrew Bible continues the Christian tradition of typology which absorbs the Old Testament, and Judaism, into the New (see especially *Bread in the Wilderness*, ch.11). Yet he did teach Heschel's book on *The Prophets* to the novices at Gethsemani and he wrote personally to the author on January 26, 1963:

> It is a privilege to be able to share your own meditations on the prophets and indeed to find very little in those pages that I would not myself want to express in much the same way. Some day perhaps I will muster up courage to try the difficult task of saying what the Prophets must mean to a Christian: difficult because of the heritage of past interpretations and allegories.

> The twentieth century makes it impossible seriously to do this any more, so perhaps we will be humble enough to dig down to a deeper and more burning truth. In so doing, we may perhaps get closer to you, whom the Lord has not allowed to find so many specious arguments in favor of complacent readings.[5]

Merton shared with Heschel his implicit dialogue with Judaism. Heschel made it explicit when he sent Merton his criticism of a draft document from the Vatican Council on the

Review XXI, 2 (January 1966), p. 117; this is Heschel's most complete definition of Jewish-Christian dialogue.
5 From the incomplete correspondence dating from 1960-1966 preserved by the Merton Collection at Bellarmine College, Louisville KY, and reproduced by the kind permission of Mrs. Sylvia Heschel and The Thomas Merton Legacy Trust.

Jews. Heschel had been closely involved with Cardinal Bea's valiant efforts to rectify the Church's denial of Judaism; here is Heschel's response: "It must be stated that *spiritual fratricide* is hardly a means for the attainment of 'fraternal discussion' or 'reciprocal understanding.' ... As I have repeatedly stated to leading personalities at the Vatican, I am ready to go to Auschwitz any time, if faced with the alternative of conversion or death" (mimeographed statement, dated September 3, 1964: see Merton-Heschel Correspondence, this volume). Merton associated himself with this prophetic rebuke: "My latent ambitions to be a true Jew under my Catholic skin will surely be realized if I continue to go through experiences like this, being spiritually slapped in the face by these blind and complacent people of whom I am nevertheless a 'collaborator.'...The Psalms have said all that need be said about this sort of thing, and you and I both pray them. In them we are one, in their truth, in their silence" (September 9, 1964). How then did Father Louis realize his latent identity as Jew?

THE CLOISTER AND THE PROPHET

Thomas Merton reached the prophetic stance within the categories of monastic tradition. He constantly strove to reconcile individual piety and social responsibility. Merton expressed his mature views in "Openness and Cloister" (1969), and stated clearly that "the radical change in the Church's attitude toward the modern world was one of the significant events that marked Vatican II. In the light of the Council it is no longer possible to take a completely negative view of the world."[6] He suggests that the Hebrew Bible, anchored so concretely in historical problems, would help transform monastic thinking:

> Today a new and more Biblical understanding of the contemplative life is called for: we must see it as a response to the dynamic Word of God in history, we must see it in the light of Biblical eschatology. The contemplative finds God not only in the embrace of "pure love" alone but in the prophetic ardor of response to the "Word of the

6 This and the next quotation are from CWA, p. 152.

Lord": not in love considered as essential good but in love that breaks through into the world of sinful men in the fire of judgment and of mercy. The contemplative must see love not only as the highest and purest experience of the human heart transformed by grace, but as God's unfailing fidelity to unfaithful man.

Merton uses the Hebrew Bible to complete the purity of contemplation with prophetic responsibility: love as essential good is completed by love as judgment and mercy in a sinful world; love as an experience of grace within the heart is completed by identification with God's fidelity to mankind. Prophetic religion removes the emphasis from personal development to voluntary imitation, within society, of God's active involvement with mankind. Merton's prophetic position fulfills his mystical journey. He meets Heschel at the crossroads of inwardness and history.

Abraham Heschel's analysis of prophetic consciousness stresses the inseparability of moral and religious thinking. The foundation of biblical prophecy is God's covenant with Israel, a reciprocal commitment to a network of moral imperatives. The prophet demands that God and the people equally conform to the ideal. God is actively involved in all human events and loves his chosen people. Heschel defines this emotional involvement as "the divine pathos," God's powerful attachment to mankind: "Prophetic religion may be defined, not as what man does with his ultimate concern, but rather *what man does with God's concern.*"[7] The prophet is overwhelmed by "a fellowship with the feelings of God, a *sympathy with the divine pathos*…. Sympathy is the prophet's answer to inspiration, the correlative to revelation." The prophet exemplifies what I now call the "recentering of subjectivity from humanity to God."[8] Instead of remaining the object of human consciousness, God becomes experienced as the Subject of which

---

7 Abraham Heschel, *The Prophets* (New York and Philadelphia: Jewish Publications Society, 1962), p. 484.

8 See my article, "Language and Reality in Abraham J. Heschel's Philosophy of Religion," *Journal of the American Academy of Religion* 41. 1 (March 1973), 94–111, in which I used the term "displacement of subjectivity." See also Maurice Friedman, "Divine Need and Human Wonder: The Philosophy of Abraham J. Heschel," *Judaism* 25, 1 (Winter 1976), 65–78.

the person is the object. The Bible is God's anthropology, not human theology. The prophet experiences and judges the world from the divine perspective.

He takes within his inner life God's love and anger and is extraordinarily moved by social ills. Through the prophet, God is present in the world:

> The prophet is a man who feels fiercely. God has thrust a burden upon his soul, and he is bowed and stunned at man's fierce greed. Frightful is the agony of man; no human voice can convey its full terror. Prophecy is the voice that God has lent to the silent agony, a voice to the plundered poor, to the profaned riches of the world. It is a form of living, a crossing point of God and man. God is raging in the prophet's words.[9]

The prophet lives at the crossroads of God, the individual, and the human community. The prophetic mediator is often torn in his loyalties and loves. He cherishes his people but must carry out God's judgment. His ultimate task is to transform: "the purpose of prophecy is to conquer callousness, to change the inner man as well as to revolutionize history."[10] The prophet participates in mankind's inner and outer lives, seeking to establish a society founded on justice and true worship.

> And what does the Lord require of you
> But to do justice, and to love kindness,
> And to walk humbly with your God?
> (Micah 6:6–8)

God's worldly kingdom requires humility and loving kindness as well as exterior justice. Personal suffering seems necessary to effect historical redemption. The Lord must punish His people repeatedly in order to eradicate callousness or hardness of heart, the root of sin.[11] Heschel talks of God in the concrete human language of biblical experience. His study of divine chastisement

9 *The Prophets*, p. 5.
10 *Ibid.*, p. 17.
11 *Ibid.*, p. 191, note.

demonstrates how the Lord's anger is an extension of His love, how divine justice is inseparable from compassion: "As great as God's wrath is, great too is His anguish," for, despite the most awful provocations, He remains devoted to the unfaithful. God suffers with the children He must punish. Heschel applies one of his most subtle analyses of the divine pathos to the book of Jeremiah in which the Lord mourns Himself: "With Israel's distress came the affliction of God, His displacement, His homelessness in the land.... Should Israel cease to be His home, then God, we might say, would be without a home in the world."[12] Both humanity and God must suffer to give God a home in the world. The prophet mediates this paradox with fear and trembling.

Suffering is more than punishment for bad behavior: "The prophets discovered that suffering does not necessarily bring about purification, nor is punishment effective as a deterrent."[13] The Bible does not understand the process of repentance in purely natural terms. Judaism and Christianity agree that suffering itself is not the solution. Heschel represents the prophetic perspective: "The extinction of evil is ... but a part of the eschatological vision. Suffering does not redeem; it only makes us worthy of redemption."[14] God's vision of human justice is the beyond to which human agony points. Thomas Merton agrees and warns Christians that "Suffering is not the cause of holiness but only its occasion. Love, expressed in sacrifice, is what makes us saints. We are made saints not by undergoing pain but by overcoming it."[15] How do we reach the love beyond agony?

Heschel explicates the prophetic answer. He finds it is God's most paradoxical punishment, his charge to Isaiah to increase the people's distance from God:

> Make the heart of this people fat,
> And their ears heavy,
> And shut their eyes;
> Lest they see with their eyes,

12 *Ibid.*, pp. 110-112.
13 *Ibid.*, p. 188.
14 *Ibid.*, p. 94.
15 Thomas Merton, *Bread in the Wilderness* (Collegeville, Minnesota: Liturgical Press, 1971), p. 79.

And hear with their ears,
And understand with their hearts,
And turn and be healed.
(Isaiah 6: 10)

How could God trap Isaiah in this "appalling contradiction"? "He is told to be a prophet, in order to thwart and to defeat the essential purpose of being a prophet."[16] God simultaneously punishes and cures the people's hardness of heart by magnifying it: "It seems that the only cure for willful hardness is to make it absolute. Half-callousness, paired with obstinate conceit, seeks no cure. When hardness is complete, it becomes despair, the end of conceit. Out of despair, out of total inability to believe, prayer bursts forth."[17]

God drives his people away in order to augment their spiritual suffering. Hopelessness may then turn into a positive intuition of radical helplessness without God: "When hardness is intensified from above, responsibility is assumed by God. He smites and He restores, bringing about a revival of sensitivity." Agony seems necessary in order to shift the human perspective from self-centered freedom to an awareness that freedom is a gift from above. Conceit humiliated, presumption painfully quelled, the fallible ego can now yearn: "Agony is the final test. When all hopes are dashed and all conceit is shattered, man begins to miss what he has long spurned. In darkness, God becomes near and clear." Seen from the perspective of divine wisdom, Israel's suffering opens its people to God's love. The prophet reminds mankind of God's eternal promise of redemption.

Christian devotion focuses more systematically on inward redemption. Thomas Merton places suffering at the heart of mystical self-transformation. The contemplative concretely participates in the Psalms as a journey from death to resurrection in Christ. The travails of the exiled Hebrews prefigure the excruciating confrontation with human limits which the liturgy exacts of the courageous celebrant: "The experience of this," writes Merton in *Bread in the Wilderness* (1953), "is an experience of union, first with Christ in suffering, then with Christ in glory. For, as St. John of the Cross says, it is the same flame that first attacks our selfishness as its

16 *The Prophets*, p. 13.
17 This and the next two quotations are from *The Prophets*, pp. 191-193.

implacable enemy, then when selfishness is gone, rewards our love by flooding it with glory."[18] Like Isaiah's flock, the Christian must be violently removed from self-concern in order to identify, like the prophet, with the divine pathos: "the more we are united to [Christ] in love the more we are united in love with one another, because there is only one charity embracing both God and our brother."

Merton's belief that mysticism was the true cure for our spiritual anguish places him, paradoxically, both deep within and far from the center of modern thought.[19] His preference for the apophatic mystical tradition – in which God is experienced as a negation of all human understanding – reflects Heschel's account of biblical chastisement. The "dark night of the soul" is the human side of an experience which even non-religious people share. Religion must respond to this real absence. What is more common today than the self-destructive arrogance and panic of humanity without God, without acknowledged meaning, and nations without justice and peace? Heschel maintained that "we must first peer through the darkness, feel strangled and entombed in the hopelessness of living without God, before we are ready to feel the presence of His living light."[20] Merton insisted that the mystic, the reflective atheist, and the agnostic may share this utter darkness and despair. The absence of God became an objective experience of Jewish history when Hitler's soldiers and bureaucrats annihilated a civilization embodied in six million individuals. We experience the eclipse of humanity as individuals. For Merton, mystical prayer can renew the prophetic vision.

OUT OF THE DEPTHS

Mysticism is the fullest of insights, for it reveals to us the glory of being human while probing our bitter depths. Merton's remarkable presentation of "Dark Lightning" in Bread in the Wilderness relives the

18 This and the next quotation are from Bread in the Wilderness, pp. 79-80.
19 See "The Contemplative and the Atheist" (1970) in CWA, pp. 180-194; and The New Man (Mentor Books, 1961), pp. 17, 27, 70.
20 Abraham Heschel, God in Search of Man (Meridian Press and The Jewish Publication Society, 1955), p.140; cf. my article, "Mysticism and Despair in Abraham J. Heschel's Religious Thought," Journal of Religion 57, 1 (January 1977), 33-47; and note 19 above.

journey from utter despair to a face to face meeting with Christ in the Psalms.[21] The anticipated meaning of Christ's Passion does not mitigate the contemplative's frightful sacrifice. It begins at the person's outer limits: "under the pressure of a very great love, or in the darkness of a conflict that exacts a heroic renunciation of our whole self, or in the ecstasy of a sudden splendid joy that does not belong to this earth, the soul will be raised out of itself." The self first experiences the ultimate powerlessness of its yearning, its conflict, or its joy. The ego is wrenched from its human center.

Merton dwells upon the moment in which the person confronts its "own appalling nonentity." He understands this terrifying plunge into the abyss, to the border of sanity, as a mystical death.[22] The insight achieved is richly paradoxical and conveys at once God's dreadful distance and His embrace:

> It can sometimes happen that we too are brought down by Christ's love, into the dust of death. Then we know, somewhat as He knew, what it is to be "poured out like water" [cf. Psalm 21:13-16]. It is a terrible experience of seeing oneself slowly turned inside out. It is a frightful taste of humility that is not merely a virtue but the very agony of truth. This ghastly emptying, this inexorable gutting of our own appalling nonentity, takes place under the piercing light of the revealed word, the light of infinite Truth. But it is something far more terrible still: we find ourselves eviscerated by our own ingratitude, under the eyes of Mercy.

From the dark night of contemplative illumination emerges a fruitful symbiosis of human nothingness and divine Mercy. One feels both more and less than human. The Christian embarks upon a deadly imitation of Christ who "emptied Himself of all His power and glory to descend into the freezing depths of darkness where we had crawled to hide ourselves, cowering in blind despair." By identifying with the negative side of the Incarnation, by dwelling in the all too human darkness of sin, we learn Christ's divine humility:

21 The following analysis treats of pp. 103-108 of *Bread in the Wilderness*.
22 Cf. *The Seven Storey Mountain*, pp.108-109, 123-125, 200-204, 356-361 for Merton's experience of the Abyss.

"Then we begin to discover that the night in which we seem to be lost is the protection of the shadow of God's wings (Ps. 16:8)....We have entered the Baptism of darkness in which we are one with His death. But to die with Christ is to rise with him."

How does Merton's conclusion that "we are able to discover the living God in the very darkness of what seems to be His utter absence" apply to us? What can we receive from mystical death? Jewish and Christian tradition both answer: our destiny as divine image.[23] Mystical death illumines our essential finitude with God's undying love for mankind.

In *The New Man* (1961), Merton traces the crucifixion and rebirth of the Promethean mystic who seeks only self-fulfillment. Liberation from willfulness painfully reconciles the person and God. The individual's resurrection from mystical death awakens his or her divine image:

> Man begins to know God as he knows his own self. The night of faith has brought us into contact with the Object of all faith, not as an object but as a Person Who is the center and life of our own being, at once His own transcendent Self and the immanent source of our own identity and life.[24]

The Christian mystic undergoes a recentering of subjectivity from his- or herself to Christ. He or she no longer experiences the divine as an object of self-fulfillment, but as a Person, a divine Subject of Whom the human being is the beloved object. Other people then appear more clearly as fellow objects of divine concern.

Merton understood all along that God loved people, but it took practice and strong doses of solitude for him to incorporate the idea. In *The Sign of Jonas* (1953), Father Louis recalls his joyful discovery that the secular society which he had so feared and

23 Thomas Merton, "The Spiritual Fathers in the Desert Tradition," CWA, p. 287: "In his surrender of himself and of his own free will, his 'death' to his worldly identity, the monk is renewed in the image and likeness of God, and becomes like a mirror filled with the divine image." Cf. *The New Man*, pp. 41-43; and Heschel, *Man Is Not Alone* (Harper Torchbooks, 1951), pp. 207-215.
24 *The New Man*, pp. 140-141.

despised was worthy of his love: "I met the world and found it no longer wicked after all. Perhaps the things I resented about the world were defects of my own that I had projected upon it. Now, on the contrary, I found that everything stirred me with a deep and mute sense of compassion."[25] He had surmounted the traditional conflict of world and cloister. Merton explains quite dramatically, in a crucial entry to *Conjectures of a Guilty Bystander* (1966), how he definitively rejected *contemptus mundi:* "The whole illusion of a separate holy existence is a dream."[26] His new human insight reflects God's view: "Then it was as if I suddenly saw the secret beauty of their hearts, the depths of their hearts where neither sin nor desire nor self-knowledge can reach, the core of their reality, the person that each one is in God's eyes."[27] Humility and compassion were no longer problems for Merton, for he spontaneously identified with God's subjectivity. When Merton first entered Gethsemani, he defensively feared the world; his awareness of others' sin was inseparable from his anxious need to escape the contamination of his own. Freed from egotism he understood why God loved mankind:

> At the center of our being is a point of nothingness which is untouched by sin and by illusion, a point of pure truth, a point or spark which belongs entirely to God, which is never at our disposal, from which God disposes of our lives, which is inaccessible to the fantasies of our mind or the brutalities of our own will. This little point of nothingness and of *absolute poverty* is the pure glory of God in us.

No conflict remained between the human will and that of God. The contemplative loves people or the world because he or she perceives their essential purity, their essence as image of the divine. (Yet, frankly, I am disturbed by Merton's need to isolate the hidden and nonhuman character of that purity, "which belongs entirely to God, which is never at our disposal.") Merton called upon contemplatives to share their inward purification

25 See Henri Nouwen, *Pray to Live* (Notre Dame: Fides, 1972).
26 *Conjectures of a Guilty Bystander* (Doubleday and Company, 1966), p. 140.
27 This and the next quotation are from *Conjectures*, pp. 141–142.

with the sinful world. The mystical journey meets Christ in the pathos of moral concern:

> Do we renounce ourselves and the world in order to find Christ, or do we renounce our alienated and false selves in order to choose our deepest truth in choosing the world and Christ at the same time? If the deepest ground of my being is love, then in that very love itself and nowhere else will I find myself and the world, and my brother and Christ.[28]

The actions of contemplatives should guide outsiders: "By their example of a truly Christian understanding of the world, expressed in a living and active application of the Christian faith to the human problems of their own time, Christians manifest the love of Christ for men (John 13:35, 17:21), and by that fact make him visibly present in the world."[29] The imitation of Christ creates a partnership with the Hebrew prophet.

Abraham Heschel's masterwork, *Man Is Not Alone* (1951), attempts to initiate that way of thinking and living. Heschel's premise is clear: "There is only one way to define Jewish religion. It is the *awareness of God's interest in man,* the awareness of a *covenant,* or a responsibility that lies on Him as well as on us. Our task is to concur with His interest, to carry out His vision of our task."[30] Heschel is the prophet's advocate. Though God has proven dramatically absent to most people, the Jew must imitate God's concern as represented in the Bible. Divine concern is transitive for it goes out to others; the person must first transcend self-concern. Full concern embraces all reality: "The self, the fellow-man and the dimension of the holy are the *three* dimensions of a mature human concern. True love of man is clandestine love of God." The three-dimensionality of existence is not just an abstract theological principle. The interdependence of God, society, and the individual establishes our inescapable partnership.

---

28 "Is the World a Problem?", in CWA, p. 171.
29 "Blessed Are the Meek: The Christian Roots of Nonviolence," in *Thomas Merton on Peace,* ed. Gordon Zahn (McCall Publishing Co., 1971), p. 209.
30 *Man Is Not Alone,* p. 214; the next quotation is from p. 139.

THE THREE DIMENSIONS OF DIALOGUE

Heschel and Merton, as Jew and Christian, understood callousness as alienation from God. Both accompany their readers to the terrifying depths of their loneliness while nurturing a sense of divine Presence which all people can share. Prayer, for both, plumbs the abyss of humanity and places us before God as responsible persons. Prayer is their touchstone of truth. Thomas Merton and Abraham Heschel stood firmly before God and spoke to the world, and to their co-religionists, with a spiritually radical conscience.

They judged society and religious institutions alike by God's standards and so realized the partnership of Judaism and Christianity in a troubled world. To society they voiced the demands of divine justice and compassion against the forces of warfare, social and economic oppression and indifference. They challenged the self-interested withdrawal fostered by religious institutionalism. Heschel sought to balance the traditional Jewish emphasis on external observance, or *halakha*, with the inner life of devotion *(agada)*. He believed ethnicity less essential to Judaism than relationship with the living God; impassioned prayer, not ethical culture, should foster a burning prophetic concern. Merton deplored the unreflective traditionalism of the American Catholic hierarchy. He sought to liberate the inner person: a mystical relationship with God would abolish the defensive self-centeredness that inhibits moral courage. Contemplatives, who specialized in devotion and personal authenticity, could become prophetic witnesses.

But we who seek to learn more from Merton should ask why he pursued dialogue with Jews less actively (or less publicly) than dialogue with atheists and religious of the East. Perhaps the concrete reality of the people Israel seemed to remain an insurmountable barrier? Christians do tend to over-spiritualize Judaism and the Jews. But surely the religion of Incarnation can appreciate the historicity and spiritual autonomy of Judaism. It must, if dialogue is to be possible. Merton's dialogue with Judaism may also have remained latent because of the politics of Synagogue and Church in North America. Whatever the reasons, Jews and Christians share a common destiny. Threats against one affect the other in the spiritual as well as social dimension. The Bible will not let us forget the inextricable partnership of our faiths. Religious cooperation must underlie action in the secular world.

Can these common undertakings remain three-dimensional and preserve the integrity – and the contradictions – of God, the individual, and collective life? Can religious institutions preserve their spiritual integrity? The Jewish and Catholic contemplatives whom we have compared, by their identification with God's involvement with humanity, answer "Yes." Merton and Heschel, from the center of their specific commitments to God, extended their love and anger to all people. Their militant devotion to the divine image of mankind is a beacon in the dark night of an anguished world. Thomas Merton and Abraham Heschel disagreed on creeds and commitments at the heart of their traditions. But they are united in their anxiety before mankind and God. Fidelity to their witness is our continuing task.

13

THOMAS MERTON'S PROPHETIC VOICE:

MERTON, HESCHEL, AND VATICAN II

Brenda Fitch Fairaday

According to Fr. Thomas F. Stransky, of all the documents prepared and discussed during the four sessions of Vatican Council II, "no draft had a more unplanned, tortuous and threatened journey than did *Nostra Aetate,* especially its No. 4 on the Jews."[1] Apparently, it had not occurred to Pope John XXIII to even consider the subject of anti-Semitism or any related item during the council. However, one week after establishing the Secretariat for Promoting Christian Unity (SPCU), the Jewish question was presented to the Pope in a half-hour conversation with Jules Isaac, a Jew and a French historian who had been director of education in France. Isaac, who had survived Nazism, had made it his mission to study the Christian scriptures and the theology of the early Church Fathers in order "to demonstrate ... the relationship between early Christian theology and anti-Semitism."[2] There was no doubt in his mind that the Holocaust had stemmed from these sources, and he presented his conclusions in an important book: *The Teaching of Contempt,* which summed up the Church's position of denunciation and theological anti-Semitism. On June 13, 1960, he urged the Pope "to show the good path by solemnly condemning the teaching of contempt as, in essence, anti-Christian," and suggested, that a papal committee should study "the Jewish

---

1 Thomas F. Stransky, C.S.P., "The Catholic-Jewish Dialogue: Twenty Years after 'Nostra Aetate,'" in *America,* February 8, 1986, p. 92. Father Stransky was a founding staff member of the Vatican Secretariat for Promoting Christian Unity.
2 Jack Bemporad and Michael Shevack, *Our Age* (New York: New City, 1996), p 16.

question." Pope John assured him that he was right in having hope, and in September of that year charged the SPCU with that task.[3]

John XXIII's vision of "aggiornamento" or "bringing up to date" now included an unanticipated topic, one which was met with disparagement and hostility in some places but welcomed as necessary in others.[4] Unlike the interchurch topics, the discussion on the Jewish question was, at the Pope's request, "sub secreto," he no doubt being aware that there would indeed be opposition. On the one hand, one could not easily forswear many centuries of papal decrees, conciliar statements, or legislation which had proscribed the Jewish population, both materially and spiritually. Catholic theology would find the shift more than a little difficult. And, on the other hand, any developments in the Catholic-Jewish relations would have enormous political implicatons in the Middle East, which was already fraught with conflicts among Jews, Christians, and Moslems.

Abraham Joshua Heschel was an active participant in the discussions in Rome, representing as he did the American Jewish Committee in its effort to improve Jewish-Christian relations and to eliminate anti-Judaism from Church teaching. Heschel's theological acumen would prove essential in discussions relating to the basic questions of theology which underpinned the Church's attitude. In November of 1961, Heschel met with Cardinal Augustin Bea, the head of the Secretariat, who invited Heschel to submit recommendations to the Council to improve Catholic-Jewish relations. According to Rabbi Fritz A. Rothschild, who was also present in Rome for these discussions,

> Heschel's memorandum, prepared in cooperation with the American Jewish Committee, made three important recommendations. It urged the Council "to reject and condemn those who assert the Jews as a people are responsible for the Crucifixion. ..." It suggested that the

3 Stransky, 92.

4 Monsignor John M. Oesterreicher, a participant and official commentator on the document *Nostra Aetate*, recounts in his book *The Rediscovery of Judaism*, his presentation introducing the "Decretum de Judaeis" to the Secretariat for Christian Unity and pleading its acceptance, which was "greeted by a standing ovation" in spite of the many arguments, alterations and dissensions.

Council "acknowledge the integrity and permanent preciousness of the Jews and Judaism" so that the Jews be accepted *as Jews*. This meant that the Church would reconsider its missionary attitude and refrain from regarding Jews primarily as potential converts. And finally, it called for programs "to eliminate abuses and derogatory stereotypes" by promoting scholarly cooperation and the creation of church agencies to combat religious prejudice.[5]

Heschel was passionately committed to basic human rights and, in this case, to fostering what he called "the new Christian understanding of Judaism."[6] He was convinced that Christians could change their traditional perspective on Judaism; his efforts were a natural offshoot of what he saw as his primary task in life: to bear witness to God.[7] He was aware of the revolution in ecumenical patterns that was occurring in the 1960s; he himself stood in the center of it. He knew that Jews had a unique opportunity, "unprecedented in nearly two thousand years, to enter into dialogue with Christians who are eager to hear the message of Jewish thought."[8] A new and more accurate understanding of Judaism would allow Christians to partake of the spiritual treasures inherent in his religion, and he himself was concerned to open Christian minds to the central realities around which Judaism revolves: God, Torah, and the People Israel.[9]

But this opportunity very nearly was scuttled by the aforementioned opponents. In a journal entry for February 29, 1964, in which he also comments on the Rolf Hochhuth play *The Deputy*, which was directed against Pope Pius XII, Thomas Merton remarks that the Church – that is, its press, the hierarchy – have remained pretty much the same in spite of the example of Pope John XXIII.

---

5 Fritz A. Rothschild, "Abraham Joshua Heschel (1907-1972): Theologian and Scholar, "*American Jewish Yearbook*, 1974, M. Fine and M. Himmelfarb, eds. (Philadelphia: Jewish Publication Society of America), 535, quoted in Rothschild, *Jewish Perspectives on Christianity* (New York: Crossroad, 1990), p. 270.
6 Abraham J. Heschel, "From Mission to Dialogue," in *Conservative Judaism* 21 (Spring 1967), 9.
7 John C. Merkle in Rothchild, *Perspectives*, p. 271.
8 Heschel, "From Mission to Dialogue," p. 11.
9 Merkle, in Rothschild, *Perspectives*, p. 272.

He goes on to say, "Now that the question of the Jews has come up in the council exactly the same roadblock is met with: one cannot go further, because to defend the Jews even on religious and spiritual grounds has political implications that are disadvantageous."[10]

Merton had become acquainted with the thought of Heschel by 1960, at which time the two men began a cordial correspondence, admiring each others' works and the depth of spiritual insight contained therein. His journal reports that Heschel sent books and "an amiable and humble letter." In Merton's estimation, Heschel "is the most significant spiritual (religious) writer in this country at the moment. I like his depth and his realism. He knows God!"[11] In his December 17 letter to Heschel, Merton comments that the "prophet Isaiah is read daily, [during] a season of longing for the fulfillment of divine promises.... I believe humbly that Christians and Jews ought to realize together something of the same urgency of expectation and desire, even though there is a radically different theological dimension to their hopes. They remain the same hopes with altered perspectives. It does not seem to me that this is ever emphasized ...And then, "I do hope you will take seriously the thought of coming to see me someday." And indeed, Heschel did go to Gethsemani, in an appeal for assistance from Merton when the wording of Chapter 4 had gone from very good and favorable to the Jews to very bad. In a mimeographed statement to the Council fathers, Heschel said,

> Chapter Four of the Schema on Ecumenism... [of November 1963] dealing with the "Attitudes of the Catholics ... toward the Jews," made special headlines around the world. Except for a few words, troublesome to the Jewish conscience, it represented a momentous declaration and was hailed as an event of historic importance.[12] Subsequently, this Chapter has been rewritten and the version now distributed ... is not only

10 T. Merton, *Dancing in the Water of Life*: The Journals of Thomas Merton, Vol. 5, 1963 (New York: Harper Collins, 1997), p. 82.
11 T. Merton, *Turning Toward the World*: The Journals of Thomas Merton, Vol. 4, 1960-1963 (New York: Harper Collins, 1996), p. 61-2.
12 See Appendix A: Texts I.

ineffective, but profoundly injurious. The omissions, attenuations, and additions are so serious that, if adopted, the new document will be interpreted as a solemn repudiation of the desire ... "to right the wrongs of a thousand years." The new document proclaims that "the Church expects in unshakable faith and with ardent desire ... the union of the Jewish people with the Church." Since this present draft document calls for "reciprocal understanding and appreciation, to be attained by theological study and fraternal discussion," between Jews and Catholics, it must be stated that *spiritual fratricide* is hardly a means for the attainment of "fraternal discussion" or "reciprocal understanding."[13]

Hard words, indeed. Heschel goes on to remark on his own bitter disappointment, citing the high price that Jews have had to pay for keeping and preserving the covenant, and he repeats his famous declaration: "I am ready to go to Auschwitz any time, if faced with the alternative of conversion or death." He states the hope that must have filled Jules Isaac's heart when he heard the response of John XXIIII: "Mutual reverence between Christians and Jews began to fill hearts. We ardently pray that this great blessing may not vanish."[14]

On September 9, 1964, Merton responded: "It is simply incredible. I don't know what to say about it. This much I will say: my latent ambitions to be a true Jew under my Catholic skin will surely be realized if I continue to go through experiences like this, being spiritually slapped in the face by these blind and complacent people of whom I am nevertheless a 'collaborator'.... I must, however, think more of people like Cardinal Bea who must certainly be crushed by this development."[15] His journal entry of September 10 complains that "all the light, all the originality" had been removed from the Council's original statement, that the

13 Noted in the Letters between Heschel and Merton as found in *Thomas Merton, Pilgrim in Process*, Donald Grayston and Michael W. Higgins, eds. Toronto, 1983. Appendix, pp. 100-101.
14 In *Thomas Merton, Pilgrim in Process*, p. 101.
15 Thomas Merton, *The Hidden Ground of Love*, Letters, ed. by William Shannon (New York: Farrar Straus & Giroux, 1985), p. 434.

chance for profound change, made through prophetic insight, had been lost. "It is precisely in prophetic and therefore deeply humiliated and humanly impoverished thirst for light that Christians and Jews can begin to find a kind of unity in seeking God's will together."[16]

Merton had written to Cardinal Bea that summer, the day following Heschel's visit in July, to offer his voice in support of the original draft, assuring Bea of the prayers of the monks for his efforts, and praying

> that God may see fit to grant his Church the very great favor and grace of understanding the true meaning of this opportunity for repentance and truth which is being offered her and which so many are ready to reject and refuse. It is true that the Chapter can do much for the Jews, but there is no question that the Church herself stands to benefit by it spiritually in incalculable ways. I am personally convinced that the grace to truly see the Church as she is in her humility and in her splendor may perhaps not be granted to the Council Fathers if they fail to take account of her relation to the anguished Synagogue.... The very words themselves should suggest that the *ekklesia* is not altogether alien from the *synagogue* and that she should be able to see herself to some extent, though darkly, in this antitypal mirror. But if she looks at the picture, what she sees is not consoling.[17]

Merton confided in Cardinal Bea "as a son to a Father," expressing his hope that the theological and biblical bases for the changes in attitude would finally carry the resolution through to the light of day, leading the Church forward. Although Heschel thought that Bea was probably too crushed to succeed and placed his hope in Bishop Jan Willebrands, Bea moved through the Fourth Session the final draft which had restored most, if not all, of the wording that Heschel had spoken well of. It was approved by 2,221

16 Merton, *Dancing in the Water of Life*, p. 142.
17 Merton, *The Hidden Gound of Love*, p. 433.

votes to 88, a stunning victory for this, the shortest but possibly the most influential document of the Second Vatican Council.

Nostra Aetate, the "Declaration on the Relationship of the Church to Non-Christian Religions" was, in the words of Rabbi Jack Bemporad, "the seed of a whole new relationship with the Jews.... The beginning of the end of theologically justified anti-Semitism.... The theological prejudice had been addressed. The roots of the Holocaust were severed."[18] These few paragraphs were the culmination of all Jules Isaac's work and of the hope that had been assured him by John XXIII.[19] This volte-face on the part of the Church was a complete restatement of and "purification of the ancient Church's teachings," forsaking "religious prejudice for religious respect."[20] Through the promulgation of *Nostra Aetate,* as well as of *Lumen Gentium (Light of the Peoples),* the Church was prepared to embrace all religions as containing, in some way and degree, the truth of God. Remarkably, the fifteen Latin sentences of Chapter Four began a shift in 1900 years of the varied and often tense relationship between Catholics and Jews. [We should note that, while the theological and pastoral horizons will change dramatically, political hindrances remain, always set to clog the wheels.]

Nostra Aetate has brought about extraordinary achievements in Jewish-Catholic relations. Some ten years later, in 1974, a follow-up document – delayed by the ever present political pressures – entitled *Guidelines on Religious Relations with the Jews,* was issued; and in 1985, the subsequent *Notes on the Correct Way to Present the Jews and Judaism in Preaching and Catechesis in the Roman Catholic Church* furthered the efforts of those who had begun work in this field.[21]

The *Notes* also reveal and address those issues which had come up in the first steps of dialogue. That document reiterated the unique place occupied by the Jewish religion vis-a-vis the doctrines of the Roman Church. It declares that the relationship between Christianity and Judaism is a "permanent reality." Using

18 Bemporad, *Our Age,* p. 17.
19 The first modern Pope to state categorically that anti-Semitism was a sin was Pius XI, in 1938. See Passelecq and Suchecky, *The Hidden Encyclical of Pius XI,* in Resources, this volume, p. 399.
20 Bemporad, p. 16.
21 For *Guidelines* and *Notes,* see Johannes Cardinal Willebrands, *Church and Jewish People*: New Considerations (New York: Paulist Press, 1992), pp. 211-239.

the words of John Paul II, it states that the Jewish people are proclaimed "the people of God of the Old Covenant, which has never been revoked." It addresses the eternal relationship between Judaism and Christianity, the deep spiritual bonds that link Jews and Christians, the great spiritual patrimony which both share in their biblical heritage. It obliges the Church to emphasize the importance of Jews and Judaism in *all* its teachings; the Jewish presence is regarded as "essential and should be organically integrated." Again, in the words of John Paul II, the Church cannot understand its mission unless it understands the Jewish people, being duly aware "of the faith and religious life of the Jewish people as they are professed and practiced still today." And it declares that one cannot understand Jesus fully unless one understands Judaism. Living Judaism, then, is essential to the life of the Church.[22]

Such statements presented, and still present, doctrinal soul-searching within the Church. What is to become of the "New Israel" when the "Old Israel" is still alive and well? Shall they be like Esau and Jacob in their final rapprochement on the banks of the Jabbok, now on the banks of the Tiber? Since the Church recognizes that people can receive salvation in other religions, how should it maintain its claim to Christ as Savior of the world, Christ as one with the Father? Building on the references to Paul's Letter to the Romans, chapters 9-11, in Chapter Four of *Nostra Aetate*, the "Notes" emphasizes even more strongly the Jewish roots of that olive branch onto which the Gentiles were grafted (quoting Romans, chapter 11); that Jesus' Jewishness informed his life, teachings, and expectations, his ministry to "the house of Israel," his sharing of the anxieties and hopes of his people. In all these documents, the Church sought to affirm its own faith in a way that also affirmed the eternal blessings given to the Jewish people.

Pope John XXIII had opened the doors to fellowship with Judaism; Paul VI had signed into being the break-through document *Nostra Aetate;* and in our time we have witnessed the further steps taken by John Paul II in shoring up the good will that had been put in place:

22 Bemporad, p. 41.

- In 1979, soon after he took office, he held an audience with representatives of Jewish organizations, reiterating then the policies set out in *Nostra Aetate* and the "Guidelines," repudiating all forms of anti-Semitism as opposed to the very spirit of Christianity; he visited Auschwitz to "kneel on this Golgatha of the modern world"; and met with other Jewish communities.
- In 1980 he again met with various groups on pastoral visits to Germany, Italy, Brazil, France, and England.
- Throughout the 1980s he continued to press for dialogue, meeting with many Jewish leaders. A watershed event was the historic visit in 1986, the first by any reigning pope, to the Synagogue of Rome, where he was received by the Chief Rabbi, Elio Toaff. In his remarkable speech, he stated again the ideals of *Nostra Aetate*, repudiating any idea that the Jews were an accursed people because of the passion and death of Christ, and declared, "You are our dearly beloved brothers and, in a certain way, it could be said that you are our elder brothers.[23,24]
- He has carried through the theme of repentance and forgiveness. In 1990 first mention was made of the need for "Teshuvah" and reconciliation on the part of Christians as "a witness to our failure to be authentic witnesses to our faith at times in the past." This statement, another about-face, was made by then Archbishop Edward Cassidy at a meeting of the International Catholic-Jewish Liaison Committee in Prague in the face of a rising anti-Semitism in Eastern Europe and Russia following the collapse of the Soviet Union.[25]

The name of that committee itself testifies to the degree of change between Rome and Jerusalem in these past 35 years. The

23 Quoted in *Pope John Paul II on Jews and Judaism*, 1979-1986, ed. Eugene Fisher (Washington, DC: US Catholic Conference, 1987), p. 79. See Appendix B.
24 It may be noted that Heschel preferred the image of mother and daughter, saying that it was appropriate that the daughter religion, Christianity, should duly honor its mother religion, Judaism, following the teaching of the Fourth Commandment to "honor your father and mother." See Heschel's "No Religion Is an Island," in Rothschild, *Jewish Perspectives*, p. 316.
25 Bemporad, pp. 65-66

278 · *Brenda Fitch Fairaday*

appeal to each party to assume a responsible posture that reflected the statement, "Both of us must realize that in our age anti-Semitism is anti-Christianity and that anti-Christianity is anti-Semitism," reveals the expectation of a common ground from which such a statement could be made, understood, and accepted – as though the bark of Peter were again comfortable on the waters of the Sea of Galilee. The Prague Statement outlined what might be done and how, closing with this revealing comment:

> "Catholic-Jewish dialogue *can become a sign of hope* and inspiration to other religions, races, and ethnic groups to turn away from contempt, toward realizing authentic human fraternity. This new spirit of friendship and caring for one another may be the most important symbol we have to offer to our troubled world."[26] [Emphasis added]

On the local level, dialogues have taken on such issues as: What is the Catholic understanding of "mission to the Jews" or the Jewish understanding of "witness to the non-Jew" without being open to charges of proselytizing? In New York City, Fordham University, in its annual "Nostra Aetate Dialogues," has been presenting each November since 1993, two speakers, one from each camp, to speak on a selected topic. These have included The Jewishness of Jesus; The Death of Jesus; Jerusalem: Heavenly City and Earthly Center in Jewish and Early Christian Thought; Abraham Joshua Heschel: Prophet of Social Activism. More recently, they have tackled such thorny issues as Pope Pius XII, and Paul: A Bond or a Barrier? The audience for these talks does not consist solely of academics or intellectuals, and the questions taken and answered have revealed very down to earth, nitty-gritty concerns.

Educational initiatives, encouraged in "Guidelines" and "Notes," have produced statements in the new Catechism, weighing in against anti-Semitism and fostering respect for the Jewish people and religion. The late Cardinal John O'Connor, a champion of the Jewish-Catholic dialogue, said: "The Catechism is not the end of the world. It does not have the authority of the *New*

26 Quoted in Bemporad, p.69.

York Times. But ... it is very serious about *Nostra Aetate* and anti-Semitism."[27] It was, by the way, Cardinal O'Connor who urged the Vatican to recognize the State of Israel, with a kind of spiritual, diplomatic recognition. He did what he could, he said, speaking in November 1993. And indeed, an accord was signed on December 30, 1993.[28]

Dr. Fritz Rothschild stated, in private conversation with this writer, that during the discussions in Rome at the time of the Second Vatican Council, he urged Heschel and Rabbi Marc Tannenbaum to base their argument, in support of the stronger wording of the Jewish Chapter, on biblical theology. The Church would only be won over, he said, by a strong theological case. They chose Paul's Letter to the Romans, chapters 9 through 11, and it is well that they did. The symbol of the good olive tree onto which the wild olive branches have been grafted was a rich one, out of which many good teachings have come, all evident and frequent in *Nostra Aetate* and the "Notes." It has also proved to be a rich source for the teaching of the Bible, both Testaments, without rancor or prejudice showing through.

It is likely that this text was one which Heschel discussed with Merton on his trip to the monastery that hot July day in 1964. In an entry in his journal, Merton says

> I am more and more convinced that Romans 9-11 (the chapters on the election of Israel) are the key to everything today. This is the point where we have to look, and press and search and listen to the word. From here we enter the understanding of Scripture, the wholeness of revelation and of the Church. Vatican II is still short of this awareness, it seems to me. The Chapter on the Jews has been woefully inadequate. It was naturally cautious, I will not say to the point of infidelity, but it was obtuse. It went nowhere. And in its inadequacy it is itself a providential sign, a "word." So we must look harder and further into this mystery.[29]

27 In *No Religion Is an Island:* The Nostra Aetate Dialogues, ed. Edward Bristow (New York: Fordham University Press, 1998), p. 114.

28 See comments in Bristow, p. 116.

29 Merton, *Dancing in the Water of Life,* p. 162.

The mystery of the olive tree and the olive branches is surely the mystery of Judaism and the Church, one in which we all partake, one which we all benefit from, one which assists in the "tikkun olam," that repair and redemption of the world which Heschel, Merton, and John XXIII all looked for, hoped for, and worked for.

Thomas Merton's encounter with Judaism began when he was in his late teens, when his exploring nature embraced three Jewish friends – Robert Lax, Seymour Freedgood, and Robert Gerdy – while they were all students at Columbia University. Their work together at the University was not, definitely not, concerned with religion, but their mutual attraction in work and study underpinned their mutual acceptance of a deeper, spiritual nature in each. Of the four friends who accompanied him at his baptism on November 16, 1938, three were these Jews. His sponsor, Ed Rice was the only Catholic he knew.[30] So when, in 1964, Merton responded wholeheartedly to Heschel's appeal, he was enunciating a long-held and deep – though unarticulated – sense of oneness with the Jews.[31] According to William Shannon, Merton was "moved to personal involvement in an issue because it affected people who were dear to him and important in his life."[32]

By the time Vatican Council II was being prepared, Merton had been asked for an article on Judaism. His letter to Rabbi Steven Schwarzschild of Feb. 24, 1962, reveals the reasons for his hesitation: "I am not worthy yet to write about the mystery of Judaism in our world. It is too vast a subject." His diffidence comes from a lack of a total immersion and study in the subject, but his appreciation was already deep. He respected the Jewish tradition and the sources of Christian knowledge about God as found in the Old Testament. Although he himself might be termed a supersessionist, still he said that the "Old Israel" was not repudiated

---

30 Eventually, Bob Lax and Bob Gerdy both joined the Catholic Church; Sy Freedgood remained a practicing Jew. Lax, Rice, and Freedgood were present at Merton's ordination.

31 This regard may also be read in his correspondence with Rabbi Zalman Schachter and other comments in various writings, i.e., between 1960 and 1964; also in *Conjectures*.

32 William H. Shannon, "Thomas Merton and Judaism," *America*, October 6, 1990, pp. 218-222. I am indebted to Msgr. Shannon and his insightful article not only for having elicited my interest in this subject but for the gist of these remarks.

by God (following Paul). Writing in *Conjectures of a Guilty Bystander,* he affirmed that "the Jews were and remain the people especially chosen and loved by God."[33]

Merton's sense for eschatology allows him to see both Christianity and Judaism on a common course which would restore the common "ground of freedom and love. The experience of the Holocaust," Merton says, "was an eschatological sign for the Jews and for the world, just as the Resurrection is one for Christians." It was a sign that Israel and Christ cannot be separated.[34] "The Suffering Servant is One: Christ, Israel .... The mystery of Israel and of the Church is ultimately to be revealed as One." And again: "There is one wedding and one wedding feast."[35]

To Cardinal Bea, Merton wrote that he hoped the Church would not lose this "opportunity for repentance and truth which is being offered." In September of that year, he deplored the weak statement of the second draft[36] crowded out as it was by "juridical niceties" and a "fantastic misunderstanding of the Church's true mission."[37]

According to Heschel,

"The prophet is a man who feels fiercely. God has thrust a burden upon his soul, and he is bowed and stunned at man's fierce greed.... Prophecy is the voice that God has lent to the silent agony [of man].... It is a form of living, a crossing point of God and man. God is raging in the prophet's words."[38]

The prophetic voices of both Merton and Heschel speak to the Church and the world of today.

---

33 T. Merton, *Conjectures of a Guilty Bystander* (New York: Doubleday, 1966), p. 171.
34 An artist's witness to this eschatological vision can be seen in Marc Chagall's many paintings of the Crucified Christ variously garbed, with prayer shawl or phylactery, surrounded by Jews of eastern or western aspect. See "Marc Chagall, Painter of the Crucified," by C. and I. Sussman, pp. 96-117, in *The Bridge:* A Yearbook of Judaeo-Christian Studies, The Institute of Judaeo-Christian Studies, vol. 1, ed. J.M. Oesterreicher (New York: Pantheon, 1956).
35 Letter to Zalman Schachter, Feb. 16, 1962, in *Hidden Ground of Love*, op. cit., p. 535.
36 See Appendix A: Text II.
37 *A Vow of Conversation*, op. cit., pp. 76-77.
38 Abraham J. Heschel, *The Prophets* (New York: Harper and Row, 1962), p. 5. Quoted in *Thomas Merton, Pilgrim in Process*, op. cit., p. 89.

"O God, in accepting one another wholeheartedly, fully, completely, we accept You, and we thank you, and we adore You, and we love You with our being, because our being is in Your being, our spirit is rooted in Your Spirit."

—from Merton's last written prayer from *Dialogues with Silence: Prayers & Drawings*

14

MERTON:
A PIONEER OF PLURALISM

Ron Miller

INTRODUCTION

Ever since I first read Diana Eck's fascinating story of her own transformation experiences in India, I have been intrigued by her categories for describing the ways in which people of faith relate to other religions. Exclusivism is the belief that no religious truth or salvation can be found outside one's own faith community. Inclusivism is the belief that other religions can indeed contain some religious truth, but such truth is at best a partial expression of what is fully articulated in one's own sacred tradition. Pluralism serves more as a hypothesis than a belief, the premise that other religious traditions operate independently of any relation to one's own belief system.

Exclusivists tend to be fundamentalists in any tradition: Jerry Falwell in Christianity, Osama bin Laden in Islam. I recall a discussion with a Christian minister in which he began our exchange with an attempt at a common ground of agreement, "Well," he announced, "we can probably agree that if one religion is right then all others are wrong." I countered by saying that if one religion was right, then there's a good likelihood that all are. At this point, the lines were clearly drawn for the rest of the night's discussions.

Not surprisingly, the center of most religions is usually peopled by inclusivists. The Jewish teaching of the covenant of Noah recognizes that all human beings can have a relationship with God, though clearly the covenant of Sinai is superior. The Catholic Church officially embraced inclusivism at the time of the Second Vatican Council, which stated that other religions contain some truth and holiness but the fullness of truth resides within the Roman Catholic communion. Islam too sees itself as having a fuller form of the revelation given to Moses and to Jesus, thus seeing Judaism and Christianity as "People of the Book" but with less complete revelatory content.

Even today, pluralism remains the "rara avis" in the contemporary religious aviary. A pluralist tends to regard religions like languages. One doesn't argue that Spanish is a better language than French, because languages do what languages do. Each language has prose and poetry, asks questions, registers surprise, adds numbers, and can soar into mystical expression. The whole point of pluralism is that you study the other on its own terms, not from the singular perspective that it exists as an inferior or deviant form of yourself.

MERTON'S PLURALISM IN GENERAL

We need to address two questions here. One has to do with Merton as a pluralist in general. The other focuses more specifically on his pluralism with special reference to his views of Jews and Judaism. In addressing either of these qustions, it is incumbent on us to keep in mind Merton's evolution as a religious thinker. There's a distance of twenty years between the Merton of *The Seven Storey Mountain* and the later Merton of the *Asian Journal*. And since Merton's Church had and continues to have an officially inclusivist position, we might have to read between the lines to find Merton's pluralism. He may indeed be revealed as a closet pluralist at best.

We begin then with a general consideration of Merton's pluralism. What I find interesting is that this consciousness is most often present without his talking about it. We all remember the famous Sherlock Holmes mystery where the clue was the dog that didn't bark, and Merton's pluralism is much the same. He doesn't parade it; it's simply around as an assumption of his discourse. I was listening recently to some of his taped talks to the novices in which he was discussing the Sufis, Muslim mystics. In these tapes, he talks about their love for God, their methods of communion with God, their special techniques for meditation and prayer. Nowhere does he say that these mystics don't enjoy as full a relation to God as one who believes in Jesus. Nor, on the other hand, does he assert that their way is an equally valid way to God. He simply proceeds from the unspoken premise that these people are finding and experiencing God as Sufi Muslims, just as the Trappist novices he is addressing are finding and experiencing God at Gethsemani as Catholic Christian monks.

Another example of this pluralism is the oft-quoted mystical experience that culminates Merton's Asian journey, and thus in some ways his life. In the posthumously published book of that name, Merton begins with the contrasting picture of himself walking barefoot through the grass to the enormous statues of the Buddha while the priest who accompanies him evinces no interest in "paganism" and instead "hangs back and sits under a tree reading the guidebook" (233). Again, it's not so much what Merton says as what he doesn't say. The contrast between the vicar general and himself presents a living parable of the contrasting paradigm of exclusivism (or a begrudging inclusivism) and pluralism. The subsequent powerful experience which he describes as purifying and clarifying his Asian pilgrimage is described with no apologies for the "pagan" statues or "non-Christian" venue. It simply exists as what it is. The implication seems to be that there is no way which may not lead to the divine mystery, just as there is no way that guarantees such success.

The ease with which Merton could adopt pluralism has a great deal to do with his starting point on these and other religious questions. This has been discussed with great acuity by Matthias Neuman, O.S.B., in his insightful article in Volume Eight of *The Merton Annual* entitled "Revisiting *Zen and the Birds of Appetite* after twenty-five years." Neuman points out (pp.142-143) that Merton begins with an experiental framework, not a doctrinal one. He begins, in other words, not with religious explanation but with religious experience. As Neuman expresses this point, "In Merton's view all great religions (in their inner reality) aspire to a direct confrontation with Absolute Being ... Absolute Love ... Absolute Mercy or Absolute Void" (p. 143).

This approach reveals Merton's kinship with the author of what many would consider the most important book on religions published in America in the twentieth century, William James'

Varieties of Religious Experience. Originally delivered as a series of prestigious Gifford lectures in Scotland at the turn of the century, the published book opened up a new direction in religious thinking. Eschewing doctrinal disputes and creedal conundrums, James wanted to drink from the fresh source of religion, the experiences of their founders and their most notable representatives. This approach seerves as a kind of end run, simply avoiding the issues that otherwise dominate the discussions of theologians. There is a beautiful expression of this implicit pluralism in *Conjectures of a Guilty Bystander*:

> If I affirm myself as a Catholic merely by denying all that is Muslim, Jewish, Protestant, Hindu, Buddhist, etc., in the end I will find that there is not much left for me to affirm as a Catholic, and certainly no breath of the Spirit with which to affirm it (p.144).

This demonstrates Merton's catholic (in the small *c* sense of universal) soul, his tendency to appreciate and celebrate diversity, not push it away out of fear or pride.

Merton's Pluralism in Relation to Jews and Judaism

Our investigation shifts now from the broader question of Merton's religious pluralism in general to the more narrowly defined question of his pluralism in relation to Jews and Judaism. As James Carroll points out so eloquently in his landmark study, *Constantine's Sword*, the Jew is defined from early on in the Christian story as the ontological other, the foil for the Christian faith. It was not that long ago that we Catholics prayed in our Holy Week liturgy for "the perfidious Jews." There is no other religion that is more typically defined by Christians by its relationship to Christianity than Judaism. It's through Christian interpretation that the Hebrew Bible becomes an "Old Testament," a book to be read, not for what it intends to say to its own community of faith, but for what it says typologically and prophetically about Jesus and the Church.

Christianity has said a great deal about Judaism in its two thousand year history, but in these instances, Judaism has inevitably been defined in terms of Christianity's own identity and faith. Just as women in our western tradition from Aristotle through Freud were defined as biologically deficient males, Jews were understood by Christians as the people who did not recognize their own Messiah when he came. Judaism was constantly Christianity's foil, the scapegoat for Christianity's failures in faith, and the projection of Christianity's shadow. From this skewed vantage point, Christianity was understood as a religion of the spirit, whereas Judaism was one of the flesh. Christians were saved by faith but Jews attempted to save themselves through their works. Christians carried the "easy yoke" of the Gospel, while Jews labored under the burdensome yoke of the Law. Christianity's good news, in other words, was always simultaneously a "bad news" for the Jews.

We describe this way of thinking as "supersessionism" or "replacement theology," resulting in a strange ambivalence towards the "Jewish other." The source of this reaches back to the first Christian writings, the letters of Saul of Tarsus whom Christians know by his Roman name, Paul. In his Letter to the Romans 11:28 Paul writes: "As regards the gospel, they [the Jews] are enemies of God for your sake; but as regards election, they are beloved for the sake of their forefathers." This juxtaposition of "enemies" and "beloved" in one verse becomes symptomatic of Christianity's posture towards Judaism. To understand this verse and the complicated man who wrote it takes us a great distance toward accessing the deepest stratum of Christian consciousness about the Jews, with its essential ambiguity of love and hate, acceptance and rejection, preservation and replacement.

On the one hand, the Jews are beloved (*agapetoi*). This reveals one side of Christian consciousness. They are forever loved by Christians "because of their forefathers." *Not for themselves, but because of their heritage.* [*V.* Ap. A, p. 360.]And what is that legacy, that gift from the fathers?

First of all, it is Jesus of Nazareth, born of the House of David. Then, it is the Hebrew Bible, the Bible of Jesus and his early followers. And finally, it is the Jewish story that connected this "new religion" to an ancient narrative, so that the great figures of the "Old Testament" become the spiritual ancestors of all the Christian men and women who are baptized, including Abraham and David, Sarah and Rebecca, Joshua and Deborah.

On the other hand, the Jews are enemies (*ecthroi*). And this discloses the other side of Christian consciousness. Jews are enemies of the gospel. Enemies through their unbelief, their stubborn clinging to the Torah, their failure to accept Jesus as their Messiah. Classical Christian theology does not work with the possibility of a variety of belief systems. In this context, one cannot argue that Jews believe the revelation of Sinai and then understand Jews in terms of what they believe. Instead, Jews are judged in terms of what they don't believe. And so it is that Jews remain forever in Christian consciousness as "beloved enemies."

Christians typically understand Jews as people who don't believe that Jesus is the Messiah. And yet in some thirty years of doing Jewish-Christian dialogue and asking Jews and Christians to identify themselves, I have yet to hear a Jew say, "I am Jewish and what I want to tell you about myself is that I don't believe that Jesus is the Messiah." Nor have I ever heard a Christian say, "I am a Christian and what I want to tell you about myself is that I don't believe the revelations made to Muhammad." Growing up Catholic, it took me a long time to realize that there are no non-Catholics in the world. When have you met someone who introduced herself as a non-Catholic? Non-Catholics, after all, exist only in the minds of Catholics.

And yet, all of these ideas that many of us are grappling with today more than thirty years after Merton's death, are those which Merton realized fairly early in his career. How did it happen? Given such a formidable tradition of exclusivism, or at best inclusivism, one wonders how Merton could have evaded it, let alone transcended it. And even if he reached a pluralistic position in relation to Buddhists or Muslims, it seems even more remarkable that he would have done so in relation to Jews. And yet, it seems to me that there is clear evidence that that is precisely what he did.

As early as October 24, 1957 we read on p. 117 of Volume Three of his journals *(The Search for Solitude)*:

One has either got to be a Jew or stop reading the Bible. For the Bible really cannot make sense to anyone who is not spiritually a "Semite." The spiritual sense of the Old Testament is not and cannot be first an emptying out of its Israelite content. The New Testament is the fulfillment of the Old, not its destruction.

It seems to me that Merton is making some significant steps here. He is beginning to understand the implications of the replacement theology that is built into the very names he has learned for the two major parts of the Christian Bible: the Old Testament and the New Testament. Even though he's not ready to challenge those terms as we would today, using Hebrew Bible and Christian Testament instead, he senses that something is wrong if the scriptures of the Jewish people are emptied of their native content.

Replacement theology comes so naturally to Christians that its irony is frequently overlooked. I remember being asked by a nearby church to give a talk on the psalms for their adult education program. Realizing that I had a conflict that evening, I recommended that they contact a rabbi I knew at a nearby synagogue to speak on the subject. There was a long pause on the other end of this phone conversation and then a somewhat pained voice queried, "But why would we ask a rabbi to talk about our psalms?" When did the song book of the Second Temple become "our" psalms? How had they ceased to be the prayerbook of the Jewish people? Where had our Latin or English translations displaced the original Hebrew poetry of these prayers?

One wonders what conclusions about replacement theology Merton might have drawn from his reflections on reading Rabbi Abraham Joshua Heschel. On June 14, 1959 (p. 292 in that same Volume Three of the journals), Merton writes:

> The Covenant – God *commits* himself without respect to what we do about it. Our infidelity cannot change the Covenant, which is *unilateral*. Our job, to receive. As Heschel says, to participate.

But Heschel is a Jew. The covenant to which God is eternally committed is the covenant of Sinai. The covenant in which Heschel is called to participate is God's covenant with the Jews. Whether Merton is fully aware of it or not, the seed planted in his mind grows into what theologians would later call "dual covenant theology," an incipiently pluralistic awareness that God covenants with Jews through the ongoing covenant of Sinai, and covenants with Christians through their relationship to Jesus. According to this view the latter does not replace the former.

On May II, 1964 (p. 247 of *Witness to Freedom),* Merton writes:

> It is a strange thing: since Pope John brought it up, I realize how much the Fathers of the Church, the "best" of them, ranted against the Jews. Their sermons are read in our refectory often, and how much of it there is! Pope John just took out one phrase in one prayer: but on Good Friday I noticed the rest of that prayer, and the context in which it came!

It's clear that the two-thousand year tradition of replacement theology is beginning to bother Merton. Merton knows the patristic literature deeply enough to realize that there was a whole genre of literature with the title *"Contra Judaeos"* ("Against the Jews"). One couldn't be a theologian without producing a work with that name. And in those essays and in the sermons preached by those same Fathers of the Church, the Jews were consistently derided as the perfidious other, a people in league with Satan by their opposition to the truth of the gospel.

The prayer he refers to was from the traditional Good Friday liturgy. In the old *Missale Romanum,* the priest prayed: "*Oremus et pro perfidis Judaeis: ut Deus et Dominus noster auferat velamen de cordibus eorum; ut et ipsi agnoscant Jesum Christum Dominum nostrum."* In English: "Let us also pray for the faithless Jews that our God and Lord take away the veil from their hearts so that they recognize Jesus Christ our Lord."

Now there is a long series of such prayers, and in all the other prayers the faithful respond "Amen," as the priest then invites them to pray, to kneel, and to get up again. After the genuflection is completed, a second prayer is said on the same theme. But in this particular case the rubrics clearly state that the "Amen," the genuflection, and the rising are to be omitted. The faithful are to go directly to the follow-up prayer which in English reads as follows:

"Almighty and eternal God, who does not exclude even Jewish faithlessness from your mercy, hear our prayers which we offer for the blindness of this people, so that recognizing the truth of your light, which is Christ, they may escape their darkness. We make this prayer through that same Lord. Amen."

The rubrical omission is telling. The mere act of genuflecting in such proximity to the declaration of Jewish blindness and faithlessness seemed too much for the literary crafters of this liturgical text. The second prayer must follow the first without interruption (*statim dicitur* are the literal words of the rubrics, i.e. "immediately said"). To genuflect at that point might seem to be honoring in some way the almost unspeakable sin of Jewish perfidy. No such humbling posture should accompany a statement about the faithless Jews.

The reference to a veil in the first prayer and blindness in the second both stem from a primary source for much of this ambivalence towards the Jews, the same Paul whose theology we briefly encountered earlier in this article. It is Paul, in Second Corinthians 3:14-16, who tells us how the Jews have been blinded.

"Indeed to this day, when they hear the reading of the old covenant, that same veil is still there, since only in Christ is it set aside. Indeed, to this very day whenever Moses is read, a veil lies over their minds; but when one turns to the Lord, the veil is removed."

Testamentum translates the Greek word for *covenant* into Latin. So it is here that we see a source of replacement theology. Not only is the Jewish covenant "an old testament" but when Jews read from the Torah (the five books of Moses), a veil lies over their minds, i.e. they are unable to interpret their Jewish scriptures unless they are willing to understand them as Christian texts.

The reformed Roman Catholic liturgy sounds a great deal better. The English of the first prayer now reads:

Let us pray for the Jewish people, the first to hear the
word of God, that they may continue to grow in the love
of his name and in faithfulness to his covenant.

This almost sounds like dual covenant theology. Are we to
presume that the Jews are called to live in faithfulness to the
covenant of Sinai?
The second prayer clarifies any ambiguity on this point:

Almighty and eternal God, long ago you gave your
promise to Abraham and his posterity. Listen to your
Church as we pray that the people you first made your
own may arrive at the fullness of redemption. We ask this
through Christ our Lord. Amen.

Inclusivism has the final word. The tip-off is the word fullness.
Something good can now be recognized in Jews and Judaism.
They are no longer a people totally blinded and lost in the
shadows. But there is only one way they can arrive at "the fullness
of redemption" and that is clearly through their acceptance of
Christ and conversion to Christianity.
It is the old dualism that is reflected here, even in the reformed
prayers. Catholic Christians still have the fullness of truth, of virtue,
and of salvation. It was on a Holy Saturday (March 28, 1964) when
Merton was reflecting on the litugy of the previous day, Good
Friday, that he wrote (p.93 in Volume Five of the journals):

More and more I see that we in the Church are deluded
and complacent about ourselves. How much there is in
our Liturgy that puts all the blame on the Jews – so that
we ourselves enter the universal guilt without realizing it.

The more Christians displace on to the Jewish shadow, the less
light is shed on their own complicity in the sins of the world. The
more we see the sliver in the Jewish eye, the less we are aware of
the log protruding from our own.
What is reflected in the language of the liturgy takes dogmatic

form in the words of the Second Vatican Council's declaration on Jews and Judaism. The "Declaration on the Relationship of the Church to Non-Christian Religions" carries a history of palace intrigue from its inception in Pope John XXIII's desire to have the Council make a statement on the Jews, to some tense moments when it looked as though there would be no statement at all, to the final compromise document which was officially voted on by some two thousand bishops and promulgated by Pope Paul VI on October 28, 1965. [See Appendix A, pp. 363-69]

In his published journals (p. 76 of *A Vow of Conversation*), Merton makes an entry for September 10, 1964:

> Abraham Heschel has sent me a memo on the new Jewish Chapter at the Vatican Council [Test II]. The new proposal is incredibly bad. All the meaning has been taken out of it. All the originality, all the light are gone and it has become a stuffy, pointless piece of formalism with the stupid addition that the Church is looking forward with hope to the union of Jews with herself. This lack of spiritual and eschatological sense, this unawareness of the real need for profound change, is what makes such statements pitiable. One feels a total lack of prophetic insight and even of elementary compunction. Where is the prophetic and therefore deeply humiliated and humanly impoverished thirst for light, that Christians and Jews may begin to find some kind of unity in seeking God's will together? But if Rome simply declares herself complacently to be the mouthpiece of God and perfect interpreter of God's will for the Jews, with the implication that he in no way ever speaks to them directly, this is simply monstrous!*

Merton's evident anger here speaks volumes. He recognizes the replacement theology that characterizes the compromise document. Merton considers it stupid to talk of the Church looking forward with hope to the union of Jews with herself. He

---

*This is the edited version of the journal entry, prepared by Thomas Merton himself. For the unedited version, see above, "The Merton-Heschel Correspondence," p. 225. – Ed.

finds it "simply monstrous" to imagine that Jews speak to God only as anonymous Christians. Surely Merton sees that Jews and Christians are both on paths that lead to God and that both of these paths are valid. For it is clear from this passage that Merton believes that God does indeed "speak to them directly." And is this not the essence of pluralism, seeing other paths in their own integrity and autonomy and not as deviant forms of one's own path?

The Second Vatican Council had clearly failed to meet Merton's expectations of a more pluralistic theology. A few months before he wrote the journal entry quoted above, on July 13, 1964, Merton received Rabbi Heschel as his guest at the Trappist monastery in Gethsemani, Kentucky. They spoke about one of the earlier and bolder proposals for a conciliar document, one that was discarded along the path of political compromise. Merton wrote in his journal on the day after that visit (p. 63 of *A Vow of Conversation*):

> Heschel thinks that the Jewish Chapter will never be accepted by the Vatican Council. We spoke of how symbolic this fact was. In my opinion, the acceptance of this Chapter and the consequent implicit act of repentance is necessary for the Church. In reality, the Church stands to benefit more by it than the Jews."

We see here, as in so much of Merton's writings, the ability to "feel the other side" that is so indispensable for deep dialogue in a pluralistic context.

There was no way that Merton could avoid having the mind and heart of a pluralist. On January 13, 1961 (p. 126 of *The Hidden Ground of Love),* Merton wrote to Doña Luisa Coomaraswamy. Doña Luisa was born of Jewish parents in Argentina and was married to Ananda Coomaraswamy, an authority on Hinduism and Buddhism. These words seem to be almost a creed for the pluralistic spirit that guided so much of Merton's writings:

> I believe that the only really valid thing that can be accomplished in the direction of world peace and unity at the moment is the preparation of the way by the formation

of men who, isolated, perhaps not accepted or understood by any "movement," are able to unite in themselves and experience in their own lives all that is best and most true in the various great spiritual traditions. Such men can become as it were "sacraments" or signs of peace, at least. They can do much to open up the ininds of their contemporaries to receive, in the future, new seeds of thought. Our task is one of very remote preparation, a kind of arduous and unthanked pioneering.

Merton will always be to me the pioneer of pluralism par excellence. I hope that these words I have written and the other essays in this volume will prove at least that one part of his statement was wrong. He was indeed an arduous pioneer but he is no longer unthanked.

GOD PURSUES ME EVERYWHERE

God pursues me everywhere,
Enmeshes me in glances,
And blinds me sightless back like flaming sun.

God, like a forest dance, pursues me.
My lips are ever tender, mute, so amazed,
So like a child in ancient sacred grove.

God pursues me like a silent shudder.
I wish for tranquility and rest – He urges: come!
And see – how visions walk like the homeless on the streets.

My thoughts walk about like a vagrant mystery –
Walks through the world's long corridor.
At times I see God's featureless face hovering over me.

God pursues me in the streetcars and cafes
Every shining apple is my crystal sphere to see
How mysteries are born and visions come to be.

—Abraham Joshua Heschel, *Human, God's Ineffable Name.*
Translated from the Yiddish by Rabbi Zalman Schachter-Shalomi

15

RENEWAL:
JEWISH AND CHRISTIAN

INTRODUCTION TO THE INTERVIEW WITH
RABBI ZALMAN SCHACHTER-SHALOMI

Edward K. Kaplan

Rabbi Zalman Meshullam Schachter-Shalomi has inspired generations of spiritual seekers, Jewish and otherwise, in the ways of prayer, study, meditation, self-transformation, joy and holiness. Known to his students and friends as Reb Zalman, he is a true religious genius and a powerful, charismatic personality. (He added Shalomi to his family name as a commitment to peace.) Ancestor of the movement of Jewish Renewal that began in the 1960s, Reb Zalman is a "trans-denominational" observant Jew with an eclectic vision, receptive to all signals of spiritual energy. He combines classical Jewish sources with other traditions in order to help people transform their particular observance. His heart welcomes Buddhism, Sufism, Christianity, and even computer science, as he follows the scent of spiritual authenticity.

Zalman is a soul brother of Thomas Merton in his enthusiasm for all voices of Spirit, his warmth, the acumen of his judgments, his vital generosity. The two guides became friends, in fact, in the 1960s. They maintained an intense correspondence for about four years and met several times at the Abbey of Gethsemani. Merton's letters to Zalman are published in *The Hidden Ground of Love* and, for the first time, the present volume includes Zalman's side of their epistolary dialogue. Merton was especially keen on Zalman's eclectic reading and Jewish teaching, especially in mysticism and Hasidism, the charismatic approach to God inspired by Rabbi Israel Ba'al Shem Tov in 18th-century Poland.

Zalman's vision is both profoundly Jewish and universal. Zalman Schachter was born in Poland in1924 and raised in Vienna before World War Two, learning both modern Hebrew and Latin, in addition to the ancient Hebrew and Aramaic of Torah and Talmud studies, the Zohar, and Hasidic sources. He also spoke the German of the majority and of course his native language, Yiddish, known as the *mame loshn*, the mother tongue. His thinking includes these languages and multicultural frames of reference.

Like Merton, Zalman lived in the belly of a paradox. Already as a young man in Europe, he harmonized Jewish cultures that were considered to be antagonistic, as he wrote: "I danced the hora with Marxist Zionists and also celebrated the farewell to the Sabbath with Orthodox anti-Zionists. My father wanted me to go to both Gymnasium (secular co-educational high school) and to yeshiva after school. My own life – not only my father's – was always full of contradiction." Zalman emerged with expanded powers of communication to a sundered world.

But not before he was almost crushed by world events. After the Nazi occupation of Vienna, his family moved to France where they were interned in a Vichy prison camp. In 1941 they were able to leave for the United States. In Brooklyn, New York, Zalman studied at the Lubavitch Yeshiva, the transplanted center of that great Hasidic dynasty from Russia, and he was ordained a rabbi in 1947. Zalman's spiritual model was the Lubavitcher Rebbe, Rabbi Joseph Schneersohn (who died in 1950, succeeded by his son-in-law, Rabbi Menahem Mendel Schneerson).

Zalman sought to broaden his skills as a spiritual advisor, studying pastoral counseling at Boston University, where he met the outstanding African-American mystic and teacher of spiritual disciplines, Howard Thurman. (He calls Thurman his "Black Rebbe.") Thurman helped open Zalman's heart to other religious paths, including his own open-minded Christianity, and taught him how to use technology in spiritual teaching, such as audiotapes and records in guided meditation exercises. In 1956 Zalman moved to Winnipeg, Canada, where he was a Hillel rabbi and taught in the department of religion at the University of Manitoba. In 1968 he earned a doctorate in pastoral counseling from the Hebrew Union College in Cincinnati, Ohio, the rabbinical seminary of the Reform Jewish movement.

Reb Zalman became a spiritual teacher of national stature during the 1960s. Still associated with Lubavitch, also known as Habad,[1] he visited many college campuses with the charismatic singer and composer Shlomo Carlebach. Zalman studied and taught with Sufi masters, Hindus, Native American elders, Buddhists, Catholic monks and nuns, humanistic and transpersonal psychologists, and more. During this time he developed considerable independence from the Hasidic authorities, experimenting with psychedelic drugs and sympathetically exploring other spiritual idioms, to the extent that Habad broke with him.

Zalman gave workshops and weekend Sabbath retreats to modern, assimilated Jews and non-Jews alike. With his mind and spirit open, he conveyed the joy of Jewish worship by retaining many of his traditional Hasidic customs, as he says in the interview, wearing his *streimel* (the fur rimmed hat) and *kappote* (kaftan or robe) on Shabbos. Zalman's ability to communicate the vitality of Jewish mysticism brought him to the attention of Thomas Merton and they began a substantive correspondence in 1961. Zalman visited Merton at the Abbey of Gethsemani, fostering a fruitful communication which he describes in his interview.

Early in the 1970s, Zalman founded a movement of Jewish Renewal, similar to Thomas Merton's vision of a Mount Olivet retreat center at the Abbey of Gethsemani, in which visitors could absorb some benefits of contemplative life. During a sabbatical leave at Brandeis University, in Waltham, MA, Zalman met Arthur Green and other founders of Havurat Shalom, an experimental Jewish community of cooperative prayer and study. Zalman first called his own community, B'nai Or ("sons of light"), and then, influenced by the Women's Movement, P'nai Or ("faces of light"). Now part of "Aleph, Alliance for Jewish Renewal," dozens of "renewal" communities on the American continent and several foreign countries make Zalman's teachings available in newsletters, in addition to his books, pamphlets, audio- and videotapes, a loose-leaf prayer book, and the famous rainbow *tallit* (prayer shawl).

1 HaBaD: Acronym of *Hochmah* (Wisdom), *Binah* (Understanding), and *Da'at* (Knowledge), emanations from the Endless One; name of the Lubavitch Movement.

Reb Zalman is both unifying and subversive, at home in many idioms, spiritual or otherwise. He transforms conventional religions into something of his own, exciting, daring, even risky. We are revitalized by his bold manner of thinking. As a strong religious personality – a virtuoso in Max Weber's phrase – Reb Zalman is above all a teacher and spiritual guide who speaks the language of his listeners, to which he joins key terms from his Hebrew and Yiddish sources.

The following interview demonstrates Reb Zalman's ability to build bridges. Central to his own life and central to his teaching, is prayer (or *davvenen* in Yiddish). Through his lifelong observance and reflection on prayer, meditation, and other forms of worship, Zalman is a practical visionary, gifted with the ability to penetrate the intimate life of other people, speak to their hearts, and, especially, to guide us into the sanctuary of holiness.

We embark upon an uncommon reading adventure. The original interview with Zalman took place, with myself and Shaul Magid of the Jewish Theological Seminary, at Zalman's home in Boulder, Colorado, in November 2001. Zalman's responses to our questions, which condensed his encyclopedic knowledge of diverse religious traditions, required careful explanation. Most of us normally wear blinders enabling us to navigate our particular traditions. William Novak sensitively transcribed and edited the transcript, which was then annotated by Beatrice Bruteau, whose informative notes read almost like Talmudic commentaries on a core document.

As we read this unusual conversation, we notice that Reb Zalman uses several languages at once to expresses his synthetic view of reality. Quite spontaneously he experiences the multiplicity of life, the plurality of religions, and uses several ways of thinking to frame his intuitions and penetrating judgments. We hope that this presentation captures some of the "spiritual intimacy" that characterizes Zalman's embracing intellect and generous heart.

16

AN INTERVIEW WITH
ZALMAN SCHACHTER-SHALOMI

THOMAS MERTON AND RENEWAL:
JEWISH AND CHRISTIAN

Edward K. Kaplan and Shaul Magid

Boulder, Colorado, November 19, 2001

THE PREPARATION

Could you tell us what prepared you to meet Thomas Merton, and could you describe your first meeting?

It happened in 1955 or 1956, when I got a job at the University of Manitoba. When I came to Winnipeg, there was already a feeling in me of, with whom am I going to hang out? The Jesuits were the ones who interested me the most. They had become my friends, the people with whom I went to the movies that my wife didn't want to see with me.

Why the Jesuits?

Because I could talk with them. I had read about St. Ignatius,[1] his *Spiritual Exercises*, and the "Ignatian method," and the story that impressed me most was this: A new pope was installed after Ignatius had founded the Jesuits, and there was some danger that

---

1 The Society of Jesus was founded in 1540 by Ignatius of Loyola (Basque) as an international missionary and educational institution of the Roman Catholic Church. It is now present in most countries of the world, operating parishes, retreat houses, high schools, colleges, and universities. It is famous for its lengthy training of its members (eleven to thirteen years) and the Thirty-Day Retreat, used by many other religious and lay people and even by other Christian denominations. The Retreat is based on a manual for the retreat director, *The Spiritual Exercises*, written by St. Ignatius. It includes what is called "the Ignatian method" of prayer.

the Society might be disbanded. Someone asked him, "Ignatius, what will you do if they disband the Society?" He said, "Fifteen minutes in the Oratory and it's all the same to me."

It's like *shiviti hashem l'neqdi tamid* [I will place God before me always]. No matter what happens, I will keep my balance through all of this, and all I need is to be in the presence of God. That was impressive.

By then I already had a fair idea of what Catholics were like. Once I was getting on a plane and a nun was boarding before me. She was alone, but usually they travel in pairs. When the stewardess came by, I give her my card and said, "Could you please ask the sister if I could talk with her?" After takeoff she invited me to come over and we talked. She was Mother Claudia of the Sisters of Zion, but I didn't know that yet. I asked, "Is this the original habit of your order?" She replied that it was. I said, "Well, it looks like France in the last century." She said, "Yes, it is so." Then I find out it's the Ratisbonne Brothers, and if I could have pulled the ejector seat at that point ...

Was this before or after Vatican II?

This was before, when they were still praying for the conversion of Jews. We start to talk, and after a while, she hadn't done her Office

This usually refers to a method of discursive meditation (discursive: moving from one idea to another; distinguished from non-discursive, holding attention fixed on one thought/feeling) in which one begins by imagining a gospel scene as concretely and vividly as possible, applying all the senses; one then watches the action, then enters into the action, then contemplates the Divine Presence in the action and the persons. One makes application to one's own life, resolves to benefit by practice, prays for grace to do so, and gathers a "spiritual bouquet" to carry away as a sense of dedication, remembrance, and consolation.

However, there are several other methods described in *The Spiritual Exercises* which may have appealed to Reb Zalman even more. Ignatius intends that one advance from reasoning to affective prayer, to "simple regard," to contemplation. The goal is that the will be converted, so that, seeing what is God's will for the person, that person will strive to fulfill it. He recommends self-examination with respect to the Commandments; another way is dwelling on each word of a formal prayer, such as 'Our,' then 'Father,' etc.; or one may put words singly on the breath, carrying them by the natural rhythm of the body. See "Three Methods of Prayer," towards the end of the *Spiritual Exercises* (various editions); also see "Contemplation for Obtaining Love," last of the formal exercises. For commentary on "other methods" and the goal of prayer see W. H. Longridge's translation and commentary on the *Exercises* (London: Roxburghe, 1922), 260–61.

yet, and I take out my *siddur* and say *tehillim* [psalms] as she is doing her Office, and we became friends. When we arrived in Winnipeg I asked what she was doing there. She was the superior of the Sisters of Zion and she was visiting the local foundation. It was on the way to Pembona, where the university was located, so I met them, too, and then several of the sisters began to take Judaic studies courses. To this day they are in touch with Rabbi Neal Rose, a professor there. It's been a wonderful relationship.

Visiting Merton

What happened on the day of your visit?

I got to Bardstown, Kentucky, and took a cab to Our Lady of Gethsemani Monastery. I had made reservations, and I'm there at the gate with my *peckelach* (baggage), and there's a rope. On the end of the rope there's a cross, and I'm standing there thinking, How am I going to ring that bell? I take the rope a little higher than the cross and I give a pull. A monk was standing inside in the shadow, but I didn't see him. He came out and said, "An interesting solution to a problem of conscience."

He led me to the dorm, and the next morning, after breakfast, I was to meet Merton. I had never seen a picture of him, and had no idea what he looked like. In those days Pius XII looked very ascetic, and I figured Merton was the same kind of person. He taps me on the shoulder and I turn around, and here's a football coach. He has a grin, a big smile, and he took me to Shangri-la, his hermitage, that he had permission to have. He had been thinking of becoming a Carthusian, but he wasn't born Catholic and the Carthusians don't accept any converts. He wrote about that. They allowed him to have that hermitage, which he had built with the help of other monks.

What did we talk about? Everything. The first thing I was interested in were the differences between meditation and contemplation. Today everything goes into the big bucket of meditation, but in those days, among Catholics, the language was precise and clear. Meditation was discursive reflection, and contemplation was something that moved away from words and got to the place where, when grace overcame a person, they would have what they called infused contemplation, meaning *Yeridat Hashefa* [the Divine influx] comes down from above and fills your mind.

We talked about the obstacles to getting there, and St. John of the Cross, and why you have to go through a dark night of the senses and a dark night of the soul. Infused contemplation isn't something you get in a box of Crackerjacks. On the other hand, I felt that when I looked at *Habad*[2] [Lubavitch Hasidism] and shared that with him, when we talked about *hitbonnenut* [meditative introspection] during the week it was very much like discursive meditation. You talk to yourself in this way and say, "There are my beliefs, these are my values."

Heschel said this wonderful thing: "It isn't enough to have conceptual meditation. You have to get into situational thinking." In *Habad* they talk about *adata d'nafshey* [soul knowledge], seeing yourself in the picture.

Another priest, a guest, was sitting there, and he looked like I imagined Augustine had looked like. They were playing, as they usually did during meals in the refectory, an audio tape of Bishop Fulton Sheen, who was saying that God deals only with corporations, and that's why there's *kahal* [congregation] and *ecclesia* [church], and this guy is sitting there, I'm keeping an eye on him, he quickly makes the sign of the cross and leaves his food and sort of bolts out of there.

I was curious: who was this stranger? I went after him and it was Dan Berrigan. In the afternoon, Dan and Philip [Berrigan][3] who was also there, and I went back to Merton and talked about how these things integrate into society. That was the other side of

2 HaBaD: Acronym for *Hokhmah* [Wisdom], *Binah* [Understanding], *Da'at* [Knowledge], from the *Sephirot* of the Tree of Life, emanations from the Endless One (God); cf. the first three of the Seven Gifts of the Holy Spirit according to the Roman catechetical tradition. See, e.g., Roman A. Foxbrunner, *Habad*: The Hasidism of Rabbi Shneur Zalman of Lyady (Northvale NJ: Aronson, 1993); Shmuel Boteach, *Wisdom, Understanding, and Knowledge*: Basic Concepts of Hasidic Thought (Aronson, 1996).

Hitbodedut: "Aloneness" with God. Religious devotions performed in seclusion for a specific period of time. Related concepts are: *devekut*, clinging to God, and *hitlahavut*, fervor.

3 The Berrigan brothers became prominent as peace activists during the Vietnam War. Dan, a Jesuit, is also an outstanding poet. Philip, now deceased, formerly a

Merton. He had large concerns. It's sad that he had to go so early, because he was just getting into a stride where his ecumenism was so rich and so full.

Do you think Merton was in danger of losing control of [his interest in other religions] at this point in his life?

No. The person who is at the growing edge of something, if he has a connection to the trunk of the tree, is safe. The trunk is mostly dead wood, but it gives structure to the tree. The growing edge gives life to the tree, and the two of them have to be together. I had the sense that he didn't want to upset that. We once had a conversation about Huysmans,[4] who had written about "the cabbage eaters," those Catholic *balabatim* [lay people, householders] who came to church, and how necessary it was for them to have the devotional experiences the Church used to offer.

But now, post–Vatican II, the Church had stripped away the little *sancta* [holy practices] that they had had. Hardly anyone was doing the rosary[5] anymore, there weren't novenas, everything had been turned into the Big Bertha – the Mass – and even that had lost its splendor and greatness.

We lamented over that and we asked, What could be done? He was more hopeful that something would happen, something that

Josephite priest, was a full-time activist, married to Elizabeth McAlister, their companion in the struggles of those early days. She has been active in Catholic Worker projects. (The Catholic Worker, founded by Peter Maurin and Dorothy Day, operates Houses of Hospitality in depressed areas of major cities; they combine service to the poor with lectures to left-wing intellectuals and demonstrations of social protest.) At present, Dan is living in a Jesuit community in New York and had been cooperating in a vigil at Union Square against the sanctions against Iraq and the war against Afghanistan. Among Dan's many publications are two books on prison life: *Light in the House of the Dead* and *Prison Poems*. Phil, who was just coming out of prison in April, 2002, died of liver and kidney cancer on December 6, 2002.

4 Joris-Karl Huysmans (1848-1907), novelist whose work epitomizes successive phases of aesthetic, spiritual, and intellectual life of late 19th-century France. His last three novels are autobiographical, using a fictional protagonist, Durtal, who recovers his Catholic faith after a prolonged period of pessimism during a retreat in a Trappist monastery, and becomes a Benedictine oblate (lay associate of an abbey).

5 Rosary: string of beads for counting repetitions of simple familiar set prayers while holding in mind the spiritual significance of a key event in the Christian revelatory story. The fifteen "mysteries" of the rosary, five joyful, five sorrowful, five glorious, can be understood as tracing the development of the spiritual life. Novena: nine days of prayer dedicated to a particular intention, originating from

later on showed itself as contemplative education, led by some other Trappists, Thomas Keating and Basil Pennington,[6] but it was only slowly beginning at that time. A kind of prayer of the heart was slowly beginning to become what is now called Centering by Prayer. Merton felt that this would give the situation a lift.

My sense was that living the liturgical year was important, and that it would be good if they came up with a kind of lay tertiary order[7] that would develop more home rituals, and so forth.

SHABBOS WITH THE MONKS

I was at Snowmass[8] and I needed to take time out, and Father Theophane and Father Thomas and Father Joseph, the Abbot, welcomed me there.

I would be up at the canonical hours and I would say my *tehillim* in the back while they were in the choir in the center of

the nine days of concentrated prayer between the Ascension of Christ and the Descent of the Holy Spirit at Pentecost (see Acts 1:9, 12-14, and 2:1-4). There were a number of other items favored in the lives of devout lay people which began to disappear at this time.

6 Both Keating and Pennington have written a number of books on prayer and the contemplative life. A useful source is Keating's *Open Mind, Open Heart* (Element, 1992), which explains Centering Prayer in great detail, together with the supporting framework of lifestyle. This movement to share the ancient tradition of Christian contemplation, somewhat eclipsed for the last few centuries, was developed by Frs. William Menninger and Basil Pennington at St. Joseph's Abbey, Spencer MA, starting in 1975. It is based on the fourteenth-century classic, *The Cloud of Unknowing* and aims at resting peacefully in the presence of God in silent attentiveness. In the mid-1980s Contemplative Outreach was organized to introduce the Centering Prayer method and to provide a support system. It proved very popular and there are now dozens, perhaps hundreds, of groups practicing it together regularly. See Resources at the end of this book.

7 Tertiary: a "third order," the first being of vowed men, the second of vowed women, the third of lay people. Trappists exist as monks and nuns, but have not formed tertiaries. Franciscans and Carmelites have had third orders for a long time: third orders *regular*, people living in community under a rule, in simple vows, and third orders *secular*, people living with their families, with still simpler guidelines and promises. Home rituals do not exist.

8 Snowmass, Colorado, St. Benedict's Abbey, where Fr. Keating went from St. Joseph's Abbey in Spencer MA. Some abbeys are spoken of by their place names and some by their dedication names (there is no significance to this, it is just a common usage that has somehow developed). Fr. Theophane was also from

the church. Came Friday, I spoke to some of the monks in the kitchen and said, "Shabbos is coming. Could I have some rolls and some grape joice and candles?" They fixed me up. We had a Friday night *tish* [table gathering] and it was a love.

The next week they said, "Would you do that again?" I said, "On one condition – if we play something. I will be Joseph of Arimethea, and you will be disciples of the Master who come from Galilee to Jerusalem, and we'll have a Shabbos together as it was in those days." It was wonderful: I lit the candles, made *kiddush* [blessed the wine], we sat around the table and sang songs that came from the Psalms. Shlomo[9] was very helpful. We sang "I Lift Up My Eyes unto the Mountains" and "For the Sake of My Brothers and Friends."

Then I said, "Well, what's the news from Galilee? What stories can you tell me from the Master?" They got so excited about that, each one telling another story, a Gospel story.

Do you think the monks need this type of change to enlarge their spiritual resources through contact with Judaism?

Not only with Judaism, but Judaism is very important. When I say with them, in Psalm 23, *bin'ot desheh yarbizeni,* normally translated as "He makes me lie down in green pastures," I translate it as "He makes me sprawl on the green lawn." There's a sense that Hebrew contains something that they don't quite get. *Ach tove va'chesed yirdefuni* they translate as "Surely goodness and mercy shall follow me [all the days of my life]" but I'm saying "chase,"

Spencer. He is the author of *Tales of a Magic Monastery,* which bears some resemblance to Hasidic stories.

9 Rabbi Shlomo Carlebach (1925-1994) was a songwriter, musician, and recording artist, performing at "peace and love" concerts in the '60s. He and Reb Zalman were fellow students of the Lubavitcher Rebbe of their day (father-in-law of the recently deceased Rabbi Schneerson). A memorable day for them both was the 19th of Kislev, December of 1949, when the Rebbe called them into his office and said, "It's time for you two to start visiting college campuses." For R. Zalman's account of how they began, see Yitta Halberstam Mandelbaum, *Holy Brother: Inspiring Stories and Enchanted Tales About Rabbi Shlomo Carlebach* (Aronson, 1997), xxix-xxxi. (Audio tapes/CDs, videos, songbooks are available.) These early efforts mark the beginning of the Jewish Renewal Movement, which retains the mysticism of Orthodoxy and adds thorough gender equality (including inclusive language and God names and images), reaching out to other religions, and developing an eco-kosher ethic.

that *yirdefuni* means almost "pursue me," or "run after me." "God pursues me everywhere," like in the Heschel poem.[10]

I want to ask about ecumenism and interfaith relations. Often dialogue comes from the "left wings" of two traditions, but here you come from the pietistic Hasidic tradition and Merton comes from the Trappist monastic tradition. What do you see as the goals of that kind of ecumenical dialogue, not only for your own communities, but in a more global way?

Let's start with talking over the fence. I once wrote something called "The Dialogue of Devoutness," in which I said that there is something about the dialogue of theology that still keeps us in disputations and takes us back to the year 170[11] with all those old issues. It doesn't work.

10 The Heschel poem runs this way:

GOD PURSUES ME EVERYWHERE

God pursues me everywhere,
Enmeshes me in glances,
And blinds me sightless back like flaming sun.

God, like a forest dense, pursues me.
My lips are ever tender, mute, so amazed,
So like a child in ancient sacred grove.

God pursues me like a silent shudder.
I wish for tranquility and rest – He urges: come!
And see – how visions walk like the homeless on the streets.

My thoughts walk about like a vagrant mystery –
Walks through the world's long corridor.
At times I see God's featureless face hovering over me.

God pursues me in the streetcars and cafes
Every shining apple is my crystal sphere to see
How mysteries are born and visions come to be.

Abraham Joshua Heschel, *Human, God's Ineffable Name* (*Der Shem Ham'forash Mentsch*, Warsaw: Intsel, 1933), freely rendered and privately published by Rabbi Zalman M. Schachter-Salomi, p. 23. See also "The Hound of Heaven," by Francis Thompson, 19th-cent. English poet.

11 One source on the Jewish-Christian relations in antiquity is Edward H. Flannery, *The Anguish of the Jews* (Paulist, 1985), chapter two: "The Conflict of Church and Synagogue." Relations worsened in the second half of the first century C.E., reflected in the progressively anti-Jewish language of the New Testament from Paul (50s) to John (90s). In the year 80, the Sanhedrin, sitting at Jabne, issued a malediction against all *minim* (heretics) which constituted the formal excommunication of all Christians. In the second century Justin composed his *Dialogue with Trypho*, apparently a record of an actual discussion with a rabbi (Rabbi Tarphon has been suggested, but this may not be true), which Flannery

What I was interested in, and what Merton was interested in, was the *upaya* [Sanskrit, lit. "means" to an end] – the "skillful means"[12] that people use for their transformation.

Here was an element of what I call generic spirituality. If you omit specific ethnicity and polity, whether it's Church government or *Halachic* government, and you ask, What is it that works, when it works, with transformation? What helps us with *tikkun hamidot* [repair of one's traits] and *conversatio morum*?[13] How do I move from my "is" to my "ought"?

Here is where yoga, Zen Buddhism, all of these, have wonderful *eitzahs* [teachings]. St. John of the Cross calls them the *cultalasas-cautelas*, the counsels that are there. My feeling was that if both of us are first of all unabashedly saying that we love God, and that if you please God, I'm happy, and hope you're happy when I please God – when that's there, we can be deep friends. And another thing, *Az nidbru yirei HaShem ish el r'ehu vayaqshev HaShem vayishma' vayikatev sefer zikkaron l'fanav l'yir' ey HaShem ulhasvey sh'mo* (Malachi 3:16). "When those who fear God and honor his name talk to one another, those dialogues are so precious to God that God has a special book in which he writes them down." So we come to dialogue not from minimizing our differences, but from maximizing our devotion.

THE LANGUAGE OF PRAYER

When I was in New Bedford, Massachusetts, and they asked if I would conduct services in English, I did, using phrases like, "Thou hast exalted my power like that of a wild ox." Those were the words in the Birnbaum *Siddur* [prayer book], which was the

says is "a model of a kind of Jewish-Christian discussion that would frequently appear throughout history" [p. 39]. The tone is irenic, courteous, and fair, and the work ends in expressions of friendship and promises of prayers for one another. The "old issues" were the messiahship of Jesus, the subsequent status of the Law, the vocation of the Church (to convert all), and the interpretation of Israelite history [p. 39], roughly summarized as "supersessionism."

12 From the Bhagavad-Gita, 2:50: "Yoga is skill in actions."

13 Sometimes rendered *conversion* but the original word in the Rule of St. Benedict is *conversatio*. It means ethical reformation of lifestyle (*mores*); it occurs frequently in primitive monastic literature; it is the classic term for signifying monachism and forms part of the Trappist vow. A Merton title is: *A Vow of Conversation*.

only one with a decent translation. Until then I had been *davvening* [praying] at home first, so I could conduct services, but then I gave up; I realized that if I don't davven, they can't davven. I started for forty days. Rabbi Elimelech says, "If you want to start something new, do it for forty days to get it going." I started saying everything on the English side of the *Siddur*. Two or three days later I was into singing it, "The soul of every being will bless Your name ..." So I was associating *nusach* [traditional prayer modes, like modes of Gregorian Chant] to those words. That made it easier for people who wanted to get into davvening to get some feeling into it. The *nusach* was there, and along with the melody were words they could understand.

Can you share with us some elements of Thomas Merton's legacy, and how it responds to problems in the Catholic or Jewish community?

For problems arising from the need to adjust ancient worldviews to our modern scientific understanding of a dynamic (evolving) world, you have to go to somebody like Teilhard de Chardin.[14] Merton did not do the big cosmological stuff. But he had something to say about problems arising from recent shifts in worship and piety.

The Roman Church lost a great deal in not paying that much attention to the daily Office. When you look at Merton's *The Seven Storey Mountain* and *The Sign of Jonas*, you find that he would always begin with some of the *piyyutim* [religious poetry] that he found in the liturgy. That's what he paid attention to and expanded on. It was a way of "inflating" – in a good sense – from *afflatus*, blowing into it. If an idea touches your heart and you breathe in, just at the beginning, when there is the slightest bit of affect coming, you welcome it and the feeling builds up.

Merton was doing this with those ideas, but today people read

14 Fr. Pierre Teilhard de Chardin (the family name is Teilhard), of the Society of Jesus (d. 1955), was a geologist and paleontologist, author of The *Phenomenon of Man* and a number of other books on evolution. Silenced by the Church in his lifetime, he enjoyed a great vogue shortly after his death as the books containing his writings began to come out and organizations were formed in various countries to promote his ideas. He took evolution to be the central dynamic of the universe, its pattern of increasing complexity and consciousness still operating to point out the future of the human race, as the "Noosphere" is urged toward an ideal society he called Omega, symbol for a messianic focus. ('Noosphere' is from the Greek *nous, noös,* mind.)

it and don't recognize what liturgy it's from, and that's a real pity. The Breviary is dry compared to what it was in other days. Also, people would read the collateral reading, the *lectio divina*, along with the Office, so that would give them access to insights of the Fathers. It's the same thing: if you davven in the Siddur, and you have studied *kavvanot*[15] [preparatory mental exercises] from various Hasidic masters, and you come across a phrase, it gets enlivened because of the interpretations you have studied. All that is lost now.

The iconography that they got rid of was a matter of taste. It was the wrong iconography, but iconography is important. I'm not talking now from a "Jewish" point of view; I have in mind windows, pictures, and images. In Frankfort-on-Main there is a church with a Pietà of brown sandstone, and I stood in front of it and started to cry. To me, that sense of Rachel *me'vackah al baneha* – weeping for her children – that's the *Shekhina* [Divine presence] in *galut* [exile]. At the same time, I see the mother and earth holding the child that is broken... it's very powerful.

What do you think the idea of monasticism has to contribute to Judaism?

One of the problems plaguing Jewish renewal is that everyone wants to be a *rebbe*. But they haven't been Hasidim long enough to live under discipline. I'm still hoping and dreaming that in my lifetime there will be a resident [religious] community that will live a liturgical year, fully. They would do everything, the works. Not that this should be the permanent *matbe'ah* [religious framework] for the people, but unless you root yourself in that totality of the liturgical life, you don't understand the possibilities for renewal, because it will be coming to you only from the outside.

The sense of days, time, time as texture, or the texture of a day when you recite *Tachanun* or *Ya'aleh v'yavoh* [two prayers that are

15 *kavvanah*: lit., intention, but in (at least) two senses: (1) the purpose or meaning of the prayer, and (2) the intensive attention or concentration with which one enters into it. Seth Kadish has subtitled his six-hundred-page study, *Kavvana*, "*Directing the Heart in Jewish Prayer*" (Aronson, 1992); it covers praying from the prayerbook, simple prayers, prayer as conversation with God, rational prayer, and mysticism, with a great deal of history and commentary from famous teachers. As "intention" it also means keeping in mind what one does in response to a Divine command, so it is not enough to consume Matzah on Passover, it needs to be baked with Kavvanah and consumed with the mindfulness that one obeys a Divine command and that one intends, according to the Zohar, to feed one's faith.

of special days and not recited daily), or the anomaly of *Hoshanah Rabba* [at the end of *Succot*] with its own liturgy – something happens in the feel of how you live in time. Heschel was so hot on that; to live in time and not in space, and I feel that's important.

I believe the Jewish calendar keeps us rooted in organic time. *Pesach* is on the full moon of the vernal equinox. *Succot* is on the full moon of the autumnal equinox, and if we live that way, then we can keep ourselves free of the trends that commodity-time imposes on us. Therefore, learning basic spiritual things, including unreasonable obedience, does something important for you. In most monastic communities, a novice would have to do menial things in order to do the kind of ego reduction that's necessary.

When Howard Thurman[16] came to Winnipeg, I offered to take him around, to show him the Parliament, but he wasn't interested. I asked him, "What would you like to see?" He said, "I understand there're some Trappists here."

I called the Abbot of the Abbey of the Prairies and asked for permission to come. He was wonderful, he gave me one of his wool gowns, and sometimes I wear it on the *Yamim Nora'im* [High Holy Days] when it's cold, and it's now *oys gedavvent* – well prayed in. He used to love to smoke cigars, but it didn't fit with him. I always pretended I liked cigars. I would bring some cigars with me, and I'd say, "May I smoke, Father Abbot?" And he would say yes, because of Benedictine hospitality. I said, "I don't want to indulge without you joining me," so he would join me.

I asked Thurman, does he want to talk with the Abbot? He says, "No, the Abbot is a manager, I want to talk with the Master of Novices." There's a conversation going on, and Thurman is asking the Master of Novices, "Tell me, what's the biggest complaint the novices have?"

16 Rev. Howard Thurman (1901-81), African-American theologian, mystic, prophet, author, founder of the Church for the Fellowship of All People in San Francisco. Beginning with the plight of black people in America, he developed a spirituality of high standards for oppressed and "disinherited" people in various categories. He believed that the life and teachings of Jesus, "the poor Jew" of Nazareth, were especially relevant to these populations: "The striking similarity between the social position of Jesus in Palestine and that of the vast majority of American Negroes is obvious. ..." He summarized the message of Jesus to the disinherited: "You must abandon your fear of each other and fear only God. You

"They say that all the great raptures come to them when they're outdoors, and nothing much is happening when they're on the floor (praying) at two-thirty in the morning, or at Chapter, and they would like to be removed from that. So I forbid them to come to anything but the obligatory Masses, and I keep them out in the field. A few weeks later they say, 'Look, I didn't come here to be a farmhand.'"

What happened to all those raptures? They realized *hazorim bedimah brinah yikzoru* ["they who sow in tears shall reap in joy," Ps.126:6]. They come to realize that what happens in the chapel that doesn't seem to be so fruitful at the time, they harvest when they're out there. That's one of the wonderful things that a monastic life can bring about.

If you could imagine the Thomas Merton and Judaism conference, what kind of conversation is really available to us at a public level?

I want to go back and mention Teilhard de Chardin. I think people need to have that in the background. We are now in the move from the Noosphere, where we have the Internet and everything else, the instantaneous communication, we are moving toward a divinization of the planet, which comes when *Melech Ha'olam* [the King of the universe] is waking up Earth. I think there's a *T'chiyat HaMeitim* [resurrection of the dead] element going on. I think we have to make peace with pantheism. Deism was on the way out. Theism is already on the way out, with a psycho-physical parallelism, the body is bad and the soul is good, and this kind of dialectic. Today we are saying, God is everything, all is God.

Let me tell you a story. *Baruch Hashem* [praise God], I'm getting older, I have a right to tell stories. In 1975, I was here in Boulder for the summer session of the Naropa Institute, and one of my colleagues, Chögiam Trungpa Rinpoche, would always needle me.

must not indulge in any deception or dishonesty. ... Hatred is destructive to hater and hated alike. Love your enemy. ... be children of your father who is in heaven." The humanizing combination of the experience of the disinherited with the religion of Jesus, he believed, made available to all an emancipatory way of being. Moving beyond the usual orthodoxies of Christianity, it also made great demands on the "inward center," the heart and soul of those who would find this liberating spirituality. (Material drawn from Vincent Harding's 1996 Foreword to Beacon Press' edition of *Jesus and the Disinherited*. Quotations from Thurman were not referenced.)

Friday night we were hanging out, I wearing my *shtreimel* [fur hat] and *kapotte* [robe]; I wore them at the time. He said, "My son asked me if there is a God, and I said, 'No, there isn't,' and he said, 'Whew!'" And he looks to me, I should give him a rebuttal.

I said, "The God you don't believe in, I don't believe in either." And that is the truth. By the time you look at the God images that people need to be iconoclastic over, I agree, they're right. What they are not right about is that they can't move into their *bhakti*,[17] their loving devotional place, without some kind of image for the heart to have.

The mind will say that God is infinite, *ein sof,* or, *Ein lo d'mut huguf v' eino quf,* that God doesn't have the appearance either of a body or of a non-body, that God is neither matter nor spirit, that God is way beyond that. At the same time, when it comes to heart, I need to have roles for Him. I have to, as it were, put a face on God, whether it is a papa face, a mama face, a son face, a daughter face.

I'm going to Kabbalah now, which takes me right back to what I call pre-patriarchal Judaism. In Canaanite religion there were *El* [Father], *Ashera* [Mother], *Ba'al* [Son], and *Anat* [Daughter], and here you have the four parts of God all over again, and you see it as old Yang, old Yin, young Yang, young Yin. How does it happen that these "foursies" come out all over the world, in *PaRDeS*[18] [Paradise, the mystical world], the four levels of interpretation (also in Christianity), all over the same? Because there's something there. I'd like to get people to acknowledge that which is there and then say, Yes, and we have these garments that It wears for our sake.

Later on in life, with Merton's engagement with the world, it became very clear — to some, anyway — that he had a real tension about his ability to remain inside the tradition. A personal question: How do you struggle with the inside/outside dichotomy in terms of your own life and work?

17 *Bhakti* (Sanskrit): One of the yogas, or "yokes," ways of union with God. *Bhakti* is devotion, worship of one's chosen form of God, as parent, child, teacher, friend, lover. Other yogas are *karma*, union through righteous and selfless action; *jnana*, through philosophy, intellectual insight; *raja yoga*, the royal way, direct control of consciousness, from ethical virtues through levels of meditation to realization of the Formless One.

18 *PaRDeS*, besides being Persian for "garden," is used as an acronym for the four levels of interpretation: *Peshat*, the plain meaning; *Remez*, the allegorical; *Deresh*, the homiletic or aggadic; and *Sod*, the mystical.

This is a rather complex issue. On the one hand, I want to make sure that we enter the new millennium with its cosmology and not stay behind in the past paradigm. One the other hand, I believe that renewal has to be in some sense downward compatible so that we don't cut ourselves off from the chthonic and non-verbal, shall I say "shamanic," treasures of the tradition. In that way I want a maximum of devotional and moral norms to be maintained in renewal. There are however some ethical and moral issues that cannot be made to be simply massaged in. The currently coming down mandate from revelation rejects some of the once needed and highly valuable traditions. From an organismic point of view chosenness of our people has a different meaning and impact than it had when we needed a high degree of surface tension dividing Jew from Non-Jew. With the rejection of the triumphalism of the past there is also a rejection of the sanctified chauvinism.

Let's first go back to Merton's case. The problem you find in Halachah [Jewish law] is that from time to time you want to make an exception because you think it's right, but they come up with what they call *lo plug* – we don't dare to make the exception, because if we do, the slippery slope, the floodgates open up, and all of discipline will disappear. They were feeling at Gethsemani that, on the one hand, the income that would come from Merton's books was good, their reputation was good, vocations were good, people came to retreats there. There was a vitality there, and they wanted to keep this going.

On the other hand, if they allowed him, they would have to allow other people the same way. And he had the vow of stability, so you can't let him have that. The people who wanted to protect the status quo kept anchoring him in ways in which he didn't want to be anchored. With a little more 'give,' the likelihood is that Merton would have stayed there, had he had the years.

Another problem the Church has now: it's not fulfilling all the capacity the human being has. You know, we have the reptilian brain, running the body; the limbic brain, mediating our emotions; and the cortex, thinking our thoughts. And our religion is supposed to have something for all of these. It used to be that when people came to church there was a sense of sanctuary. You could feel safe in sacred space, which meant that the dinosaur in you was relaxed, that it didn't

316 · Edward K. Kaplan and Shaul Magid

go Jurassic Park on you. And for the limbic: there were wonderful things that had to do with music, and I'm not talking about fancy Roman music, but about what I saw in Seville, in Spain – Gloria, Gloria! – where the Masses were alive. From the Kyrie to the Gloria they had what I call "Forepray."

When you got into the deeper parts of prayer, you could be contemplative, you could go to higher places, but the body was present and the heart was present, so first the body has to feel safe, and then you lift up your heart. But today, when they don't do much *p'sukei dezimrah* [preliminary psalms], there's no *birchot HaShachar* [early morning blessings for the functions and use of the body], they're not getting the body there. The genuflections have become smaller, the sign of the cross is a little dip into the holy water stoup at the door, a little on the finger, a quick motion of the hand – there isn't that sense that we have crossed a threshold, that we are entering into the Divine home with feeling. That has cooled a lot of stuff down.

If I could give some *eitzahs* [advice] to the Church, it would be, Make sure that you don't put down the raves of the kids. The top brass did a really stupid job by throwing out somebody like Matt Fox,[19] because he understood a lot better what was needed in the reformatting of Roman theology by bringing in unconventional, extra-ecclesial materials. Look, we always do it, throw out the people who are different, like the mystics. But what's the problem with the mystic? Gershom Scholem says that most of the time we prefer our mystics housebroken.

---

19 Matthew Fox is a spiritual theologian who has been an ordained priest since 1967. He holds Master's degrees in philosophy and theology from Aquinas Institute and a Doctorate in spirituality, summa cum laude, from the Institut Catholique de Paris. A liberation theologian and progressive visionary, he was silenced by the Vatican and later dismissed from the Dominican order. After dismissal he was received as an Episcopal priest by Bishop William Swing of the Diocese of California. Fox is author of 24 books, including the best selling *Original Blessing*; his most recent is *One River, Many Wells*. He lectures in North America, Central America, Europe, and Australia. He is the founder and president of the University of Creation Spirituality, located in downtown Oakland, CA.

Fox received the 1994 New York Open Center Tenth Anniversary Award for Achievement in Creative Spirituality. In 1995 he was presented the Courage of Conscience Award by the Peace Abbey of Sherborn, Mass. Other recipients of

Of course, Meister Eckhart and John of the Cross weren't so housebroken. Sometimes the authorities want to have the charismatic gifts present, like in Padre Pio,[20] but they silence him at the same time: You can do your praying and your healing, but you mustn't preach. Why? Because the mystic doesn't color inside the lines. He sees bigger than the people who made the lines. This is what we need. So it's necessary for the Church to start looking beyond a renewal that is merely on the outside, because that's what they have been doing. They didn't do the renewal from the inside.

So that's where Thomas Merton would fit in?

That's right. Thomas Merton already had to learn as an adult. The Church was trying to do some things with a secular institute named Opus Dei,[21] and this was like doing a fundamentalist trip. They were trying to put on the headscrews so that you really think inside the channels, instead of giving people a chance to learn from the inside, to do gazing.

this award include the Dalai Lama, Mother Theresa, Ernesto Cardenal, and Rosa Parks. In 1996 he received the Tikkun National Ethics Award in recognition of contributions made to the spiritual life of our society. Fox has twice received the Body Mind Spirit Award of Excellence for outstanding books in print: in 1996 for *The Reinvention of Work* and in 1997 for *Confessions: The Making of a Post-Denominational Priest*. (This information was obtained from the web site www.creationspirituality.com/matthew.html)

20 Meister Eckhart (1260-1329), Dominican theologian and mystic, eminent scholar, held the chair at the University of Paris previously occupied by Thomas Aquinas. Accused of heresies based on his attempts to speak of the union of the soul with God, often in paradox; the way to such union is by emptying and detachment from finite values, including concepts of God. Thomas Merton remarked on the similarity of Eckhart's thought to that of Zen Buddhism.

St. John of the Cross, Carmelite, friend of St. Teresa of Avila, (1542-1591), mystic and doctor (teacher) of the church. Author of *The Ascent of Mt. Carmel, The Dark Night of the Soul,* and *Living Flame of Love.* This was the era of the Inquisition in Spain, a dangerous time for religious innovators, which Teresa and John were. He was imprisoned and abused by his own religious congregation. His poetry celebrates the purification of the soul and its ecstatic union with God. His analysis explains in detail the psychology of this movement.

Padre Pio, Italian, Capuchin friar and stigmatic (1887-1968). Traditional in theology, he possessed various charisms in addition to the stigmata (bleeding hands, feet, side): healing miracles, knowing people's secret thoughts and deeds, prophecy – in 1947, hearing the confession of Karol Wojtyla, he told the young man he would one day be pope. He attracted crowds of pilgrims, which disturbed the authorities in the Vatican, who forbade him to say Mass in public (for a time).

21 Opus Dei (not to be confused with these words meaning the Divine Office, the

I know that Christians won't want to hear this at this point, but this is my witness to you: You don't know the difference between *Halachah* [law] and *Aggadah* [parable]. Jesus was a teacher of Aggadah. The mistake is to say that he taught "with authority."[22] The phrase is, *k'echad hamoshlim*, one of the *moshlim*. A *moshel* is somebody who teaches with parables – an aggadic teacher.

When somebody is ogling a woman and asks, "What do you say about divorce?" Jesus says, "Whatsoever God put together don't you put asunder.[23] That's an aggadic statement, but people take it as legalistic. But when Jesus says, "If your eye offends you, cast it out," I haven't seen any fundamentalist go to the eye doctor and say, "This eye offends me, I'd like you to cut it out." Everybody understands that the statement is aggadic, not halachic.

A lot of stuff that Christians have made into halachah should not have been made into halachah. The unhappiness you have caused people, and the subterfuge you had to use to annul marriages! If only you had gone with the House of Shammai at least, and said, "Yes, for adultery you can have a divorce," then people could start a new life.

But you [Christians] haven't consulted us [Jews] about this ... and other questions. For instance, now we are all dealing with the issue of Frankenfoods [as in Frankenstein's monster] and genetic manipulation – what's kosher and what's not kosher, and I wish you

---

prayers appointed for the various hours of the day, according to the season) is a *secular* institute, as distinguished from a *religious* institute, such as a monastic order or a conventual congregation. It sees itself as doing the "work of God," in close obedience to the Vatican authority. The people who belong to it are usually well placed in society and conservative/orthodox in their views. See www.opusdei.org.

22 Mark 1:22, repeated in Matthew 7:29: *hos exousian echon*. *Exousia* means authority or power, usually in a governmental context, as having the right to make judgments and take actions. The text continues ." .. and not as the scribes," perhaps suggesting not citing other authorities for a doctrine or an interpretation, but speaking out of one's own experience.

23 Divorce: Mark 10:2-9, with reference to Deut. 24:1-4. Shammai interpreted this strictly, divorce possible only for severe offense; Hillel loosely, for any displeasure or preference for another. Some commentators say Jesus shifted the ground of the question; others say he was concerned to protect women. Offensive eye: Matthew 18:9 – *skandalizei*, cause to stumble, put difficulties in the way, scandalize. The context suggests that if any *part* of your life is putting difficulties in the way of your righteousness, it is better to give that up than to lose your *whole* life.

would join us in a project of eco-kosher.[24]

Here's another one that we could get together on. Based on the Talmud, we have a stupid misinterpretation – that you shouldn't teach Torah to girls, because if you do, you will teach them how to be foolish and how to skirt the law. But it's important to pay attention to what women think and say. Look at the Acts of the Apostles, how women were important elders of the early Church. It's very clear that woman-mind is now necessary to keep the Church healthy and to heal the planet.[25]

So this is my witness to you, that you need to be in dialogue with us about these kinds of things, and we need to be in dialogue with you from medical ethics to everything having to do with ecology. I need your mind, and you need my mind, and the stereoscopic effect gives us three-dimensional vision. I have a feeling we could go to yet other dimensions, too, if we at least did the glorification of God together, if we did the sharing of the ways of piety with each other, and if we all understood that whatever we do, we do in exile.

24 The Jewish Renewal Movement has expanded the category of "fit" foods to include any consumer items harmful in themselves or produced and marketed by harmful or unethical means. This covers the general field of planetary ecology; worker rights, protection and compensation; and prevention of cruelty to animals. See Michael Lerner, *Jewish Renewal* (New York: Putnam, 1994), p.336: "Rabbi Zalman Schachter-Shalomi suggests that we should add a new code of eco-kosher practices to our practice of *kashrut* [fitness for use]. Products that are grown using earth-destroying pesticides may not be eco-kosher. Newsprint made by chopping down an ancient and irreplaceable forest may not be eco-kosher. Products that are made out of irreplaceable natural resources may not be eco-kosher." Corporations that pollute the environment or use excessive amounts of fuel may not be eco-kosher. Investments in companies that pollute the environment or are otherwise ecologically insensitive may not be eco-kosher. See also Arthur Waskow, in *New Menorah*, Spring 1993, p.1: ". . . for the next several generations the Jewish people should shape itself into an intergenerational, international 'movement' with the goal of protecting the web of life on earth. We should shape our prayers, our celebrations, our spiritual practices, the rearing of our children, and our public policy with this purpose in mind." *New Menorah* is the magazine of Aleph, Alliance for Jewish Renewal, 7000 Lincoln Dr., B2; Philadelphia PA 19119; www.aleph.org.

25 Jewish Renewal opens all functions in religious life to both sexes. It uses inclusive language in worship and uses names, titles, and images for God that are masculine, feminine, neither. Reb Zalman recommends "Yah" as a name of God that can be either feminine or masculine. (He also writes "G!D"!)

Many people in the Church don't see themselves in exile; but look at the way they sing the *Salve Regina* ["Hail, Queen," hymn to the Blessed Virgin Mary, sung by the Trappists (and many others) last thing before retiring for the night – it includes the phrases "*exsules, filii Hevae*" and "*hoc exsilium*"], that we are the "exiles, children of Eve." See yourselves in exile. In exile we don't know yet what's necessary. We need the *Mashiach* [Messiah] to come for the first time, and you need him to come for the second time. All of that means that we don't have it all together yet, that we need still more. It looks to me that God has given each one a vitamin that the other one needs, and we won't be able to survive in health if we don't get the exchange of vitamins from each other.

Since you gave musar [ethical advice] to the Christians, would you give a little musar to the Jews? Jews generally have a fear of Christianity that results from a long history[26] of oppression, persecution and darkness. How can Jews overcome their natural aversion to Christian ideas and to Christianity that would enable them to open up to the kind of dialogue you're talking about?

Sometimes, in pastoral work, I have to deal with people who were abused as children, especially incestual abuse and sexual abuse. It is so hard to help the people get to the place where they're willing to let go and forgive, because they were so twisted. My sense is that it'll take a while until we can do that [between Jews and Christians].

I do want to repeat something that we need to hear. We had a meeting in Berkeley some years ago, called "Torah and Dharma," and Shlomo [Carlebach], *alav hashalom* [may he rest in peace], could not attend, so I sat with him in the car and I said, "Would you at least give me a message?"

He said:

The rule is that, from the lips of the priest you should get knowledge and awareness. It is also forbidden for a *cohen* [priest] to touch the dead. The Ishbitzer Rebbe[27] asks,

26 In addition to James Carroll's *Sword of Constantine*, see, e.g., Edward Flannery, *The Anguish of the Jews*, and William Nicholls, *Christian Antisemitism*. For the social effect here and now, see, e.g., Allen Secher, "The 'J' Word," in Beatrice Bruteau, ed., *Jesus Through Jewish Eyes*.

27 The Ishbitzer Rebbe, Rabbi Mordechai Yossef Lajner (1800-1842) was a

"Why is that so? Because if you see the dead before you, if you touch the dead, you can't help but be angry at God. And when a teacher who is angry at God teaches Torah, the Torah is bitter." In order to keep the teacher unpolluted, he must not touch the dead. After the Holocaust, all our teachers were polluted. We are still polluted. So God, in His mercy, sent us teachers from the Far East who were not polluted by death, and they were able to teach us so that we would have access to God and to the Spirit.

I thought this was a wonderful teaching.

With regard to this, we haven't yet had a *Klal Yisrael* [wider community of Israel] meeting on how to clean up the thing. There are still [Emil] Fackenheim-ish[28] people who say that if we clean this out, we will give Hitler a posthumous victory. There's a *koan* we have: When you get to the land, erase the memory of Amalek, don't forget [Deut. 25:19 (cf. 17)]. I believe this is what it means: Erase the memory, the traumatic part of the memory, the "ouch" part that makes you reactive, but don't forget the lesson that you learned.

I think we need to remember that lesson. We should have applied it in the case of the Ibos, the Hutus and the Tutsis, and there's so much more that we didn't do, didn't do what we should have learned, *Ki gerim hayitem b'eretz Mitzrayim* [Because you were slaves and strangers in the land of Egypt, Ex. 22:21; 23:9 adds, "You know the heart of a stranger, for you were ..." See also the Passover liturgy], so remember to treat the slaves right. You were persecuted, so remember to treat the persecuted right.

disciple, colleague, and later dissident of Rabbi Menachem Mendl Morgenstern of Kotzk. His teachings are available in translation in *All Is in the Hands of Heaven*, tr. Morris M. Faierstein (Ktav, 1989), and in *Living Water*, tr. Betzallel Phillip Edwards (Aronson, 2001). He is regarded as among the most original thinkers of Hasidism. He opposed the mechanical performance of *mitzvot*, saying they are devoid of meaning, adding that the rabbi should be a spiritual guide rather than a miracle worker. Informed faith, he said, is superior to blind faith; for God should be served with intelligence as well as with devotion. He recognized the human shortcomings of biblical heroes but felt that they did not detract from their moral stature. In many ways, his thought parallels that of de Caussade in his *Abandonment to Divine Providence* (classic of Christian spirituality, various editions).

28 Emil L. Fackenheim, *God's Presence in History* (Aronson, 1997): Preface to the

In 1967 I proposed that we should put away a penny per gallon of gasoline, which then cost 39 cents, for the UJA [United Jewish Appeal] to resettle the Palestinian refugees, and that we should declare Jerusalem an international city, and that the UN should move there. I think it would have been a healthy thing, but I don't think we have gotten rid of our memory that gets our immune system so reactive that we break out in a rash. You say "Krishna," it's not so bad. But if you say "Jesus," right away it gets us to be reactive and upset.

I want to remind the Jewish community that there are some people whose souls were touched by the Gospels. I think I want to reclaim Jesus as one of the extra-canonical *maggidim* [teachers] of that time, and to say that at least some of the stuff in the Gospels should be seen as a Jewish book, although maybe not canonical. And if some people are Nazarene Hasidim, they shouldn't be any worse than Lubavitcher or Bratzlaver Hasidim, having their deceased *rebbe* (teacher, guru). The Jews for Jesus [a denomination], however, are seeking to proselytize us and are really hanging in with the Christian fundamentalists. They start quoting Romans and Galatians and that sort of thing even after they read from the Torah, then show that it is now superseded, and that doesn't feel right.

So, coming to the concept of the Noosphere again at the end, I think if we can all get together and recognize that just as the lungs, or the brain, or the liver can't be the whole body, and every vital organ is needed, so every religion is a vital organ of the planet. Once we understand this, we can all work together for the divinization of

New Edition, "No Posthumous Victories for Hitler," pp. ix ff. Cf. Lerner, *Jewish Renewal*, pp. 202 ff, "The 614th Commandment: Don't Give Hitler a Posthumous Victory" (ref. Fackenheim, p.xi), and pp.216 ff, "Healing the Trauma": First step: Be realistic – "There will never be an end to Jewish vulnerability until there is a world of justice, caring, ethical and spiritual sensitivity, mutual recognition, and ecologial responsibility" . . . Second step: Create therapeutic communities to process the rage, grief, and mistaken internalizations of disvalue; mourn *thoroughly* for all that has been lost. Third step: Complete, finish, the mourning; no longer build life around it (traditional teaching on death, grief), but return to our vocation of witnessing to God's presence in the world; don't give in to denial of meaning, but don't be naively optimistic, and don't compensate for injury by chauvinism. Understand where the evil comes from and struggle against it intelligently and compassionately, with faith in God's help. (Step Two may take a long time.)

the planet, converging toward Teilhard's "Omega Point." And the means for that movement we can find in Merton's spiritual direction.

Which means prayer, openness to other traditions, and to poetry.

And to let your own tradition work through you.

"The important thing for me is ... opening up the depths of my own heart. The rest is secondary."

— Thomas Merton, *The School of Charity*

"The word 'God,' then, is in reality a non-word; yet behind it is a presence which fills the whole Bible like the smoke that filled Solomon's temple or the pillar of fire and cloud over the tabernacle."

—Thomas Merton, *Opening the Bible*

I7

THOMAS MERTON and
JEWISH/CHRISTIAN
EXISTENTIALISM

Transcribed and Edited by Paul M. Pearson.

In late 1967 Thomas Merton was speaking to the monastic community at Gethsemani in his regular Sunday afternoon conferences about the Islamic Sufis. In a lecture he gave on October 29, 1967 he broke off from this series to speak about the Hasidic movement within Judaism. His lecture stems from his reading of a recent article published in the journal *Commentary*, "A Symposium: The State of Jewish Belief"[1] in which, after an introduction by Milton Himmelfarb, thirty-eight leading Jewish thinkers addressed their own and contemporary religious thought. Merton moves on quickly to examine the thought of Zalman Schachter, one of the commentators in the article, especially his thinking on Jewish existentialism. Merton's comments in this lecture relate only to the first part of Schachter's answers to the questions raised by the editors of *Commentary*. In Merton's final comment to the monastic community, after the bell has rung signaling the end of the session, he says he will return to this topic again. However there is no evidence in the tapes held at the Merton Center that he ever did this but returned in the following session to his talks on the Islamic Sufis.

---

1 The article was subsequently reprinted as a book, *The Condition of Jewish Belief: A Symposium Compiled by the Editors of Commentary Magazine*, (New York: Macmillan, 1966). Zalman Schachter's response to the questions can be found on pages 207-216. Quotations from Schachter referred to in this transcript will refer to the book version of this article.

Zalman Schachter, along with another famous Rabbi, Lou Silberman,[2] had visited Gethsemani in the summer of 1962 and, at Merton's request both had addressed Merton's novitiate classes – Schachter on the subject of holiness and Silberman on the Dead Sea Scrolls.[3] Merton described their visit saying: "Last week was tremendous, busy, exciting...Zalman Schachter came with Rabbi L. Silverman from Vanderbilt, who talked about the Dead Sea Scrolls."[4]

This conference by Thomas Merton was previously published as side B of cassette ten of Electronic Paperbacks' *The Mystic Life* tapes, produced in 1976 by Norman Kramer.

The transcript of the conference reproduced here has been done with the minimum of editing so as to keep as closely as possible to Merton's spoken word while, however, omitting certain repeated words and phrases which were characteristic of Merton's lecturing style but which would have distracted from his overall message. At times quotes Merton attributes to Schachter are paraphrases of what Schachter wrote in the *Commentary* article; where this is the case Schachter's exact words are given in the footnotes. As with many of Merton's lectures at Gethsemani he ends abruptly when the monastery bell rings.

Jewish Hasidism
Thomas Merton.

Today I have something quite good. It is not Sufism but it is like Sufism in a way. It is Jewish spirituality in the line of Hasidism. Now, Hasidism is like Sufism only it is Jewish. The Jewish Hasids are the Jewish mystics. The man who is giving this thing out is Zalman Schachter. He's been here and given talks in the novitiate. You all know him with his beard, he's a completely orthodox Jew. He is a Hasid and he has an Hasidic master. Like Sufism, the Hasids have their own Ravi, which is their master, and they go pretty

---

2 In Merton's journal entry for August 21, 1962 he incorrectly refers to Silberman as Silverman.

3 These conferences were given to Merton's classes of novices in August 1962 and recordings of these conferences are held in the collection of the Thomas Merton Center at Bellarmine University, Louisville, Kentucky.

4 Merton, Thomas. *Turning Toward the World: The Pivotal Years*, ed. Victor A. Kramer (San Francisco: Harper Collins, 1996), 238.

much for dancing and self-expression and a very expressive kind of religion. And they're mystical. Just like the Sufis get to the heart of the Moslem way of life, so the Hasids really are at the heart of Judaism. This is the real live Judaism, the Hasidim, just as we monks should be right at the heart of Christianity. I mean, there always should be a nucleus of people who go right to the heart of the thing. And the heart of it is pretty much the same for all of us, really, in one way or another. Quite apart from the theological implications, it gets down to be pretty much the same thing.

I happened to come across an article written by Zalman Schachter in reply to a questionnaire from the best Jewish magazine in the country, a magazine called *Commentary*. This magazine, *Commentary*, got 10 or 20 important Jews to answer a question. The question was something like this, "Where is Judaism going, or have we still got any reason to function, or should we quit?" You know the sort of question that everybody's asking everywhere in one form or another – "What ought we to be doing? Are we making sense or are we not?" And so, what you come down to here then is a different formulation of the same kind of question that everybody is asking everywhere. And Zalman Schachter, being a sort of Buberite Jew, a student of Buber, is therefore a Jewish existentialist. So here you get a little bit of Jewish existentialism, which can come pretty close to Christian existentialism, and I think you'll find this useful.

So that's what I want to talk about. And the thing that he is talking about is one of the great problems that you always run into in religion and in monasticism and everywhere, and it is something that we all know and we all think about. And he expresses it in this way: "It's the dialectic between *is* and *ought* …"[5]

Now what that really is, is just simply the dialectic between what I am and what I ought to be, where I am and then how far I meet demands that one never perfectly meets. For each one of us in the community we have demands that we should meet, they are objective demands to meet, and then we all come more or less close and there is no such thing as everybody being absolutely, word perfect, right on the line all of the time, and it should not be that way. One of the tricks about this is it is not supposed to be that way

---

5 Schachter in *The Condition of Jewish Belief* speaks of "the tension between ought and is," 210.

either. Because what you have here is dialectical thinking. And what is important in dialectical thinking is that you have got two poles, two things, and it is not that you are supposed to move from one to the other and leave one behind. It is that those two poles are supposed to maintain a tension. And what is important in dialectical thinking is not the resolution of the problem but the tension of the problem. So dialectical thinking is tension thinking, and therefore it is real thinking. Because in real life you do not solve problems. You live them, or you live your way through them, or they solve themselves. But in living reality what is important is the quality of this tension and the honesty and authenticity of the tension. And of course, tension means discomfort.

What we are starting out with is this fact that for a Jew, as for a Trappist, as for anybody else who takes the spiritual life seriously, there is a basic tension. The life sets up a tension which is supposed to be there. We're supposed to be biting our nails to some extent. It may be artificial, it shouldn't be too artificial, but it does exist. The life sets up a tension between a norm that you're supposed to aim at and how far you are capable of approaching that yourself. And that tension is maintained all the time. And one of the places where this kind of tension is maintained is choir. Choir, that is the source of nervous tension and any other kind of tension in choir. You are always supposed to be hitting some sort of a norm, and you never quite hit it, and it never completely works. The more you get this on your mind, of course, it can be too much. You can have too much tension on this particular point. But there has always got to be some. Life is tension. But life is not all tension. It is also relaxation. Life is tension and relaxation. So therefore, what one has to do: it is wrong thinking – I'm not going to go and repeat this all over again because I've said it thousands of times – it is wrong, and it is stupid, and it is destructive and useless to try to live your life in such a way that you just simply solve one problem after another, and you go step by step from problem to problem leaving behind you the debris of solved problems. This is not it. What it is, is a constant alternation between tension and relaxation, and struggle and rest, and keeping this thing going in such a way that it is realistic and true to you.

Schachter says that there is a double temptation. One temptation, which is not usually presented as a temptation at all, it is usually presented as the right thing, is to so conform to the norm that the tension disappears and you have rest. Now, let us face the fact that this is something that is built into our mentality here and it is wrong. You get the feeling that, "If only I could perfectly hit, perfectly meet, the demands that are made of me by this life," ("the demands" in the abstract terms, in sort of a general way) "if only I could." What it amounts to in the end is, "If only I could be somebody totally approved by everybody as having met the norm, they would all say, 'There's the man who's met the norm.'" I guess the reason why we do not do that is that we are not crazy enough to really want it that badly because it's not real! There is something in us that says, "Really, that is not it." But conscience says, "Yeah, maybe you should." We all develop a slightly scrupulous conscience on this point, and conscience sort of nags us and says, "Well, you really should be perfect in that sense." Then life says, "Nuts! You can't. That's not real." But what is important is the tension, because you have got to remember both. Because then what happens if you throw this out and everybody gets extremely existentialistic about the thing and they say, "There are no objective demands. The heck with the objective demands. Throw them out. They're useless." Then the tension disappears. But you are in a mess, because you don't know whether you are up or down or sideways or backwards. You do not know where you are going. There have to be objective demands. If there are no objective demands, there is no tension.

Now, what do these objective demands consist in? We are now Jews, so let's approach it from the Jewish point of view. For the Jew where do you find your objective demands? Obviously the first place is the Torah, the Torah and the Talmud and all those 631 commandments.[6] The things you have to do. And right away there

---

6 Merton here transposes the numbers. Schachter had referred (p. 211) to the standard Jewish tradition that there are "613 commandments," or precepts in the Torah, a figure corresponding to the 365 days of the year and the 248 limbs and organs of the human body. See, e.g., Ephraim E. Urbach, *The Sages: Their Concepts and Beliefs*, tr. Israel Abrahams (Cambridge, MA: Harvard UP, 1995), 342-365, on The Number, Classification, and Evaluation of the Precepts. Catholic Canon Law has far more than 613 precepts. The Talmud (*Sotah* 22b) expressly condemns a "cut and dried" attitude. What is important is purity of heart, a loving participation in God's creative intention. This theme has a long history in Jewish spiritual classics, beginning with the Bible, and is developed at length by Heschel, e.g. in *God in Search of Man*, chapter 30.

330 · Paul M. Pearson

are plenty of those. They have got even more than we have, and we have cut down on what we've got, but they always had about twice as many as we had anyway. That is an objective norm. You have to meet these rules. They are things you have to do. For a Jew it is all cut and dried. I mean, there are a lot of things that you have to do, and a lot of things that you just do not do. On Yom Kippur you fast from sunset to sunset. It's the Day of Atonement. I've been to the synagogue on Yom Kippur when they blow the shofar, a big trumpet.[7] They are all very hungry and they are all singing the Psalms and then they blow this trumpet and they all barrel out of there and go home and have a big dinner. And that is fine. That is great. And they say the prayers. I have been with a real Orthodox family for supper on Yom Kippur. It is beautiful, it is really great. And there is joy, and they drink some wine and all that. Very nice!

Another one of the objective norms that Zalman talks about is what he calls "the practice of the pious."[8] This is an objective norm. Now, what I was saying a minute ago that we should try to be good religious, and that we can't perfectly attain it, but it is nevertheless a reality. There is a certain norm of what constitutes a good religious. And someone says, "How do you know?" Well, the mentality of the community, in so far as it is more or less sane, has in it a picture of what a good religious is. In that picture there are sometimes screwy elements that have to be gotten rid of. But on

---

7 The shofar is a ram's horn, which of its nature could vary in size. It is used as a musical instrument to make three different sounds: *t'kiah*, a long uninterrupted sound; *shevorim*, a sound broken into three; and *t'ruah*, a sound broken into nine tiny notes. The steady sound connects our lives strongly to the Divine realm. The broken sounds represent our creaturehood, fragmented lives, faults and erring ways, which are mended and transformed during the Days of Awe (the ten days from Rosh Hashanah – the "Head of the Year" – to Yom Kippur – the Day of Atonement). Even on Rosh Hashanah the shofar sound, which the Torah commands that the People "hear," concludes with another long steady blast announcing the coming of God as King and Judge, who takes His seat on the throne of loving-kindness, promising our total redemption. At the very end of the Yom Kippur observance there is a long strong continuous blast which proclaims God's sovereignty and the People's renewed freedom and dignity as the Children of God. (See, e.g., Moshe Braun, *The Jewish Holy Days: Their Spiritual Significance* [Northvale NJ: Aronson, 1996], 12-21.)

8 Schachter speaks of the "consensus of the pious," 210. This is not an objective norm as Merton then goes on to suggest it is; Schachter calls it an "objective standard," 209.

the whole there is a sort of a sensible, sane idea in the community, and people know what a good religious is. And they can tell, "This guy is a good religious." Now this is an objective norm. But we have to remember that if somebody thinks of so and so, "He's a good religious. This guy is a real good religious," okay, he is a real good religious, but he may have some tensions going on there that you do not know about. He may be a very peaceful looking guy and very balanced and all that sort of thing. And then one of these days maybe you may see what kind of tensions are going on behind the man's peaceful look. You cannot judge by that.

What I am saying now is that you cannot say that these things are absolutely objective. We know what they are, but they are never objectively fulfilled. We may think they are. But they are not really. What happens is this tension is maintained. And then he says another thing. Of course, when you meet an objective demand like this, what happens is you are forced to alter your life to some extent in order to meet some kind of demand, and you make that adjustment. When you do that, then you are doing something which honors God (we are now in a religious context), you do something which gives glory to God because you are obeying God, you are obeying an objective demand of God. When you give glory to God and obey God, you also come closer to Him, and you know Him better. This is standard but it has to be recalled.

Now Zalman says there are other commands of God, deeper and more inexplicable ones, which you cannot formulate, which you cannot rationalize, but are very important. This is the kind of thing where God himself, without having written out any rule or any blueprint for it, simply breaks into your life and says, "Look, I want this from you." Usually it is a question of some providential event that comes along: somebody dies or something happens, and then your situation changes, and God is telling you, "This is what I ask from you. Do this." And these are sometimes extremely difficult. We have been talking about this in one of the other conferences, how God will ask you to undergo an insupportable trial or something like that. This is one of the objective demands, one of the things that we meet in life. God breaks into our life with a big demand; we know that this is it, and we have to meet it, and we never quite do. There is a tension set up there. This is from the outside, this is something that we don't control. It is just dished out to us, and here it is, dumped in your lap. What are you going to do with it?

Then, on the subjective side, there is what comes from within ourselves. Again, I'm following Zalman because I like the way he thinks this out, and he does a very nice job with it. He says, "From within ourselves we meet these demands in terms of" – this is his language and this is good, this is the kind of thing we ought to think about more – "in terms of decisions which fit our covenant with God."[9]

We ought to be more covenant-centered in our thinking. Each one of us has a covenant with God. And as an institution we have a covenant with God. This is something objective. There is a kind of agreement; there's an understanding between us and God as individuals and as a community. And we are supposed to be people who are living in terms of this understanding, who make decisions on the basis of our understanding with God.

I remember a Protestant, when I was dealing with these Protestants that came here, a very pious one from Asbury. This is a little Methodist seminary where they are all really devout. I was talking to this very devout Methodist minister and he was asking me could I ever come over there or something like that, and he said, "Could you do that or would that not be in accordance with your covenant?" That is a very good way of putting it, looking at things in terms of a covenant we have made with God. We have covenanted to do this and not that, and so forth. This is the Jewish way of looking at the thing too.

Then, there is another thing that Zalman says that can arise in terms of our subjective response. This is what he calls "the reckless love of God"[10] which is different from the covenant response. In other words, I have in me, we should all have in ourselves, the capacity to meet these objective obligations or just no obligation at all. There should be within us a capacity for covenant response, a covenant awareness, a sense that we have come to an agreement with God, and that there are certain things that he can ask of us, because we have made an agreement, not because of our human

---

9 Schachter says, "Rather is it rooted in the subjective self that makes these decisions as part of the calculus of its covenant with God," 210.
10 Schachter, 210.

nature. This idea of covenant is completely different from natural law, for example. I would say there should be much more of this in peace-thinking and race-thinking, and so forth. The Christians, the Catholics, never seem to bring this idea of a covenant up in terms of these things. We have got a covenant with God to be peaceful people. We've got a covenant with God to love our brother and a covenant with God to treat our brother fairly even though he has got a different color skin, and that sort of thing. You never hear that. Who ever bothers with that? Covenant! Natural law! You invoke natural law then ignore it. But we have a covenant with God on these particular points.

Then he says there is this reckless love of God.[11] Well, we all get a little bit of that. We don't get an awful lot but, every once in a while, something will spring up from within you that kind of prompts you to give God something that He hasn't asked for – usually He doesn't want it. But very often you will make some kind of a reckless offer and He will say, "Listen, keep it, kid. I'll give you the merit but I don't want that. You're nuts!" There is in us this reckless love of God, once in a while. There should be something of this. There should be a little recklessness and, every once in a while, we do some kind of crazy thing out of love for God. But don't do too many crazy things out of love for God, because it may not work too well.

Now, when you add up these things that he's lined up there, and you consider the tension between them, then you get a pretty good picture of the spiritual life. This gives you a good, healthy, dynamic view of the spiritual life – objective obligations, unpredictable demands from God, covenant decisions, and movements of reckless love. This, I would say, is a good way to look at the spiritual life to see it in terms of these elements added up together and working together.

11 Schachter illustrates this "reckless love of God" saying: "This recklessness is closer to the Great Maggid's 'now that I have no more part in the world to come, I can serve You the more lovingly,' than to Calvin's being damned for God's greater glory. Some of R. Zussia's readiness to go to hell because 'in this I can fulfill one more *mitzvah*' is stronger than a Kierkegaardian suspension of the ethical," 210. The Great Maggid (Storyteller) was Dov-Baer of Mezeritch, Poland (1710-1772), successor-disciple of the Ba'al Shem Tov (Master of the Good Name, one who sees all beings in their union with God), founder of the Hasidic revival in the eighteenth century. See, e.g., Elie Wiesel, *Souls on Fire: Portraits and Legends of Hasidic Masters* (Northvale NJ: Aronson, 1993).

334 · *Paul M. Pearson*

Then there is another tension that is established by the constant norm of the law, which is the same all of the time. I mean a commandment is a commandment. The first commandment is the same on Tuesday as it is on Wednesday. You know, it's the same. It doesn't change. And then there are what Zalman calls "The teachings of the hour." Now that doesn't mean to say the latest, fashionable article that came out about situation ethics, or something. But it does refer to the situation. You've got your norm of the law, and you have the demands of special circumstances, the demands of the hour, the time, the place, and so forth, which are an exception, which constitute an exception.

This is good moral thinking. This you have to remember in making moral decisions. You have the norm, and you have also to take into account the possible exception – a mother's got children to take care of so she doesn't go to Mass on Sunday, or something like that. In other words, circumstances come in and it's not that you're excused from the general law, but it is more virtuous not to obey the general law at that point, because this is a virtue which is the virtue of following exceptions. The virtue of spotting and following exceptions is called *epicheia*. If there is nothing but exceptions, then the tension disappears. That's what is wrong. Incidentally, the greatest laxist was a Cistercian called Caramuel. He is called in moral theology "the Prince of Laxists." But I don't know what he taught.

The exception makes sense when there is a norm. You maintain the objective norm, and for it to be meaningful it has to be constant. Then the exception is meaningful when you've got a constant norm. If you don't have a constant norm, then you don't have any exception either, you've got nothing, the tension disappears. Now what happens, he's got a very good point here, is that if you don't insist on being strict, if there is no strictness at all, then there's no tension at all, then the whole thing collapses. Now, this is one thing you have to remember.

Right now we are dealing with a lot of loose talk in this whole thing. You get someone who will stand up and say, "In human development, to really flower and blossom as a human being, there should be nothing holding me down." But if nothing holds you down, you are never going to be any kind of a human being. What makes a human being is this tension. A human being is made by facing obstacles and handling obstacles.

This is one of the problems that you've got with the method that a certain Dr. Spock thought up of bringing up children. They're all grown up now. This guy came along after World War II and said, "The way to bring kids up is to let them do what they want. I mean, don't hinder them in anything. Just let them go ahead." Spock himself, when they started growing up, said, "Well listen, I should have said, 'You should spank them once in a while.' There are certain things that you really should stop them from doing." The point is you're not doing a person a favor when you just let him follow every whim. This is not good for him! That's not what makes a human being. There has to be a tension. He has to be held back. Suppose you want to play tennis with somebody. What do you do? If you've got a three-year-old child that can't hold a racket well, you'll sure win, you'll win every game. There's no tennis game. If you want to play tennis, you have to find somebody who is more or less equally matched so that you'll be able to play. And so it is with life. You have to meet up with obstacles. You are not doing anybody a favor if you take all of the obstacles out of his life, because sometimes you have to put obstacles there, sometimes you have to get in the guy's way and say, "Stop! You're doing wrong. This is not the way to do it. This is the wrong way. There are other ways of doing it."

Zalman has a little point here, that it is good to be tough and to make demands. "In making a rule for others, I must be guided by the same scale. If the other is informed, committed, willing, and capable of observance …I cannot invent theological tricks to save me or him from our moral bankruptcy."[12] In other words, what he's saying is, you've got to make it tough, not in order so that you can all prove yourselves to be extremely virtuous, but in order that you get a real grasp of your own weakness. That is the point that he's making. The dialectic between the tough demands of the law and the defects which this brings out in us so that we have to fight, not each other, but our own defects. That is the way he's really arguing this thing. He is making a great point out of what he calls the revelation of the "crooked heart." When you get into these situations

12 Schachter, 211.

where you have to meet obstacles then what happens is that everybody who gets into this situation recognizes in himself the fact that he is not virtuous and that he is a sort of a prevaricator, because we all are. We are all sinners, we are all to some extent prevaricators. We are all to some extent unfaithful. It is good that the situation should be tough and we should be forced to admit this. Then we are dealing with reality. That is the point that he makes. But now, he turns it around too! He says, if you've got a situation where everybody has got it down to a fine point so that they are keeping all the rules in such a way that nobody ever slips up, this is the worst thing that could happen, because then, for all practical purposes, for these people, God is dead. They are living according to a system. They are never forced to meet up with the existential realities of their situation. They never have to face the wrong that is in themselves. They don't need God!

Now the thing about Zalman is that Zalman cannot stand St. Paul. But what he is saying here is exactly the teaching of St. Paul. This is exactly the teaching of Romans. These difficult chapters in Romans and Galatians where St. Paul is saying, "Where sin abounded, grace has super-abounded" and all that sort of thing, "Therefore, should I break the law to get more grace? No! God forbid!" You know all that stuff where you go through in a fog wondering what he's talking about. This is what he's talking about. He's saying that there has to be a law. But the law doesn't justify you. The law makes you experience the tension between your own nothingness and the law and it makes you cry out, not for the law, but for God. That's the point. That is the way he puts it. He does a very good job on it.

Here is where he brings in Prometheus. Nietzsche and Sartre and these people have come along. The great thing about Nietzsche and Sartre is they throw away objective demands. Nietzsche says, "Look, this objective demand stuff is just holding you back." Nietzsche and Sartre both say this. They are not saying what you think. They are not just saying throw away the objective demands and have a good time. It is quite the opposite. They are saying, "With this objective demand business you are making it too easy, because as long as you've got objective demands you can kid yourselves. If you meet the objective demands you can say, 'Oh. I was a good boy. I met the objective demands.' And there are no objective demands. You've got to be brutally honest with every situation. You've got to decide the whole thing for yourself." In other words, the reason why it is wrong is you've practically got to be God. It is very difficult for us to conceive what this means because we just never have thought in these terms. But Nietzsche throws you into a position where you have to practically be God. There is no objective norm. You have got to decide with your own will what is right and wrong.

The key to Sartre's existentialist ethics is this: that you have to act at every moment without any objective norms, there are no laws, but you have to make a law for yourself every time you act. And you make it by this standard. You say, "I will now do what I think ought to be binding on everybody in such a situation."

"In other words, you are God. You have to act in such a way that you invent a moral law in acting. Now, to us, this is inconceivable. This never occurs to us. We just don't think in these terms. These people say, "You guys with your objective norms have got it much too easy. You don't have to think. All you have to do is remember that rule 225 says this, and you just do that without even thinking. So that's lazy." But Zalman says, in a nice, quiet way, "To Sartre this is no occasion for rejoicing." See, this freedom. "Sartre must take on infinite responsibilities." Who wants to take on infinite responsibilities? We don't even do too good with very limited ones. "There is no exit; and looking at those who take no responsibilities at all" – that is to say, those who shove the responsibilities off onto the law – "he is affected with nausea. This is no problem for me. *Halakha*," that is to say *observance*, "limits my responsibility. I am not infinitely responsible. In responding to God through the *halakha*," by keeping the law, "my responsibility is finite."[13]

13 Schachter, 212. In this quotation Schachter is alluding specifically to Sartre's book *Nausea* and his play *No Exit*.

"It is through piety that there comes the real revelation of the self, the disclosure of what is most delicate in the human soul, the unfolding of the purest elements in the human venture."

—Heschel, *An Analysis of Piety*

"Under My Skin"

I've got to get to
the good Jew
beneath my Catholic skin.

I've got to get to
the sincere humanist
beneath my
Jewish skin.

I've got to get
beneath my
humanist skin
to my original face.

The good Jew
finds my Catholic skin
unbelievable.

The sincere humanist
finds my Jewish skin
superfluous.

My original face
Finds all skins
magnificent.

Paul Quenon, 2002

"'Come let us reach an understanding,' saith the Lord."
  —Isaiah 1:18 JPS

"Let us go into the House of the Lord"
  —Psalms 122:1

THE SUCCESSIVE VERSIONS
of NOSTRA AETATE

*Translation, Outline Analysis, Chronology,
Commentary by James M. Somerville*

Text I

The Fourth Chapter of the ecumenism decree, November 1963: De Catholicorum habitudine ad nonchristianos et maxime ad Iudaeos:

Postquam de Oecumenismi Catholici principiis tractavimus, silentio praeterire nolumus, quod eadem, habita ratione diversae condicionis, applicari debent, cum agitur de modo colloquendi et cooperandi cum hominibus non-christianis, qui tamen Deum colunt, vel saltem bona animati voluntate, legem moralein hominis naturae insitam, pro conscientia servare student.

After having treated the principles governing Catholic ecumenism, we do not wish to pass over in silence the fact that these principles should be applied, with due respect for varying circumstances, whenever there is a question of how to converse and cooperate with non-Christians who, nevertheless, worship God, or at least, animated by good will strive in good conscience to observe the moral law innate in human nature.

Maxime autem hoc valet cum de Iudaeis agitur, quippe qui cum Ecclesia Christi speciali ratione coniungantur.

This holds true above all when it comes to the Jews, who are especially linked to the Church of Christ.

Ecclesia Christi grato animo agnoscit fidei et electionis suae initia iuxta Dei salutare mysterium iam inter Patriarchas et Prophetas inveniri. Omnes enim Christifideles, Abrahae filios secundum fidem [Gal. 3:71] in eiusdem Patriarchae vocatione includi et in populi electi exitu ex terra servitutis Ecclesiae salutem mystice praesignari confitetur. Nequit Ecclesia, nova in Christo creatura [Eph. 2:15], oblivisci se continuationem esse populi illius quocum olim Deus ex ineffabili misericordia sua Antiquum Foedus concludere dignatus est.

The Church of Christ gratefully acknowledges that the beginnings of its own faith and election in connection with the saving mystery of God is already to be found in the Patriarchs and Prophets. All believing Christians, sons of Abraham in faith [Gal. 3:7], are regarded as included in the vocation of the same Patriarch, and the salvation of the Church is mystically prefigured in the exodus of the Chosen People from the Land of Bondage. Nor can the Church, a new creature in Christ [Eph. 2:17], forget that it is a continuation of that People with whom God out of his ineffable mercy deigned to enter into an Ancient Covenant.

Credit insuper Ecclesia Christum, Pacem nostram, uno amore et Iudaeos et Gentes complecti et utraque fecisse unum [Eph. 2:14] atque amborum in uno corpore unione [Eph. 2:17] annuntiari totius orbis terrarum in Christo reconciliationem. Etsi populi electi magna pars interim longe a Christo, iniuria tamen diceretur populus maledictus, cum Deo maneat carissimus propter Patres et dona eis data [Rom. 11:28], vel gens deicida, quia omnium hominum peccata, quae causa fuerunt passionis et mortis Iesu Christi, Dominus passione et morte sua luit [Lk. 23:34; Act. 3:17; 1 Cor. 2:8]. Mors tamen Christi non a toto populo tunc vivente, et multo minus ab hodierno populo adducta est. Ideo caveant sacerdotes ne quid dicant in instructione catechetica, neque in praedicatone, quod in cordibus auditorum, odium aut despectionem erga Iudaeos gignere possit. Neque obliviscitur Ecclesia ex hoc populo natum esse Christum Iesum secundum carnem, natam esse Mariam Virginem, Christi Matrem, natos esse Apostolos, Ecclesiae fundamentum et columnas.

The Church believes, moreover, that Christ, our Peace, embraced with a single love both Jews and Gentiles, and has made both groups into one [Eph. 2:14], uniting them in a single body [Eph. 2:27], and announcing the reconciliation of the entire world in Christ. And although the Chosen People, meanwhile, have for the most part been far from Christ, it is, nonetheless, unfair to speak of a people under a curse, since they remain most dear to God for the sake of the Fathers and because of the gifts they have received [Rom. 11:28]. Nor should they be regarded as a deicidal race, for the Lord by his passion and death expiates for all men's sins which were the cause of his passion and death [Lk. 23:34; Acts 3:17; I Cor. 2:8]. The death of Christ is not to be attributed to any whole people then living, and even less to a people today. Therefore, let priests take care lest they say anything in catechetical instruction or in preaching that could give rise in the hearts of hearers to hatred and contempt of Jews. Nor should the Church forget that it is from this People that Christ was born according to the flesh, that the Virgin Mary, the Mother of Christ, was born, and that the apostles, the foundation stones and pillars of the Church were born.

Quare eum tantum Ecclesia sit cum synagoga, commune patrimonium, Sacra haec Synodus etriusque mutuam cognitionem et aestimationem, quae studiis theologicis et colloquiis fraternis obtinetur, omnino fovere et commendare intendit et insuper, sicut iniurias hominibus ubicumque inflictas severe reprobat, ita etiam magis odia et persecutiones contra Iudaeos, sive olim sive nostris temporibus perpetratas, materno animo deplorat et damnat.

Therefore, since the Church and the Synagogue hold so much of their patrimony in common, this Sacred Synod intends to foster in every way and commend the mutual recognition and esteem stemming from both theological studies and brotherly dialogue. Beyond that, just as it reprobates severely any injuries inflicted on men anywhere, so all the more does it deplore and condemn hatred and persecutions against Jews, whether carried out in times past or in our own day.

TEXT II

Sections 32-34 of the ecumenism decree, September 1964; *De Iudaeis et de non-christianis*:

32. (De communi patrimonio Christianorum cum Iudaeis.) Ecclesia Christi libenter agnoscit fidei et electionis suae initia iam apud Patriarchas et Prophetas, iuxta salutare Dei mysterium, inveniri. Confitetur enim omnes Christifideles, Abrahae filios secundum fidem [Gal. 3:7], in eiusdem Patriarachae vocatione includi et in populi electi exitu e terra servitutis salutem Ecclesiae mystice praesignari. Quare nequit Ecclesia, nova in Christo creatura [Eph. 2:15] et populus Novi Foederis, oblivisci se continuationem esse populi illius, quocum olim Deus ex ineffabili misericordia sua Antiquum Foedus inire dignatus est, et cui revelationem in Libris Veteris Testamenti contentam concredere voluit.

(Concerning the common patrimony of Christians with Jews.) The Church of Christ freely acknowledges that the beginnings of its faith and election are to be found with the Patriarchs and Prophets in connection with God's saving mystery. It is further acknowledged that all believing Christians, sons of Abraham in faith [Gal. 3:7], are to be regarded as included in the vocation of the same Patriarch, and that the salvation of the Church is mystically prefigured in the exodus of the Chosen People from the Land of Bondage. Nor can the Church, a new creature in Christ [Eph. 2:15] and the people of the New Covenant, forget that it is a continuation of that People with whom God out of his ineffable mercy deigned to enter into an Ancient Covenant, and to whom he willed to entrust the revelation contained in the books of the Old Testament.

Neque obliviscitur Ecclesia ex populo iudaico Christum natum esse secundum carnem, natam esse Christi Matrem, Mariam Virginem, et natos esse Apostolos, Ecclesiae fundamentum et columnas.

Nor should the Church forget that it was from the Jewish People that Christ was born according to the flesh, that the Mother of Christ, the Virgin Mary, was born, and that the apostles, the foundation stones and pillars of the Church, were born.

Verba quoque Apostoli Pauli semper habet et habebit prae oculis Ecclesia de Iudaeis "quorum adoptio est filiorum et gloria et testamentum et legislatio et obsequium et promissa" [Rom. 9:4].

The Church also has and will always have before its eyes the words of the Apostle Paul concerning the Jews, to whom belong "the adoption as sons and the glory and the covenant[s] [Gk. (Paul):*diathēkai*] and the giving of the Law and the worship [Gk.(Paul) *latreia*] and the promises" [Rom. 9:4].

Cum igitur tantum patrimonium Christiani ex Iudaeis acceperint, Sacra haec Synodus mutuam utriusque cognitionem et aestimationem, quae et studiis theologiciis et fraternis colloquiis obtinetur, omnino fovere vult et commendare, atque insuper, sicut iniurias hominibus ubicumque illatas severe reprobat, ita enim odia et vexationem contra Iudaeos deplorat et damnat.

Therefore, since Christians have received so great a patrimony from the Jews, this Sacred Synod wishes to foster and commend in every way the mutual recognition and esteem stemming from theological studies and brotherly dialogue, and just as it severely reprobates injuries inflicted on men everywhere, so also does it deplore and condemn hatred and abuse leveled against Jews.

Memoria insuper dignum est adunationem populi iudaici cum Ecclesia partem spei christianae esse. Ecclesia enim, docente apostolo Paulo [Rom. 11:25], fide inconcussa ac desiderio magno accessum huius populi exspectat ad plenitudinem populi Dei, quam Christus instauravit.

Moreover, it is proper to keep in mind that the union of the Jewish People with the Church is part of Christian hope. For the Church, following the teaching of the Apostle Paul, awaits with firm faith and great desire the addition of this People to the full complement of the People of God which Christ initiated. [This paragraph does not appear in Text I. It is the one to which Abraham Joshua Heschel particularly objected, since it calls for Judaism to disappear and be absorbed into the Catholic Church. It was withdrawn and does not appear in in Text III and was replaced by less offensive language in Text IV.]

Ideo curent omnes ne, sive in catechesi impertienda et Verbi Dei praedicatione sive in quotidianis colloquiis, populum iudaicum ut gentem reprobatam exhibeant, neve aliud quid dicant aut faciant, quod animos a Iudaeis alienare possit. Caveant praeterea ne Iudaeis nostrorum temporum quae in Passione Christi perpetrata sunt imputentur.

Therefore, let all take care, whether in catechetical instruction or in preaching the Word of God, or whether in daily conversation, lest the Jewish People be represented as a rejected nation. Neither should anything be said or done that could alienate human minds from the Jews. In addition, let all take care lest there be imputed to Jews of our day what was done during the Passion of Christ.

33. (Omnes homines Deum ut Patrem habeant.) Dominus Iesus omnium hominum Patrem esse Deum, sicut iam Scripturae Veteris Testamenti statuunt et ipsa innuit ratio, luculenter confirmavit. Nequimus vero Deum omnium Patrem vocare vel orare, si erga quosdam homines, ad imaginem Dei creatos, fraterne nos gerere renuimus. Ita enim arcte connectuntur habitudo hominis ad Deum Patrem et eiusdem habitudo hominis ad homines fratres, ut omnis negatio humanae fraternitatis negationem ipsius Dei, apud quem non est acceptio personarum [2 Chr. 19:7; Rom. 2:11; Eph. 6:9; Col. 3:25; 1 Pet. 1:17], secumferat vel ad eam ducat. Nam prius mandatum eum altero ita coalescit, ut nobis nequeant dimitti debita nostra, nisi nosmetipsi ex corde debitoribus nostris dimittamus. Iamvero in Lege Veteri dicitur: "Numquid non

346 · Merton and Judaism

Pater unus omnium nostrum? numquid non Deus unus creavit nos? quare ergo despicit unusquisque nostrum fratrem suum?" [Mal. 2:10]; idque in Nova Lege clarius affirmatur: "Qui non diligit fratrem suum quem videt, Deum quem non videt quomodo potest diligere? Et hoc mandatum habemus a Deo ut qui diligit Deum diligat et fratrem suum" [I Jn. 4:20-21].

33. (All men have God as Father.) The Lord Jesus has amply confirmed the fact that God is the Father of all men, even as the writings of the Old Testament declare and reason itself intimates. We cannot truly call God the Father of all and pray to him, if we refuse to relate in a friendly way to certain men created in the image of God. Thus, so closely linked are man's relation to God the Father and the relation of man to his fellowman that every denial of human fraternity is a denial of God himself for whom there can be no favoritism [2 Chr. 19:7; Rom. 2:11; Eph. 6:9; Col. 3:25; 1 Pet. 1:17]. For the first commandment is so linked to the second that our offenses cannot be forgiven unless we forgive from the heart those who have offended us. Indeed, we read in the Old Law, "Have we not all one Father? Has not one God created us? Why then does each one of us despise his brother?" [Mal. 2:10]. The same is clearly affirmed in the New Law: "How can those who do not love a brother whom they see, love God whom they do not see? This is the commandment we have from God, that the one who loves God also loves his brother" [1 Jn. 4:20-21].

Hac caritate erga fratres nostros compulsi, magna cum observantia consideremus opiniones et doctrines quae quamvis a nostris in multis discrepent, tamen in multis referunt radium illius Veritatis quae illuminat omnem hominem venientem in hunc mundum.

Impelled by this charity towards our brothers, we consider with great care those opinions and doctrines which, although they differ from ours in many ways, nevertheless in many others reflect a ray of that Truth which enlightens every man coming into this world.

Sic amplectamur imprimis etiam Musulmanos qui unicum Deum personalem atque remuneratorem adorant et sensu religioso atque permultis humanae culturae communicationibus propius ad nos accesserunt.

So, we embrace in a special way Moslems, who adore the one personal God and Remunerator and who have come near us in virtue of their religious sense and many shared views on human culture.

34. (Omnis species discriminationis damnatur.) Fundamentum ergo tollitur omni theoriae vel praxi quae inter hominem et hominem, inter gentem et gentem discrimen quoad humanam dignitatem et iura exinde dimanantia inducunt.

34. (Every semblance of discrimination is condemned.) The foundation is thus removed from every theory or practice that introduces a discrimination between man and man, between nation and nation where human dignity and the rights that flow from it are concerned.

Abstineant ergo necesse est omnes bene cordati homines et praesertim Christiani a quavis hominum discriminatione aut vexatione propter stirpem eorum, colorem, condicionem vel religionem. At contra Christifideles Sacra Synodos ardenter obsecrat ut "conversationem inter gentes habeant bonam" [1 Pet. 2:12] si fieri potest, quod in eis est, cum omnibus hominibus pacem habeant [Rom. 12:18]; immo eisdem praescribit ut diligant, non tantum proximum suum, sed et inimicos, si quos se habere censeant, ita ut vere sint filii Patris qui in caelis est et qui solem suum oriri facit super omnes [Mt. 5: 44-45].

It is necessary, then, that all good-hearted men, and especially Christians, refrain from any kind of discrimination among men or form of abuse because of an individual's race, color, condition in life, or religion. On the contrary, this Sacred Synod ardently entreats believing Christians that "maintaining friendly relations with non-Christians" [1 Pet. 2:12], they, if possible as far as in them lies, remain at peace with all men [Rom. 12:18]. Indeed, it is further enjoined on them not only to love their neighbor, but even their enemies, insofar as they are aware of having any, so that they may be true children of the Father in heaven who causes his sun to rise on all [Mt. 5:44-45].

Text III

Declaration, November 1964: *De Ecclesiae habitudine ad religiones non-christianas:*

1. *(Prooemium.) Nostra aetate, in qua genus humanum in dies arctius unitur et necessitudines inter varios populos augentur, Ecclesia attente considerat quae sit sua habitudo ad religiones non-christianas.*

1. (Preamble.) In our day [*Nostra Aetate*], when the human race is day by day more closely united and the ties between various peoples are on the increase, the Church carefully considers the

nature of her relationship to non-Christian religions.

Una enim communitas sunt omnes gentes, unam habent originem, cum Deus omne genus hominum inhabitare fecerit super universam faciem terrae [Act. 17:26], unum etiam habent finem ultimum, Deum, cuius providentia ac bonitatis testimonium et consilia salutis ad omnes se extendunt [Wis. 8:1; Act. 14:17; Rom. 2:6-7; 1 Tim. 2:4], donec uniantur electi in Civitate Sancta, quam claritas Dei illuminabit, ubi gentes ambulabunt in lumine eius [Rev. 21:23-24].

For all nations constitute a single community and have a single origin, since God ordained that the human race should dwell over the entire face of the earth. They have but one final end, God, whose providence, the evidence of whose goodness, and saving designs are extended to all men in anticipation of the day when the elect will be united in the Holy City which will be illumined by the splendor of God, where the nations will walk in his light.

Homines a variis religionibus responsum exspectant de reconditis conditionis humanae aenigmatibus, quae sicut olim et hodie corda hominum intime commovent: quid sit homo, quis sensus et finis vitae nostrae, quid bonum et quid peccatum, quae sit via ad veram felicitatem obtinendam, quid mors, iudicium et retributio post mortem, quid demum illud ultimum et ineffabile mysterium quod nostram existentiam amplectitur, ex quo ortum sumimus et quo tendimus.

Men look to various religions for an answer to those profound mysteries of the human condition which in times past and still today deeply move the human heart: What is man? What is the meaning and purpose of our existence? What is goodness and what is sinful? What is the right path for obtaining true happiness? What about death, judgment, and postmortem retribution? What, in fine, is that ultimate and ineffable mystery that encompasses our existence, whence we take our origin and whither we tend?

2. (De diversis religionibus non-christianis.) Iam ab antiquo apud diversas gentes invenitur quaedam perceptio illius arcanae virtutis, quae cursui rerum et eventibus vitae humanae praesens est, immo aliquando agnitio Summi Numinis ac Patris. Religiones vero cum progresso culturae connexae subtilioribus notionibus et lingua magis exculta ad easdem quaestiones respondere satagunt. Ita in Hinduismo homines mysterium divinum scrutantur et exprimunt inexhausta foecunditate mythorum et acutis conatibus philosophiae, atque liberationem quaerunt ab angustiis nostrae conditionis per formas vitae asceticae, per profundam meditationem,

necnon per refugium ad Deum cum amore et confidentia. In Buddhismo
radicalis insufficientia mundi huius mutabilis agnoscitur et via docetur qua
homines, animo devoto et confidente, se abnegando et purificando a rebus
transitoriis liberari et statum permanentis quietis attingere valeant. Sic
ceterae quoque religiones, quae per totum mundum inveniuntur,
inquietudini cordis hominum variis modis occurrent proponendo vias,
doctrines scilicet ac praecepta vitae, necnon ritus sacros.

2. (Concerning various non-Christian religions.) Already in
ancient times, there could be found among different peoples a
certain perception of that hidden power which is present in the
course of things and in the events of human life, resulting at times
in the recognition of a Supreme Divinity and Father. Religions
associated with the advance of human culture have struggled to
reply to these same questions with more refined concepts and in a
more highly developed language. Thus in Hinduism men plumb the
depths of the divine mystery and express it in the inexhaustible
fecundity of myths and through keen philosophical efforts, while
they seek liberation from the anguish of our human condition by
various forms of ascetical practice, profound meditation, and by
taking refuge in God with love and confidence. In Buddhism the
radical insufficiency of this mutable world is recognized and a path
is taught by which men of devout and confident spirit can, by self-
denial and purification from transitory things, achieve a state of
permanent tranquility. Similarly, other religions found throughout
the world approach the inquietude of the human heart in various
ways by offering paths, teachings, precepts for living, and sacred rites.

Ecclesia catholica nihil eorum, quae in his religionibus vera et sancta
sunt, reicit. Annuntiat enim indesinenter Christum, qui es "via, veritas et
vita" [Jn. 14:6] et in quo Deus omnia sibi reconciliavit [2 Cor. 5:1]. De
variis salutis dispositionibus edocta, sincera cum observantia considerat
modos agendi et vivendi, praecepta et doctrines, quae quamvis ab iis quae
ipsa proponit in multis discrepent, referunt tamen radium illius Veritatis
quae illuminat omnes homines.

The Catholic Church rejects none of the things that are true
and holy in these religions, while she unfailingly proclaims Christ
who is "the way, the truth, and the life" [Jn. 14:6], in whom God
has reconciled all things to himself. Informed about various paths
of salvation, the Church considers with sincere regard their

manner of acting and living, and their precepts and doctrines which, though in many ways not in accord with what she holds, do reflect, however, a ray of that Truth that illumines all men.

Filios suos, hortatur igitur, ut per colloquia et collaborationem cum asseclis aliarum religionum, salva integritate fidei catholicae, illa bona spiritualia et moralia necnon illos valores socio-culturales, quae apud eos inveniuntur, servent et promoveant.

She exhorts her sons, therefore, that they, through conversations and collaboration with followers of other religions, with due regard for the integrity of the Catholic faith, preserve and promote those spiritual and moral goods and socio-cultural values found among them.

3. (De Musulmanis.) Cum aestimatione quoque Musulmanos respicit Ecclesia qui unicum Deum adorant, viventem et subsistentem, omnipotentem, Creatorem caeli et terrae, homines allocutum, cuius occultis etiam decretis toto animo se submittere student, sicut Deo se submisit Abraham ad quem fides musulmana libenter sese refert. Iesum, quem quidem ut Deum non agnoscunt, ut Prophetam tamen venerantur, matremque eius virginalem honorant Mariam et aliquando eam devote etiam invocant. Diem insuper iudicii expectant cum Deus omnes homines resuscitatos remunerabit. Exinde Deum colunt maxime in oratione, eleemosynis et ieiunio; vitam quoque moralem tam individualem quam familialem et socialem in obsequium Dei ducere conantur.

3. (Concerning Moslems.) The Church regards with esteem Moslems who adore the one God, living and enduring, the omnipotent Creator of heaven and earth, who has converse with men, to whose inscrutable decrees they strive to submit, just as did Abraham, to whom the Islamic faith gladly traces its lineage. Though they do not acknowledge the divinity of Jesus, they nevertheless venerate him as a Prophet, and honor his virgin mother Mary and at times invoke her with devotion. They await, moreover, the day of judgment when God will recompense all men in the resurrection. Consequently, they honor God in prayer, almsgiving, and fasting, and seek to serve him through moral living on the individual, family, and social levels.

Quodsi in decurso saeculorum inter Christianos et Musulmanos non paucae dissensiones et inimicitae exortae sint, Sacrosancta Synodus omnes exhortatur, ut, praeterita obliviscentes, se ad comprehensionem mutuam sincere exerceant et pro omnibus hominibus iustitiam socialem, bona moralia necnon pacem et libertatem communiter tueantur et promoveant.

Although in the course of the centuries quarrels and hostilities have arisen between Christians and Moslems, this most Sacred Synod urges all, forgetting the past, to work sincerely together toward mutual understanding, so as to guard and advance for all men the cause of morality, peace, and freedom.

4. (De Iudaeis.) Mysterium Ecclesiae perscrutans, Sacra haec Synodus meminit vinculi, quo populus Novi Testamenti cum stirpe Abraham coniunctus est.

4. (Concerning Jews.) As this Sacred Synod searches into the mystery of the Church, it remembers the bond by which the people of the New Testament is conjoined with the stock of Abraham.

Ecclesiae enim Christi grato animo agnoscit fidei et electionis suae initia iam apud Patriarchas, Moysen et Prophetas, iuxta salutare Dei mysterium, inveniri. Confitetur omnes Christifideles, Abrahae filios secundum fidem [Gal. 3:7], in eiusdem Patriarchae vocatione includi et salutem Ecclesiae in populi electi exitu de terra servitutis mystice praesignari. Quare nequit Ecclesia oblivisci se a populo illo, quocum Deus ex ineffabili misericordia sua Antiquum Foedus inire dignatus est, Revelationem Veteris Testamenti accepisse et nutriri radice bonae olivae, in quam inserti sunt rami oleastri Gentium [Rom. 11:17-24]. Credit enim Ecclesia Christum, Pacem nostram, per crucem Iudaeos et Gentes reconciliasse et utraque fecisse unum [Eph. 2:14-16].

The Church of Christ gratefully acknowledges that the beginnings of her faith and election are to be found with the Patriarchs, Moses, and the Prophets, in connection with God's saving mystery. It is further acknowledged that all believing Christians, children of Abraham in faith [Gal. 3:71, are to be regarded as included in the vocation of the same Patriarch, and that the salvation of the Church is mystically prefigured in the exodus of the Chosen People from the Land of Bondage. Nor can the Church forget that it was through this People, with whom God, in his ineffable mercy deigned to establish the Ancient Covenant, that she has received the revelation of the Old Testament, and that she draws sustenance from the root of that good olive tree onto which have been grafted the wild olive branches of the Gentiles [Rom. 11:17-24; this is the first

appearance in the *Nostra Aetate* Texts of this image and reference.]
Indeed, the Church believes that Christ, our Peace, by his cross
reconciled Jews and Gentiles and made them one [Eph. 2:14-16].

*Semper quoque prae oculis habet Ecclesia verba Apostoll Pauli de cognatis
eius, "quorum adoptio est filiorum et gloria et testamentum et legislatio et
obsequium et promissa, quorum patres et ex quibus est Christus secundum
carnem" [Rom. 9:4-5], filius Mariae Virginis. Recordatur etiam ex populo
iudaico natos esse Apostolos, Ecclesiae fundamenta et columnas, atque plurimos
illos primos discipulos, qui Evangelium Christi mundo annuntiaverunt.*

The Church also has always before her eyes the words of the
Apostle Paul concerning his kinsmen, to whom belong "the
adoption as sons and the glory and the covenants and the giving
of the Law and the worship and the promises, and from whom is
Christ according to the flesh [Rom. 9:4-5], the Son of the Virgin
Mary. The Church also recalls that it was from the Jewish People
that the Apostles, the foundation stones and pillars, were born, as
well as most of those early disciples who proclaimed the Gospel of
Christ to the world.

*Etsi Iudaei magna parte Evangelium non acceperunt, tamen, Apostolo
testante, Deo, cuius dona et vocatio sine poenitentia sunt, adhuc carissimi
manent propter patres [Rom. 11:28-29]. Una cum Prophetis eodemque
Apostolo Ecclesia diem Deo soli notum expectat, quo populi omnes una voce
Dominum invocabunt et "servient ei humero uno" [Wis. 3:9. cf. Is. 66:23;
Ps. 65:4; Rom. 11:11-12].*

And although the Jews for the most part did not accept the
Gospel, nevertheless, they remain, on the word of the Apostle,
most dear to God for the sake of the Fathers, since the gifts and
calling of God are without regret. In company with the Prophets
and the same Apostle, the Church awaits the day known to God
alone when all people will call on the Lord with a single voice and
"serve him with one accord" [Wis. 3:9].

*Cum igitur adeo magnum sit patrimonium spirituale Christianis et
Iudaeis commune, Sacra haec Synodus mutuam utriusque cognitionem et
aestimationem, quae praesertim studiis biblicis et theologicis atque fraternis
colloquiis obtinetur, fovere vult et commendare. Praeteria iniurias
hominibus ubicumque inflictas severe reprobans, Synodus, huius patrimonii
communis memor, odia et persecutiones contra Iudaeos, sive olim sive
nostris temporibus perpetratas, deplorat et damnat.*

Since the spiritual patrimony common to Christians and Jews is thus so great, this Sacred Synod wishes to foster and commend that mutual recognition and esteem which is the fruit above all of biblical and theological studies and of brotherly conversations. Moreover, severely reprobating injuries inflicted on men anywhere, and mindful of our common patrimony, it deplores and condemns hatred and persecutions directed against Jews, whether perpetrated in the past or in our own day. [This is now the third time that the Text has used the words "deplorat et damnat."]

Ideo curent omnes ne in catechesi impertienda seu in Verbi Dei praedicatione aliquid doceant, quod in cordibus fidelium odium aut despectionem erga Iudaeos gignere possit; numquam populus iudaicus ut gens reprobata vel maledicta aut deicidii reu exhibeatur. Ea enim quae in passione Christi perpatrata sunt minime toti populo tunc viventi, multo minus hodierno populo imputar possint. Ceterum semper tenuit et tenet Ecclesia, Christum voluntarie propter omnium hominum peccata passionem suam et mortem immensa caritate obiisse. Ecclesiae praedicantis ergo est annuntiare crucem Christi tamquam signum universalis Dei amoris et fontem omnis gratiae.

So, let all take care in catechetical instruction or in preaching the Word of God lest they teach anything that could give rise in the hearts of the faithful to either hatred or contempt against the Jews. The Jewish People is never to be represented as a reprobate race or accursed or as guilty of deicide. What was done during the passion of Christ can scarcely be blamed on the whole People living then, much less on the People of today. In addition, the Church has always held and still holds that Christ, out of a spirit of great love, freely underwent his passion and death for the sins of all men. Therefore, the Church's preaching is to proclaim the cross of Christ as a sign of God's universal love and the font of every grace.

5. (De fraternitate universale, quavis discriminatione exclusa.) Nequimus vero Deum omnium Patrem invocare, si erga quosdam homines, ad imaginem Dei creatos, fraterne nos gerere renuimus. Habitudo hominis ad Deum Patrem et habitudo hominis ad homines fratres ita connectuntur: qui non diligit, non novit Deum [1 Jn. 4:8; 2:9-11; Lk. 10:25-37].

5. (Concerning universal brotherhood which excludes any kind of discrimination.) Truly we dare not call upon God the Father of all, if we refuse to behave in a brotherly manner toward certain men created in God's image. The relation of men to God

and the relation of man to his brother men are so bound together that the one who does not love does not know God.

Fundamentum ergo tollitur omni theoriae vel praxi quae inter hominem et hominem, inter gentem et gentem, discrimen quoad humanam dignitatem et iura exinde dimanantia inducunt.

The ground is thus removed from any theory or practice that would introduce a discrimination between man and man or between people and people where human dignity and the rights that flow from it are concerned.

Abstineat ergo necesse est omnes homines et praesertim Christiani a quavis hominum discriminatione aut vexatione propter stirpem eorum, colorem, condicionem vel religionem. At contra, Christifideles Sacra Synodus, vestigia Sanctorum Apostolorum Petri et Pauli premens, ardenter obsecrat ut, "conversationem inter gentes habentes bonam" [1 Pet. 2:12], si fieri potest, quod in eis est cum omnibus hominibus pacem habeant [Rom. 12:18], ita ut vere sint filii Patris qui in caelis est [Mt. 5: 44-45].

It follows that all men and especially Christians must refrain from any kind of discrimination or abuse because of anyone's race, color, [social] condition, or religion. On the contrary, this Sacred Synod, following in the footsteps of the Apostles Peter and Paul, ardently entreats believing Christians that, "maintaining friendly relations with the non-Christians" [1 Pet. 2:12], they, if possible and as far as in them lies, be at peace with all men, so that they may be sons of the Father who is in heaven.

TEXT IV

The final text of the declaration, October 1965: approved by Pope Paul VI: *Declaratio de Ecclesiae habitudine ad religiones non-christianos.*

Paul, Bishop
Servant of the Servants of God
Together with the Fathers of the Sacred Council
For Everlasting Memory

1. Nostra aetate, in qua genus humanum in dies arctius unitur et necessitudines inter varios populos augentur, Ecclesia attentius considerat quae sit sua habitudo ad religiones non-christianias. In suo munere unitatem et caritatem inter homines immo et inter gentes, fovendi, ea imprimis hic considerat quae hominibus sunt communia et ad mutuum consortium ducunt.

1. In our day, when the human race is being daily drawn together and the ties between various peoples are increasing, the Church carefully considers what should be its relation to non-Christian religions. In her role of fostering unity and love among men, even among nations, she gives primary consideration in this document to what human beings have in common and what leads to cooperation among them.

Una enim communitas sunt omnes gentes, unam habent originem, cum Deus omne genus hominum inhabitare fecerit super universam faciem terrae [Acts17:26]; unum etiam habent finem ultimum, Deum, cuius providentia ac bonitatis testimonium et consilia salutis ad omnes se extendunt [Wis. 8:1; Acts 14:17; Rom. 2:6-7; 1 Tim. 2:4], donec uniantur electi in Civitate Sancta, quam claritas Dei illuminabit, ubi gentes ambulabunt in lumine eius [Rev. 21: 23-24].

All people comprise a single community and have a single origin since God made the whole human race dwell over the entire face of the earth. One also is their final end, God, whose providence, evidence of goodness and his designs for salvation are extended to all, until the elect are united in the Holy City, which God's splendor will illumine and the peoples will walk in his light.

Homines a variis religionibus responsum expectant de reconditis conditionis humanae aenigmatibus, quae sicut olim et hodie corda hominum intime commovent: quid sit homo, quis sensus et finis vitae nostrae, quid bonum et quid peccatum, quem ortum habeant dolores et quem finem, quae sit via ad veram felicitatem obtinendam, quid mors, iudicium et retributio post mortem, quid demum illud ultimum et ineffabile mysterium quod nostram existentiam amplectitur, ex quo ortum sumimus et quo tendimus.

Men look to various religions for an answer to the profound mysteries of the human condition which, as in the past, still today deeply move the human heart: what is man, what is the meaning and end of our life, what is goodness and what is sinful, what is the path for obtaining true happiness, what about death, judgment, post-mortem retribution, what, finally, is to be said about that ultimate and ineffable mystery that encompasses our existence, whence we take our origin and whither we tend?

2. Iam ab antiquo usque ad tempus hodiernum apud diversas gentes invenitur quaedam perceptio illius arcanae virtutis, quae cursui rerum et eventibus vitae humanae presens est, immo aliquando agnitio Summi Numinis vel etiam Patris. Quae perceptio atque agnitio vitam earum intimo sensu religioso penetrant. Religiones vera cum progressu culturae connexae subtilioribus notionibus et lingua magis exculta ad easdem quaestiones respondere satagunt. Ita in Hinduismo homines mysterium divinum scrutantur et exprimunt inexhausta foecunditate mythorum et acutis conatibus philosophiae, atque liberationem quaerunt ab angustiis nostrae condicionis vel per formas vitae asceticae vel per profundam meditationem vel per refugium ad Deum cum amore et confidentia. In Buddhismo secundum variis eius formas radicalis insufficientia mundi hius mutabilis agnoscitur et via docetur qua homines, animo devoto et confidente, sive statum perfectae liberationis acquirere, sive, vel propriis conatibus vel superiore auxilio innixi, ad summam illuminationem pertingere valeant. Sic ceterae quoque religiones, quae per totum mundum inveniuntur, inquietudini cordis hominum variis modis occurrere nituntur proponendo vias, doctrinas scilicet ac praecepta vitae, necnon ritus sacros.

From ancient times down to the present, there could be found among different peoples a certain perception of that hidden power which is present in the course of things and in the events of human life, resulting at times in the recognition of a Supreme Numinous Spirit and even of a Father. This perception and recognition penetrates their life with a profound religious sense. Indeed, religions associated with the advance of human culture have struggled to reply to these same questions with more refined concepts and in a more highly developed language. Thus, in Hinduism men search into the divine mystery and express it in the inexhaustible fecundity of myths and through keen philosophical efforts, while they seek liberation from the anguish of our human condition by various forms of asceticism, or profound meditation, or by taking refuge in God with love and confidence. In Buddhism, according to its various forms, the radical insufficiency of this mutable world is recognized and a path is taught by which men of devout and confident spirit can achieve either a state of perfect freedom or, relying on their own efforts or superior assistance, attain supreme enlightenment. Similarly, other religions found throughout the world strive to come to grips with the inquietude of the human heart in various ways by proposing paths, teachings, precepts for living, and sacred rites.

Ecclesia catholica nihil eorum, quae in his religionibus vera et sancta sunt, reicit. Sincera cum observantia considerat illos modos agendi et vivendi, illa praecepta et doctrinas, quae, quamvis ab iis quae ipsa tenet et proponit in multis discrepent, haud raro referunt tamen radium illius Veritatis, quae illuminat omnes homines. Annuntiat vero et annuntiare tenetur indesinenter Christum, qui es "via, veritas et vita" (Jn.14:6), in quo homines plenitudinem vitae religiosae inveniunt, et in quo Deus omnia sibi reconciliavit [2 Cor. 5:18-19].

The Catholic Church rejects none of the things that are true and holy in these religions. She considers with sincere respect those ways of acting and living, those precepts and doctrines which, although they differ in many ways from what she holds and proposes, not infrequently reflect a ray of that Truth which illumines all men. Indeed, the Church proclaims and is bound always to proclaim Christ, who is "the way, the truth, and the life" [Jn. 14:6] in whom men find the plenitude of religious life, and in whom God has reconciled all things to himself [2 Cor. 5:18-19].

Filios suos igitur hortatur, ut cum prudentia et caritate per colloquia et collaborationem cum asseclis aliarum religionum, fidem et vitam christianam testantes, illa bona spiritualia et moralia necnon illos valores socio-culturales, quae apud eos inveniuntur, agnoscant, servent et promoveant.

The Church, therefore, exhorts her sons that, with prudence and charity, through conversations and collaboration with the followers of other religions, always bearing witness to Christian faith and life, they acknowledge, preserve and promote those spiritual and moral goods and the socio-cultural values found among them.

3. Ecclesia cum aestimatione quoque Musilmos respicit qui unicum Deum adorant, viventem et subsistentem, misericordem and omnipotentem, Creatorem caeli et terrae, homines allocutum, cuius occulis etiam decretis toto animo se submittere student, sicut Deo se submisit Abraham ad quem fides islamica libenter se refert. Iesum, quem quidem ut Deum non agnoscunt, ut prophetam tamen venerantur, matremque eius virginalem honorant Mariam et aliquando eam devote etiam invocant. Diem insuper iudicii expectant cum Deus omnes homines resuscitatos remunerabit. Exinde vitam moralem aestimant et Deum maxime in oratione, eleemosynis et ieiunio colunt.

The Church regards with esteem Moslems who adore the one God, living and enduring, the omnipotent Creator of heaven and earth, who has converse with men, to whose inscrutable decrees they strive to submit, just as did Abraham, to whom the Islamic faith gladly traces its lineage. Though they do not acknowledge the

358 · *Merton and Judaism*

divinity of Jesus, they nevertheless venerate him as a Prophet, and honor his virgin mother Mary and at times invoke her with devotion. They, moreover await the day of judgment when God will recompense all men in the resurrection. Consequently, they esteem the moral life and honor God in prayer, almsgiving, and fasting.

Quodsi in decursu saeculorum inter Christianos et Muslimos non paucae dissensiones et inimicitae exortae sint, Sacrosancta Synodus omnes exhortatur, ut, praeterita obliviscentes, se ad comprehensionem mutuam sincere exerceant et pro omnibus hominibus iustitiam socialem, bona moralia necnon pacem et libertatem communiter tueantur et promoveant.

Although in the course of the centuries many disagreements and hostilities have arisen, this most Holy Synod exhorts all, forgetting the past, to work sincerely toward mutual understanding, and together protect and promote social justice and moral values along with peace and freedom for all men.

4. Mysterium Eccleiae perscrutans, Sacra haec Synodus meminit vinculi quo populus Novi Testamenti cum stirpe Abraham spiritualiter coniunctus est.

4. As this Sacred Synod searches into the mystery of the Church, it remembers the bond that links the people of the New Testament with the stock of Abraham.

Ecclesia enim Christi agnoscit fidei et electionis suae initia iam apus Patriarchas, Moysen et Prophetas, iuxta salutare Dei mysterium, inveniri. Confitetur omnes Christifideles, Abrahae filios secundum fidem [Gal. 3:7], in eiusdem Patriarchae vocatione includi et salutem Ecclesiae in populi electi exitu de terra servitutis mystice praesignari. Quare nequit Ecclesia oblivisci se per populum illum, quocum Deus ex ineffabili misericordia sua Antiquum Foedus inire dignatus est, revelationem Veteris Testamenti accepisse et nutriri radice bonae olivae, in quam inserti sunt rami oleastri Gentium [Rom. 11:17-24]. Credit enim Ecclesia Christum, Pacem nostram, per crucem Iudaeos et Gentes reconciliasse et utraque in semetipso fecisse unum [Eph. 2:14-16].

Indeed, the Church of Christ acknowledges that the beginnings of its own faith and election is already found in the Patriarchs, Moses and the Prophets in accord with God's saving mystery. She professes that all believing Christians, sons of Abraham in faith, are included in the vocation of the same Patriarch and that the salvation of the Church is mystically prefigured in the exodus of the Chosen People from the Land of

Bondage. Consequently, the Church cannot forget that it was through this People, with whom God, in his ineffable mercy deigned to establish the Ancient Covenant, that she received the revelation of the Old Testament, and that she draws sustenance from the root of that good olive tree onto which have been grafted the wild olive branches of the Gentiles. For the Church believes that Christ, our Peace, by his cross reconciled Jews and Gentiles and united both of them in himself.

Semper quoque prae oculis habet Ecclesia verba Apostoli Pauli de cognatis eius, "quorum adoptio est filiorum et gloria et testamentum et legislatio et obsequium et promissa, quorum patres et ex quibus est Christus secundum carnem" [Rom. 9:5], filius Mariae Virginis. Recordatur etiam ex populo iudaico natos esse Apostolos, Ecclesiae fundamenta et columnas, atque plurimos illos primos discipulos, qui Evangelium Christi mundo annuntiaverunt.

The Church also always has before her eyes the words of the Apostle Paul concerning his kinsmen, to whom belong "the adoption as sons and the glory and the covenant[s] and the giving of the Law and the worship and the promises, and from whom is Christ according to the flesh" [Rom. 9:4–5], the Son of the Virgin Mary. The Church also recalls that it was from the Jewish People that the Apostles, the foundation stones and pillars of the Church, were born, as well as most of those early disciples who proclaimed the Gospel of Christ to the world.

Teste Sacra Scriptura, Ierusalem tempus visitationis suae non cognovit [Lk. 19:44], atque Iudaei magna parte Evangelium non acceperunt, immo non pauci diffusioni eius se opposuerunt [Rom. 11:28]. Nihilominus, secundum Apostolum, Iudaei Deo, cuius dona et vocatione sine poenitentia sunt, adhuc carissimi manent propter Patres [Rom. 11:28-29]. Una cum Prophetis eodemque Apostolo Ecclesia diem Deo soli notum expectat, quo populi omnes una voce Dominum invocabunt et "servient ei humero uno" [Wis. 3:9].

Sacred Scripture testifies that Jerusalem did not know the time of her visitation [Lk. 19:44] and that the Jews for the most part did not accept the Gospel. Indeed, not a few opposed its spread [Rom. 11:28]. Nevertheless, on the word of the Apostle, the Jews remain for the sake of the Fathers most dear to God whose gifts and calling are without regret. In the company of the prophets and the same Apostle, the Church awaits the day, known to God alone, when all people will call upon the Lord with a single voice and "serve him with one accord" [Wis. 3: 9)].

Cum igitur adeo magnum sit patrimonium spirituale Christianis et Iudaeis commune, Sacra haec Synodus mutuam utriusque cognitionem et aestimationem, quae praesertim studiis biblicis et theologicis atque fraternis colloquiis obtinetur, fovere vult et commendare.

Since the spiritual patrimony common to Christians and Jews is thus so great, this Sacred Synod wishes to foster and commend that mutual recognition and esteem which is the fruit above all of biblical and theological studies and of brotherly conversations.

Etsi auctoritates Iudaeorum cum suis asseclis mortem Christi urserunt, tamen ea quae in passione eius perpetrata sunt nec omnibus indistincte Iudaeis tunc viventibus, nec Iudaeis hodiernis imputari possunt. Licet autem Ecclesia sit novus Populus Dei, Iudaei tamen neque ut a Deo reprobati neque ut maledicti exhibeantur, quasi hoc ex Sacris Litteris sequatur. Ideo curent omnes ne in catechesi et in Verbi Dei praedicatione habenda quidquam doceant, quod cum veritate evangelica et spiritu Christi non congruat.

Even though Jewish authorities with their followers pressed for the death of Christ, still the things done in his passion cannot be imputed without distinction to all Jews then living nor to today's Jews. While the Church is the new People of God, still the Jews should neither be represented as rejected by God nor as accursed, as if this follows from Sacred Scripture. So let all take care in catechetical instruction and in preaching the Word of God lest they teach anything not in accord with evangelical truth and the spirit of Christ.

Praeterea, Ecclesia, quae omnes persecutiones in quosvis homines reprobat, memor communis cum Iudaeis patrimonii, nec rationibus politicis sed religiosa caritate evangelica impulsa, odia, persecutiones, antisemitismi manifestationes, quovis tempore et a quibusvis in Iudaeos habita, deplorat.

Moreover, the Church reprobates [*reprobat*] all persecutions against any men whatsoever, and keeping in mind her common patrimony with Jews, impelled not by political considerations but by evangelical religious charity, deplores [*deplorat*] hatreds, persecutions, manifestations of anti-Semitism against Jews at any time and by anyone whatsoever. [*Reprobat* and *deplorat* here seem a little weaker than the *deplorat* and *damnat* of versions two and three.]

Ceterum Christus, uti semper tenuit et tenet Ecclesia, propter peccata omnium hominum voluntarie passionem suam et morten immensa caritate obiit, ut omnes salutem consequantur. Ecclesiae praedicantis ergo est annutiare crucem Christi tamquam signum universalis Dei amoris et fontem omnis gratiae.

In addition, the Church has always held and still holds that Christ, because of the sins of all men, out of a spirit of great love, freely underwent his passion and death in order that all might attain salvation. Therefore, the Church's preaching is to proclaim the cross of Christ as a sign of God's universal love and the font of every grace.

5. Nequimus vero Deum omnium Patrem invocare, si erga quosdam homines, ad imaginem Dei creatos, fraterne nos gerere renuimus. Habitudo hominis ad Deum Patrem et habitudo hominis ad homines fratres adeo connectuntur, ut Scriptura dicat: "qui non diligit, non novit Deum" [1 Jn. 4:8].

5. Truly we dare not call upon God the Father of all, if we refuse to behave in a brotherly manner toward certain men, created in God's image. The relation of men to God as Father and the relation of man to his brother men are so bound together that, as Scripture says, "who does not love, does not know God" (1 Jn. 4:8).

Fundamentum ergo tollitur omni theoriae vel praxi quae inter hominem et hominem, inter gentem et gentem, discrimen quoad humanam dignitatem et iura exinde dimanantia inducit.

The ground is thus removed from every theory or practice that would introduce a discrimination between man and man or between people and people where human dignity and the rights that flow from it are concerned.

Ecclesia igitur quamvis hominum discriminationem aut vexationem stirpis vel coloris, condictionis vel religionis cause factam tamquam a Christi mente alienam reprobat. Proinde, Christifideles Sacra Synodus, vestigia Sanctorum Apostolorum Petri et Pauli premens, ardenter obsecrat ut, "conversationem inter gentes habentes bonam" [1 Pet. 2:12], si fieri potest, quod in eis est cum omnibus hominibus pacem habeant [Rom. 12:18], ita ut vere sint filii patris qui in caelis est.

The Church therefore repudiates every kind of discrimination or abuse of men on the basis of race or color, social condition or religion, as alien to the mind of Christ. Hence, this Sacred Synod, following in the footsteps of the Holy Apostles Peter and Paul, ardently entreats believing Christians that, "maintaining friendly relations with the non-Christians," [1 Pet. 2:12], they, if possible and as far as in them lies, be at peace with all men, so that they may be true sons of the Father who is in heaven.

Sequence of Changes in the Editing of the Four Vatican II Texts on Non-Christian Religions, Especially the Jews

The first timid draft covered but a single page. The three that followed became progressively longer, each picking up much of what was said in the earlier drafts, while occasionally dropping a phrase or rewording a passage.

Text I: November 1962

There are approximately 13 distinct items in Text I:

1. How converse with Jews?
2. Church owes its beginnings to Patriarchs and the faith of Abraham
3. And is a continuation of that lineage.
4. Her salvation is mystically prefigured in the Exodus from the Land of Bondage.
5. Christ embraced Jews and Gentiles in a single love, making them one.
6. The whole world, Jews and Gentiles, are reconciled in Christ.
7. Though Jews are far from Christ, they are dear to God because of the Fathers.
8. Jews are not to be called deicides or accursed.
9. Christ's death is not to be blamed on all Jews who lived then or now
10. Take care not to teach anything leading to hate of Jews in catechesis or preaching.
11. Jesus, Mary, and Apostles are all Jews according to the flesh.
12. Christians and Jews have a common patrimony in scripure and the Patriarchs.
13. Church deplores and condemns (*damnat*) persecution of Jews.

Text II: September 1963

Most of the items in Text I are repeated in later ones. The sentence in Text I which had explicitly denied that the Jews were deicides and accursed is missing in Text II. However, it is said that they must never, in formal teaching or in everyday talk, be "represented as reprobate," that is, rejected by God.

The following items are additions that did not appear in Text I:

1. According to St. Paul, the Jews are blessed because they are God's adopted children, gifted with the Covenant, the Law, and the promises.
2. Church awaits the "addition" of the Jews to herself in order to complete the People of God. This implies the disappearance of Judaism and was dropped in later versions.
3. No one who mistreats a fellowman created in God's image can call God Father.
4. Those who do not love neighbor whom they can see, cannot love God who is invisible.
5. God does not discriminate in his love; he doesn't play favorites.
6. Religions differing from the Christian faith may display a ray of that Truth that illumines every man coming into the world.
7. The Church esteems Moslems who believe in the one, remunerating God.
8. The foundation is cut from under any theory or practice that introduces a discrimination among men as regards their dignity or the rights flowing from it.
9. Let there be no discrimination based on race, color, or religion.
10. Believing Christians are to "promote good relations among the nations" [1 Pet. 2:12].
11. There is no repudiation of "deicide."

Text III: September 1964

Text III drops the idea that the Church expects to add the Jewish People to its membership. The section on Islam is much expanded. Statements about Hinduism and Buddhism remain the same.

1. World is smaller now. So the Church needs to give thought to its relations to non–Christian religions.
2. We all have the same end: God, and the Holy City where God's splendor will shine.
3. Men rely on religions for the meaning of life and destiny.
4. Ancient men had a perception of God's true Divinity.
5. Hinduism and Buddhism are not changed in this text.
6. The Church rejects nothing that is true and holy in other religions.
7. Moslem section is much expanded. They accept Jesus as prophet though not as God and honor Mary, even praying to her. Let hostilities be a thing of the past.
8. Let all remember Paul's observation that the Gentiles are wild olive branches grafted onto that good Jewish olive tree.
9. Jews did not accept the gospel, but are still most dear to God whose gifts are without regret.
10. God alone knows the day of judgment. Eventually, all will praise him with one voice.
11. Jews are not accursed or guilty of deicide (reintroduced from Text I).
12. Christ voluntarily died for all men, meaning also for Jews.
13. The cross is a sign of God's love.

Text IV: September 1965

The final text picks up most of the "new" material introduced from Texts II and III. The truly new material is minimal but significant and somewhat controversial.

1. The Buddhists strive for enlightenment either with help or "on their own efforts." [This seems to take into account that some Buddhist sects do not rely on divine help. The Buddha had said that men should work out their salvation with diligence, with no mention of divine help.]

2. Jerusalem did not recognize the time of her visitation and the majority of Jews did not accept the gospel. [This could be interpreted as introducing a negative note. The failure to recognize implies a kind of spiritual blindness.]

3. The Jewish authorities pressed for the death of Christ. [Another negative note, perhaps, though it might be seen as limiting culpability to the Jewish authorities alone.]

4. The Church is the "New People of God."[Another questionable item, since it could imply that the Jews had lost standing before God and had been replaced, in spite of the fact that God does not repent of his gifts.]

5. But the Jews should not be represented as rejected or cursed by God. However, repudiation of "deicide" is omitted.

6. This Declaration is issued out of a spirit of religious good fellowship, "not for any political reason." [Perhaps, but the statement itself could be seen as introduced lest the laudatory passage on Islam seem to have been inserted to counterbalance the favorable approach to the Jews in the light of the foundation of the Jewish State in a largely Moslem region.]

COMMENTARY

There was a first draft of this document prepared in 1961 which was never presented to the Council because it was halted in 1962 in the Central Commission of the Council, through which all decrees had to pass. The reason – which continued to be the reason why the document had trouble – was partly diplomatic pressure from the governments of Arab countries fearing the Vatican would grant diplomatic recognition to the State of Israel, and partly worry on the part of Catholic bishops in those same countries that their people would suffer and their pastoral activities would become more difficult. It is important to recognize that the hesitation about the Decree on the Jews was based on such extraneous political concerns and not on any misgivings about Judaism or the Jewish People themselves. Cardinal Bea said, in his address to the Council presenting Text I, that this earlier version was dropped "not because of the ideas or doctrine expressed in the schema, but only because of certain unhappy political conditions at that time [June 1962] .... There is no question of recognition of the State of Israel by the Holy See." No such question was broached at all. "The schema treats exclusively of a purely religious question."[1]

That earliest draft covered many of the same points made in Texts I-IV: The Church claims an unbroken continuity from the original Covenant between God and the Jewish People and acknowledges that its faith in its own chosenness is rooted in that of the Jewish People. In this context the Church hopes for unity among all of God's people. The Church stresses that Jews must never be regarded as rejected or cursed and deplores any and all contempt and persecution they have suffered.

On June 13, 1960 Jules Isaac, a noted French scholar, in a meeting with Pope John XXIII, had requested that the Council take up the question of the Church and Judaism with a view to reversing all past teaching that approved of any form of anti-Semitism. The Pope subsequently spoke to Cardinal Bea, who was heading the Secretariat on Christian Unity, on September 18, 1960, and told him to prepare a Declaration on the Jews. This was a follow-up on what the Pope had done on Good Friday, 1959, when he had ordered removed from the prayer for the Jews the word 'perfidious.' Originally meaning simply "unbelieving," the word had acquired a pejorative sense that the Church repudiated. This move had raised Jewish hopes and the Pope wished to press forward.[2] When the earliest draft, preceding our Text I, was removed from the Council's agenda because of Arab protests against Jewish representation in Rome in connection with the Council, Bea went to Pope John again, and the Pope wrote to the Council [December 13, 1962]: "We unreservedly associate ourselves with the burden and responsibility of a concern which we must make our own."[3]

A draft of Text I was then prepared and circulated. Carried in newspapers, it caused a great deal of excitement and satisfaction when it appeared, showing as it did against the background of the

1 Augustin Cardinal Bea, S.J., *The Church and the Jewish People: Commentary on the Second Vatican Council's Declaration on the Relation to Non-Christian Religions*, tr. Philip Loretz, S.J. (New York: Harper & Row, 1966), p. 541.
2 Bea, p. 22.
3 Bea, p. 23.

centuries of theologically based Christian persecution of Jews. In the opinion of some, this first Text was "the strongest version of the schema that ever existed" for "reversing traditional theological rationale for anti-Semitism."[4] However, Text I was never discussed on the Council floor, because Pope Paul VI (John XXIII had died on June 3, 1963) feared it might prejudice his Holy Land pilgrimage of January 1964.

A new draft, Text II, was prepared, in which the formula *gens deicida* was omitted. Some Council fathers felt that this was a serious omission, because these words had traditionally been used by the Church in description of the Jewish People and the Church's position with respect to them. Others urged that the whole idea should be dropped, for no one people could be charged with what was – by the Church's own faith – the guilt of all. But Text II also muted *reprobata vel maledicta* and reduced the condemnation of anything provoking "hatred or contempt" to what "could alienate ... minds." "Xavier Rynne" [Fr. Francis Xavier Murphy, CSSR], reporting on the Second Session of the Council, wrote: "What specifically irked observers at the time was that he [Pope Paul VI] saw fit to give no assurance that it [The Declaration on the Jews] would be taken up again as part of the agenda at the Third Session. In view of the tactics of the minority, it seemed dangerous not to make some public statement."[5]

There was a good deal of complaint among the Fathers about these omissions and reductions. There was also a new idea. Text II had attempted to "hide" the declaration on the Jews as one case among other "non-Christian religions," and this raised demands that these other religions receive more attention. Thus Text III was composed to meet these expectations. Responsive to the complaints, the words *gens reprobata vel maledicta aut deicidii rea* were all restored, along with the strong condemnation of inciting "hatred or contempt." The judgment against all kinds of discrimination was strengthened. This version, put to the vote on November 20, 1964, received, out of 1996 votes, 1651 'Yes,' 99 'no,' and 242 'yes, with reservations.'[6]

4 Mikka Ruokanen, *The Catholic Doctrine of Non-Christian Religions: According to the Second Vatican Council* (New York: Brill, 1992), p. 37.

5 Xavier Rynne, *The Second Session. The Debates and Decrees of Vatican Council II. September 29 to December 8, 1963* (New York: Farrar, Straus, 1964), p. 267.

6 Bea, p. 24.

Between the Third and Fourth Sessions, there was vigorous activity aimed at suppressing the schema. Mikka Ruokanen, rehearsing this history, tells us that "all possible means, diplomatic and undiplomatic, sympathetic and unsympathetic, were exploited in order that the schema would be dropped or at least altered," and he refers us for a full account to John M. Oesterreicher. [7]

Text IV undertook to satisfy those 242 'yes, with reservations' votes. Cardinal Bea points out that there was still trouble in the Near East, "largely due to misunderstandings arising mainly from lack of sufficient information, which left the public at the mercy of irresponsible propaganda ..."[8] Bea reports that "a series of visits were made to the Near East to make contact with the principal Catholic and non-Catholic ecclesial authorities in order to ascertain their difficulties and their wishes in the matter."

Text IV was presented to the Council on October 14, 1965. Bea's own view of the amended Text was that it was intended only to clarify and render more precise the sense of Text III already approved by a large majority.[9] However, the formula of deicide had again been dropped for "pastoral prudence and evangelical charity": "It is known," Bea explained in his presentation address to the Council, "that difficulties and controversies – for example, that the schema might seem to contradict the Gospel – have in fact arisen, especially because of the use of this word. On the other hand, it is obvious ... that the substance of what we wished in the earlier text to express by this word is found exactly and completely expressed in the new text." The new text says that "the Jewish authorities and those who followed their lead pressed for the death of Christ (cf. John 19:6)" but that this "cannot be attributed to all Jews, without distinction, then alive, nor to the Jews of today," and that "the Jews should not be presented as rejected by God or accursed, as if this follows from the Holy Scriptures."

Bea argued that this "preserves ... the truth of the Gospel," but at the same time "excludes unjust ... accusations," and permits the Council to exhort everyone "to say only what accords with the

7 Johannes (John) Oesterreicher, Die Erklärung über das Verhältnis der Kirche zu den nichtchristlichen Religionen, Kommentierende Einleitung. Lexikon für Theologie und Kirche, Das Zweite Vatikanishe Konzil 2, 406–487.
8 Bea, p. 25
9 Bea, p. 25.

truth of the Gospel and with the spirit of Christ."[10] This final phrase is not here defined, but Bea had earlier argued that Christ had prayed for the forgiveness of those guilty of his death and had affirmed that his prayers were always heard.[11]

The words *deplorat et damnat* were deleted and so was *severe reprobans*. Ruokanen explains that *damnat* was changed to *reprobat* because *damnare* was normally used only against heresies, and anti-Semitism, however deserving of the strongest possible rejection, was not exactly a "heresy" (although some felt that it was), and besides, Pope John had explicitly asked that the Council not declare any condemnations.[12]

Text IV, on the first ballot (October 14–15, 1965) produced, out of 2023 votes, 1763 'yes,' 250 'no,' and 10 abstentions. We need to remember in this connection that the Text covered all "non-Christian religions," and mentioned explicitly Hinduism, Buddhism, Islam, and animism, as well as Judaism. The 250 'no' votes include those who had objections to the way those other religions were treated by the schema as well as reservations on the Judaism chapter.

The final ballot, on October 28, 1965, showed a total of 2312, of which 2221 were 'yes,' 88 'no,' with 2 reservations (disallowed) and 1 abstention. Bea comments that, compared with the first ballot in 1964, this is a "massive increase of 328" votes in favor. The promulgation, which followed, was, in his view, for the most part "calmly received" and "correctly interpreted."[13]

In some final reflections we may note that the claim that the Church is "the new People of God," joined to the assessment that the Jewish People did not "recognize the time of their visitation," would seem to suggest their being left out and left behind, while a new group supersedes them. The intention to add the Jewish People to this new People of God is not declared in Text IV as it had been in Text II, but it is not clear that this version is any improvement. Understandably, some Vatican II observers found the final version of the Declaration, the one approved by Pope Paul VI, more controversial than earlier ones.

10 Bea, p. 171.
11 Bea, p. 156.
12 Ruokanen, p. 42.
13 Bea, p. 26.

On the other hand, Text III had introduced the image of the Gentiles being "grafted onto" the "good olive tree" of the Jewish People [Rom. 11:17-24], which would seem to put the relationship the other way around. Text IV does not fail to repeat this image and acknowledges that the Church "draws sustenance" from that "root." Text III had called attention to the bond that sees the people of the New Testament as joined together, "coniuntus," with the "stirpe," the stock, or race, of Abraham, in the sense that that stock is the foundation, the basic reality, the source from which others derive; this would seem to be consistent with the idea of the olive graft.

Text I had brought a sense of relief and expectation; its replacement by Text II was a corresponding disappointment and the cause of distress. Hope had been aroused that at last there would be some acknowledgment of the truths of history and some real resolve to recognize companion religions with respect. Text III did set the whole matter in the context of the current worldwide interest and concern to honor and learn from other religions. And Text III does make positive remarks about all the other religions, but does not suggest that their members really ought to become Christians.

The Jews, however, seem to have had a unique responsibility to have become Christians in the beginning and chose not to do so. They "did not accept the Gospel." Nor did the Moslems, despite their "conjunction" with the "stock of Abraham," join the Church. Yet the Church, in these documents, does not express the hope or expectation that the Moslems in particular will do so. They, together with Hindus and Buddhists and everyone else, are conceived as retaining their identity, while joining the whole human race in praising God "with one voice."

On the other hand, the uniqueness of the Christian relation to the Jews can be seen in the fact that of all the "non-Christian religions," only Judaism is linked by *Nostra Aetate* to Christianity by what Ruokanen calls "the very substance of religion itself." The sacred scriptures of the Jewish People are, for Christians, documents of divine revelation. The term "revelation" is not used by the Decree in speaking of any other religion. It is worth mentioning also that the schema does not support the still popular view that Judaism is a "religion of law" whereas Christianity is a "religion of love." In these Texts Judaism is expressly seen as a religion of (what

Christians call) "grace," that is, divine election, God's special love, covenants, and promises. Here the Church lays claim to a common "patrimony" with the Jews, a kinship it does not admit with any other. Thus in the Decree on the Relation of the Church to the Non-Christian Religions, Judaism is in a class by itself.[14]

POSTSCRIPT

"In 1994 the Roman CatholicChurch entered into diplomatic relations with Israel. In March 1998, Pope John Paul II issued 'We Remember: a Reflection on the *Shoah*' seeking forgiveness for the failure of Catholics to stop the mass deportations and the killings of Jews during the Holocaust. Also, the Lutheran Church in the United States has explicitly rejected Martin Luther's anti-Semitic teachings."[15]

See also Appendix C, beginning on page 377, especially page 381, where the U.S. Bishops renounce "the wish to absorb the Jewish faith into Christianity."

---

14 Ruokanen, pp. 80–81.
15 Lewis D. Solomon, *Jewish Spirituality: Revitalizing Judaism for the Twenty-first Century* (Northvale, NJ: Jason Aronson, 2000) 21.

And the Lord said to Moses: 'Come up to Me in the mountain, and be there.'" (Exodus 24:12).

"And the mountain burned with fire to the heart of Heaven." (Deuteronomy 4:11)

"Is there a 'heart of Heaven'?
And did the flames of Mount Sinai actually reach
'to the heart of Heaven'?
The fire of Mount Sinai blazed so and inflamed so
that the heart of flesh
of each of those present at the Revelation
became a 'heart of Heaven' –
the heart became Heaven."

— *The Sayings of Menahem Mendel of Kotsk*

HISTORIC VISIT of JOHN PAUL II TO THE SYNAGOGUE of ROME

April 13, 1986

On Sunday, April 13, 1986, Pope John Paul II made an historic visit to the Synagogue of Rome. He was welcomed by Professor Giacomo Saban, President of the Jewish Community of Rome. Chief Rabbi Elio Toaff addressed the Pope and the congregation in a fairly lengthy speech on Jewish history, ancient and recent, scripture and theology, ethics and aspirations. This formed a background for his remarks on the significance of the Church's new attitude toward Judaism.

He began by remembering how Pope John XXIII had appeared in the street outside the synagogue as the people were leaving after Sabbath worship. He had greeted and blessed them, something that had never happened before. Rabbi Toaff mentioned in this connection Jules Isaac, who had visited Pope John and brought to his attention the moral disvalue of the Church's teaching on the Jews. Through the centuries, under the shadow of this teaching, Jewish martyrs had sustained their faith, surrendering their lives if necessary for the Sanctification of God's Name.

The vocation of Israel is to teach monotheism to the world, with its spiritual and moral values, so that all humankind may be united with the one God of all in goodness and peace. Human beings have the honor of bearing the image of the divine benevolence and must cultivate mutual respect and care. Prejudice, racial injustice, and even terrorism are still with us and must be opposed until they are banished forever, said the Rabbi, and praised Vatican II for its strong statements condemning anti-Semitism.

In the context of this aspiration to universal mutuality, Rabbi Toaff expressed his conviction that the return of the Jewish people to the Land of Israel is a good for the whole world because of its role in the final redemption and comprehensive righteousness.

He went on to speak of human rights, the freedom that belongs to every person, and the equality that all enjoy owing to their divine origin. He developed the theme of the right to life including a right to subsistence, which involves attention to the distribution of wealth and resources, and protection against violence and disease. It also means, he said, protection against prejudice, hatred, and contempt, pointing out that in Judaism an attack on a person's self-respect is equivalent to bloodshed. Freedom, for its part, has to include freedom of religion and of conscience and conviction.

Because of the Church's new attitude toward the Jews and their religion, expressed in *Nostra Aetate*, the Jewish People take hope that we are entering a new phase. Without forgetting the past, Rabbi Toaff said, we have turned toward equality and mutual respect as a basis for pursuing joint actions in concern for all humanity. There is a foundation of common faith in God the Creator and Parent of all, who urges all people to love one another. He quoted Deuteronomy's assertion that all are children of the one God, and concluded with Isaiah 61 and the vision of joy in salvation and righteousness in a world that brings forth justice and goodness as a garden produces life.

Pope John Paul II then replied that his visit was to be understood as a significant movement toward respectful and cooperative relations between Jews and Roman Catholics, grounded in a common heritage and united in common aspirations. He called *Nostra Aetate* a decisive turning-point.

The new attitude is based also on mutual respect and support for the right of each to its own faith and convictions, its own identity, recognizing differences and particularities as well as shared features. Acknowledging that a thorough transformation in feelings and expressions would take time and continued earnest effort, the Pope urged both parties to exert themselves to represent the other correctly and fairly, based on accurate information. In this connection he drew the attention of Catholics to the Guidelines that the Church had issued for putting the new attitude into appropriate practice.

The Pope had recourse to the text of *Nostra Aetate*, as he has had in other speeches on this theme, in expressing his desire for continuing dialogue and deeper sharing and trusting.

He concentrated on his hopes for working together on issues of general human and world concern. He echoed the sentiments of Rabbi Toaff on freedom, human rights, justice and peace, using that rich word *shalom*.

He spoke of the problems of the present time (1986), saying the crisis in individual and social ethics was acute, faith declining and selfishness increasing, expressed in more violence. He asked for cooperation between the two great faith communities in addressing what he saw as a duty imposed on both to correct these terrible ills. In acting together in such ways, he suggested, we will each be faithful to our respective religious allegiances. Like Chief Rabbi Toaff, he also quoted Deuteronomy on justice to the needy and powerless, including strangers, and concluded with the image from Ezekiel 47 of the miraculous river flowing from the Temple in Jerusalem to the Dead Sea, bringing new life and health.

For the full texts of these speeches and others, together with useful narrative and commentary, see *Pope John Paul II on Jews and Judaism, 1979-1986*, prepared by Dr. Eugene Fisher, Executive Secretary of the Secretariat for Catholic-Jewish Relations, in cooperation with Rabbi Leon Klenicki of the Anti-Defamation League of B'nai B'rith, and published by the National Council of Catholic Bishops and the United States Catholic Conference, Inc.

NATIONAL COUNCIL of SYNAGOGUES and DELEGATES of the U.S. CATHOLIC BISHOPS' COMMITTEE on ECUMENICAL and INTERRELIGIOUS AFFAIRS "REFLECTIONS on COVENANT and MISSION"

August 12, 2002

PRESS RELEASE: Washington – Leaders of the Jewish and Roman Catholic communities in the United States, who have been meeting to discuss topics affecting Catholic-Jewish relations twice a year for more than two decades, made public today (August 12) a document entitled *Reflections on Covenant and Mission*.

Citing the growing respect for the Jewish tradition that has unfolded since the Second Vatican Council, and the deepening Catholic appreciation of the eternal covenant between God and the Jewish people, the Catholic portion of the *Reflections* says that "campaigns that target Jews for conversion to Christianity are no longer theologically acceptable in the Catholic Church."

"This joint reflection marks a significant step forward in the dialogue between the Catholic Church and the Jewish community in this country," said Cardinal William Keeler, the U.S. Bishops' Moderator for Catholic-Jewish relations. "Here one can see, perhaps more clearly than ever before, an essential compatibility, along with equally significant differences, between the Christian and Jewish understandings of God's call to both our peoples to witness to the

Name of the One God to the world in harmony. This echoes the words of Pope John Paul II, praying that as Christians and Jews we may be a blessing to one another" so that, together, we may be "a blessing to the world."' (Pope John Paul II On the 50th Anniversary of the Warsaw Ghetto Uprising, April 6, 1993).

Rabbi Gilbert Rosenthal, Executive Director of the National Council of Synagogues, said: "The joint Catholic-Jewish statement on mission is yet another step in turning a new page in the often stormy relationship between the Jewish people and the Roman Catholic Church. Neither faith group believes that we should missionize among the other in order to save souls via conversion. Quite the contrary: we believe both faith groups are beloved of God and assured of His grace. The joint mission statement has articulated a new goal, namely the healing of a sick world and the imperative to repair the damage we humans have caused to God's creations. We believe we are partners in bringing blessings to all humankind for this is God's will."

Participants in the ongoing consultation are delegates of the Bishops' Committee for Ecumenical and Interreligious Affairs (BCEIA) of the United States Conference of Catholic Bishops (USCCB) and the National Council of Synagogues (NCS). The NCS represents the Central Conference of American Rabbis, the Rabbinical Assembly of Conservative Judaism, the Union of American Hebrew Congregations, and the United Synagogue of Conservative Judaism. The Consultation is co-chaired by Cardinal Keeler and Rabbi Joel Zaiman of the Rabbinical Assembly of Conservative Judaism and Rabbi Michael Signer of the Union of American Hebrew Congregations.

The Reflections derive from a meeting which the BCEIA-NCS Consultation held in New York last March. Participants examined how the Jewish and Roman Catholic traditions currently understand the subjects of Covenant and Mission. Each delegation prepared reflections on the current state of the question in each community. The Consultation voted to issue its considerations publicly in order to encourage serious reflection on these matters by Jews and Catholics throughout the United States. The Roman Catholic and Jewish reflections are presented separately in the document.

The Roman Catholic reflections describe the growing respect

for the Jewish tradition that has unfolded since the Second Vatican Council. "A deepening Catholic appreciation of the eternal covenant between God and the Jewish people, together with a recognition of a divinely-given mission to Jews to witness to God's faithful love, lead to the conclusion that campaigns that target Jews for conversion to Christianity are no longer theologically acceptable in the Catholic Church," they state.

The Jewish reflections describe the mission of the Jews and the perfection of the world. "This mission is seen to have three aspects. First, there are the obligations that arise as a result of the loving election of the Jewish people into a covenant with God. Second, there is a mission of witness to God's redeeming power in the world. Third, the Jewish people have a mission that is addressed to all human beings." The Jewish reflections conclude by urging Jews and Christians to articulate a common agenda to heal the world.

The NCS-BCEIA Consultation expressed concern about the continuing ignorance and caricatures of one another that still prevail in many segments of the Catholic and Jewish communities, and reaffirmed its commitment to deepen the dialogue and promote amity between these two communities in the United States.

The Dialogues have previously produced public statements on such issues as Children and the Environment and Acts of Religious Hatred.

[Excerpts from the Consultation Document]
ROMAN CATHOLIC REFLECTIONS

The post-*Nostra Aetate* Catholic recognition of the permanence of the Jewish people's covenant relationship to God has led to a new positive regard for the post-biblical or rabbinic Jewish tradition that is unprecedented in Christian history. The Vatican's 1974 *Guidelines* insisted that Christians "must strive to learn by what essential traits Jews define themselves in the light of their own religious experience."[1] The 1985 Vatican *Notes* praised

[Roman numerals were used in the original text for footnotes. They are included after the Arabic numerals for easy reference.]

1 (v): Pontifical Commission for Religious Relations with the Jews: Guidelines and Suggestions for Implementing the Conciliar Declaration *Nostra Aetate*, No. 4 (1974), Prologue.

post-biblical Judaism for carrying "to the whole world a witness – often heroic – of its fidelity to the one God and to 'exalt Him in the presence of all the living' [Tobit 13:4]."[2] The *Notes* went on to refer to John Paul II in urging Christians to remember "how the permanence of Israel is accompanied by a continuous spiritual fecundity, in the rabbinical period, in the Middle Ages and in modern times, taking its start from a patrimony which we long shared, so much so that 'the faith and religious life of the Jewish people as they are professed and practiced still today, can greatly help us to understand better certain aspects of the life of the Church'" (John Paul II, 6 March 1982).[3] This theme has been taken up in statements by the United States Catholic bishops, such as *God's Mercy Endures Forever*, which advised preachers to "be free to draw on Jewish sources (rabbinic, medieval, and modern) in expounding the meaning of the Hebrew Scriptures and the apostolic writings."[4]

In a remarkable and still most pertinent study paper presented at the sixth meeting of the International Catholic-Jewish Liason Committee in Venice twenty-five years ago, Prof. Tommaso Federici examined the missiological implications of *Nostra Aetate*. He argued on historical and theological grounds that there should be in the Church no organization of any kind dedicated to the conversion of Jews. This has over the ensuing years been the *de facto* practice of the Catholic Church.

More recently Cardinal Walter Kasper, President of the Pontifical Commission for Religious Relations with the Jews, explained this practice. In a formal statement made first at the seventeenth meeting of the International Catholic-Jewish Liason Committee in May 2001, and repeated later in the year in Jerusalem, Cardinal Kasper spoke of "mission" in the narrow sense to mean "proclamation," or the invitation to baptism and catechesis. He showed why such initiatives are not appropriately directed at Jews:

> The term mission, in its proper sense, refers to conversion
> from false gods and idols to the true and one God, who

2 (vi) Pontifical Commission for Religious Relations with the Jews, Notes on the Correct Way to Present Jews and Judaism in Preaching and Teaching in the Roman Catholic Church (1985), VI, 25 .

3 (vii) Ibid.

4 (viii) NCCB, *God's Mercy Endures Forever* (1988), 31i.

revealed Himself in the salvation history of His elected people. Thus mission, in the strict sense, cannot be used with regard to Jews, who believe in the true and one God. Therefore, and this is characteristic, there exists dialogue but there does not exist any Catholic missionary organization for Jews.

As we said previously, dialogue is not mere objective information; dialogue involves the whole person. So in dialogue Jews give witness of their faith, witness of what supported them in the dark periods of their history and their life, and Christians give account of the hope they have in Jesus Christ. In doing so, both are far away from any kind of proselytism, but both can learn from each other and enrich each other. We both want to share our deepest concerns to an often-disoriented world that needs such witness and searches for it.[5]

From the point of view of the Catholic Church, Judaism is a religion that springs from divine revelation. As Cardinal Kasper noted,…"The Church believes that Judaism, i.e. the faithful response of the Jewish people to God's irrevocable covenant, is salvific for them."[6]

[The Church's] evangelizing task no longer includes the wish to absorb the Jewish faith into Christianity and so end the distinctive witness of Jews to God in human history.

[It] recognizes that Jews are also called by God to prepare the world for God's kingdom. Their witness to the kingdom…must not be curtailed by seeking the conversion of the Jewish people to Christianity. The distinctive Jewish witness must be sustained.…

5 (xx) Walter Cardinal Kasper, "Dominus Iesus." Address delivered at the 17th meeting of the International Catholic-Jewish Liason Committee, New York, May 1, 2001.
6 (xxi) Ibid.

JEWISH REFLECTIONS

The Jews are, for better or for worse, for richer or poorer, partners with God in a sometimes stormy and sometimes idyllic romance, in a loving marriage that binds God and the People of Israel together forever and which gives the deepest possible meaning to Jewish existence.

The practical result of all this is that the first mission of the Jews is toward the Jews. It means that the Jewish community is intent upon preserving its identity. Since that does not always happen naturally, it is the reason why Jews talk to each other constantly about institutional strengths and the community's ability to educate its children. It creates an abhorrence of intermarriage. It explains the passion to study the Torah. The stakes are high in Jewish life and in order not to abandon God, the Jewish community expends a great deal of energy seeing to it that the covenantal community works.

The message of the Bible is a message and a vision not only to Israel but to all of humanity. Isaiah speaks…of the Jews as a "covenant people and a light to nations…[The light is] the light of the Torah…Since the message of the Torah is peace, the light that comes forth conveys a message of the blessings of peace that ought to reign throughout the world.[7]

The God of the Bible is the God of the world. His visions are visions for all of humanity. His love is a love that extends to every creature.

Therefore, in Judaism, the absolute value of human beings, their creation in the divine image, as well as God's overriding concern for justice and mercy is at the basis of a universal joint community of the created, a community called to respond to the love of God by loving other human beings, by setting up the structures of society that maximize the practice of justice and mercy and by engaging unendingly in the religious quest to bring healing to the broken world.

7 (xxxv) Rabbi David Kimhi, known as Radak (Provençal scholar of the late twelfth to early thirteenth centuries) in his comment on Isaiah 42:6.

At the same time, it is important to stress that notwithstanding the covenant, there is no need for the nations of the world to embrace Judaism. While there are theological verities such as belief in God's unity, and practical social values that lead to the creation of a good society that are possible and necessary for humanity at large to grasp, they do not require Judaism in order to redeem the individual or society. *The pious of all nations of the world have a place in the world to come.*

Just as important, however, is the idea that the world needs perfection. While Christians and Jews understand the messianic hope…differently,…we share the belief that we live in an unredeemed world that longs for repair.

Why not articulate a common agenda? Why not join together our spiritual forces to state and act upon the values we share in common and that lead to repair of the unredeemed world? We have worked together in the past in advancing the cause of social justice. We have marched together for civil rights, we have championed the cause of the poor and homeless; and we have called on our country's leader to seek nuclear disarmament. These are but a few of the issues we Jews and Christians have addressed in concert with each other.

To hint at what we might yet do together let us look at some of the concrete ways that classical Judaism takes theological ideas and transforms them into ways of living. And, if these be stones in a pavement on which we might together walk, then we will be able to fashion a highway that is a route we share in common toward humanity's repair and the world's perfection.

Though the prophetic concern for the needy is well known, it should be stressed that it is in the Talmud that the specifics of doing good are laid out in such a way that they become the cornerstones of life.

Tzedakah (charity) and deeds of kindness are weighed in the balance as equal to all the commandments of the Torah. The obligation of charity is directed at the poor and deeds of kindness are directed at the poor and the rich. Charity is directed at the living and deeds of kindness are rendered to the living and to the dead. Charity utilizes one's money while deeds of kindness utilize one's money and one's self.[8]

Already in Talmudic times, charitable institutions to care for the poor were an established and essential part of the community's life. When, for example, the Mishnah teaches that a Jew must celebrate the Passover Seder with four cups of wine,[9] it notes that the public dole "*tamhui*" must provide that wine for the poor. The poor must celebrate and feel the dignity of being free people – and that is the responsibility of the community.[10] Yet as much as charitable institutions are a central part of the community's life, Maimonides makes it clear that the highest form of charity is to make it possible for someone to earn a living himself.[11]

The large section of the Talmud that deals with civil and criminal law, *Nezikin,* or damages, specifies and protects workers' compensation.[12] It gives concrete form to the Torah's prohibitions against interest[13] and extends the laws prohibiting interest to include many types of financial transactions that appear to be interest, even when they are not. All this is done in order to create an economy where people are encouraged to help each other financially as an expression of their common fellowship, rather than as a way of making money. Financial instruments are created that enable people without funds to become partners with others rather than borrowers – another way of protecting human dignity and encouraging the development of a society where this dignity is manifested in everyday life.[14]

Acts of kindness that are required and developed in detail by the law include the obligations to visit the sick and to comfort mourners. Jews are required to redeem captives and to provide for brides, to bury the dead and to welcome people to their tables.[15] The Talmud details the obligation of Jews to show deference to the old. "Standing up" and showing special signs of respect to the old

---

8 (li) Jerusalem Talmud, Peah 1:1.
9 (lii) To remember the four verbs of God's deliverance in Exodus 6:6-7: ["free...deliver...redeem...take," NRSV—ed.]
10 (liii) Mishnah Pesahim 10:1
11 (liv) *Maimonides, Mishneh Torah,* "Laws of Gifts to the Poor," 10:6.
12 (lv) BT Bava Metzia, Ch. 7.
13 (lvi) Exodus 22:24, Leviticus 25:6, Deuteronomy 23:20 and 23:21.
14 (lvii) BT Bava Metzia, Ch. 7
15 (lviii) BT Shabbat 121.

are responses to the physical problems of aging.[16] As a person's own sense of dignity diminishes, the community is asked to reinforce the individual's dignity.[17]

Of course Jewish law is directed at Jews and its primary concern is to encourage the expression of love to the members of the community. It deals not in sentiments but, principally, in actions. But it is important to note that many of these actions are mandatory toward all people. Thus the Talmud says: "One must provide for the needs of the gentile poor with the Jewish poor. One must visit the gentile sick as one visits the Jewish sick. One must care for the burial of a gentile, just as one must care for the burial of a Jew. [These obligations are universal] because these are the ways of peace."[18]

The Torah's ways of peace manifest a practical response to the sacred creation of humanity in the divine image. They help perfect the world into the Kingdom of the Almighty.

Does not humanity need a common path that seeks the ways of peace? Does not humanity need a common vision of the sacred nature of our human existence that we can teach our children and that we can foster in our communities in order to further the ways of peace? Does not humanity need a commitment of its religious leadership within each faith and beyond each faith, to join hands and to create bonds that will inspire and guide humanity to reach toward its sacred promise? For Jews and Christians who heard the call of God to be a blessing and a light to the world, the challenge and mission are clear.

Nothing less should be our challenge – and that is the true meaning of the mission which we all need to share.

16 (lix) Leviticus 19:32. The Talmud develops these ideas particularly in BT Kiddushin 32b-33a.
17 (lx) See Harlan J. Wechsler, *Old Is Good*.
18 (lxi) BT Gittin 61a.

RESOURCES FOR FURTHER STUDY

I:

WORKS BY CONTRIBUTORS TO
Merton & Judaism

Thomas Merton and Judaism: An Interfaith Conference held in Louisville, KY and sponsored by The Thomas Merton Foundation and Congregation Adath Jeshurun. Audiotape No. 8: Panel discussion, featuring Brenda Finch Fairday, Donald Grayston, Edward Kaplan, Lucien Miller, Karl Plank, and Mary Heléne Rosenbaum. Moderated by Sherry Israel of Brandeis University. Available from The Thomas Merton Foundation, 2117 Payne St., Louisville, KY 40206. FAX (502) 899-1907.

Carroll, James. *Constantine's Sword: The Church and the Jews: A History.* Boston: Houghton Mifflin, 2001.

Grayston, Donald and Michael W. Higgins, eds. *Thomas Merton: Pilgrim in Process.* Toronto: Griffin House, 1983.

Kaplan, Edward K. and Samuel H. Dresner. *Abraham Joshua Heschel: Prophetic Witness.* New Haven: Yale University Press, 1998.

Kaplan, Edward K. "Martin Buber and the Drama of Otherness: The Dynamics of Love, Art, and Faith," *Judaism* 27,2 (Spring 1978), 196-206.

—. "Sacred versus Symbolic Religion: Herschel versus Buber," *Modern Judaism* 14,3 (Fall 1994), 213-231.

—. *Holiness in Words: Abraham Joshua Heschel's Poetics of Piety.* Albany, NY: State University of New York Press, 1996.

Kramer, Victor A. *Thomas Merton: Monk and Artist.* Boston: Twayne, 1984. Prof. Kramer has edited or coedited successive editions of The Merton Annual: Studies in Thomas Merton, Religion, Culture, Literature & Social Concerns since its inception in 1988. New York: AMS Press, 1988.

Magid, Shaul. "Abraham Joshua Heschel and Thomas Merton: Heretics of Modernity," *Conservative Judaism* 1, 2-3 (Winter-Spring 1998), 112-125.

—. "Monastic Liberation as Counter-Cultural Critique in the Life and Thought of Thomas Merton," *Cross Currents* 49,4 (Winter 1999-2000), 445-461.

Miller, Lucien. "Merton's *Chuang Tzu,*" Thomas Merton Center, Bellarmine University, Louisville, Kentucky.

Pearson, Paul M. *Thomas Merton: A Mind Awake in the Dark.* Abergavenny, Wales: Three Peaks Press, 2001.

Plank, Karl A. "The Survivor's Return: Reflections on Memory and Place," *Judaism* 38 (1989), 266 ff.

—. "Thomas Merton and Hannah Arendt," *The Merton Annual* 3 (1990), 121-150.

—. "Thomas Merton and the Ethic Edge of Contemplation," *Anglican Theological Review* 84,1 (2002), 113-126.

—. *Mother of the Wire Fence: Inside and Outside the Holocaust.* Louisville: Westminster John Knox, 1994.

Schachter, Zalman. "The Condition of Jewish Belief." Zalman Schachter's answer to the question proposed in *The Condition of Jewish Belief: A Symposium Compiled by the Editors of Commentary Magazine.* New York: Macmillan, 1966, pp. 207-216.

—. *Fragments of a Future-Scroll: Hasidism for the Aquarian Age*, ed. Philip Mandelkorn and Stephen Gerstman. Germantown: PA: Leaves of Grass Press, 1975.

—. Zalman Schachter-Shalomi and Donald Gropman, *The First Step: A Guide to the New Jewish Spirit*. New York: Bantam Books, 1983.

—. Zalman Schachter-Shalomi and Edward Hoffman, *Sparks of Light: Counseling in the Hasidic Tradition*. Boulder CO: Shambala, 1983.

—. *Spiritual Intimacy: A Study of Counseling in Hasidism*. Northvale, NJ: Jason Aronson, 1991.

—. *Paradigm Shift: From the Jewish Renewal Teachings of Reb Zalman Schachter-Shalomi*. Ellen Singer, ed. Northvale, NJ: Jason Aronson, 1993.

—.Zalman Schachter-Shalomi and Ronald Miller, *From Age-ing to Sage-ing: A Profound New Vision of Growing Older*. New York: Warner Books, 1995.

Shannon, William. *Thomas Merton's Dark Past*. New York: Farrar, Straus, Giroux, 1987.

II:
Merton Resources

Merton Vade Mecum: A Quick-Reference Bibliographic Handbook. By Patricia Burton, with a Foreword by Patrick F. O'Connell. Louisville, KY: The Thomas Merton Foundation, Second Edition, 2001. This is an exhaustive 164 page reference book. It contains lists of all Merton's writings, letters, and journal entries.

A Thomas Merton Reader. Thomas P. McDonnell, ed., with an Introduction by M. Scott Peck. New York: Doubleday Image, 1989.

Thomas Merton: Essential Writings. Selected with an Introduction by Christine M. Bochen. Maryknoll, NY: Orbis Books, 2000.

MERTON TITLES MOST FREQUENTLY CITED IN THIS BOOK

—. *Conjectures of a Guilty Bystander.* New York: Doubleday, 1966.

—. *Dancing in the Waters of Life.* New York: Harper Collins, 1997.

—. *The Hidden Ground of Love.* New York: Farrar, Straus, Giroux, 1985.

—. *Opening the Bible.* Collegeville, MN: Liturgical Press, 19170.

—. *A Vow of Conversation: Journals 1964-1965*, Noami Burton Stone, ed. New York: Farrar, Straus, Giroux, 1988.

[Specialist in retailing Merton Books: Bardstown Art Gallery, P.O. Box 417, Bardstown, KY 40004; (502) 348-6488/fax (502) 349-1920. Art Gallery website: http://www.thomasmertonbooks.com].

BOOKS ABOUT MERTON MENTIONED IN THIS BOOK

Cunningham, Lawrence S., ed. *Thomas Merton: Spiritual Master.* Mahwah, NJ: Paulist Press, 1992.

Finley, James. *Merton's Palace of Nowhere: A Search for God Through Awareness of the True Self,* with a Foreword by Henri Nouwen. Notre Dame, IN: Ave Maria Press, 1978.

Griffin, John Howard. *A Hidden Wholeness: The Visual World of Thomas Merton.* Boston: Houghton Mifflin, 1970.

—. *Follow the Ecstasy: Thomas Merton, The Hermitage Years, 1965-1968.*

Patrick Hart, ed. *Thomas Merton, Monk.* New York: Sheed & Ward, 1974.

Kelly, Timothy. "Epilogue: A Memoir," in *The Legacy of Thomas Merton*, Patrick Hart, ed. Kalamazoo, MI: Cistercian Publications, 1986.

Labrie, Ross. *Thomas Merton and the Inclusive Imagination.* Columbia, MO: University of Missouri Press, 2001.

Matt, Michael. *The Seven Mountains of Thomas Merton.* Boston: Houghton Mifflin, 1984.

Padovano, Anthony. "The Eight Conversions of Thomas Merton," *The Merton Seasonal* 25,2 (Summer 2000), 9-15.

Zahn, Gordon C., ed. *The Non-Violent Alternative.* New York. Farrar, Straus, Giroux, 1980.

III
JEWISH RESOURCES

(a) General

Baeck, Leo. *The Essence of Judaism.* New York: Schocken Books, 1948.

Bauman, Zygmunt. *Modernity and the Holocaust.* Ithaca, NY: Cornell University Press, 1991.

Ben-Chorin, Schalom. *Brother Jesus: The Nazarene Through Jewish Eyes.* Jared Klein and Max Reinhart, transl. Athens: University of Georgia Press, 2001.

Braun, Moshe. *The Jewish Holy Days: Their Spiritual Significance.* Northvale, NJ: Jason Aronson, 1996.

Bruteau, Beatrice, ed. *Jesus Through Jewish Eyes: Rabbis and Scholars Engage an Ancient Brother in a New Conversation.* Maryknoll, NY: Orbis Books, 2001.

Green, Arthur. "Abraham Joshua Heschel: Recasting Hasidism for Moderns," *Tikkun* 14, 1 (Jan.-Feb. 1999), 63-69.

Niewyk, Donald L. *The Holocaust: Problems and Perspectives of Interpretations*. Lexington, MA: Heath, 1992.

Solomon, Lewis D. *Jewish Spirituality: Revitalizing Judaism for the Twenty-first Century*. Northvale, NJ: Jason Aronson, 200.

Wiener, Shohama Harris and Jonathan Omer-Man, eds. *Worlds of Jewish Prayer: A Festschrift in Honor of Rabbi Zalman M. Schachter-Shalomi*. Northvale, NJ: Jason Aronson, 1993.

(b) Martin Buber

Buber, Martin. *The Tales of Rabbi Nachman*. Maurice Friedman, transl. New York: Horizon Press, 1956 [orig. 1907].

—. *The Legend of the Baal-Shem*. Maurice Friedman, trans. Princeton University Press, 1996. [orig. 1908].

—. *Chinese Tales*. Alex Page, transl. Atlantic Highlands, NJ: Humanities Press International, 1991.

—. *I and Thou*. Walter Kaufmann, transl. New York: Charles Scribner's Sons, 1970 [orig. 1927].

—. *Hasidism and Modern Man*. Maurice Friedman, ed. & transl. New York: Harper & Row, 1966. [orig. 1947].

—. *Tales of the Hasidim*. Book One: *The Early Masters*. Book Two: *The Later Masters*. Olga Marx, transl. New York: Schocken Books, 1991. [orig. 1947 & 1948].

—. *The Prophetic Faith*. Carlyle Witton-Davies, transl. New York: Harper & Row, 1949.

—. The Way of Modern Man According to the Teaching of Hasidism. Secaucus, NJ: Citadel Press, 1976 [orig. 1950].

——. *Two Types of Faith*. Norman P. Goldhawk, transl. London: Routledge & Kegan Paul, 1951.

——. *Between Man and Man*. Ronald G. Smith, transl. Boston: Beacon Paperback, 1955.

——. *The Origin and Meaning of Hasidism*. Maurice Friedman, ed. & transl. New York: Horizon Press, 1960.

——. *On the Bible*. New York: Schocken, 1982.

——. "People Today and the Jewish Bible," in Martin Buber and Franz Rosenzweig, *Scripture and Tradition*, L. Rosenwald, transl. Bloomington, IN: Indiana University Press, 1994.

Friedman, Maurice S. *Martin Buber: The Life of Dialogue*. New York: Harper & Row, 1960. First published by The University of Chicago Press, 1955.

——. *Martin Buber's Life and Work*. New York: Schocken, 1967.

(c) Abraham Joshua Heschel

Heschel, Abraham Joshua. *The Sabbath: Its Meaning for Modern Man*. New York: 1951; expanded edition 1963.

——. *Man Is Not Alone: A Philosophy of Religion*. New York: Farrar, Straus, Giroux, 1972 [orig. 1951].

——. *Man's Quest for God: Studies in Prayer and Symbolism*. New York: Charles Scribner's Sons, 1954.

——. *God's Search for Man: A Philosophy of Judaism*. New York: Harper & Row, 1955.

——. *The Prophets*. New York: Harper & Row, 1962.

—. *Who Is Man?* Stanford, 1965.

—. *The Insecurity of Freedom: Essays on Human Existence.* New York: Farrar, Straus, Giroux, 1966.

—. "No Religion Is an Island," *Union Seminary Quarterly Review* 21,2 (Jan., 1966).

—. *A Passion for Truth.* New York: Farrar, Straus, Giroux, 1973.

—. *The Circle of the Baal Shem Tov.* Samuel H. Dresner, ed. Chicago: Chicago University Press, 1986.

ANTHOLOGIES, BOOKS, ESSAYS DEALING WITH HESCHEL

Between God and Man: An Interpretation of Judaism. Selected and Edited by Fritz A. Rothchild. New York, 1959 [revised 1976].

Abraham Joshua Heschel: Exploring His Life and Thought. John C. Merkle, ed. New York: Macmillan, 1985.

I Asked for Wonder: A Spiritual Anthology [of] Abraham Joshua Heschel. Samuel H. Dresner, ed. New York: Crossroad, 1992.

Moral Grandeur and Spiritual Audacity: Essays of Abraham Joshua Heschel. Susannah Heschel, ed. New York: Farrar, Straus, Giroux, 1996.

"Abraham Joshua Heschel: A Twenty-fifth Yahrzeit Tribute," in *Conservative Judaism*, Vol. L, no.2-3, Winter-Spring, 1998.

For further references, see Edward K. Kaplan's *Holiness in Words.* Annotated Bibliography in English, 197-202. Lists books, anthologies, selected articles by Heschel, interviews, books in English, and articles on Heschel.

IV:
CHRISTIAN RESOURCES

Albergo, Giuseppe, ed. *History of Vatican II*. Vol. I. English Version editor, Joseph A. Komonchak. Leuven: Peeters, 1995.

Bea, Augustin Cardinal. *The Church and the Jewish People:* A Commentary on the Second Vatican Council's Declaration on the Relation of the Church to Non-Christian Religions. Philip Loretz, SJ, transl. New York: Harper & Row, 1966.(Includes Bea's addresses to the Council.)

Bomporad, Jack and Michael Shevack. *Our Age*. New York: New City Press, 1996.

Council Daybook. Floyd Anderson, ed. Washington, DC: National Catholic Welfare Conference. Vatican II: Sessions 1&2, Session 3; 1965.

Flannery, Austin, ed. *Vatican Council: The Conciliar and Post-Conciliar Documents*. Collegeville, MN: The Liturgical Press, 1975.

Oesterreicher, John M. *The Rediscovery of Judaism*. New Jersey: Institute of Judaeo-Christian Studies: Seton Hall University, 1971.

Passelecq, George and Bernard Suchecky, *The Hidden Encyclical of Pius XI:* The Vatican's Lost Opportunity to Oppose Nazi Racial Policies That Led to the Holocaust, with an Introduction by Gary Wills, tr. from French by Stevan Rendall. New York: Harcourt Brace, 1997.

Rynne, Xavier. *Vatican Council II*. New introduction by author. Maryknoll, NY: Orbis, 2003.

Ruokanen, Mikka, *The Catholic Doctrine of Non-Christian Religions According to the Second Vatican Council*. Leiden: E.J. Brill, 1992. Contains Latin texts.

Stacpoole, Alberic, ed. *Vatican II by Those Who Were There.* London: Geoffrey Chapman, 1986.

Willebrands, Johannes Cardinal. *Church and Jewish People: New Considerations.* New York: Paulist Press, 1992. See his Selected Bibliography on Christian-Jewish Relations (1975–1990).

V

JEWISH–CHRISTIAN RELATIONS, BY YEARS

Cohen, Arthur D. *The Myth of the Judaeo-Christian Tradition.* New York: Harper & Row, 1963.

Mussner, Franz. *Tractate on the Jews: The Significance of Judaism for Christian Faith,* Leonard Swidler, transl. Philadelphia, Fortress, 1984.

Stransky, Thomas F., CSP. "The Catholic-Jewish Dialogue: Twenty Years after *Nostra Aetate,*" *America,* Feb. 8, 1986.

Schwartz, G. David, "Explorations and Responses: Is There a Jewish Reclamation of Jesus?," *Journal of Ecumenical Studies* 24, 1 (Winter 1987).

Jewish Perspectives on Christianity. Fritz A. Rothschild, ed. New York: Crossroad, 1990.

Interwoven Destinies: Jews and Christians Through the Ages. Eugene J. Fisher, ed. Mahwah, NJ: Paulist Press, 1993.

Wallis, James H. *Post-Holocaust Christianity: Paul Van Buren's Theology and the Jewish-Christian Reality.* New York: University Press of America, 1997.

Anti-Judaism in the Gospels. William R. Farmer, ed. Harrisburg, PA: Trinity Press International, 1999.

Christianity in Jewish Terms, eds. Tikva Fryer-Kensky, David Novak, Peter W. Ochs, David F. Sandmel, Michael A. Signer.

Boulder, CO: Westview, 2001.

Irreconcilable Differences: A Learning Resource for Jews and Christians, eds. David F. Sandmel, Rosann M. Catalano, and Christopher M. Leighton. Boulder, CO: Westview Press, 2001.

"Catholic-Jewish Statement on Conversion Draws Controversy," *America,* Sept. 9, 2002 [cf. Appendix C, this book].
"Covenant and Mission," by Cardinal Avery Dulles, SJ, and "Theology's Sacred Obligation: A Reply to Cardinal Avery Dulles on Evangelization," by Mary C. Boys, Philip A. Cunningham, and John T. Pawlikowski, *America,* Oct. 21, 2002 [cf. Appendix C, this book].

VI:
PERIODICALS AND SOURCEBOOKS

Menorah Review. Center for Judaic Studies of Virginia Commonwealth University.

The Merton Annual: Studies in Thomas Merton, Religion, Culture, Literature, and Social Concerns. Fifteen volumes. New York, AMS Press,

Dalin, David G. "The Jewish Theology of Abraham Joshua Heschel," *The Weekly Standard* (Jan. 4/Jan. 11, 1999).

Friedman, Maurice. "Divine Need and Human Wonder: The Philosophy of Abraham Joshua Heschel," *Judaism* 25 (Winter 1976), 65–78.

Mirsky, Yehudah, "The Rhapsodist," *The New Republic* (April 19, 1999), 36–42. Review of Abraham Joshua Heschel: *Prophetic Witness* by Edward K. Kaplan and Samuel H. Dresner, and *Moral Grandeur and Spiritual Audacity: Essays by Abraham Joshua Heschel,* Susannah Heschel, ed.

SourceBook of the World's Religions: An Interfaith Guide to Religion and Spirituality, ed. Joel Beversluis. Novato: New World Library, 2000.

VII:
ORGANIZATIONS, WEBSITES

Aleph: Alliance for Jewish Renewal, 7318 Germantown Ave., Philadelphia, PA 19119-1795. *New Menorah* is the quarterly journal of Aleph. www.jewishrenewal.org.

Christian Meditation Center, 23 Kensington Square, London W8 5HN, England. Fax: 011-44-171-937-6790. *Christian Meditation Newsletter,* International Centre, St. Mark's, Middleton Square, London EC1R 1XX. John Main Institute, 7315 Brookville Rd, Chevy Chase, MD 20815. Christian Meditation Center, 1080 West Irving Park Rd., Roselle, Il 60172.

CLAL; The National Jewish Center for Learning and Leadership, 440 Park Ave. So. 4th floor. New York, NY 10016-8012.

Contemplative Outreach News. St. Benedict's Monastery, Snowmass, Colorado 81654. International Headquarters: Contemplative Outreach, 10 Park Place, P.O. Box 737, Butler, NJ 07405.

Creation Spirituality: Matthew Fox:http://www.creation-spirituality.com/matthew.html

Dovetail Institute for Interfaith Family Relations, 775 Simon Greenwell Lane, Boston, KY 40107. Institute offers conferences and consultation. Newletter carries articles and editorials on Jewish-Christian marriages.

The Institute for Christian and Jewish Studies. Baltimore, MD: http://www.icjs.edu

Metivta: A Center for Contemplative Judaism, 2001 S. Barrington Ave., Suite 106, Los Angeles, CA 90025-5363. www.metivta.org

CONTRIBUTORS

Beatrice Bruteau has a Ph.D. in philosophy from Fordham University (B.A., Math., Univ. of Missouri; M. Litt., Math., Univ. of Pittsburgh). She is the author of twelve books and more than a hundred articles. Her writings and lectures typically feature an integrated study of science, mathematics, philosophy and religion in an East-West context. Her essays have appeared in journals such *as International Philosophical Quarterly* and *Cross Currents* in the United States, *Blackfriars* in the United Kingdom, and *Mother India* and *Prabuddha Bharata* in India. Among her books, *Evolution Toward Divinity* has been translated into Spanish and *What We Can Learn from the East* into German. A survey of her most recent books includes: *God's Ecstasy: The Creation of a Self-Creating World* (Crosssroad, 1997), *The Grand Option* (Univ. of Notre Dame Press, 2001), *Jesus Through Jewish Eyes: Rabbis and Scholars Engage an Ancient Brother in a New Conversation* (Orbis, 2001), and *Radical Optimism* (Sentient Publications, 2002).

James Carroll is the author of the best-selling book *Constantine's Sword*, which won the 2001 National Jewish Book Award in History. The book explores the long and often troubled relationship between Christians and Jews. In a cover story in the January 14, 2001 edition of *The New York Times Book Review* Andrew Sullivan wrote, "What Carroll wants to show us above all is that the relationship with the Jews is not merely one issue among many for the modern church. It is the central issue in church history, and is inextricable from the core of what Christianity is about." Carroll is the author of nine novels and the memoir, *An American Requiem*, which won the National Book Award. His column on culture and politics appears weekly in the *Boston Globe*.

Photo © Lisa Kohler

Brenda Fitch Fairaday, M.M., M.A., is a graduate of Union Theological Seminary in Church History and of the University of Southern California in Music. She is enrolled at Jewish Theological Seminary for advanced studies in Judaism, where she continues her study of Abraham Joshua Heschel's works. In 1997, as chair of the Thomas Merton Conference at Corpus Christi Church in New York, she organized a symposium on Merton and Heschel: "Thomas Merton's Prophetic Voice," and in 1998 she co-sponsored a day-long conference commemorating Merton's baptism: "The Conversios of Thomas Merton." She lectures on the development and progress in Catholic-Jewish Relations since Vatican II, leads retreats, and teaches courses on Merton's life, thought, and spirituality, and on the spirituality of the medieval mystics.

Donald Grayston is Director of the Institute for the Humanities at Simon Fraser University in Vancouver, BC, where he teaches Religious Studies in the Humanities Department. He received his Ph.D. from the University of St. Michael's College in the Toronto School of Theology with a dissertation on Thomas Merton. His publications on Merton include: *Pilgrim in Process*, co-edited with Michael W. Higgins (1983; a revised edition is scheduled for this year); *Thomas Merton: The Development of a Spiritual Theologian* (1985), and *Thomas Merton's Rewritings* (1989). He serves as vicar of St. Oswald's Anglican Church in Port Kells, southeast of Vancouver.

Dr. Edward K. Kaplan is Kaiserman Professor in the Humanities at Brandeis University and chair of the new Program in Religious Studies at that instution. He has published two books on Abraham Joshua Heschel and essays on Thomas Merton, Martin Buber, and Howard Thurman. Volume One of his intellectual and cultural biography of Heschel, co-authored with Samuel Dresner, *Abraham Joshua Heschel, Prophetic Witness* (Yale, 1998), was a finalist in Jewish Scholarship in the National Jewish Book Awards. Kaplan's foundational book, *Holiness in Words: Abraham Joshua Heschel's Poetics of Piety* (SUNY, 1996), appeared in French translation as *La sainteté en parole: Abraham Heschel: piété, poetique, action* (Paris: Ed. du Cerf, 1999). Kaplan helped organize the first francophone colloquium on Abraham Heschel, which took place in Paris, January 15-17, 2000. Prof. Kaplan is a Research Associate at the Tauber Institute for the Study of European Jewery at Brandeis and a professor of French and Comparative Literature.

Victor A. Kramer is Exectuive Director of the Aquinas Center of Theology at Emory University, where he also serves as Editor of *The Meron Annual: Studies in Spirituality, Culture and Social Concerns.* He is an adjunct professor at Emory University and also teaches for Spring Hill College, Mobile, Alabama. Dr. Kramer's books focus on Southern literature, literary criticism, literature in relation to religion and spirituality, and particular authors, including Thomas Merton.

Shaul Magid is Associate Professor and Chair of the Department of Jewish Philosophy at The Jewish Theological Seminary of America where he teaches Jewish philosophy, Kabbala, and Hasidism. He is editor of *God's Voice from the Void: Old and New Essays on Bratslav Hasidism* (SUNY, 2001); co-editor (with Aryeh Cohen) of *Beginning/Again: Toward a Hermeneutics of Jewish Texts* (Seven Bridges Press, 2002); and author of the forthcoming, *Hasidism on the Margin: Reconciliation, Antinomianism, and Messianism in Izbica and Radzin Hasidism* (Univ. of Wisconsin Press, 2003). He is co-editor of the *Journal of Textual Reasoning* and a founding member of ChAI (Children of Abraham Institute) dedicated to dialogue between Jewish, Christian, and Muslim scholars. He also serves as the rabbi of the Fire Island Synagogue in Sea View, New York.

Lucien Miller is Professor of Comparative Literature at the University of Massachusetts, where he also serves as deacon at the campus Catholic Center. He received his Ph.D. in Comparative Literature from the University of California, Berkeley, in 1970. His specialties in Comparative Literature and East-West literary relations include: cross-cultural studies, colonial and post-colonial literature, ethnic minority cultures and folk literature, ethics and literature, translation studies and comparative religion. Dr. Miller is the author of a number of books, including *Exiles at Home: Short Stories by Ch'en Ying-Chen, Masks of Fiction in Dream of the Red Chamber: Myth, Mimesis, and Persona,* and *South of the Clouds: Tales from Yunnan.* He teaches courses that include: Contemplative Literature, International Literary Relations, and Ethics and Literature.

Ron Miller Chairs the Religion Department at Lake Forest College, IL., where he has taught for twenty-four years. He is co-founder and co-director of Common Ground, Chicago, an adult center for interreligious dialogue. He has written numerous articles and books, including *Wisdom of the Carpenter* (Ulysses Press, 2003).

Paul M. Pearson is Director and Archivist at the Thomas Merton Center and Assistant Professor in the Faculty of Arts and Sciences at Bellarmine University, Louisville. He is Resident Secretary of ITMS, the International Thomas Merton Society. His Ph.D. on Merton was completed at Heythrop College, University of London. Dr. Pearson is a founding member and first secretary of the Thomas Merton Society of Great Britain and Ireland. He is editorial advisor to *The Merton Journal,* editor of *Thomas Merton: Poet, Monk, Prophet* (Three Peaks Press, 1998); *Thomas Merton: A Mind Awake in the Dark* (Three Peaks Press, 2001); and a compiler of *About Merton: Secondary Sources 1945-2000: A Bibliographic Workbook.* He is a regular contributor to Merton conferences in Europe and the USA. In 1999 he was awarded a "Louie" by ITMS for his contribution on an international level to the promotion of Merton's writings and the presentation of his ideas.

Karl A. Plank, the J.W. Cannon Professor of Religion at Davidson College, NC, teaches biblical studies and Jewish literature and thought. He is the author of *Mother of the Wire Fence: Inside and Outside the Holocaust* (1994) and has published a number of key articles in such journals as *Judaism, Literature and Theology, Cistercian Studies,* and *The Augustinian Theological Review*. His writings on Thomas Merton include: "Thomas Merton and Hannah Arendt: Contemplation after Eichmann," *The Merton Annual* 3 (1990), 121-150; "The Eclipse of Difference: Merton's Encounter with Judaism," *Cistercian* Studies 28/2 (1993), 179-191; and "Thomas Merton and the Ethical Edge of Contemplation," *Anglican Theological* Review 83/1 (2002), 113-126.

Brother Paul Quenon, OCSO, is a monk of the Abbey of Gethsemani and received his novitiate training under Thomas Merton. He is community cook, photographer, and Director of Education. He has published several books of poetry and is editor of Monkscript, a new series of literary collections.

Mary Heléne Rosenbaum is Executive Director of the Dovetail Institute for Interfaith Recources and editor of *Dovetail: A Journal By and For Jewish/Christian Families*. With her husband, Dr. Stanley Ned Rosenbaum, she co-authored the book *Celebrating Our Differences: Living Two Faiths in One Marriage* (Ragged Edge Press, Shippensburg, PA. 1994, with a Foreword by Martin Marty; paperback ed., 1999). Mary Heléne is a practicing Roman Catholic, a lector in her church for over 20 years, who has also served as executive director of Congregation Beth Tikvah (Reform), Carlisle, PA. She has published articles on religious topics ranging from euthanasia to the spiritual vision of Stephen King, in such magazines as *Redbook, The Christian Century, Christian Ministry, Daughters of Sarah,* and *The Other Side*. She has spoken to Jewish, Christian, and secular groups in nine states and in England, and has been interviewed on radio and TV programs, including National Public Radio, CBS *This Morning*, the NBC *Today Show*, and two appearances on the *Sally Jessy Raphael Show*. Most recently, she contributed the article on interaith marriage to the forthcoming second edition of *Macmillan International Encyclopedia of Marriage and Family Relations*.

Rabbi Zalman Schachter-Shalomi is the founder and guiding spirit in the Jewish Renewal Movement in North America. He was ordained in the Habad (Lubavitch) Hasidic movement and has formed friendships with spiritual leaders of many traditions. His more recent books are *Paradigm Shift* (Jason Aronson, 1993) and *From Age-ing to Sage-ing* (Time-Warner, 1998). His correspondence with Thomas Merton can be found in the collection of Merton's lectures entitled, *The Hidden Ground of Love* (1985).

Monsignor William H. Shannon, Professor Emeritus in the Religious Studies Department of Nazareth College, Rochester, NY, is the Founding President of the International Thomas Merton Society and General Editor of the Merton Letters. He is the author of the acclaimed Merton biography, *Silent Lamp* (Crossroad, 1992), and other works on Thomas Merton.

Robert B. Slosberg is Rabbi of Congregation Adath Jeshurun in Louisville, Kentucky, where he has served since his ordination in 1981. Nationally, he serves on the Chancellors Rabbinic Cabinet of the Jewish Theological Seminary. In 1996-1997, he was chairman of the Rabbinical Assembly Campaign. In 1992, Rabbi Slosberg became the first annual recipient of the Rabbi Simon Greenberg Achievement Award of the Jewish Theological Seminary. In 2002, he was elected chairman of the Board of Overseers of Albert A. List College, on whose board he has served since 1995.

James M. Somerville, Professor Emeritus of Philosophy, Xavier University, Cincinnati, began his teaching career at Fordham, where he was Chair of the Philosophy Department for many years and co-founder and executive editor of *International Philosophical Quarterly*. From 1984 to 2001 he edited *The Roll,* a review of philosophy, science, and religion for contemplatives. Among his recent publications are *The Mystical Sense of the Gospels* (Crossroad, 1997) and *Jesus: A Man for Others* (Univ. of Scranton Press, 2003).

(Note: The word listed in the Index may not appear at the place referenced in the body of the text, but the general idea will be found there.)

"Fill us then with love and let us be bound together with love as we go our diverse ways, united in this one Spirit which makes You present to the world, and which makes You witness to the ultimate reality that is love. Love has overcome. Love is victorious. Amen."

—Merton's *Last Written Prayer*

"Grant us to see your face in the lightening of this cosmic storm, O God of holiness, merciful to all. Grant us to seek peace where it is truly found! In Your will, O God, is our peace! Amen."

—Merton's *Prayer for Peace* from *Dialogues with Silence: Prayers & Drawings*